CLS 25

Papers from the
25th Annual Regional Meeting of the
Chicago Linguistic Society

Part Two:
Parasession on Language in Context

Chicago Linguistic Society
1989

edited by
Bradley Music
Randolph Graczyk
Caroline Wiltshire

First Edition

First printing 1000 copies September, 1989

Library of Congress Catalog Card Number 76-27943

ISSN: 0577-7240
ISBN: 0-914203-33-9

Acknowledgments

The CLS conference and the production of the two volumes of proceedings could not have taken place without sacrifices of time, talent and energy from many people. We would like to thank all of those who have worked diligently to bring this year's conference and proceedings to a successful completion.

Special thanks go to Lynn Nichols, Paul Manning, Manuela Noske, and Eddy Gaytan for organizing the housing arrangements and conference party, and to Diane Brentari, Bill Eilfort, Anne Farley, Karl-Erik McCullough, Barbara Need, Eric Schiller, Elisa Steinberg, Bob Sprott, and David Testen for contributions above and beyond the call of duty.

We also thank Asif Agha, Tista Bagchi, Anna Bosch, Justine Cassell, Stuart Creason, Karen Deaton, Jenny deGroot, Lise Dobrin, Nancy Dray, Zixin Jiang, Kyunghwan Kim, Paul Kroeber, Gretchen Lai, Gary Larson, Jeff Lear, Lynn McCleod, Cynthia Miller, Bert Vaux, James Yoon, and Mike Ziolkowski for their work before the conference reading abstracts, at the conference registering participants and selling books, and after the conference proofreading papers. In addition, the resourceful assistance provided by Mary Pollard and Valerie Jones during the conference in Ida Noyes was greatly appreciated.

We are grateful to the Linguistics Department of the University of Chicago, especially chair Jerrold Sadock; and to Dean Stuart M. Tave, Ena Miller, and the other staff of the Division of the Humanities. Finally, we thank our department secretary Iretha Phillips and CLS coordinator Milan Panic for their ongoing assistance.

The Editors

Bradley Music
Randy Graczyk
Caroline Wiltshire

Contents†

---

† Michael Silverstein, "Oenophily and Oinoglossia" is not contained
in this volume.

* indicates that the paper was not presented at the 25th Annual
Regional Meeting of the Chicago Linguistic Society.

Autonomy and Modularity in a Pragmatic Model

Ellen L. Barton
Wayne State University

In this paper, I discuss a theory of the structure and interpretation of nonsentential constituents (defined as independent NPs, VPs, and so on) developed within the general framework of generative linguistic theory, working out some of the consequences of assuming a distinction between linguistic competence and pragmatic competence.[1] I interpret this distinction both narrowly and broadly, following a narrow definition of autonomous linguistic competence as a description of the ability to derive a single structure out of context and following a broad definition of pragmatic competence as a description of the ability to interpret an utterance within context. Further, I assume that models of these abilities are essentially modular in nature, making different contributions to an explanation of how speakers produce and understand expressions of a language, in this case nonsentential constituents.

It is difficult to decide how to start defending an approach using the concepts of autonomy and modularity in pragmatics since there are many research traditions to respond to. In work in conversation analysis, for example, Schiffrin (1984: 314) points to "the difficulty of maintaining an assumption of autonomous levels," and Levinson (1983: 286) warns against "premature theory construction." In work in functional linguistics, Hopper (1988: 132) claims that "the term 'pragmatics' itself must be put on probation as long as it is understood to be opposed to syntax and semantics as discrete modules," and Givon, speaking at the 1987 Linguistic Institute, characterizes such a modular approach as "the height of in-group folly." In work within generative linguistics, too, this approach must respond to criticisms that pragmatic theory is essentially unconstrained and therefore should, using Hornstein's (1986: 234) terms, be "scrapped" from the domain of linguistic research. And even beyond autonomy and modularity are under critique; the work of Belenky et al. (1986), for instance, argues that autonomy is an intellectual assumption driven largely by the hegemonic institutions of Western culture and education. Nevertheless, I would like to describe an approach to pragmatics that incorporates autonomy and modularity, proceeding as follows: I first briefly describe a theory of nonsentential constituents which consists of interacting competence and pragmatic models and then discuss what I see as the strengths and weaknesses of this approach and the ways in which it compares and contrasts with other research approaches. I know that I will not address all of the issues arising from a consideration of autonomy and modularity in pragmatics, but I hope to show that this approach holds some promise to contribute to our understanding of the interpretation of language in context.

In a larger work (Barton, in press), I describe a theory of nonsentential constituents in English. Arguing against the work of Morgan (1973) and Sag (1976), and extending the work of Shopen (1972), Brame (1979), Yanofsky (1978) and Napoli (1982), I claim that nonsentential constituents like the examples in (1) are not derived through ellipsis, since there is no controller to trigger recoverable deletion, but are dominated by their own maximal projections, that is, the initial node of great sadness in (1a) is NP; the initial node of ask for another Grand Jury in (1b) is VP; and so on:

>   (1a)   D: Apparently she [Mrs. Hunt] was the pillar of strength in that
>   family before the death.

1

P: Great sadness.
[$_{N''}$ [$_{N'}$ [$_{ADJ''}$ great] [$_N$ sadness]]]

(1b) D: One way to do it is for you to tell the Attorney General that you finally know. Really, this is the first time you are getting all the pieces together.

P: Ask for another Grand Jury?
[$_{V''}$ [$_{V'}$ [$_V$ ask] [$_{P''}$ for another Grand Jury]]]

(1c) P: The <u>Post</u> didn't have it until after you continued to the back section. It is the (adjective omitted) thing I ever saw.

D: Typical.
[$_{ADJ''}$ [$_{ADJ'}$ [$_{ADJ}$ typical]]]

(1d) D: Hunt and Libby were in his office.

H: In Colson's office?
[$_{P''}$ [$_{P'}$ [$_P$ in] [$_{N''}$ Colson's office]]]

(1e) E: This grand jury started focusing on the aftermath and he might be involved..

H: Exactly.
[$_{ADV''}$ [$_{ADV'}$ [$_{ADV}$ exactly]]]

(1f) D: He said, "Well, I was pushed without mercy by Magruder to get in there and to get more information. That the information was not satisfactory. That Magruder said, 'The White House is not happy with what we are getting'."
[$_{S'}$ [$_{COMP}$ that] [$_S$ the information was not satisfactory]]
[$_{S'}$ [$_{COMP}$ that] [$_S$ Magruder said the White House is not happy with what we are getting]]

(<u>Transcripts</u>, 1974: 109, 116, 46, 124, 232, 103)[2]

To generate these nonsentential structures within an autonomous competence model of grammar, I propose that the initial node of a generative grammar is the X-bar theory construct X^{max}, which allows any maximal projection to function as an initial node: an initial node of S generates sentence structures; an initial node of S' generates independent clausal structures like those in (1f); and an initial node of a major lexical category generates nonsentential constituent structures like those in (1a) - (1e). Under the initial node of X^{max}, then, the grammar generates the set of well-formed sentential and nonsentential structures.[3]

Within the theory of nonsentential constituents, the competence model and the pragmatic model interact in order to provide a modular account of meaning: the output of an autonomous competence model is a Logical Form representation of minimal context-free semantic meaning, which becomes the input to a pragmatic model; the output of a pragmatic model is a representation of meaning broadly defined as interpretation within context. The competence model and the pragmatic model contrast in a number of ways: first, a competence model is strictly autonomous because its operation is context-free, but a pragmatic model is only partially autonomous because its operations crucially involve interactions with context; second, the central operation of a competence model is derivation, which leads to a representation of determinate semantic meaning (albeit minimal), but the central operation of a pragmatic model is non-deductive inference, which leads to a representation of indeterminate meaning in context; and third, a competence model is strictly modular, with an internal organization of separate submodules, but a pragmatic model is only partially modular, with an internal organization of two separate submodules which share crucial properties, notably the operation of non-deductive inference.

There are two separate submodules within the pragmatic model because each one incorporates a different type of non-deductive inference which is based on a different kind of contextual information, reflecting the differences in interpretation across examples like those in (2a) and (2b):

(2a)   P: Who grants immunity? The judges?
(2b)   P: The Post didn't have it until after you continued to the back
        section. It is the (adjective omitted) thing I ever saw.
        D: Typical.
        (Transcripts, 1974: 210, 46)

A submodule of Linguistic Context describes the discourse-based interpretation of the example in (2a), where the NP the judges could be interpreted as functioning in the discourse role of Agent for the predicate grant through a generalized operation of discourse inference. A submodule of Conversational Context describes the information-based interpretation of the example in (2b), where the ADJP typical could be interpreted through a particularized operation of cooperative inference based in part on the shared background knowledge of the interlocutors that the Washington Post is the newspaper most dedicated to publishing unfavorable reports about the conduct of the Nixon administration during the Watergate affair. Although the two submodules of the pragmatic model describe different types of interpretation, the internal organization of each submodule is similar as shown in Figure 1: each submodule has a principle that describes the structure of context, and each principle has an associated operation of inference that elaborates that structure of context; each submodule also includes a condition of acceptability which governs the results of the operation of inference. In Figure 1, the horizontal dotted lines indicate where the interactions within the pragmatic model take place, and the vertical dotted lines and double arrows indicate where the pragmatic model interacts with external systems of information.

Using Zwicky's (1984) terms, the interaction between the competence model and the pragmatic model is both weakly and fuzzily autonomous: its weakly autonomous interaction takes place by means of the interface representation of Logical Form; this interaction is fuzzily autonomous as well because certain properties of Logical Form representation, specifically the expansion possibilities of lexical items for selecting argument roles and occurring with modifiers (which I see as aspects of determinate semantic content), are relevant for discourse-based interpretation. The structure-building principle within the submodule is the Principle of Linguistic Context in (3), which associates the individual utterances within a discourse sequence together:

(3)   The Principle of Linguistic Context
        In a discourse sequence, the Logical Form representation of each
        structure becomes the representation of each utterance within a
        structure of linguistic context.

The Principle of Linguistic Context creates the structure for discourse-based interpretation, which elaborates the linguistic context according the operation of Discourse Inference in (4):

4

Figure 1

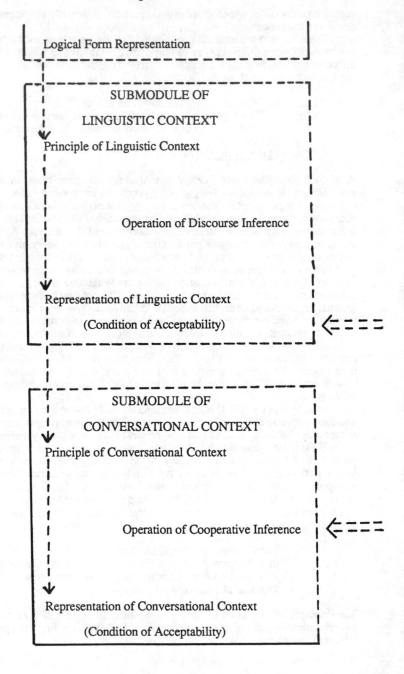

(4) Discourse Inference
If a discourse sequence includes an independent constituent utterance that potentially matches an expansion possibility of a previous element within the structure of linguistic context, then assign the constituent utterance to function as that expansion possibility in an elaboration of the structure of linguistic context.

The operation of Discourse Inference creates a representation that consists of an elaborated structure of linguistic context; the representation in (5') is the elaborated structure for the sequence in (5):

(5) P: Mitchell has given a sworn statement, hasn't he?
    D: Yes, Sir.
    P: To the Jury?
    D: To the Grand Jury.
    (Transcripts, 1974: 105)

(5') P: [s [NP Mitchell]   [VP [V has given]   [NP a sworn statement]
         SOURCE   [SRC, PT, (GOAL)] PATIENT
         [S' hasn't he]]

     P: [PP [P to] [NP the Jury]]

     D: [PP [P to] [NP the Grand Jury]]

In this representation, the dotted arrows represent the inferred match between an independent constituent utterance and its discourse function within an elaborated representation of linguistic context. The submodule of Linguistic Context accounts for a number of types of interpretation based on matching linguistic properties between independent constituents and previous elements, as shown in the representations of (6), where a constituent utterance functions as an answer to a wh-question in (6a), as a specification of a pronoun in (6b), and as a modifier in (6c):

(6a) P: Who grants immunity? The judges?
(6b) E: Everybody knew about it?
     H: Mitchell, Haldeman, Colson, Dean, the President.
(6c) P: Yeah, in other words, you stay in the job.
     K: Until the trial.
     (Transcripts, 1974: 210, 234, 397)

(6a') P: [S' [for which other persons, x]
          AGENT
          [s x [VP [V grants]   [NP immunity]]]]
                 [AG, PT]   [PATIENT]

      P: [NP the judges]

(6b') E: [s [NP everybody]   [VP [V knew]   [PP about it]]]
           EXPERIENCER   [EXP, PT]   PATIENT

      H: [NP [NP Mitchell] [NP Haldeman] [NP Colson] [NP Dean]
         [NP the President]]

(6c')   P: [$_{S'}$ [$_{ADVP}$ yeah] [$_{PP}$ in other words]   [$_S$ [$_{NP}$ you]
                                                        THEME
       [$_{VP}$ [$_V$ stay]   [$_{PP}$ in the job]]]]
    ↗   [TH, LOC]   LOCATION
    ⟍
       K: [$_{PP}$ [$_P$ until] [$_{NP}$ the trial]]

The operation of Discourse Inference clearly has the potential to overgenerate interpretations; consider the sequences in (7), where the PP <u>by the deadline</u> is unacceptable with a reading as an Agent but acceptable with a reading as a modifier of time:[4]

(7a)   A: John's dissertation was approved.
       B: By the whole committee?
(7b)   B: (#)By the deadline? (with reading as Agent)
(7c)   B: By the deadline? (with reading as modifier of time)

A nonformal explanation of these intuitions about pragmatic acceptability and unacceptability rests upon what Miller (1977: 400) calls "practical knowledge": in the world, committees approve dissertations, but deadlines do not, although dissertations are approved within time limitations. Within the partially autonomous submodule of Linguistic Context, such knowledge about the world operates to confirm the inferred discourse function of a constituent utterance as acceptable or overrule it as unacceptable. The Condition of Acceptability in (8) describes this limited interaction between the submodule and a model of knowledge about the world:

(8)   Condition of Acceptability (Submodule of Linguistic Context)
       Within a representation of linguistic context, an independent
       constituent utterance is pragmatically acceptable if it can perform its
       implicated discourse function according to the operation of Discourse
       Inference; otherwise, it is deemed unacceptable (and marked #). The
       basis for a judgment of acceptability or unacceptability is knowledge
       about the world.

The division of labor proposed here allows a generalized operation of Discourse Inference to take place, but constrains the resulting interpretation based on knowledge about the world.
       The partial autonomy of the submodule of Linguistic Context is restricted to the operation of the Condition of Acceptability. The submodule of Conversational Context, however, describes interpretation based directly on information from beyond the linguistic context, so its partial autonomy has to allow the interaction of knowledge about the world and the operation of inference itself.
       The structure-building principle within the submodule is the Principle of Conversational Context in (9) which incorporates Grice's (1975) Cooperative Principle and the notion of relevance as the basis for particularized pragmatic interpretation:[5]

(9)   Principle of Conversational Context
       In a discourse sequence, the representation of linguistic context for
       each utterance becomes the representation of an utterance with a

potential structure of implicatures explaining its relevance as a
cooperative contribution within the conversational context.

An operation of Cooperative Inference elaborates a structure of conversational
context, creating implicatures that explain how an utterance is a relevant and therefore
cooperative contribution to a discourse; these implicatures include what Levinson
(1983: 104) calls "standard" implicatures that follow from observing the Cooperative
Principle as well as conversational implicatures that follow from exploiting the
Cooperative Principle. The notion of conversational context here is necessarily a
broad one which has to encompass a great deal of contextual information, and a
determination of relevance can be based on subsets of contextual information, so I
propose that a number of specific domains of relevance are associated with the
operation of Cooperative Inference. These domains correspond to subsets of
information that interlocutors use as a set of boundaries for an operation of
particularized inference; the four subtypes of Cooperative Inference in (10) are based
on domains of the physical context of situation, the topic of conversation, the shared
background knowledge of the interlocutors, and their general knowledge about the
world:[6]

(10) Cooperative Inference
  (i)   If the utterance is relevant based on information from
         knowledge of the physical context of situation, then . . .
  (ii)   If the utterance is relevant based on information from
         knowledge of the topic of conversation, then . . .
  (iii) If the utterance is relevant based on information from the
         background knowledge of the interlocutors, then . . .
  (iv)   If the utterance is relevant based on information from
         knowledge about the world, then . . .

The subtypes of Cooperative Inference are open-ended if-then statements because
they describe the general form of a particularized inference outside of the specific
context that will instantiate both the if and the then portions of a particular inference.
    To illustrate interpretation within the conversational context, I will discuss the
examples in (11), where interpretation is based on the domain of topic plus the
domain of the shared background knowledge of the interlocutors:[7]

(11) H: The Post didn't have it until after you continued to the back
          section. It is the (adjective omitted) thing I ever saw.
      D: Typical.
      (Transcripts, 1974: 116, 46)

As Brown and Yule (1983: 68 ff.) note, the notion of topic is an intuitively
powerful one in discourse analysis, but one which is difficult to describe precisely or
formally. Keenan and Schieffelin (1976 (1983: 68)) define discourse topic as "the
proposition (or set of propositions) about which the speaker is either providing or
requesting new information." Following Strawson (1964: 104), who defined topic
as "what is of current interest or concern," Gundel (1985: 89-90) notes that the
primary function of a topic is "to establish the relevance of an utterance." Consider,
then, the example in (11), which occurs within a discussion about the topic of the
return of a Robert Vesco campaign contribution; the intuitive statement of the topic
provides the basis for an inference interpreting the ADJP typical as shown in the

representation of (12) (following Levinson (1983: 105), the symbol +> means 'implicates'):

(12)   P: Somebody is after him [Maurice Stans, chair of the Finance Committee within the Committee to Re-Elect the President] about Vesco. I first read the story briefly in the <u>Post</u>. I read, naturally, the first page and turned to the Times to read it. The <u>Times</u> had in the second paragraph that [Vesco's] money had been returned, but the <u>Post</u> didn't have it.
       D: That is correct.
       H: The <u>Post</u> didn't have it until after you continued to the back section. It is the (adjective omitted) thing I ever saw.
       D: Typical.
           Topic: return of Vesco contribution
           [ADJP typical]
           +>RELEVANCE If the utterance is relevant based on information about the topic of the conversation, then it is typical of the <u>Post</u> not to emphasize the return of Vesco's contribution.

This interpretation connects the constituent utterance to the specific topic, but it does not fully explain why it is typical of the <u>Post</u> not to emphasize the return of the contribution. Additional implicatures, however, could result from an operation of Cooperative Inference based on the background knowledge that Dean, Haldeman, and the President share about the <u>Washington Post</u>. If this shared knowledge is represented as an assumption in effect as the basis of an inference, the representation in (13) describes further interpretation of the ADJP <u>typical</u>:

(13)   Background Assumptions
       -In general, the <u>Post</u> does not regard the Nixon Administration favorably.
       [ADJP typical]
       +>RELEVANCE If the utterance is relevant based on information from the background knowledge of the interlocutors, then it is typical of the <u>Post</u> not to emphasize the return of Vesco's contribution because this is unfavorable to the Nixon administration.

The full interpretation of the ADJP, then, is composed of two implicatures based on the topic and the shared background knowledge of the discourse participants: information from the topic generates an implicature that is specific to the fact under discussion; information from shared background knowledge generates an implicature that connects this fact to a larger pattern.

The operation of Cooperative Inference is triggered by the assumption of cooperation incorporated into the Principle of Conversational Context, reflecting what Levinson (1983: 109) calls the "remarkable robustness" of the assumption of cooperation. It is possible, though, to construct some sequences in which intuitions of pragmatic acceptability are violated as in the examples of (14):

(14a) A: Nixon was President from 1968 to 1974.
       B: #Stickball
       A: What?/Huh?/What are you talking about?/ I don't know what you mean./(silence)

(14b) A: John Mitchell was Attorney General during the Nixon administration.
       B: #Stained glass windows
       A: What?/Huh?/We're talking about politics here./
          What do windows have to do with politics?/(silence)

The different responses in (14) all function as requests for clarification within a kind of breakdown in communication, which indicates that the problem with an unacceptable constituent utterance seems to be an inability to infer a set of implicatures determining the relevance of an utterance. The Condition of Acceptability in (15) describes these circumstances:

(15) Condition of Acceptability (Submodule of Conversational Context)
      A constituent utterance is pragmatically acceptable if a set of implicatures establishes its relevance as a cooperative contribution in the representation of conversational context; otherwise, it is deemed unacceptable (and marked #) because a set of implicatures cannot be inferred to establish relevance.

An unacceptable constituent utterance, followed by silence or a breakdown in communication, requires an overt clarification of the implicatures that make it a relevant contribution to the conversation.

This has been a brief overview of the partially autonomous and partially modular pragmatic model of the context-dependent interpretation of independent constituent utterances, and I would now like to discuss what I see as the major strengths and weaknesses of this approach to pragmatics. First, I believe that one strength of this approach is its modular distinction between a minimal representation of determinate semantic meaning and a maximal representation of indeterminate meaning in context. Through the interacting competence and pragmatic models, the theory of nonsentential constituents actually incorporates a view of interpretation in which context is primary because the burden of accounting for the majority of interpretation is formally shifted from a context-free grammar to a context-dependent pragmatics. Second, I believe that another strength of this approach is its modular distinction between pragmatic interpretation based on information solely from the linguistic context and interpretation based on information from beyond the linguistic context, which is reflected in the internal organization of the pragmatic model. Through separate submodules, the pragmatic model associates different types of inference with the contexts in which they operate. This association between types of inference and types of context is developed further with the association of particularized inference to different domains of relevance. I believe that yet another strength of this approach is its characterization of pragmatic inference as non-deductive.

I also, however, see the major weakness in this work as its lack of a formal description of this operation of non-deductive pragmatic inference, especially for the particularized inferences within domains of relevance. The statements describing the subtypes of Cooperative Inference in (10) ultimately are vague because they do not explain what information from the world is involved in making an inference within a domain of relevance and because they do not specify a conclusion within their if-then statements. Some of this vagueness is necessary because the pragmatic model cannot provide an unchanging and determinate representation of the conversational context. When information from different conversational contexts varies, the resulting implicatures vary as well. Levinson (1985: 4) notes that one of the unique characteristics of pragmatic inference is its ability to invoke premises in the interpretation of an utterance. As I see it, these premises consist of assumptions that can be drawn from the conversational context of an utterance. A domain of relevance thus functions as an area within which an inference takes place based on assumptions drawn from that domain. So I regard the form of the rules of Cooperative Inference as only an initial attempt to describe pragmatic inference as non-deductive and context-dependent. Nevertheless, in a crucial way, these rules do not provide an account of the activation of assumptions from context and the operation of non-deductive inference that follows, and the pragmatic model needs to specify these operations in more detail, if this is, in fact, possible.

The development of the pragmatic model in general follows work in neo-Gricean pragmatics by Horn (1984) and Levinson (1985, 1987). The use of an independent constituent utterance is an example of Levinson's (1987) maxim of Minimization, where the speaker says as little as necessary, and his maxim of Enrichment, where the hearer finds a more specific interpretation for what is said. Within the submodule of Linguistic Context, the operation of Discourse Inference is a type of generalized inference to a specific, informationally enriching implicature, namely, an implicature of discourse function. Within the submodule of Conversational Context, the operation of Cooperative Inference is a type of particularized inference to an informationally enriched interpretation, namely, a set of implicatures explaining relevance.

The work presented here is in general opposition to the pragmatic theory of Sperber and Wilson (1986), where relevance is viewed as a way to arrive at one unique interpretation for an utterance. Although the concept of relevance figures prominently in the pragmatic model presented here, it follows Levinson's (1987: 78) idea that there are multiple types of relevance, which I see as leading to the concept of domains of relevance generating different interpretations for an utterance, thereby accounting for some of the indeterminacy that characterizes pragmatic interpretation (where the definition of indeterminacy used here is the possibility of different interpretations for an utterance). Indeterminacy within the pragmatic model arises from interpretations from different submodules, from different domains of relevance, and from different assumptions drawn from the conversational context. This view of pragmatic interpretation is modular, and one of the benefits of modularity in the pragmatic model is that it accounts for this kind of indeterminacy through the devices of separate submodules and multiple domains of relevance. My difference with Sperber and Wilson can be summed up with an analogy: just as a model of grammar has to provide a way to arrive at more than one structural description of an ambiguous syntactic structure, so a pragmatic model has to provide a way to arrive at more than one interpretive representation of the indeterminate meaning of an utterance.

To compare the work presented here with other approaches to research on language in context, I would like to focus upon some points drawn from work in conversation analysis and functional linguistics because I (at least) see a few interesting parallels in basic concepts and views despite differences in methods. First, both my work within generative linguistic theory and Merritt's (1976) work within conversation analysis point to non-ellipsis-based accounts of what I have termed independent or nonsentential constituents; Merritt (1976: 327), in fact, calls an ellipsis-based approach "quite hopeless," and I have argued in support of this characterization. Also, recent work in functional linguistics has pointed out the difficulty of assuming that the category S is the only syntactic category of legitimate interest, especially for discourse analysis; DuBois (1985: 357), for instance, notes that S may not be validated for some languages, and I have proposed the alternative that a grammar actually generates all major category structures, including sentences, clauses, and nonsentential constituents.

With respect to the submodule of Linguistic Context, I see the view of discourse-based interpretation presented here as connected to the view of discourse as interaction presented in work on conversation analysis (cf. Schiffrin (1988) for a recent review article). Using an independent constituent utterance could be viewed as one of many ways in which participants interact to achieve joint meanings through the sequential unfolding of locally-managed turns: since most sequences containing independent constituent utterances consist of adjacent or near-adjacent utterances, one turn-possibility seems to be the use of a constituent utterance to function in combination with a previous utterance within the linguistic context. Thus, discourse-based interpretation describes a dynamic interaction of utterance, context, and inference, capable of growing and changing as participants add, elaborate, modify, repair, and even contradict utterances through the use of constituent utterances.

Schiffrin (1988: 256) notes that a central question in conversation analysis asks how we know that a sequence of utterances is a connected whole rather than unconnected parts, and it is possible that coherence, like joint meaning, arises in part out of local relations. Levinson (1983: 107) points out that the notions of relevance and coherence are fundamentally connected, and I see the Conditions of Acceptability discussed above as presenting two local definitions of coherence, at least with respect to discourse sequences containing nonsentential constituents: we know that a sequence is coherent if a determination of discourse function can be made for an independent constituent within its linguistic context, and/or we know that a discourse is coherent if a set of implicatures explaining relevance can be made for any particular constituent utterance within its conversational context.

Finally, I also see the pragmatic model presented here as complementary to the concept of context discussed in diverse areas of linguistic research. Working in functional linguistics, Givon (1983: 16) presents a view of context with three aspects: generically shared knowledge coded in the culturally shared lexicon and known semantic likelihoods; specifically shared knowledge of the particular discourse; and specifically shared knowledge of the particular speaker and hearer, what they know or tend to assume about each other. Working in conversation analysis, Gumperz (1982: 153) also describes context with a similar set of distinctions, including grammatical and lexical knowledge plus the physical setting, participants' personal background knowledge, and their socio-cultural knowledge of status and value. Working in linguistic semantics, Partee (1989) distinguishes between sentential, discourse, and utterance context, which recalls the body of research on the distinction between anaphoric and deictic contexts (Hankamer and Sag, 1976; Lyons, 1977). I see all these views of context as similar to the view of context operationalized here, where lexical or grammatical knowledge is the input provided by an autonomous grammar, knowledge of discourse is the linguistic context, and shared knowledge and knowledge about the world are included in the conversational context. Although there might be considerable disagreement on the autonomous nature of grammatical or lexical knowledge, I believe there is a shared view on several important distinctions within a concept of context, including a distinction between the linguistic and extra-linguistic context as well as a distinction between specifically shared and generally shared knowledge within that extra-linguistic context.

In my work, I see the concepts of autonomy and modularity as contributing to the development of one perspective on the notion of context: the emphasis here is on the operation of pragmatic inference within bounded areas of contextual information. Within this view, the partial autonomy of the pragmatic model identifies the places where knowledge of context is used in inferential interpretation, which, I have suggested, is crucially important in providing the assumptions that form the basis for premise-invoking non-deductive pragmatic inference; the partial modularity of the pragmatic model connects types of inference with specific types of context, which I think is a crucial step in describing the nature of non-deductive inference operating within boundaries. I do not mean to imply, however, that this view of context is the only legitimate view or that a pragmatic model has to account for this view and no others. In his discussion of autonomy and modularity, Sadock (1983) suggests that languages are characterized by Redundancy of Function, which means that a language may incorporate more than one way of communicating the same information. I believe that research on context has to explore its Redundancy of Function, which leads to a view of context as providing many interpretive paths for interlocutors to follow. My emphasis here has been on the interaction of context and inference; this is only one function of context, however, and this perspective needs to be integrated into a view of context that incorporates many different, and possibly redundant, perspectives.

In conclusion, as I mentioned at the beginning of this paper, I know that I have not addressed all concerns about the use of autonomy and modularity in pragmatics; I hope, however, that the articulation of such an approach presents an interesting account of some aspects of the interpretation of nonsentential constituents in context. I am, no doubt, guilty of "premature theorizing"; I believe, though, that this theory may raise questions and address issues of interest to practitioners of many different approaches towards research on language in context.

Notes

[1]Chomsky (1980) proposed this distinction, although he, of course, was not the first or the only person to suggest that the concept of competence extends to domains other than grammar and that one of these domains is the use and interpretation of language in context. Hymes (1964, 1972), for example, originally proposed the concept of communicative competence, defining it as the ability to use language appropriately in sociocultural situations, an idea which seems to have informed Chomsky's later definitions of pragmatic competence. More recently, Gumperz (1982, 1984) has continued to explore the notion of communicative competence, relating the use of language to its reflections of social order.

[2]My study of nonsentential constituents is based on discourse sequences taken from The Presidential Transcripts of the Watergate conversations between President Richard Nixon and the members of his Executive staff. Discourse participants are identified by initial:

P: President Richard Nixon
D: John W. Dean, Counsel to the President
H: H.R. Haldeman, White House Chief of Staff
E: John D. Ehrlichman, Assistant to the President
K: Richard G. Kleindienst, U.S. Attorney General

I recognize that the version of the Transcripts I am using presents regularized data; in other words, the transcripts do not include stress, intonation, pauses, overlap, and other features as do the detailed transcripts of conversation analysis (for a discussion of the superior nature of such transcripts, cf. Ochs, 1979; DuBois, Cumming, and Schuetze-Coburn, 1988). My use of the published Transcripts is a compromise: on the one hand, it is a problematic source of conversational data because the method of transcription is deficient; on the other hand, it is a rich source of conversational data with many interesting examples of independent constituent utterances.

[3]For a detailed description of the grammar of nonsentential constituent structures, see Barton (in press).

[4]I am indebted to Judy Levi (personal communication) for this example.

[5]Sperber and Wilson (1986) propose that relevance is central to pragmatic interpretation, which is the general idea that I follow here. I do not, however, agree with the nature of the theory that Sperber and Wilson have built from this idea, and I offer arguments against their approach later in the paper and in Barton (in press).
[6]It is entirely possible that these four areas do not exhaust the domains of relevance; however, I leave the number and nature of additional domains of relevance as an open issue for future research.
[7]For additional examples of interpretation within the submodule of Conversational Context, see Barton (in press).

References

Barton, E. In press. A Theory of the Grammatical Structure and Pragmatic Interpretation of Nonsentential Constituents. Pragmatics and Beyond New Series. Amsterdam: John Benjamins.

Belenky, M., B. Clinchy, N. Goldberger, J. Tarule. 1986. Women's Ways of Knowing. New York: Basic Books.

Brame, M. 1979. "A Note on COMP S Grammar vs. Sentence Grammar," Linguistic Analysis 5:383-386.

Brown, G. and G. Yule, 1983. Discourse Analysis. Cambridge: Cambridge University Press.

Chomsky, N. 1980. Rules and Representations. New York: Columbia University Press.

DuBois, J. 1985. "Competing Motivations," in Iconicity in Syntax ed. by J. Haiman. Amsterdam: John Benjamins.

DuBois, J., S. Cumming, and S. Schuetze-Coburn. 1988. "Discourse Transcription," in Santa Barbara Papers in Linguistics Vol. 2: Discourse and Grammar ed. by S. Thompson. Santa Barbara: Department of Linguistics, University of California Santa Barbara.

Givon, T., ed. 1983. Topic Continuity in Discourse: A Quantitative Cross-Language Study. Amsterdam: John Benjamins.

Grice, H. P. 1975. "Logic and Conversation," in Syntax and Semantics 3: Speech Acts ed. by P. Cole and J. Morgan. New York: Academic Press.

Gumperz, J. 1982. Discourse Strategies. Cambridge University Press.

Gumperz, J. 1984. "Communicative Competence Revisited," in Meaning, Form, and Use in Context: Linguistic Applications ed. by D. Schiffrin. Washington, DC: Georgetown University Press.

Gundel, J. 1985. "Shared Knowledge and Topicality," Journal of Pragmatics 9: 83-107.

Hankamer, J. and I. Sag. 1976. "Deep and Surface Anaphora," Linguistic Inquiry 4: 17-68.

Hopper, P. 1988. "Emergent Grammar and the A Priori Grammar Postulate," in Linguistics in Context: Connecting Observation and Understanding ed. by D. Tannen. Norwood, NJ: Ablex.

Horn, L. 1984. "Toward a New Taxonomy for Pragmatic Inference: Q-Based and R-Based Implicature," in Meaning, Form, and Use in Context ed. by D. Schiffrin. Washington, DC: Georgetown University Press.

Horn, L. 1988. "Pragmatic Theory," in Linguistics: The Cambridge Survey: Linguistic Theory: Foundations ed. by F. Newmeyer. Cambridge: Cambridge University Press.

Hornstein, N. 1986. "Pragmatics and Grammatical Theory," in Papers from the Parasession on Pragmatics and Grammatical Theory. Chicago: Chicago Linguistic Society.

14

Hymes, D. 1964. "Toward Ethnographies of Communication: The Analysis of Communicative Events," rpt. in Language and Social Context (1972) ed. by P. Giglioli. Harmondsworth: Penguin.

Hymes, D. 1972. "Models of the Interaction of Language and Social Life," in Directions in Sociolinguistics: The Ethnography of Communication ed. by J. Gumperz and D. Hymes. New York: Holt, Rinehart and Winston.

Keenan, E. Ochs and B. Schieffelin. 1976. "Topic as a Discourse Notion: A Study of Topic in the Conversations of Children and Adults," rpt. in Acquiring Communicative Competence (1983) ed. by E. Keenan and B. Schieffelin. London: Routledge and Kegan Paul.

Levinson, S. 1983. Pragmatics. Cambridge: Cambridge University Press.

Levinson, S. 1985. "What's So Special about Conversational Inference?" Paper presented to the Annual Conference of the British Psychological Society.

Levinson, S. 1987. "Minimization and Conversational Inference," in The Pragmatic Perspective ed. by J. Verschueren and M. Bertucelli-Papi. Amsterdam: John Benjamins.

Lyons, J. 1977. Semantics. Cambridge: Cambridge University Press.

Merritt, M. 1976. "On Questions Following Questions in Service Encounters," Language in Society 5:315-357.

Miller, G. 1977. "Practical and Lexical Knowledge," in Thinking: Readings in Cognitive Science ed. by P. Johnson-Laird and P. Wason. Cambridge: Cambridge University Press.

Morgan, J. 1973. "Sentence Fragments and the Notion 'Sentence'," in Issues in Linguistics ed. by B. Kachru et al. Urbana, IL: University of Illinois Press.

Napoli, D. 1982. "Initial Material Deletion in English, Glossa 16: 85-111.

Ochs, E. 1979. "Transcription as Theory," in Developmental Pragmatics ed. by E. Ochs and B. Schieffelin. New York: Academic Press.

Partee, B. 1989. "Implicit Variables in Quantified Contexts," Paper presented at the 25th Annual Regional Meeting of the Chicago Linguistics Society.

The Presidential Transcripts. 1974. New York: Dell.

Sadock, J. 1983. "The Necessary Overlapping of Grammatical Components," in Papers from the Parasession on the Interplay of Phonology, Morphology, and Syntax. Chicago: Chicago Linguistics Society.

Sag, I. 1976. Deletion and Logical Form. New York: Garland.

Schiffrin, D. 1984. "How a Story Says What It Means and Does," Text 4: 313-346.

Schiffrin, D. 1988. "Conversation Analysis," in Linguistics: The Cambridge Survey: Language: The Socio-cultural Context ed. by F. Newmeyer. Cambridge University Press.

Shopen, T. 1972. A Generative Theory of Ellipsis. Ph.D. dissertation, UCLA.

Sperber, D. and D. Wilson. 1986. Relevance: Communication and Cognition. Cambridge, MA: Harvard University Press.

Strawson, P. 1964. "Identifying Reference and Truth-Values," rpt. in Semantics ed. by D. Steinberg and L. Jakobovits. Cambridge: Cambridge University Press.

Yanofsky, N. 1978. "NP Utterances," in CLS 14. Chicago: Chicago Linguistic Society.

Zwicky, A. 1984. "Autonomous Components and Limited Interfacing," in Papers from the Twentieth Regional Meeting of the Chicago Linguistic Society. Chicago: Chicago Linguistics Society.

Discourse Markers in Tojolabal Mayan

Jill Brody

Louisiana State University

I. Introduction

Schiffrin (1987:31) defines discourse markers as "sequentially dependent elements which bracket units of talk." English discourse markers identified by Schiffrin are independent particles, conjunctions, phrases, or other elements that function to promote cohesion and structure in discourse. These are elements like and, oh, well, but, because, so, or, now, then, I mean and y'know. These signpost elements occur with high frequency in discourse, and while their meaning is vague, it resides in their discourse patterning. Such markers are one aspect of language that is especially sensitive to both linguistic context and cultural settings.

In this paper I explore ways in which Schiffrin's notion of discourse marker may be universal and how it may need to be expanded to account for languages other than English. I analyze the operation and occurrence of discourse markers in Tojolabal, a Mayan language of Chiapas, Mexico, with special attention to the ways discourse markers characterize speech genres and to their role in the structure and cohesion of discourse. In Tojolabal, discourse markers include conjunctions, particles, phrases, grammatically dependent particles, and particles and conjunctions borrowed from Spanish (Brody 1987b, Brody in press a.). Many of these may combine with each other in various ways that create an array of different qualities of discourse marking. They may occur at the beginning or at the end of an utterance. Although we would not expect discourse markers in any two languages to be isomorphic, we can learn more about their universal and particular features by examining discourse markers in Tojolabal.

II. Terminology Clarification

Before turning to the Tojolabal data, it will be useful to contrast terms and definitions of concepts from various authors that are similar to Schiffrin's definition of discourse markers.

Dell Hymes' (1981) insight into the function of "initial particles" revealed that they partition Chinookan myths into segments of "lines" and other units (also 1987 for Takelma). He argued that the identification of these units indicated by "initial particles" allows us to recognize Chinookan myths as poetry. However, Bright (1981, 1982) has questioned whether segmentation of Native American narrative can

15

be established exclusively on the basis of these
markers, and whether the use of "initial particles" is
sufficient to define a poetic genre as distinguished
from prose. He suggested that the way to determine
whether "initial particles" characterize the poetic
genre is to examine natural discourse.

Dell Hymes also pointed out that Hoijer (1949, in
Hymes 1987) recognized a discourse function for the
interaction of particles and syntactic suffixes in
Tonkawa.

Longacre (1976, 1983), taking a different tack,
analyzed the role of particles in the cohesive
structure of narrative, with special focus on the use
in South American languages of "mystery particles and
affixes" that operate in narrative discourse to
indicate the main story line. What seemed mysterious
in terms of morphology or syntax alone was de-
mystified and seen to make perfect sense from a
discourse perspective.

Grimes (1975) may have been the first to identify
cross-linguistically the category of discourse markers,
which he labeled "Pesky Little Particles":

> Most languages have particles whose use seems
> to be related to gluing the parts of
> discourses together but which are never easy
> to pin down. In English they are words like
> now, either, moreover, when used to relate
> more than one sentence (1975:93).

He also noted that in languages other than English (his
example is the Uto-Aztecan language Huichol), this
cohesive function may be carried out by enclitics and
affixes as well as by full lexical items. Levinson
(1983:87), too, recognizes a process of "discourse
deixis," carried out by particles, words, phrases, or
morphemes, which "indicate the relationship between an
utterance and the prior discourse."

A more encompassing view is provided by Gumperz'
(1982:131) "contextualization cues," defined as "any
feature of linguistic form that contributes to the
signalling of contextual presuppositions." This
definition not only takes into account a wider range of
elements than particles, but it also specifically
locates the function of the cues in context. Discourse
is the aspect of context that is most central to both
contextualization cues and to discourse markers, but
other aspects of context are important as well.

Schiffrin's definition of discourse markers links
them explicitly with both discourse context and
discourse sequencing. I will use Schiffrin's term
"discourse marker" throughout. Schiffrin offers
"tentative suggestions" regarding the conditions for
the use of an expression as a discourse marker:

> it has to be syntactically detachable from a
> sentence
> it has to be commonly used in initial position of
> an utterance
> it has to have a range of prosodic contours
> e.g. tonic stress and followed by a pause,
> phonological reduction
> it has to be able to operate at both local and
> global levels of discourse, and on different
> planes of discourse
> this means that it either has to have no
> meaning, a vague meaning, or to be reflexive
> (of the language, of the speaker) (Schiffrin
> 1987:328)

This list makes clear that it is primarily the pattern
of occurrence rather than the particular form of an
element that allows it to operate as a discourse
marker.

The various concepts and approaches considered
above show that there have been two characterizations
of what is apparently the same range of phenomena: one
which stresses the role of discourse markers in
structure, and the other which emphasizes their
cohesive function. The definitions of "initial
particles" (Hymes) and "mystery particles and affixes"
(Longacre) locate the function of these elements in the
structuring of discourse through the way they mark
sections and divisions in narrative. On the other
hand, "discourse deixis" (Levinson), "discourse
markers" (Schiffrin), "Pesky Little Particles"
(Grimes), and "contextualization cues" (Gumperz) are
characterized as manifesting discourse coherence.
However, this distinction between structure and
cohesion is, I believe, a false one. Cohesion and
structure are two aspects of the same process.
Structure is cohesive; it is what holds discourse
together. Cohesion is structural in that the units
defined by structure are indicated through markers of
cohesion.

In this paper I show how this necessary connection
between structure and cohesion is enacted by discourse
markers in a range of Tojolabal speech genres. Through
an examination of discourse markers in three different
genres, I will show that Tojolabal discourse markers
function not only to indicate segmentations in formal
narrative discourse or poetry, but that there are
everyday conversational functions for discourse
markers, on the order of those described for English by
Schiffrin. I want to point out the differences in
discourse markers for narrative, ritual speech and
everyday conversation, as well as to underscore the
similarities of their function. I am following up on
Bright's (1981, 1982) suggestion to clarify the role of
"initial particles" in genre definition through the

investigation of natural discourse. The consideration
of discourse markers in various Tojolabal genres
suggests some solutions. I also hope to show that what
characterizes discourse markers formally may differ by
language, as may their location in discourse.

III. Tojolabal Discourse Markers
    When applied to Tojolabal discourse, Schiffrin's
"tentative suggestions" identify a set of Tojolabal
expressions as clear discourse markers, and suggest
that several other expressions may also be candidates.
Yet to label an expression as a discourse marker is not
to tie it to a single function; in fact, discourse
markers are multifunctional. They may operate at the
syntactic level and discourse level in similar ways.
Several Tojolabal discourse markers have grammatical
meaning and function syntactically as conjunctions or
disjunctions: <u>sok</u> 'and'; <u>i</u> 'and'; and <u>pero</u> 'but'.
These expressions are syntactically cohesive, joining
clauses as conjunctions. They also reinforce cohesion
as discourse markers, associating and dissociating
larger discourse units.
    Other discourse markers have meaning and function
as sequentials: <u>ti</u> 'then'; <u>entonse</u> 'then'; <u>yajni</u>
'when'; <u>kwando</u> 'when', <u>ya7n</u> 'now'. These expressions
carry out coherence in discourse by making connections
through time. Discourse markers that combine
sequentiality with evaluation are <u>ja7ch</u>/<u>jach'</u>/<u>jachuk</u>
'thus'; <u>porke</u> 'because'; and <u>ja7-0 y-uj</u> (cleft-3a 3e-
relN)[1] 'therefore'.
    A third type of discourse marker has no meaning
other than its discourse meaning or as an exclamation:
<u>pwes</u>/<u>pwe</u>/<u>pes</u>/<u>pe</u> 'well'; <u>este</u> 'um'; <u>bweno</u> 'well'; <u>ja7-</u>
<u>0(=i)</u> (cleft-3a=npt) 'it is, [cleft marker], yes'; <u>lek</u>
'good'; <u>e</u> 'oh'; <u>a</u> 'oh'. These discourse marker may
function simultaneously in their lexical, grammatical,
and discourse meanings.

IV. Tojolabal discourse marker functions in three
speech genres
    1) Organization of narrative
    Tojolabal discourse markers help organize
discourse into constituent units. In narrative, they
help demarcate the beginning and end of narrative
units. They help move narratives through their
development, mark the climax, and signal the
denouement. This is the function highlighted by
Longacre (1976, 1983) and Hymes (1981). This is
illustrated in the structure of Tojolabal folktales.
Tojolabal folktales (Brody 1986b, 1987b, in press) are
framed by formulaic openings and closings, which could
themselves be considered discourse markers. Episodes
within the development of the narrative are generally
indicated by the use of a discourse marker such as <u>pwes</u>

or <u>entonse</u>, or by a phrase that combines a number of discourse markers and other elements, such as <u>ora ya7n=ni jaw=i</u> (now now=emp that=npt) or <u>entonses ti=b'i ya7n=ni jaw=a</u> (then then=rpt now-emp that=clt). Within episodes, discourse markers such as <u>pero</u> and <u>pwes</u> frequently function as paragraph markers, indicating change of topic. The denouement of the folktale is marked by the evaluative or explanatory discourse markers <u>ja7ch/jach'/jachuk/</u>, <u>porke</u>, and <u>ja7-0 y-uj</u>. Within the units just described, discourse markers that carry out functions of narrative sequencing are <u>entonse</u>, <u>ya7n</u>, <u>ti</u>, <u>yajni</u> and <u>kwando</u>. Which discourse marker is used at any particular point of segmentation varies among speakers. Although I have characterized these discourse markers as demarcating discourse segments, they also simultaneously indicate the cohesion between the segments.

2) Turn-taking in conversation and ritual speech
Interactive discourse is also structured. Discourse markers reveal this structure, and reflect the coherence of the interaction. Discourse markers with specifically interactive function occur at the beginning of turns or bids for turns, where they connect the new turn to the previous talk. The ends of conversational turns are also frequently marked by characteristic particles and phrases which I want to argue are discourse markers. In addition to meeting most of the qualifications set forth by Schiffrin (above), these turn-final particles and phrases are also cohesive in at least two ways. They relate the turn being completed to the previous talk by indicating that it is finished. They also link the turn being finished to the subsequent talk by indicating that the next turn may begin. Smooth negotiation of turns is cohesive in dialogue, whether conversational or ritual.

Not every conversational turn is initiated by a discourse marker, but these expressions are very frequent, and conversations typically exhibit long sequences of turns all beginning with a discourse marker, as in the conversational segment below.

```
1.
JL:  ya7n=a  0-jak--k-i7-0--ko7            ja
     now=clt com-ARRIVE--1e-TAKE-3a--DOWNWARD det
     ermana teresa.
     SISTER TERESA
     And then I went to take sister Teresa down.

J:   a.
     Oh.
```

```
JL:  pes  pes  jutz'in=i    0-waj-i-e7--ko7=a.
     well well QUICKLY=npt com-GO-ivm-3apl--
                                         DOWNWARD=clt
     Well, well they went down with me quickly.


J:   a  bweno ya7n=ni jaw=a.
     ah GOOD  now=emp THAT=clt
     Oh so that's what happened. [lit. oh good then
     that]
JL:  e  lom=xta    x-lumul-j-i-0         ja7ch-uk-0
     oh REALLY=dur inc-STOMP-pas-ivm-3a thus-sbj-3a

     ja  ala winik=i.
     det dim MAN=npt
     Oh, he really went stomping along like this, the
     poor man.


J:   pe  ay-0=ni    nochan     ixuk-e7    0-waj-0=ta.
     but BE-3a=emp FOLLOWING WOMEN-3pl com-GO-3a=
                                                already
     But the women really kept following after him.


JL:  e  baya ixuk=i    x-kelel-i-e7--ek'=e.
     oh yeah WOMAN=npt inc-SCREAM-ivm-3apl--PASS=term
     Oh yeah, the women were screaming as they went by.
```

A distinctively interactive type of linguistic
element is the back-channel, which functions to
negotiate turn-taking. There are two characteristic
types of back-channels in Tojolabal conversation:
stereotypic phrases and back-channel repetitions (Brody
1986a). These are characteristic ways that co-
conversationalists let each other know that whoever has
the turn at speaking may continue. This creates
cohesion in conversation in that the back-channel
utterance refers back to the previous utterance, and
communicates that the other conversational participant
may continue speaking. Because of this cohesive
function and their role in structuring turn-taking, and
because they meet the conditions of Schiffrin's
"tentative suggestions," I consider back-channels to be
discourse markers. Stereotypical conversational back-
channels may consist of a single discourse marker, as
in the use of ja7-0=i in the last three turns in
example (8.) below. In an emphatic response, they may
also take the form of an accumulation of discourse
markers into a discourse marker phrase; an example is a
bweno ya7n=ni jaw=a in the conversational segment (1.)
above. Back-channel repetitions are discourse markers
whose form is particularly closely tied to the
linguistic context, in that they are direct or
abbreviated repetitions of a previous utterance.

2.
E: oj=xa   wa-s-lok-ow-on-e7=ta.
     fut=now pro-3e-INVITE-tvm-1a-3epl=already
     Yes, they are inviting me.

JL: a wa-s-lok-ow-a.
     oh pro-3e-INVITE-tvm-2a
     Oh, they are inviting you.
E: wa-s-lok-ow-on.
     pro-3e-INVITE-tvm-1a
     They are inviting me.

The same verb is repeated in each turn, with
appropriate alterations of person.
     Another place where discourse markers operate
interactively is in Tojolabal ritual speech. Most
ritual speech, such as the marriage petitions and
Carnaval petitions, have dialogue structure and a
characteristic use of a distinctive set of discourse
markers. Occurring formulaically throughout ritual
speech, discourse markers mark the beginning and the
end of the turns in the ritual exchange. For example,
a turn by the spokesman for the groom at an enactment
of the wedding petition begins with a heavy accretion
of discourse markers (line breaks reflect intonation
and pauses):

3.   bweno k-ermano
     GOOD 1e-BROTHER

     ya7n=ni ermano
     NOW=emp BROTHER

     lek ay-0
     GOOD BE-3a

     tz'akatal.
     THANK YOU

Each line is a conventional phrase that functions as a
discourse marker to open this turn at ritual speech;
the turn then continues.
     Sometimes the same discourse marker can frame an
entire turn in the ritual speech dialogue.

4.   lekil ab'al
     GOOD SPEECH
     'Well spoken,

     senyor santo testigo
     MISTER HOLY WITNESS
     Lord Holy Witness,

```
mi   mal ab'al-uk-0     ja jaw=i
neg BAD SPEECH-sbj-3a det THIS=npt
This was not badly spoken.

lekil ab'al.
GOOD  SPEECH
Well spoken.'
```

The same phrase is repeated at the beginning and end of
(4.), which is a complete turn in the marriage
petition.   These (and other) markers occur repeatedly
throughout the marriage petition.   As discourse
markers, they carry the meaning of indicating turn
change in the formulaic interaction; they also signal
the genre of ritual speech.
Discourse markers in ritual speech tend to
accumulate, much in the fashion of the discourse
markers in emphatic conversational back-channels. Many
ritual speech discourse markers are built around or
incorporate narrative and conversational discourse
markers, with distinctive ritual speech components
added on. Discourse markers particular to ritual
speech include lekil ab'al 'well spoken'; tz'akatal
'thank you'; jastal miyuk 'of course' [lit. 'why
not?']. The discourse marker ya7n=ni 'now=emp' occurs
with exceptionally high frequency in the marriage
petition; its function seems to be to help indicate the
taking up of the various actions of the marriage ritual
as they occur in the sequence of the ritual petition
dialogue.
Since, as Schiffrin has shown for English, and as
we have seen above for Tojolabal, discourse markers can
have grammatical or lexical meaning as well as
discourse meaning, they are ultimately defined by their
patterning and what the discourse marker comes to mean
through use. This allows for a particular genre to
have a distinctive set of markers, and for the same
discourse markers to indicate at one instance a new
episode in a narration, and at another a new turn in
conversation. The definition of a discourse marker
through its pattern of use also captures the
individuality, even idiosyncracy, of speakers' use of
discourse markers while still maintaining mutual
comprehension.

V. Clitic particles as discourse markers
Defining discourse markers by their patterning and
their meaning in use requires us to consider the
discourse marker function of other elements besides
those which are "syntactically detachable from a
sentence." Schiffrin's emphasis on the syntactic
detachability of the expressions neglects discourse
markers in languages which make heavy use of
cliticization. Clitics do not meet most of the

"tentative suggestions" put forth by Schiffrin for
characterizing discourse markers. Yet Hoijer (1949, in
D. Hymes 1987) stressed the interaction between
particles and syntactic elements, Longacre (1976)
included affixes in his "mystery" category, and Grimes
(1975) made mention of the functional similarity of
free-standing elements and dependent particles in
Huichol. In Tojolabal, two categories of clitics
function as discourse markers.
     The first type, temporal/aspectual clitic
particles, typically attach to the end of the first
non-fronted element in a clause (Brody 1987a). These
clitics are syntactically optional, but occur with high
frequency in discourse. They carry out discourse
functions that overlap to a large extent with those of
discourse markers.

5.
temporal/aspectual clitic particles
=xa   now
=ta   already
=to   still
=xta   durative
=cha/cho   repetitive

From the glosses of the temporal/aspectual clitics it
is clear that their meanings are similar to those of
many of the free-standing discourse markers. The fact
that the meaning and patterns of occurrence of
temporal/aspectual clitics are similar to those of the
syntactically independent particles, suggests that they
reinforce the structural and cohesive effect of the
free-standing discourse markers. These clitics operate
to indicate subtle interactions between the sequencing
of discourse and speaker's attitudes toward that
sequence, such as whether the action was unexpected or
anticipated. They often are cliticized to or occur in
aggregates with other discourse markers of sequence
such as entonse and ti in discourse marker phrases.
The clitic =cha/cho is conjunctive, and frequently
occurs along with the free-standing discourse markers i
and sok.
     The meaning of a discourse marker phrase is a
distinctive product of the interaction of its component
parts and the context of its use. For example, the
sentence below begins with three discourse markers and
two clitics.

6. <u>ja=xa   yajni ti=xa</u>   yaman-0   y-uj=i
    det=now when then=now GRIPPED-3a 3e-relN=npt

ti=b'i   0-s-t'aj-a--y-i7-0
then=rpt com-3e-SPLIT-tvm--3e-TAKE-3a

ja   s-lukum   ja ayin=i.
det 3e-STOMACH det ALLIGATOR=npt
As for as soon as he had it grasped, he then supposedly
split open the alligator's stomach.

This is from a story where a man is swallowed by an
alligator and frees himself. This particular
constellation of discourse markers and clitics conveys
very strongly the sense that the action described -
cutting open the alligator's stomach - took place just
as soon as the man got the knife in his hand. The
discourse markers <u>yajni</u> 'when' and <u>ti</u> 'then' indicate
the sequence and its dependency on previous action.
The clitic =<u>xa</u> occurs twice to allow us to understand
the immediacy of the action in sequence.
     Borrowed Spanish particles do not take clitics
directly, but native Tojolabal discourse markers
frequently do. This helps create a discourse marker
phrase at the beginning of an utterance, with a typical
and frequently occurring concatenation including a
conjunction borrowed from Spanish, an indigenous
discourse marker, and a clitic discourse marker. The
following is a segment from a Rabbit and Coyote myth
narration.

7.
49. kastigo   0-ajyi-0--k-i7-0"   x-chi-i-0=b'i.
    PUNISHMENT com-BE-3a--1e-TAKE-3a inc-SAY-ivm-3a=rpt
What I got was punishment," (it is said) he said.

50. <u>entonses yajni jaw=a</u>.
    then   when THAT=clt
Then when that happened.

51. "pwes bweno si=ta   oj=cho wa7an-0 mas la7"
    well GOOD if=con fut=rep EAT-3a   MORE COME!
"Well good, if you want to eat more, come on!"

Here the particular set of discourse markers is used to
summarize the preceding sequence of events, which were
Coyote's lamentations about the miseries he had endured
on Rabbit's account, and marks the transition to the
quote from Rabbit, which leads cohesively into the next
episode of the story.
     The meaning of each of these discourse marker
phrases is in part a factor of the way in which the
particular discourse markers comprising the phrase
interact with one another. This allows for a wide

range of subtly different types of cohesion. Schiffrin
hints at a similar process of combination of discourse
markers in English, but the fact that she deals only
with English discourse markers that are syntactically
detachable elements allows her to avoid the
combinations and to treat each discourse marker in
isolation or as one in a series rather than as forming
an aggregate with distinctive meaning.[2] The fact that
the Tojolabal discourse marker phrases are composed of
an accumulation of discourse markers through
cliticization forces us to deal with their nature as
complex units.

   The second category of Tojolabal clitics
considered here occurs only at the end of an utterance.
After utterance-initial position, utterance-final is
the most salient position in discourse. Virginia Hymes
(1987) has noted that line-final particles function in
the organization of Warm Springs Sahaptin discourse.
There are at least three Tojolabal utterance-final
clitics that are arguably discourse markers. They are
=tak '[emphasis], anyway'; =b'a '[contrast],
[emphasis]'; and =ye7/=ye7n '[emphasis], anyway'.
Discourse markers are tricky to define, but these have
been the most difficult in the Tojolabal inventory. As
far as I can determine, all three are used exclusively
in conversation, and all generally occur utterance-
finally at the very end of a conversational
contribution. In (8.), E's final comment ends with
=tak, which terminates the string of back-channels.

8.
JL: ja7-0 y-uj   oj=xa=cha   y-a7-0--y-i7-0
    cl-3a 3e-AGENCY fut=now=rpt 3e-MAKE-3a--3e-TAKE-3a

    ja   jach'oj=i.
    det HARVEST=npt
    That's why they're going to harvest.

E: ja7-0=i   ermana.
    cl-3a=npt SISTER
    Yes, sister.

JL: ja7-0=i.
    cl-3a=npt
    Yes.

E: ja7-0=i   ja7-0 y-uj   wa-s-le7-aj-0
    cl-3a=npt cl-3a 3e-AGENCY pro-3e-SEEK-tvm-3a

    s-moj-e7=tak.
    3e-COMPANION-3pl=anyway
    Yes, that's why they're looking for companions,
    anyway.

Exceptions to the turn-final occurrence are
particularly emphatic conversational responses, as in
this excerpt from a joking conversation:

9.
A: w-e7n   lom   gana   wa
      2e-indpn BECAUSE REALLY pro

      x-w-a7--yakb'i-k-on--kan=ta.
      inc-2e-MAKE--DRUNK-sbj-1a--STAY=already
      Because it's you who really makes me get drunk.

L: 0-ko7-0=ta   jun ala b'is=i.
      com-DOWN-3a=already ONE dim SHOT=npt
      He's already downed a shot [of liquor].

A: jach=ni=tak=a.
      thus=emp=anyway=clt
      That's really right anyway.

      0-jak-a--w-a7-0--kan   trawo.
      com-ARRIVE-2a--2e-MAKE-3a--STAY TRAGO
      You came to make people drink liquor [lit. you
      came to leave liquor].
      b'a lom=xta   oj w-a7--yakb'-uk-0
      loc FOR NO REASON=dur fut 2e-MAKE--DRUNK-sbj-3a

      ja kristiyano.
      det PEOPLE
      Just to make people drunk.

The function of these utterance-final discourse markers
is directly parallel to the end-of-turn use of phrases
as discourse markers in ritual speech. Part of their
meaning is to signal that the speaker is relinquishing
his or her turn, and that someone else should take the
next turn.

VI. Conclusion
     The "tentative conditions" that Schiffrin outlined
for the use of an expression as a discourse marker
appear to be biased toward English in at least two
ways: syntactic detachability and sentence initial
position. Comparison of several genres of discourse
also extends the notion of what discourse markers can
be and perhaps also enhances the understanding of what
they accomplish in discourse. While there are
similarities in the way that discourse markers operate
in conversation, narrative, and ritual speech, there
are also aspects of distinctiveness in each genre.
While there are perhaps universals of discourse
markers, there are also language-specific features in
their form and function.

What was a dilemma for Bright, the question of
whether demarcation of discourse units made for poetry
in Native American myth narratives, is clarified with
the understanding that the demarcators are discourse
markers, which have similar functions but perhaps
different manifestations in different speech genres.
Comparing the discourse structure of speech genres
helps resolve the kind of problem lamented by Bright in
his analysis of Karok, where he wanted to recognize and
show the value of the poetic structure of Native
American oral tradition but puzzled about how to
determine distinctions between narrative and poetry.
Bright found "initial particles" in Karok myths to
operate similarly to those Hymes analyzed as revealing
poetry in Chinookan, but he was dismayed to find the
same "initial particles" in ethnographic texts. He
wondered,

> Does this mean that I was actually getting
> ethnographic poetry? Probably not; the
> situation in which a Karok speaker dictated
> texts to me, word by word, was analogous to
> the native situation in which stories were
> told to children for piece-by-piece
> repetition, and so the style of narrative may
> have artificially been extended to
> descriptions of salmon-fishing and
> sweathouses (1982:280-1)

I think that the distribution of "initial particles"
that Bright found was neither a product of ethnographic
poetry nor a factor of the form of dictation. Rather,
it is evidence that in Karok, as in Tojolabal,
discourse markers operate to enhance structure and
cohesion in various genres.

Karok is a language without a vital speech
community, and hence it is difficult to obtain a range
of speech genres to carry out a comparison of the form
and function of discourse markers. For Tojolabal,
where a vital speech community does exit, I have shown
that while different genres are characterized by
different discourse markers, the same functions of
cohesion and structure are carried out by discourse
markers in all genres. Discourse markers seem to be
essential to the cohesive structure of language in
general. It is not surprising that discourse markers
might be most salient and regular in the poetic genres
of Chinookan, Karok and Tojolabal myth, as Jakobson
(1968:599) has shown, "grammatical concepts...find
their widest application in poetry as the most
formalized manifestation of language." Tannen (1982)
and Friedrich (1986) point out that the relationship
between conversation and poetry is along a continuum.
Discourse markers are signposts along this continuum.

Acknowledgements:

I am grateful to Lyle Campbell, Laura Martin, Walter
Pitts, and Miles Richardson for rewarding interactive
discourse and for helpful criticism on various versions
of this paper.

Notes:

1. Abbreviations used in text examples are as follows:
1,2,3a - first, second, third person absolutive; 1,2,3e
- first, second, third person ergative; cl - cleft; clt
- clause terminal; com - completive aspect; det -
determiner; dur - durative; emp - emphatic; fut -
future; inc - incompletive aspect; indpn - independent
pronoun; ivm -intransitive verb marker; npt - noun
phrase terminal; pas - passive; pl - plural; pro -
progressive; relN - relational noun; rep - repetitive;
rpt - reportative; sbj - subjunctive; term - terminal;
tvm - transitive verb marker.
2. Laura Martin pointed this out to me.

Bibliography:

Brody, Jill. 1986a. Repetition as a rhetorical and
     conversational device in Tojolabal (Mayan).
     International Journal of American Linguistics
     52(3):255-274.
Brody, Jill. 1986b. Tojolabal Maya folktales: Discourse
     structure and variation. Paper presented at the
     American Anthropological Association meetings.
Brody, Jill. 1987a. Particles in Tojolabal Mayan
     discourse. Kansas Working Papers in Linguistics
     12:1-12.
Brody, Jill. 1987b. Particles borrowed from Spanish as
     discourse markers in Mayan languages.
     Anthropological Linguistics 29(4):507-21.
Brody, Jill. In press. Incipient literacy: From
     involvement to integration in Tojolabal. Oral
     Tradition.
Brody, Jill. forthcoming. Conversation as the matrix
     for Mayan discourse analysis. Current Issues in
     Mayan Discourse Analysis, ed. by Laura Martin.
     John Benjamins.
Bright, William. 1981. Poetic structure in oral
     narrative. Spoken and Written Language, ed. by
     Deborah Tannen, 171-84. Norwood, N.J.: Ablex.

Bright, William. 1982. Literature: Written and Oral.
    Analyzing Discourse: Text and Talk, Georgetown
    University Round Table on Languages and
    Linguistics, 1981, ed. by Deborah Tannen, 271-
    285. Washington, D.C.: Georgetown University
    Press.
Friedrich, Paul. 1986. The Language Parallax:
    Linguistic Relativism and Poetic Indeterminacy.
    Austin: University of Texas Press.
Grimes, Joseph E. 1975. The Thread of Discourse.
    Berlin: Mouton.
Gumperz, John J. 1982. Discourse Strategies. Cambridge:
    Cambridge University Press.
Hymes, Dell. 1981. 'In Vain I Tried to Tell You':
    Essays in Native American Ethnopoetics.
    Philadelphia: University of Pennsylvania Press.
Hymes, Dell. 1987. Tonkawa poetics: John Rush Buffalo's
    "Coyote and Eagle's Daughter." Native American
    Discourse: Poetics and Rhetoric, ed. by Joel
    Sherzer and Anthony C. Woodbury, 17-61. Cambridge:
    Cambridge University Press.
Hymes, Virginia. 1987. Warm Springs Sahaptin narrative
    analysis. Native American Discourse: Poetics and
    Rhetoric, ed. by Joel Sherzer and Anthony C.
    Woodbury, 62-102. Cambridge: Cambridge University
    Press.
Jakobson, Roman. 1968. Poetry of grammar and grammar of
    poetry. Lingua 21:597-609.
Levinson, Stephen C. 1983. Pragmatics. Cambridge:
    Cambridge University Press.
Longacre, Robert E. 1976. 'Mystery' particles and
    affixes. Papers for the Twelfth Regional Meeting
    Chicago Linguistic Society, ed. by Salikoko S.
    Mufwene, Carol A. Walker and Sanford B. Steever,
    468-75. Chicago: Chicago Linguistic Society.
Schiffrin, Deborah. 1987. Discourse Markers. Cambridge:
    Cambridge University Press.
Tannen, Deborah, ed. 1982. Spoken and Written Language:
    Exploring Orality and Literacy, Vol. 9 of Advances
    in Discourse Processes, ed. by Roy O. Freedle.
    Norwood, NJ: Ablex.

DISCOURSE FUNCTIONS AND SYNTAX

Jan Terje Faarlund
University of Chicago

1. Introduction. The aim of this paper is twofold: based
on data from colloquial Norwegian (cf. Appendix), I will
present an inventory of discourse functions, and I will
attempt to characterize the level of linguistic
representation where they associate with syntactic
structure. In order to account for the distribution of
discourse functions in the sentence, we need a set of
precisely defined categories both for those functions
and for sentence elements at the level where discourse
functions are relevant.

2. Discourse functional sentence structure. It is
generally accepted that in cases where the syntax of a
given language allows for variable constituent order,
given elements typically precede elements which carry
new information - or, to use a different set of terms,
topic precedes comment. Terms that refer to discourse
related notions such as topic and comment, are used on
at least two different levels of linguistic description,
which often may lead to a pernicious ambiguity. 'Topic'
may on the one hand be used to refer to sentence elements
that are grammatically marked as such, for example by
occupying the first position in the sentence, as in
Chinese or Scandinavian, or by having a certain morpheme
attached to them, as in Japanese or Cebuano. In this
sense 'topic' and 'comment' are (morpho)syntactic
categories. On the other hand, 'topic' may be used to
refer to an element with certain discourse functional
properties, whether or not the element is grammatically
marked as topic. In this paper, the terms will be used
in this latter sense.
  The exact definition of topic and comment as
discourse functions is of course more problematic. I
cannot go into that in detail here; I will merely adopt
the more or less standard interpretation of 'topic' as
that part of the sentence that carries information that
the speaker assumes that he shares with the hearer. This
includes then elements that are existentially presupposed, given in the context or in the communicative
situation, or at least presented as if they were given.
'Comment' is what introduces new information. For the
purpose of the work that I am reporting on here, the
distinction between two kinds of topics is as important
as the distinction between topic and comment.

3. <u>Discourse functional categories</u>. The categories that turn out to be relevant at the level where they associate with syntactic structure can be defined as follows:

i)   <u>Anaphoric topics</u> (A): Sentence elements that refer to entities introduced in the previous linguistic context, i.e. third person pronouns, definite NPs, and certain temporal and locative adverbials anchored in the time or place of the narrative.

ii) <u>Deictic topics</u> (D): Sentence elements that refer to entities in the context of the speech act or communicative situation, i.e. first and second person pronouns, tense markers, certain temporal and locative adverbials anchored in the place or time of the speech act, modal verbs and modal adverbs.

iii) <u>Empty topics</u> (0): Semantically empty elements that occupy typical topic positions by virtue of not being comments or new information, such as the dummy elements 'there' and 'it'.

iv) <u>Comment</u> (C): Sentence elements introducing new information.

v)   <u>Expressives</u> (X): Sentence elements highlighting or contrasting certain parts of the given or new information. An expressive element may refer to a member of an already given set, contrasting this member to the other members of the set.

Below is a demonstration of how the various discourse functions are distributed over sentences from spoken Norwegian. The numbers refer to the numbering in the Appendix, where the sentences are given in their full context.

```
    A         D                                    C
5  Det  hadde vi  hver vår törn hver fredag å pusse,
   that had   we  each our turn each Friday to polish


    A          0                    C
14 Der  stod   det  en sånn en gammal krakk,
   there stood there a  such an old   bench


    A        C
7  ho  var  reingjöringskone.
   she was  cleaning-woman
```

```
     D              C
32 Jeg var liten jentunge.
   I   was little girl

     X          D     C
24 de  andre hadde liksom  ordna  opp hjemme
   the others had   sort-of tidied up  at-home

     0              C
4  Det   var ikke noe  som hette å kjöpe elektrisk omn
   there was not anything called to buy electric stove
```

4. "The Sentence Schema". The Danish linguist Paul
Diderichsen in his work in the forties and the fifties
(Diderichsen 1946) introduced a model for syntactic
analysis of Scandinavian called the "sentence schema"
(Sætningsskemaet), which won wide recognition among
Scandinavian structuralist linguists and educators as a
method of accounting for the word order properties of
Scandinavian languages. Diderichsen and his followers
observed and described several interesting syntactic
implications of this model. (About some of these
results, as well as the history and most recent develop-
ments of the theory, see Heltoft and Andersen 1986, and
the references there.) In view of more recent linguistic
theory, particularly autolexical syntax (Sadock,
forthcoming, and personal communication), Diderichsen's
sentence schema may be seen as a level of representation
where the syntactic module associates with the discourse
functional module.

      According to Diderichsen, Danish sentences can be
divided into three parts, which he called "fields", and
each field - except the first one - consists of three
positions. Figure 1 shows the schema analysis of three
different word order versions of a Norwegian declarative
main sentence.

FUNDA MENT	NEXUS FIELD			CONTENT FIELD		
	v	n	a	V	N	A
Ho she	hadde had	x	ikkje not	treft met	han him	i fjor last-year
I fjor	hadde	ho	ikkje	treft	han	x
Han	hadde	ho	ikkje	treft	x	i fjor

Fig. 1. The Sentence Schema: Main Declarative Sentences.

The Nexus field and the Content field each have three positions, one for the verb, one for NPs, and one for any adverbials. Diderichsen used lower case letters as symbols for the Nexus field positions and capital letters for the Content field positions. For example, n stands for the NP position in the Nexus field, which is the subject position. Thus grammatical relations are defined in terms of fields and positions. As can be seen from Figure 1, two of the fields start with a verb. The verb therefore marks the boundary between the fields, and there is a striking parallelism in that the three positions for verb, nominal, and adverbial occur in the same order in the two fields. Although the model is strictly monostratal, the names of the fields reflect semantic or deep syntactic considerations, while the partition itself and the definition of the fields and positions are motivated on the basis of surface syntax.

5. _Associations of syntactic surface structure and discourse functions_. I will assume that the relevant discourse functional categories for Scandinavian are the ones listed and defined in Section 3 above, and that the relevant syntactic units that associate with them are defined in terms of the Sentence Schema given in Figure 1. The hypothesis to be supported in the following says basically that each of the three fields in declarative sentences, delineated by (the position of) the verbs, is the domain of different types of discourse functions: expressive elements and anaphoric topics belong in the Fundament, deictic topics in the Nexus field, and the comment in the Content field. This can be formalized in terms of an association chart as in Figure 2.

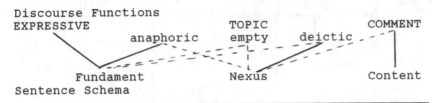

Fig. 2. Association Chart: Discourse Functions and Surface Syntax.

Exceptions to this general rule are due to strict requirements of the syntax of the language. Syntactic constraints that overrule the discourse functional principles are:

i)   one and only one constituent can be in the Fundament (Scandinavian is a strict verb second language),
ii) finite auxiliary verbs and most modal adverbs cannot occur in the Fundament.
iii) non-cliticized object noun phrases, subcategorized adverbials, nonfinite verbs, and obligatory predicate complements cannot occur in the Nexus field,
iv) the subject cannot occur in the Content field.

The role of the empty topic is to fill positions that cannot remain empty for syntactic reasons, and for which there is no other topic available. The empty topic is therefore found in the Fundament if there is no deictic or anaphoric topic in the sentence, or in the NP position in the Nexus field (the subject position) if the only topic is a non-subject.

Obviously, claims of the sort that are made here are claims about tendencies, not about absolute rules of grammar. Therefore they cannot technically be refuted in a Popperian sense, let alone "proven". Hypotheses or theories about discourse structure can only be made plausible by being tested on massive amounts of data. All I can do in this context is to show how the theory is supported by the text excerpt given in the Appendix. The Appendix is a transcript from spontaneous speech in Oslo dialect, recorded during a major sociolinguistic project at the University of Oslo in the 1970s (Hanssen et al. 1978). My original study is based on a larger corpus and also on different genres, including folk tales. The results so far support the hypothesis. In addition, a graduate thesis from the University of

Trondheim, (Våtevik 1988), confirms my findings on the basis of a larger and different corpus.

5.1. The Fundament. In most of the sentences the Fundament clearly contains an anaphoric topic, for example in sentence 1, where det refers to the kitchen mentioned in the question; in 3 inni der refers to the hood mentioned in 2; in 8 ho refers to the mother mentioned in 7, where ho is also in the Fundament because it has been introduced immediately before by left dislocation.

Not all the sentences have an anaphoric topic in the fundament, however. In 2 it is the pronoun vi, which is deictic; in this sentence there is no anaphoric topic, the rest is a finite verb and a piece of new information. Since the Fundament is obligatorily filled, it is filled by the deictic topic if there is no anaphoric topic available. 25 and 32 are similar cases.

In 4 the Fundament consists of the dummy word det, which is an empty topic. Here again there is no anaphoric topic, except maybe the adverbial den gangen, but the fact that it is placed at the end of the sentence gives it special focal emphasis. It would, however, also have been equally natural to treat the adverbial as an anaphoric topic, placing it in the Fundament, as in 17.

The reason why expressive elements compete with anaphoric topics about the Fundament position can be seen clearly from the present text. Expressive elements are topical in the sense that they refer to members of sets already introduced, or to concepts evoked indirectly. De andre in 24 are contrasted to the persons already mentioned, her brother and herself. De andre therefore also carries given information in the sense that it refers to members of an already known set. The phrases noen in 26-28 are also expressive elements, in that they pick out definite members of the same set. The phrase telefon in 30 has not been mentioned previously, and can hardly be said to carry given information. But notice the context of this. The interviewee talks about when her mother was sick, and is going to tell about what happened then. Then it is just as if she expects the interviewer to ask why she did not call the doctor, and that is how the telephone becomes topical, although the interviewer did not say a word. Rather than presenting a counterexample, sentences like 30 in fact support the hypothesis, precisely because the occurrence of the word 'telephone' in the Fundament leads the reader or listener to infer that question from the interviewer.

5.2. The Nexus field. Certain elements obligatorily belong in the Nexus field, first of all the finite verb.

Part of the finite verb is the tense marker, which by
definition is deictic in main declarative sentences.
When there is no auxiliary verb in the sentence, the main
verb attaches to the tense marker, and that way we may
obligatorily get non-topical elements into the Nexus
field because of this syntactic requirement. This is the
case for example in 16, 22 and 34. Sentences 9, 10, 15,
and 23 have a special Scandinavian aspectual construction
which I cannot go into here.

The negators, ikke 'not' and aldri 'never' also
obligatorily belong in the nexus field, as in 4, 30, and
34. They normally have no other place to go when they
have the whole sentence as their scope, except that aldri
may also occur in the Fundament if it is expressive.
Modal adverbials belong in the Nexus field, being deictic
in the sense that they refer to the speaker's attitude
towards the content of the sentence or to the hearer,
rather than convey new information. The adverb vel in
21 is such a modal. It would have to be rendered in
English as something like 'I suppose'; and jo in 30 means
roughly 'as you know'. Da in 3 is a kind of narrative
particle, just signaling that I am now in the middle of
an exposé, and expect to continue uninterrupted. In 12,
24, and 25 liksom serves as a hedge, modifying the
content of the sentences.

Subjects in spoken Norwegian are necessarily topics,
either anaphoric, deictic, or empty, and a subject phrase
which is not in the Fundament has no other choice than
the Nexus field. Of the 35 sentences in the text
excerpt, almost half have a Nexus field subject. In four
of these sentences, the subject is a third person,
anaphoric pronoun; see for example sentence 18, which has
the adverb så in the Fundament. Så is the anaphoric
adverb par excellence in Norwegian, and is used exten-
sively in the spoken language to mark temporal or causal
sequence in a narrative. Since this adverbial occupies
the Fundament, then, the subject has to stay in the Nexus
field even though it, too, is anaphoric. This follows
from a general principle discussed in Faarlund (1981).
According to that principle, whenever two elements of the
same discourse functional category compete for the
Fundament position, the one that otherwise would be last
will end up in the Fundament. This means that adverbials
precede nominals if they are of equal discourse functional status. The remaining Nexus field subjects are
either the dummy subject det or a first person pronoun,
which of course is deictic. In 22 there is in addition
a first person clitic object or reflexive pronoun, which
is also deictic, of course.

5.3. The Content field. As expected, the comment is typically to be found in the Content field, which comprises the final part of the sentence. To the extent that we find topical elements also in the content field, it is because they have to be there by requirements of the syntax, or because other possible options are taken up by other topical elements. For example in sentence 1, the word innreda is repeated from the preceding question, and is thus an anaphoric topic. It is a nonfinite verb (or a predicate adjective), and can therefore not occur in the Nexus field, and the Fundament is taken up by another anaphoric element.

Conversely, parts of the comment may occur in the Nexus field due to syntactic requirements, as we have seen in the case of finite main verbs, e.g. in 34. Consequently, it is possible for a declarative sentence not to have a Content field at all, as can also be seen from 34.

6. Discourse functions overriding syntax. As we have seen, discourse functional principles are normally restricted by the syntactic rules of the language, and can thus operate only within the limits of the word order options offered by the syntax. At least one syntactic phenomenon of Modern Norwegian, however, seems to indicate that the opposite may be the case. Consider the examples (a-c) below.

    a. Eg trudde [det hadde kommi mange gjester]
       I thought that there had arrived many guests
    b. Alle gjestene trudde eg [_ hadde kommi]
       all the guests thought I that had arrived
       'I thought all the guests had arrived'
    c. *Det trudde eg [_ hadde kommi mange gjester]
       there thought I that had arrived many guests
       (with same reading as (a))

The interesting fact here is the ungrammaticality of sentence (c). The reason is that the subject extracted from the embedded sentence is the dummy det. Such dummies are possible in embedded sentences, as shown in (a). Subjects may be extracted from embedded object clauses, as shown in (b), but the dummy subject may not be extracted, (c). The explanation is that the resulting structure has an empty subject in the Fundament of the higher clause, followed by the matrix subject, which must always be either an anaphoric or a deictic topic. This then violates the order predicted by the chart in Fig. 2. The result this time is not only a certain oddity, but a very definite grammatical unacceptability.

7. <u>Conclusion</u>. As always, the answers you get depend on the questions you ask. Asking questions about the relationship between syntax and discourse functions involves also defining not only syntactic, but also discourse functional categories. The categories introduced in this paper have turned out to reveal connections between syntactic surface structure and discourse functional structure beyond the obvious and well known fact that given information precedes new information.

APPENDIX

Sample text in approximated standard orthography (adapted from Hanssen et al. 1976), with interlinear word-by-word translation. Slashes mark the boundaries between the fields; material that does not belong inside the frames of a declarative sentence is put between parentheses.

```
(Hvordan var kjökkenet innreda?)
how was the-kitchen equipped
1  Det / var / innreda akkurat som et gammalt kjökken.
   it   was   equipped just like an old      kitchen
2  Vi / hadde / ei damphette av mur,
   we   had     a hood (over the stove made) of stone
3  (og) inni der / var det da / en omn.
   and  in  there was there then a stove
4  Det / var ikke / noe som hette å kjöpe elektrisk omn
   there was not anything called to buy electric stove
   den gangen.
   that time
   (there was no such thing as buying an electric stove
   in those days)
   (Og mye kobber på veggane.)
   and much brass on the-walls
5  Det / hadde vi / hver vår törn hver fredag å pusse,
   that had  we    each our turn each Friday to polish
6  Det / var / et ganske allminnelig kjökken,
   it   was   a quite    ordinary     kitchen
7  (men ho mamma,) ho / var / reingjöringskone.
   but     mama,  she was   cleaning-woman
8  Ho / har / vært vaskekone for alle disse store
   she  has   been cleaning-woman for all those great
   familiene oppe på vestkanten, (ho)
   families  up  on the-westend
9  Ho / gikk bort / og vaska enda ho stelte oss ungane.
   she went out    washing although she took-care-of us
   children
10 Ho / var borte / og sleit og vaska.
   she  was out     toiling and washing
```

11 Da / var det / den yngste broren min, da, også jeg,
   then was it   the youngest brother mine then and I,
12 Så / skulle liksom vi / möte ho, da, om eftan
   then should sort-of we meet her then in the-evening
   når ho kom
   when she came
13 Da / gikk vi som regel / bort på Etterstadgaten der
   then went we as rule over to Etterstad-street there
14 Der / stod det / en sånn en gammal krakk,
   there stood there a such an old bench
15 (og) der / satt han Olaf og jeg / og venta på mamma
    and there sat   Olaf and I   waiting for mama
16 Da / kom ho, (da,)
   then came she
17 (og) den gangen / var det / hestetrikk.
    and that time   was there horse-tram
18 Så / kom 'a, (da,)
   then came she
19 (og) da / hadde 'a / korga på armen,
    and then had she the-basket on the-arm
20 (og) oppi der / hadde 'a / fått litt godt,
    and in   there had she got some goodies,
21 (for) dem / hadde vel / litt ekstra,
    for they had (I-suppose) some extra,
   (disse her storfolka.)
   these here high-up-people
22 (Og) da / kosa vi oss / når vi kom hjem.
    and then enjoyed we ourselves when we got home
23 Da / satt vi to / og venta på henne, (da,)
   then sat we two waiting for her
24 (mens) de andre / hadde liksom / ordna opp hjemme
    while the others had   sort-of tidied up at-home
25 Vi / hadde liksom / hver vår oppgave.
   we   had   sort-of each our task
26 Noen / skurte / golver
   some   mopped   floors
27 (og) noen / törka / stöv
    and some   wiped   dust (dusted off)
28 (og) noen / gikk / ærender
    and some   went   shopping
29 Så / var det / en gang som ho mamma var blitt syk.
   then was there one time that mama   had gotten sick
30 (Og) telefon / var det jo ikke / å snakke om å ha.
    and telephone was there not to talk about to have
   (there was no question of having a telephone)
31 Så / var jeg / ute i gården og lekte.
   then was I   out in the-backyard playing
32 Jeg / var / liten jentunge.
   I   was   little girl

40

33 Så / var jeg / ute i gården.
   then was I   out in the-backyard
34 Det / glömmer jeg aldri.
   that forget I   never
35 (Og) så / kommer det / to sånne flotte hester.
   and then come   there two such beautiful horses

REFERENCES

Diderichsen, Paul. 1946: Elementær Dansk Grammatik.
Gyldendal. Copenhagen.

Faarlund, Jan Terje. 1981: Obligatory fronting in a
verb initial language: an attempt at pragmatic syntax.
R. A. Hendrick et al., eds.: Papers from the 17th
Regional Meeting of the Chicago Linguistic Society,
45-58. Chicago.

Hanssen, Eskil, et al. 1976: vanli osjlomål vel,
Talemålsundersokelsen i Oslo (TAUS). Novus. Oslo.

Hanssen, Eskil, et al. 1978: Oslomål. Novus. Oslo.

Heltoft, Lars, John E. Andersen, eds. 1986: Sætningsskemaet og dets stilling - 50 år efter. Nydanske
studier & almen kommunikationsteori 16-17. Akademisk
forlag. Copenhagen.

Sadock, Jerrold M. (forthcoming): Autolexical Syntax.

Våtevik, Marie Johanne. 1988: Anafori og deiksis.
Cand.philol. thesis. University of Trondheim.
Trondheim.

NON-PROPOSITIONAL ADDRESSEES

ZYGMUNT FRAJZYNGIER
UNIVERSITY OF COLORADO AT BOULDER

1 Introduction

In current (and past) syntactic theories, both "formal" and "functional," all constituents of a sentence are assigned to either the propositional component or the Tense, Aspect, Modality components. Most theories are stated as if they were exhaustive i.e., they are supposed to account for every lexical item and morpheme occurring in the sentence. Relational Grammar appears to be slightly less exhaustive than others in that it provides the formal apparatus for the description of only the propositional component of the clause. In view of this situation the existence of elements of the clause lying outside of the scope of those theories is implicitly ruled out. The purpose of this brief paper is to present the first evidence for the existence of elements that are constituents neither of the propositional structure nor of the TAM components of the sentence. The existence of such elements constitutes a challenge for linguistic theories: either they must allow for the possibility that there are elements that the theories do not account for, or else the theories must be adjusted so as to incorporate those elements into the existing paradigms.[1] Although the elements in question can be found in a number of languages (to be described a later paper), the present paper deals only with the data from Mupun, a West Chadic language spoken in the Plateau State of Nigeria. The focus of the paper is a function of a pronominal-like element. Such elements in all theories, including RG, are treated as lying in the domain of the propositional component. In what follows I will first provide an outline of the relevant structures of Mupun, and then I will discuss the evidence for the existence of a non-propositional addressee, i.e. a pronominal form that refers to the addressee of the discourse but that is not part of the propositional structure.

2 The indicative and the interrogative in Mupun

Mupun is an SVO language. There is no nominal inflection and the grammatical relations and semantic roles of arguments are marked either by position with respect to the verb (for core arguments) or by prepositions. The indirect object as well as most locative arguments are marked by preposition n- and occur after the direct object. In the pronominal system there is gender distinction in second and third person singular only. In plural the gender distinction is neutralized. Adverbs of manner and time occur clause finally. The language has serial verb constructions used for a variety of functions, such as marking of certain locative arguments and marking of some adverbial characteristics. Sentential adverbs, which in Mupun

41

have all modal functions, occur clause initially. The category of tense is marked through morphemes derived from adverbs of time. All tense markers are an optional category and occur at the beginning of the clause. Perfective and habitual aspect markers occur before the verb when the subject is third person, and before the subject pronoun when the subject is first or second person. The progressive aspect marker, derived from the locative preposition pǝ, occurs before the verb regardless of the person of the subject. Mood is marked by several devices; imperative is marked by tone on the pronominal subjects marking second person; optative (mainly in the embedded clauses) is marked by a construction consisting of the clause initial kɔ́ and clause final marker ɗi. The complete scheme of an indicative clause in Mupun has therefore one of the following forms (optional elements in parentheses): (T) (S) A V (O) (IO) (Adv) (PP).

There are several types of interrogative sentences in Mupun. Yes/no questions without any presupposition as to the possible answer are marked by the clause final vowel i and high tone. Other vocalic markers are used to express surprise and presupposed negative answer. In specific interrogatives ("wh-questions") the argument of the proposition that the question is about is marked by the copula a. Such markers remain in situ, as this is the only way to indicate the role of argument. The specific interrogatives encode whether the argument is human (marker -w-), non-human (-m-), place (-n-), or cause/reason (-r-). The latter is also used to mark surprise. The clause final interrogative marker is the same as in yes/no questions, viz. -i. The specific interrogative marker has the form a - w/m/n/r-i. If the question is not about the subject, the specific interrogative will usually occur at the end of the clause. The above structure may be expanded by only one element, nuwa, described in the following section.

3 Hypothesis about the function of nuwa

The use of the clause final nuwa is pragmatically conditioned. It never occurs in narrative texts of any kind and it did not occur in elicited sentences until the present author became aware of its existence through an analysis of recorded conversations among several speakers of the language.

In clause final position, the position that is of interest in the present paper, the morpheme occurred only in interrogative sentences. The use of nuwa in affirmative sentences produces an ungrammatical sentence, e.g.:

(1) a   wun mu   wu ji   a   ɓuon fun a r-i   nuwa
    COP 2PL EMPH 2PL come PREP after 1PL INTERR PL

    'as far as you are concerned, you came after us, didn't you?'

cf.:

```
*a     wun mu    wu ji    a    ɓuon  fun nuwa
COP 2PL EMPH 2PL come PREP after   1PL   PL
```
'as far as you are concerned, you came after us'

I would like to propose that in the interrogative sentence as illustrated in sentence (1) the morpheme <u>nuwa</u> is added in clause final position when the question is addressed to more than one hearer. Note here that I am not claiming that the morpheme is used when there is more than one hearer. The evidence for the above hypothesis is provided by the following sentences where the hearer is also the argument of the clause: With a hearer in the singular <u>nuwa</u> cannot be used. <u>Nuwa</u> is used with a hearer in the plural when a question is addressed to more than one hearer; <u>nuwa</u> can also be used with a singular hearer when the question involves the hearer and some people with him/her, e.g.:

(2) *yi man   nə   wur lap   mpuo a r-i   nuwa

    2F know COMP 3M marry another INTERR PL

    for 'do you (F SG) know that he has married another one?'

cf.

    yi man   nə   wur lap   mpuo a r-i

    2F know COMP 3M marry another INTERR

    'do you (F SG) know that he has married another one?'

(3) wu   man   nə   wur lap   mpuo a r-i   nuwa

    2PL know COMP 3M marry another INTERR

    'do you (PL) know that he has married another one?'

The above sentences not only provide the evidence for the hypothesis that <u>nuwa</u> encodes the plural number of the addressees, but at the same time they also provide evidence that the unmarked interrogative sentence is by default addressed to a singular addressee.

Although <u>nuwa</u> in the sentences above refers to hearers that are also part of the proposition expressed by the clause, such an interpretation of this reference is not due to the inherent meaning or the syntactic position of <u>nuwa</u> but rather to the fact that the subject of the clause is second person plural.

The addressees, however, do not have to be an argument of the proposition. The following sentences do not allow for an interpretation in which the addressee(s) could also be an argument of the clause. Compare (4) with (1) above and compare (5), where the number of addressees is plural, with (6), where it is singular:

(4) mo ji   a   ɓuon fun a-r-i   nuwa

    3PL come PREP after   1PL INTERR PL

    'did they come after us?'

(5) wur lap mat ɗi mpuo a r-i nuwa
3M marry wife REL another COP why PL
'has he married another one?'

(6) wur lap mat ɗi mpuo a-r-i
'has he married another one?'

Compare also the following pair of sentences, where (7) differs from (8) in the number of the addressee only:

(7) a-w-i lap namwes-i
who marry Namwes-Interr
'who married Namwes?'

(8) a-w-i lap namwes-i nuwa
PL
'who married Namwes?'

Now that we have established what nuwa refers to, we should examine the categorial status of this morpheme in this specific position. I would like to propose that morpheme nuwa in the interrogative clause final position as illustrated in (1) represents a category that has not yet been explicitly described in the literature. It is the category that encodes one of the aspects of the speech situation, namely the number of addressees. It is thus a deictic category, but it differs from the deictic categories noted so far in that it does not have to be a constituent of the proposition.

All the examples discussed so far constitute the evidence for the hypothesis. Additional evidence for the deictic character of the plural addressee marker is provided by interrogative embedded clauses. In such clauses the plural marker nuwa does not occur, even if the addressee is an argument of the proposition, e.g.:

(9) wu tal pə mun nə war n-jiŋ-e
3M ask PREP 1PL COMP 3SG PREP-Jing-INTERR
'he asked us whether she is in Jing'

(10) n-tal pə wu nə war n-jiŋ-e
1SG-ask PREP 2PL COMP 3SG PREP-Jing-INTERR
'I asked you whether she is in Jing'

Thus the embedded interrogatives with a plural addressee do not differ from interrogatives with a singular addressee, e.g.:

(11) wu   tal pə   an   nə   war n-jiŋ-e

    3SG ask PREP 1SG COMP 3F PREP-Jing-INTERR

    'he asked me whether she is in Jing'

The explanation for these facts is as follows: One cannot use <u>nuwa</u> in embedded clauses because <u>nuwa</u> is a deictic category. Embedded clauses after a verb of saying, such as <u>tal,</u> do not provide a proper environment for deixis. When the embedded clauses in the sentences above were used as main clauses, the plural addressee marker was used in the context that suggested a plural addressee, viz.:

(12) wur n-jiŋ-e

    3M PREP-Jing-INTERR

    'is he in Jing?'

(13) wur n-jiŋ-e nuwa

    'is he in Jing?' (Plural addressee)

4 The polysemy and the origin of <u>nuwa</u>

The only other place in the grammatical system of Mupun where <u>nuwa</u> occurs is in the context of embedded clauses when the verb of the main clause is a verb of saying. In such clauses <u>nuwa</u> refers to the plural number of addressees. In the following example <u>nuwa</u> serves as the subject of the embedded clause:

(14) n-sat   mo nə   nuwa naa kə   n-kes   makaranta

    1SG-say 3Pl COMP PL look PERF 1SG-finish school

    'I told them, look, I have finished school' (Frajzyngier 1985:29)

Note that if the verb of the matrix clause is not a verb of saying, then <u>nuwa</u> cannot occur, and instead the usual discourse anaphora third person plural morpheme occurs, e.g.:

(15) n-pet mo ɓe mo/*nuwa ji

    1SG-call 3PL CONS 3PL came

    'I called them and they came'

In the following examples <u>nuwa</u> is a possessive pronoun. The antecedent with which <u>nuwa</u> is bound is in boldface:

(16) datar sat n-**dapus** kə **napus**   nə   ɗi
  Datar say PREP-D CONJ Napus   COMP 3M LOG
  naa la   rep <u>nuwa</u>
  see DIMIN girl 3PL.AD
  'Datar₁ told Dapus₂ and Napus₂ that he₁ saw their₂ daughter'
cf.

(17) datar sat n-dapus kə napus nə ɗi   naa la   rep mo

  'Datar₁ told Dapus₂ and Napus₂ that he₁ saw their∗₂ daughter'

Even if the addressee is singular, <u>nuwa</u> can still be used in the possessive form. In such a case it indicates that its referent is the addressee and some people with him/her, e.g.:

(18) datar   sat n-**napus**   nə   ɗi   naa la   rep <u>nuwa</u>
  Datar   say PREP-Napus COMP 3M LOG see DIMIN girl 3PL
  'Datar₁ told Napus₂ that he₁ saw their₂ daughter' (Frajzyngier 1989)

The interrogative clause final position of <u>nuwa</u> cannot be occupied by either verbs or nouns. In environments other than embedded clauses after a verb of saying, <u>nuwa</u> cannot occur as either a subject or an object of a clause, or as an object of a prepositional phrase. The following sentences contrast the ungrammatical use of <u>nuwa</u> in the two syntactic positions with the grammatical use of other referring expressions:

(19) *nuwa nas an

     beat 1SG

  for 'you(pl) beat me'

cf.

  wu nas an

  2PL beat 1SG

  'you pl. beat me'

  mo nas an

  'they beat me'

(20) *n-nas nuwa

   1SG beat

   for 'I beat you'

cf.

    n-nas wu

    1SG beat 2PL

    'I beat you'

    n-nas mo

    'I beat them'

The morpheme <u>nuwa</u> cannot be used as an argument of an equational sentence, in the function of either subject or predicate, e.g.:

(21) *nuwa a miskoom
          COP

    for 'you (pl) are chiefs'

cf. wu a miskoom
    'you PL are chiefs'

    mo a miskoom

    'they are chiefs'

The following examples contrast the ungrammaticality of prepositional phrases with <u>nuwa</u> with the grammaticality of prepositional phrases with other referring expressions, once again in an environment outside of the embedded clause after a verb of saying:

(22) *pə -nuwa
     at -
     for 'at your place'

cf.

    pə wu

    at you (pl)

    'at your place'

    pə mo

    'at their place'

(23) *mo kə́ nuwa

    3PL ASSOC

    for 'they and you'

48

cf.

mo kɔ́ wu

3Pl ASSOC 2PL

'they and you'

We are dealing with two different usages of <u>nuwa:</u> one in the embedded clauses after verbs of saying and the other in interrogative matrix clauses. The two functions are quite different. In the first, <u>nuwa</u> refers to the addressee of the main clause; in the second it refers to the addressee of the speech situation. Even if the embedded clause is a complement of a verb of saying in the main clause, <u>nuwa</u> cannot be used in the interrogative clauses, as illustrated in sentences (9)-(10), because this is not the proper environment for deixis. A possible question as to the diachronic primacy of one function over another cannot be answered with certainty. Note, however, that in the function of marking the anaphoric addressee, <u>nuwa</u> is a part of the rich system of anaphoric expressions that also includes logophoric pronouns (cf. Frajzyngier 1989). In the function of marking a deictic addressee, <u>nuwa</u> seems to be an isolated morpheme. The synchronic polysemy can be explained if one postulates that the language has encoded the grammatical function of the addressee and that the function includes both the anaphoric as well as the deictic addressee.

5 Implications

The paper has shown the existence of elements that do not form part either of the proposition or of the Tense/Aspect/Modal component. Current syntactic theories are ill equipped to accommodate such elements. More specifically, the deictic addressee bears no grammatical relations to the verb at any level; hence it is outside of the domain of Relational Grammar. The deictic addressee cannot have assigned Case or a Theta role, therefore it is outside the domain of GB theory. The deictic addressee cannot be described within the system of features and the ID/LP format of the GPSG theory. It cannot be described in the Lexical-Functional framework, which also assumes that every constituent of a clause is a part of either the TAM component or of the propositional component. It appears that functional models can be more easily modified to include elements discussed in the present paper. One would have to expand sentence structure to include, along with TAM and Propositional components, a component that encodes the environment of the speech situation. The elements of such an environment may but do not have to be elements of the propositional or TAM components. Possible modifications of the formal systems are much more complicated because of the possibility of seriously disturbing the remaining elements of the system.

6 Footnotes

*The work on this paper was partially supported by the NSF Grant Nr. BNS-84 18923. I would like to thank my Mupun assistants Wesley Kumtong Damar and Sylvanus Dashwa for their patience and help during the work on the Grammar of Mupun.

(1) It is not easy to find explicit statements as to the intended scope of the given theory. It appears that there is a governing tacit assumption that a syntactic theory is complete, i.e. that it accounts for every element of the sentence. A reading of Chomsky 1982a and b, Gazdar et al. 1985, Kaplan and Bresnan 1982, confirms this interpretation.

7 References

Bresnan, Joan (ed.). 1982. The mental representation of grammatical relations. Cambridge, Mass.: MIT Press.

Chomsky, Noam. 1982a. Lectures on government and binding. Dordrecht: Foris.

Chomsky, Noam. 1982b. Some concepts and consequences of the theory of government and binding. Cambridge, Mass.: MIT Press.

Frajzyngier, Zygmunt. 1985. 'Logophoric systems in Chadic'. Journal of African Languages and Linguistics, 7:23-37.

Frajzyngier, Zygmunt. 1989. 'Three types of anaphora' in Current Progress in African Linguistics, Isabelle Haik and Laurice Tuller, eds. Amsterdam: Foris.

Gazdar, Gerald, Ewan Klein, Geoffrey Pullum, and Ivan Sag. 1985. Generalized phrase structure grammar. Cambridge, Mass.: Harvard University Press.

Kaplan, Ronald, and Joan Bresnan. 1982. 'Lexical-Functional grammar: A formal system of grammatical representation'. In Bresnan 1982.

A Linguistically Motivated
Theory of Conversational Sequences

Michael L. Geis
The Ohio State University

A central concept in the analysis of conversation is the **adjacency pair** (Schegloff and Sacks 1973), which consists of a pair of turns in conversation such that utterance of the first member of the pair makes the second immediately relevant and expectable. Thus, utterance of a question makes an answer immediately relevant and expectable and utterance of a request makes an acceptance or rejection immediately relevant and expectable. The second turn of an adjacency pair might not follow the first immediately, as in cases in which the two utterances are interrupted by what Schegloff (1972) has called an Insertion Sequence. In (1) the adjacency pair consisting of turns $<T_2, T_3>$ interrupts the question-answer pair $<T_1, T_4>$.

(1) Merritt, 1976: 333
    A: May I have a bottle of Mich? T_1
    B: Are you twenty one? T_2
    C: No T_3
    D: No T_4

Even in this sort of case, the pair-wise organization of the turns that comprise conversation is maintained, for after the intrusive sequence has run its course, the relevant and expected next turn occurs.

Although the pair-wise organization of utterances is quite real, it is clear that there exist larger groupings of turns. Thus, while a request can be made and accepted utilizing a single pair of utterances, as in (2), these occur in what I (Geis 1989a, mss-a, mss-b) have elsewhere called "information rich" contexts in which most of the conditions that must be satisfied for a request to be made successfully are satisfied by the context.

(2)   A: Could I have some hot chocolate with whipped cream?
        B: Sure.

I would suggest that cases like (2) are much less representative of requests than are cases like (3), in which the request is worked out over four or more turns, and I would suggest that we begin to think of requesting, not as a property of specific utterances that somehow **count as** requests, but as an emergent property of conversational exchanges.

(3) Levinson, 1983: 347, from Merritt, 1976, 337.
        C: Do you have hot chocolate? T_1
        S: mmhmm T_2
        C: Can I have hot chocolate with whipped cream? T_3
        S: Sure ((leaves to get)). T_4

The following problems emerge concerning such sequences:

I.   We must have some way of identifying initial and terminal elements
     of sequences.
II. We must have some way of distinguishing one type of sequence from
     another, e. g. proposal sequences from invitation sequences, offer
     sequences from promise sequences, etc.
III. We must be able to account for the sequencing of subsequences
     inside sequences.

IV. We must account for the make up and the nature of the connection between the first and second turns of the adjacency pairs that make up each subsequence.

V. We must be able to identify intrusive sequences such as Insertion Sequences as being intrusive.

There are two approaches to solving these problems which I would like to consider here, one based on the theory of sequences advanced by Conversation Analysts and a neoSearlean account that I have been developing (Geis 1989; mss-a, mss-b) which is based on speech-act-theoretic principles.[1]

According to the Conversation Analysts, Schegloff and Levinson, a conversation like (3) consists of two subsequences, a pre-request sequence consisting of a question (*Do you have hot chocolate?*) followed by its go ahead (*mmhmm*), followed by a request sequence consisting of a request (*Can I have hot chocolate with whipped cream?*) followed by an acceptance (*Sure*). They see the claim that a conversational sequence might consist of a pre-sequence of a certain type followed by a primary sequence of the same type as a substantive claim about the internal structure of such conversational exchanges.

Schegloff (1984: 34f) has argued that at least two of the sacred cows of linguistics -- syntactic form and speech act theory -- are of problematic utility to our understanding of how utterances are interpreted in conversation. He has brought into question the thesis that "linguistic form supplies a prima facie basis for the analysis of an utterance, which will hold unless superseded by other features," arguing, for instance, that "what distinguishes questions from first pair parts of other sorts [of adjacency pairs] does not seem in any straightforward way to be sought from linguistic resources" and that "if the question form can be used for actions other than questioning, and questioning can be accomplished by linguistic forms other than questions, then a relevant problem can be posed not only about how a question does something other than questioning, but about how it does questioning." His own proposal is that the "structural location [of an utterance] can have attached to its slot a set of features that may overwhelm its syntactic or prosodic structure in primacy." Thus, he would say that an utterance like

(4) Why don't you come see me sometime?

is more likely to be used to register a complaint or make an invitation than to request information despite its interrogative form.

Schegloff seems not to appreciate the full import of his attack on the utility of linguistic form and prosody in the analysis of how utterances are used and interpreted in conversation, for in claiming that positional considerations can overwhelm form and prosody, he is also saying, whether he likes it or not, that positional considerations can also overwhelm utterance meaning. Observe that if one takes away from a sentence like (5)

(5) Will you help me?

its interrogative form and its rising intonation, all one has left is its "bare bones" propositional content, e. g.,

(6) $(\exists t)(At(Help (Hearer, Speaker), t) \& Laterthan(t, now))$

Thus, when Schegloff says that the interrogative form of an utterance can be overwhelmed by positional factors, he is also saying that its interrogative meaning can also be overwhelmed. Now, I would invite Schegloff to develop a theory of conversation in which all an utterance normally contributes to its interpretation in conversation is its "bare bones" propositional content, with all other aspects of its interpretation being accounted for by its sequential location. The implausibility of this view is quite staggering. To see this, consider the following representation of the propositional content of a homemade conversation

(7) Homemade Conversation
A: (∃t)(At(Bill go to Boston, t) & Laterthan(t, now) & In(t, tonight))
B: Yeah.

Given this representation, it would be quite impossible for us, as analysts, to tell whether A has asked a question (*Will Bill go to Boston tonight?*) which B has answered or has made an assertion (*Bill will go to Boston tonight*) that B has signaled prior knowledge of. What Schegloff fails to appreciate is that if linguistic form does not supply a prima facie basis for the interpretation of utterances in conversation, it isn't relevant at all, for what form is quintessentially is a prima facie, linguistic given.

In my view, the arguments that Schegloff (1984) advances in support of his quite remarkable views on the relevance of form to the interpretation of sentences in conversation are, in each case, based on a misanalysis of the data he cites in support of it. In Geis (1989a), I deal with one such example at length. I shall deal with a second here. Consider the following extract of a conversation.

(8) Schegloff (1984: 31)
B: Why don't you <u>come</u> and see me some⎰times T_1
A: ⎱I would
        like to T_2
B: I would like you to. Lemme ⎰just T_3
A: ⎱I don't know just
        where the-us-this address <u>is</u>. T_4

Schegloff writes (31) that "although B's first utterance in the excerpt looks syntactically like a question, it is not a "question" that A "answers," but an "invitation" (in question form) that she "accepts."

Why not-Interrogatives are particularly interesting, for, contra Schegloff, they exhibit important syntactic and semantic properties of Interrogatives even though they are normally used to make suggestions, which can function as invitations, as in the case of T_1 in (8), or requests, as in the case of

(9) Why don't you pick up some beer on the way over?

Schegloff's view that T_1 is not a question is very far from being correct. Negative *Why*-Interrogatives exhibit three important properties of questions beyond their inverted word order and the presence of the sentence-initial *Wh*-word *why*. First, they exhibit a presupposition characteristic of negative *Why*-Interrogatives. Note that just as the clearly Interrogative sentence (10.a) presupposes (10.b)

(10) a. Why didn't you use a hammer?
b. You didn't use a hammer.

a *Why not*-Interrogative being used to make a suggestion like (11.a) presupposes (11.b)

(11) a. Why don't you use a hammer?
b. You aren't using a hammer.

and the *Why not*-Invitation (12.a) of Schegloff's example presupposes the negative proposition (12.b)

(12)   a. Why don't you come see me sometimes.
       b. You don't (often enough/ever) come see me.

Second, *Why not*-Interrogatives, like negative questions generally, carry with them a deontic conventional implicature. Just as (13.a) conventionally implicates (13.b)

(13)   a. Isn't John here yet?
       b. John should be here by now.

and the *Why not*-Question (14.a) implicates (14.b)

(14)   a. Why didn't you use a hammer?
       b. You should have used a hammer.

and the *Why not*-Suggestion (15.a) implicates (15.b)

(15)   a. Why don't you use a hammer?
       b. You should use a hammer.

the *Why not*-Invitation of Schegloff's example (16.a) implicates the deontic proposition (16.b).

(16)   a. Why don't you come see me sometimes.
       b. You should come see me sometimes.

Thus, if we do not say that Schegloff's *Why not*-Interrogative is a genuine Interrogative, we shall be quite unable to account for the fact that it shares these important semantic properties with genuine Interrogatives even when being used to make an invitation.

Finally, the most compelling reason for saying that *Why not* constructions are genuine Interrogatives no matter how they are being used is that they are quite routinely answered as if they were questions. Observe that the pattern of positive and negative answers in the case of clear cases of *Why not*-Interrogatives, such as (17), extends to *Why not*-Interrogatives used to make suggestions (18) and to Schegloff's case (19).

(17) A: Why didn't you use a hammer?
       a. I did.
       b. Because it might have broken.
(18) A: Why don't you use a hammer?
       a. I'm going to.
       b. Because it might break.
(19) A. Why don't you come see me sometimes?
       a. I do.
       b. Because I have no way of getting to your place.

How is it that T_1 in conversation (8) counts as an invitation? This *Why not*-Interrogative conventionally implicates the deontic proposition (16.b) and it is this implicature that effects the invitation, for if the hearer accepts this implicature, as she does overtly in turn T_2, this establishes a willingness to visit the speaker. If she then concedes an ability to visit the speaker, the focus of turn T_4, she will be committed to visiting the speaker. The principle that governs such behavior is (20).

(20) If a person P_1 has a contextually given or expressed need or desire, and another person P_2 concedes an ability and willingness to satisfy it, then P_2 is obligated to satisfy it.

Thus, contrary to what Schegloff would have us believe, one cannot account for the force of T_1 without supposing that T_1 is a genuine Interrogative. However, it is clear that B did not provide either of the responses of (19). Instead, she responded to the conventional implicature (16.b). Notice in this connection how natural the following conversation is:

(21) Homemade conversation
       A: You should come see me sometimes.
       B: I would like to. (cf. T_2 in (8))

But, of course, to say that T_1 in (8) is a genuine Interrogative is not to say that it is a mere information question.
       In regard to data like

(22) Do you know who's going to that meeting?

Schegloff (1988) notes that speech act theory can account for its use as a direct *Yes-No*-Interrogative or as an indirect *Wh*-Interrogative, but claims that it cannot account for the fact that it can be used to make a pre-announcement, which is how Russ mistakenly construed it in the following excerpt of a conversation cited by Schegloff.

(23) Schegloff (1988: 57) -- Family dinner
       Mother: Do you know who's going to that meeting? T_1
       Russ: Who. T_2
       Mother: I don't kno:w. T_3
       Russ: Oh::. Prob'ly Missiz McOwen ('n detsa) en prob'ly Missiz
               Cadry and some of the teachers. (0.4) and the counsellors T_4

Schegloff (1988: 61) argues that "what a rudimentary speech act theoretic analysis misses, and I suspect a sophisticated one will miss as well, is that parties to real conversations are always talking in some sequential context," where a "sequential context" is taken by him to be the (p. 61) "more or less proximately preceding and projectably ensuing talk." He then goes on to say that (p. 61) "although it could be argued that speech act theory can incorporate another category of speech act like 'pre-announcement' and establish its felicity conditions and incorporate the result into future analysis, this is not the same as incorporating sequential connectedness itself. Here the outlook is not hopeful, for speech act theory has inherited from traditional philosophy the single act or utterance as its fundamental unit." What Schegloff (Schegloff and Sacks 1973: 313) is primarily claiming, in sum, is that "no analysis, grammatical, semantic, pragmatic, etc., of these utterances taken singly and out of sequence, will yield their import in use, will show what co-participants might make of them and do about them."
       I would like to agree with Schegloff that no grammatical or semantic analysis of utterances considered in isolation from the conversational contexts in which they occur can, taken alone, yield their import in **use**. However, it does not follow from this that form and literal meaning are not of critical importance to understanding how utterances are used. My analysis of Schegloff's *Why not*-Invitation illustrates the folly of this inference, for in order to explain how it is that an Interrogative can be used to make an invitation, one must assume that

it **is** an Interrogative, semantically and sytactically. What is required is a theory that allows us to distinguish what sentences are from how they are used.

There is a way out of this difficulty that will, I think, appeal to Schegloff. In the work cited earlier, I have made a distinction between what I call l-meaning, which is literal, linguistic meaning, and s-meaning, which concerns the significance of an utterance or its social meaning, and I would argue that one cannot account for the s-meaning of an utterance in a conversation without appealing to its l-meaning, but that an account of l-meaning is insufficient by itself to account for s-meaning. In this work, I make a fundamental distinction between certain basic linguistic constructions that have what I call "social action potential" -- Declaratives, Interrogatives, and Directives -- and the wide range of Social Actions that we perform using these constructions such as making promises, making offers, issuing invitations, giving warnings, making threats, as well as making assertions, asking questions, and making requests or giving orders, the last three being the respective default social actions associated with Declaratives, Interrogatives, and Directives. Thus, the sorts of things that previous theorists have called "speech acts" are treated here as being fundamentally social in nature and as making no contribution to the meanings of utterances.

Teun van Diyk has suggested to me, however, that the fact that certain actions, like questioning, promising, requesting, and offering invitations, etc. cannot be performed other than linguistically necessarily makes them speech acts. However, there is substantial social, and very little linguistic, content to what has been called speech acts. There is, for instance, no interesting linguistic difference whatever between (24.a) and (24.b), beyond the difference in reference of I and *Bill*, yet the first can easily be used to make a promise, while the second would normally not be so used.

(24)   a. I will be in my office at noon.
       b. Bill will be in his office at noon.

And, whether an assertion like *The bridge is out* is intended to convey information simpliciter or to give a warning by conveying information seems to be determined by context, rather than any purely linguistic factor, though prosody will sometimes offer a clue. And, whether or not a Directive might be a command or suggestion is sometimes determinable only by context -- by who is talking to whom. Thus, if a parent says (25) to a child it is an order, but if an advertiser says it, it must be construed as a suggestion.

(25) Brush your teeth with Crest.

But if essentially social factors determine what sort of action an utterance performs, then I think we must recognize that the action is basically social in nature and thus what is most important about such actions is not how they are performed (through speaking) but what they do (perform social actions).

I shall argue that any given conversational sequence will be a social action sequence -- a sequence intended to perform some social action like make a promise or request -- and that the sentences that occur in any such sequence will normally be meant literally, with the social force or import or significance, i.e., the s-meaning, of the utterances making up the sequence being predictable given

> the literal meaning (l-meaning) of the sentences (which includes truth-conditional aspects of meaning, presuppositions, conventional implicature, and most aspects of deixis)
> contextual information (including what has preceded conversationally, aspects of the social and epistemic context)

shared background knowledge
a set of conditions on social actions
common sense reasoning of a Gricean sort
principles governing the conduct of conversation, e.g., turn taking rules

On this view, such social actions as making promises or offers or giving warnings or making threats, etc., are seen primarily not as properties of utterances, but as properties of sequences.

I shall argue that Declaratives, Interrogatives, and Directives have associated with them truth-related sincerity conditions, which are conditions on their social action potential. Consider

(26) Sincerity Conditions
    a. Declaratives: for S asserts P to H: S must have a warranted belief that P is true.
    b. Interrogatives: for S asks H whether or not P: S must have a warranted belief that P is true or P is false.
        for S asks H an Interrogative of the form "WH-X, ...X...": S must have a warranted belief that there is an instantiation of "...X..." which is true.
    c. Directives: If S directs that H do A, under a description P, then S must have a warranted belief that H can act in such a way to cause P to come to be true.

This approach allows us to distinguish what a sentence is from how it is used.

Suppose that we say that the social purpose of promising and the conditions on the social action of promising are as in (27).[2]

(27) Promising (S-Commissive): S makes a promise to H to do A
    Purpose: to make a commitment to H to do A
    Sincerity Condition:
        S intends to do A C_1
    Preparatory conditions:
        H wishes S to do A C_2
        S is able to do A C_3

In this light, observe that, a Declarative like *I will be in my office at noon* (cf. (24.a)) constitutes a prediction about the future behavior of the speaker while *Bill will be in his office at noon* (cf. (24.b)) constitutes a prediction about the future behavior of someone else. Now, satisfaction of sincerity condition (26.a) on Declaratives -- the speaker has a warranted belief in the truth of what he says -- is possible in the case of a future prediction by a speaker about his or her own behavior just in case the speaker has an **intention** (cf. C_1 in (27)) to behave in the asserted way, which implicates an ability to do so (cf. C_3 in (27)). This intention is entailed by (24.a), then, given that it is a future, active Declarative with a first person subject. In a context in which the speaker believes the behavior **benefits** the hearer (cf. C_2 in (27)), then the utterance will count as a promise (social action), for both the sincerity and preparatory conditions on promises will have been satisfied. Now, *Bill will be in his office at noon* cannot be used to make a promise directly for there is no entailment of a speaker intention to perform some action. Instead, the speaker is giving his or her assurances that Bill will be in his office at noon. Thus, we can account for the different ways in which utterances like (24.a) and (24.b) can be used while assuming that these sentences are semantically identical up to the difference in reference of *I* and *Bill*. As this example illustrates, whether or not a sentence is a promise can be predicted simply given its literal meaning as a Declarative and facts about context and need not -- indeed, should not -- be treated as a property of the sentences employed. I take this to be an exceedingly important virtue of the proposed theory.

Given the theory advanced in this paper, it would be quite incorrect to say that the Interrogative of turn T_3 in conversation (3) **is** a request, as Levinson (1983: 361) would. In a commercial exchange like this, the willingness to satisfy reasonable consumer requests is assumed in the context, thus, all that is required (cf. principle (20)) is to determine whether or not the clerk is able to supply hot chocolate (cf. T_1) with whipped cream (cf. T_3). In my view, a view defended at length in the papers cited earlier, T_1 and T_3 are Interrogatives being used to request information within a larger sequence, the social intent of which is to make a request. In conversation, the whole is typically more than the sum of its parts.

Recall Schegloff's claim that speech act theory cannot account for the so-called pre-announcement interpretation of a sentence like (22). It is clear that although the Mother's question in T_1 was intended as an indirect *Wh*-Interrogative, this was not how Russ interpreted it. Instead, he construes it as being what Schegloff calls a "pre-announcement". Schegloff says that (p. 58) "pre-announcements regularly take such formats as "Guess what/who..." or "Y'know what/who..." etc." This sounds very much like he might be suggesting that such utterance patterns might be **conventionally** used to make pre-announcements. If we wish to maintain this position, we must say that T_1 in (23) is triply ambiguous in force, being conventionally usable as a direct *Yes-No*-Interrogative, indirect *Wh*-Interrogative, or pre-announcement. Since Schegloff (1984) has earlier used the term "ambiguity" to refer to alternative interpretations of what I am calling social force, I suspect that this is what he would have in mind. However, at most what can be said is that it is a property of an utterance that it can be used to make a pre-announcement **in certain particular types of contexts.** Thus, a sentence like T_1 in conversation (23) will be usable as a pre-announcement in virtue of some property *Pu* of the sentence and some property *Pc* of the context. The question arises as to what *Pu* and *Pc* are.

Consider the following revised scenarios.

(28) The indirect *Wh*-Interrogative interpretation
       Mother: I need to know who's going to that meeting. Do you
            know who's going?
       Russ: Yeah, Missiz McOwen, Missiz Cadry, ...
(29) A *Yes-No*-Interrogative interpretation
       Mother: I want you to phone everyone who is going to that
            meeting. Do you know who's going?
       Russ: Yeah.
(30) A pre-announcement interpretation
       Mother: I want you to phone everyone who is going to that
            meeting. Do you know who's going?
       Russ: No, who.
       Mother: Missiz McOwen, Missiz Cadry, ...
(31) A pre-request interpretation
       Mother: I want you to phone everyone who is going to that
            meeting. Do you know who's going?
       Russ: No, who.
       Mother: I don't know. Maybe you should phone Billy to see if
            he knows.

In order to account for these four scenarios, we need know only the *l*-meanings of the sentences that comprise it and certain facts about the context. We have no need whatever for the notion "pre-announcement." If it is clear to speaker and hearer that it is **the speaker who needs the information**, as in scenario (28), a sentence like T_1 in (23) must be interpreted as an indirect *Wh*-Interrogative. Why is this? Before answering this question, let us first consider a situation in which the person who needs this information may actually know that the hearer has it. In such a case, it would be appropriate to ask a **direct** *Wh*-Interrogative like *Who is going to the meeting?* On the other hand, if the speaker does not know whether or not the hearer has the information then he or she must first determine whether or not the hearer does have this information, and, as a result, a sentence like T_1 in (23) is in order. Now, the hearer will assume that this is not an idle question and will recognize that the only conceivable purpose in asking it, in this context, is to find out who is going to the meeting. If, in fact, the hearer has the information, a response like that in (28), where Russ replies first to the literal meaning (*l*-meaning) of the question, and then to the intended social force (*s*-meaning), is called for.

On the other hand, if it is **the hearer who needs the information**, as in scenarios (29), (30), and (31), then two responses are possible. If the hearer actually knows the information, he or she will presumably indicate this by saying *yes* or some variant thereof, as in (29). That will be the end of the matter. Notice that even had the mother intended what she said to be a pre-announcement, it will fail to be one in this case for Russ's response will have aborted it. Thus, an utterance's being a pre-announcement depends not on any intrinsic property of the utterance, as Schegloff's remark on the syntactic patterns employed might suggest, or any property of the turn in which it occurs or prior turns, but solely on how it is responded to in a **later** turn. On the other hand, if the hearer does not know this information, a response like *No*, or *No, who*, or *Who* is in order. In scenarios (30) and (31) we have two situations, one in which the mother has the information (namely (30)) and one in which she does not (namely (31)). If she does have the information, principle (20) will obligate her to supply it. In this case, the original question could be said to be a pre-announcement though saying this would contribute nothing to our understanding of what is going on. However, if the mother does not have this information, then she may come up with a request or suggestion along the lines of that in scenario (31). In this case, what she said originally would now have to be viewed as a pre-request.

Clearly, the concept "pre-sequence" contributes nothing whatever to an account of how utterances like T_1 in (23) are interpreted in conversation. Instead, how such an utterance is to be interpreted depends on its **literal meaning** as an Interrogative and on **who is to put the knowledge to use** and **what the states of knowledge of the speaker and hearer** are. There is nothing left to be accounted for for which the notion pre-announcement would be of any use.

It is worth asking, nevertheless, why Russ responds as he does to his mother's question. To answer this question, we would need to know a good deal about the social relationship between Russ and his mother, which ironically the sociologist, Schegloff, does not supply us. Russ's mother initiates the conversational sequence at hand by saying

> (32) Daddy 'n I have t- both go in different directions, en I wanna talk ta you about where I'm going (t'night).

This claim that the mother is going to do some telling of things could dispose a polite-acting Russ to allow his mother to tell him what he already knows. We sometimes, out of politeness, let people tell us things we already know, for to preempt someone's telling us something by announcing that we already know this thing can be deflating, especially when "hot news" is involved. Or there could be some other social explanation for Russ's insincere response arising out of the relationship between Russ and his mother. In any event, we can account for how a sentence like T_1 in conversation (23) will normally be interpreted, given only the *l*-meaning of this utterance and facts about the social context. We do not need positional information per se at all. And, certainly, we do not need the notion of a "pre-announcement."

Levinson (1981), in his attack on the utility of speech act theory in understanding how language is used in conversation, claims that (475) "speech act types are not the relevant categories over which to define the regularities of conversation." One problem, according to Levinson is (p. 476) that "utterance units often seem to involve more than one speech act in a number of different ways." He claims (p. 476) that "the first utterance in (33) is not just a question:

> (33) A: What are you doing tonight?
> B: Nothing, why?
> A: I was thinking of going to a movie, wanna come?

It is also as Sacks, Schegloff and associates have pointed out, a **pre-offer**. If we were to characterize A's first utterance as just a question, we would have to consider B's 'nothing' palpably false, which it isn't of course under the interpretation that it is a response to a question that is a pre-offer and that it therefore means essentially "nothing that would make the offer of an evening's entertainment irrelevant'." Levinson argues that (p. 477) "multiple assignments of force actually lies not in the utterance taken singly, but in the slot it occupies in a conversation sequence."

Now, Levinson says that *What are you doing tonight?* is a pre-offer in conversation (33). Though A's second turn might seem to legitimize this thesis, at the time it is uttered, B has no way of knowing that it is a pre-offer. It is certainly not a pre-offer for him or her at the moment he or she hears it. An utterance like this might reasonably be a pre-invitation, if followed by something like, *I'm giving a come as you are party tonight. Wanna come?* or a pre-request, if followed by something like, *I need someone to take me to the airport. Could you do it?* How are we to tell what sort of pre-sequence we have in any given situation?

The thesis that it is the "slots" utterances occupy, rather than the syntactic and semantic properties of those utterances, that determines their force, if this is to be of genuine explanatory value, presupposes that it is possible to characterize the properties of slots independently of a characterization of the syntactic and semantic properties of the utterances that occupy these slots. It is quite clear that this is impossible. Levinson (1983: 346f), who provides the criteria in (34) for identifying pre-sequences (T_1 and T_2) and sequences (T_3 and T_4), makes my point for me.

> (34) a. T_1 (Position 1): a **question** checking whether some **precondition** obtains for the **action** to be performed in T_3. (Emphasis added)
> T_2 (Position 2): an answer indicating that the precondition obtains, often with a question or request to proceed to T_3.
> T_3 (Position 3): the prefigured action, conditional on the 'go ahead' in T_2.
> T_4 (Position 4): response to the action in T_3.
> b. *distribution rule*: one party, A, addresses T_1 and T_3 to another party, B, and B addresses T_2 and T_4 to A.

It would seem from the statement of T_1 that we cannot know what sort of pre-sequence we have in any given case unless we look ahead to turn T_3. But, of course, the person hearing the utterances that comprise T_1 cannot possibly know what will be said in turn T_3. Thus, while a criterion like this might be of interest to those doing an after the fact linguistic analysis, it cannot stand as a hearer's criterion. Levinson's criterion should read "a question checking whether some precondition obtains for some social action." That is all that is warranted.

In his statement in T_1, Levinson makes reference to "a question checking whether some precondition obtains for the action to be performed in T_3." Now, despite Schegloff's assault on the utility of the notion "question" in the analysis of conversation, we discover from what Levinson says that T_1 will contain a question, presumably an information question such as T_1 in conversation (3). Moreover, we cannot know what precondition is being questioned without knowing the l-meaning of this question. And, despite both Schegloff's and Levinson's assaults on the utility of speech act theory in the analysis of conversation, Levinson's statement of T_1 is precisely what one would get from a Searlean approach to the problem, where the "precondition" in question is a felicity condition on the speech act being performed in T_3. In the framework I am advancing, we would say instead that the precondition in question is a felicity condition on the **social** action of a sequence as a whole, rather than the speech act being performed in T_3. So much for Levinson's assault on speech act theory.

Levinson's claim that *nothing* means "nothing that would make the offer of an evening's entertainment irrelevant" in (33) is quite spectacularly false, for as I noted earlier, at the time this utterance is made, B could have no idea what A had in mind. It l-means 'nothing important,' and s-means 'nothing that makes me **unable** to engage in some sort of activity.' Levinson's claim that "if we were to characterize A's first utterance as just a question, we would have to consider B's 'nothing' palpably false" is itself palpably false. The word *nothing* here, as is usually the case in ordinary language, is a restricted quantifier, l-meaning, as noted, 'nothing important.'

I submit that we cannot characterize the slots or positions utterances occur in without making reference to the l-meanings of the utterances that comprise them and to a theory of social action of the sort I am advancing here. Reconsider (33). I would argue that all we can say about the question *What are you doing tonight?* is that it initiates, or potentially initiates a social action sequence in which the more or less immediate availability of the hearer to engage in some activity is involved. The social action could be a request, an invitation, an offer, or a proposal, etc. The conversational utility of such an opening to the speaker is clear: if the hearer is to be able to take advantage of any invitation that might be forthcoming, the hearer must concede his or her present availability, a concession that will make it difficult to turn down a request (recall principle (20)), should that be what the speaker actually has in mind.

Now, Levinson says that *I was thinking of going to a movie, wanna come?* is an offer. I would like to suggest that it is not an offer, in fact, but rather, a proposal, for it involves a mutual commitment by speaker and hearer to engage in a joint activity, while offers, like promises, normally involve only a speaker commitment. In fact, in dealing with this class of social actions, it is useful to speak of Speaker Commissives (promises and offers), Hearer Commissives (requests, orders, and suggestions), and Speaker-Hearer Commissives (mutual promises to engage in some sort of activity, such as proposals -- nobody is host -- and invitations -- speaker is host).

I would characterize proposals (Speaker-Hearer Commissives with no host) as follows:

    (35) Proposal (S/H-Commissive, no host): S proposes to H that S and H do A

            Purpose: to secure a commitment from H to do A with S and make a commitment to H to do A with H.

            Sincerity Condition:

                S can do A. C_1

Preparatory Conditions:

S wishes to do A.	C_2
S wishes H to do A with S.	C_3
H is able to do A	C_4
H is willing to do A with S	C_5

B's response to A's initial Interrogative establishes that condition C_4 is possibly true, and his assertion, *I was thinking of going to a movie*, entails that condition C_2 is satisfied and implicates that condition C_1 is satisfied. All that is required is establishment that condition C_5 holds. That is the purpose of the Interrogative *wanna come?*, which is a literal inquiry about the hearer's willingness to engage in the activity in question. The sequence as a whole is recognizably a proposal then because what is said entails a speaker desire to engage in some activity and implicates his or her ability to do so, and it inquires about a hearer desire to engage in that same activity and it does these things in virtue of the literal meanings of the utterances involved.

Levinson provides still another homemade example, with which I suppose we must deal. He offers four possible replies by Mildred to John's assertion.

(36)   John: It's getting late, Mildred.
       Mildred:
           a.   It's only 11.15 darling.
           b.   But I'm having such a good time.
           c.   Do you want to go?
           d.   Aren't you enjoying yourself dear?

To discuss this properly, it would be helpful to be told something about the behavior patterns of the couple. But since this is a homemade example, we will never know this. Nevertheless, let us proceed.

One may respond to an assertion by agreeing or disagreeing with it and/or by exhibiting appreciation (possibly negative) for the information provided. Now, A's remark is a Declarative. As such, it can be taken as a mere statement of fact or as being an assessment, among other things. Let us take a look at the properties of assessments.[3]

(37)   Assessment: S asserts A to H, where A claims that some person, thing, action, or state of affairs X has some property P to some especially noteworthy degree D
       Purpose: to cause H to come to share S's view that A is true
       Sincerity Condition:

S has a warranted belief that A is true	C_1

       Preparatory Conditions:

H has not recognized that A is true	C_2
H possibly wishes to know that A is true.	C_3

On this analysis, it is an essential property of an assessment that it be intended to generate a shared judgment.

A claim like *It's getting late* can constitute a subjective judgment. The hour of 11:15 might be late if one has a baby sitter and one has promised to be home at 11:30, but not if the promise to the baby sitter was for 1:00 a.m., or it might be late if one is accustomed to going to bed at 10:30 or 11:00, but not if one is accustomed to going to bed at 1:00 or 2:00. There are two scenarios in which this utterance might be used of interest to us here. In one scenario, the time in question is indisputably late for Mildred, but not necessarily for John. In this case, John might be saying *It's getting late* merely to remind Mildred that it is late. In this case, *It's getting late* is intended merely to convey information, the default s-meaning of a Declarative, for John can expect Mildred to agree that it is late once this is pointed out to her. Suppose, on the other hand, that the time in question is late for John, but not necessarily for Mildred. This fact makes John's assertion an assessment, rather than a simple assertion of fact, for John cannot antecedently expect Mildred to share his view that it is late. In both cases, however, the intent of John would be to **propose** that Mildred and he leave.

How do we get from an assessment to a proposal? It involves movement from a mutually agreed to judgment that it is late to a mutually agreed to desire to leave. The claim that it is late implicates, in this context, a speaker desire to leave the party (cf. C_2 in (35)). Since the couple came together, the man must persuade the woman to engage in the joint activity of leaving (cf. condition C_3). They are, one presumes, fully able to leave the party, as is required by conditions C_1 and C_4. However, since John cannot assume that Mildred wishes to leave, his claim can be seen as an effort to generate such a desire (cf. C_5). Should Mildred have conceded that it is late, this would implicate that she **may** share John's implicated desire to leave, and we can expect that John would say something like *Should we go then?*

Given this second scenario, (36.a) is a dispreferred counter-judgment -- 11:15 isn't late -- entailing rejection of the proposal, for if it is not late, then there is no need for them to leave. Response, (36.b) counts as conceding the correctness of the judgment that it is late (cf. *but*), but counts as a dispreferred response to the implied proposal in that it establishes an unwillingness to leave (condition C_5 of (35)). Response (36.c) is the first turn of an Insertion Sequence and seems to be intended simply to assess whether or not the hearer has picked up the speaker's s-meaning (cf. the purpose statement and condition C_3 of (35)). And, (36.d), I would argue, is also the first turn of an Insertion Sequence and would seem to question John's sincerity in making the assessment, for it suggests that she thinks that it is not actually late for John. In this case, Mildred would seem to be searching for John's "real" reason for having this implied desire to leave. As in the case of response (36.c), Mildred is responding to condition C_3 of proposals. Notice that what we have said depends not at all on positional information per se.

It is clear from what has just been said that in order to understand how language is used in conversation, one must be willing to recognize that utterances have l-meaning and s-meaning and that responses to utterances will normally have l-meaning and s-meaning as well and that one cannot determine the s-meaning of an utterance or its response without taking l-meaning quite seriously. On the other hand, one cannot understand why anyone ever says anything without a theory of social action, which will include both conditions on social actions (felicity conditions) and a theory of preference. Thus, the best theory of conversational sequences will, in my view, combine elements of linguistic analysis -- a theory of l-meaning which will assume the existence of the three major Declarative, Interrogative, and Directive constructions and a theory of how l-meaning is realized syntactically and prosodically -- with sociological elements including the theory of social actions, including felicity and preference, and a theory of turn-taking.

I would like to conclude by returning to the five desiderata of a theory of conversational sequences identified earlier and roughly sketch how such a theory might be developed.

I. I would argue that the initial element of any sequence will normally be a first utterance addressing a felicity condition on some social action. Thus, a request sequence might begin with a Declarative asserting satisfaction of some precondition or an Interrogative like that of T_1 in conversation (3) inquiring whether some precondition of some social action is satisfied. As we saw in connection with our discussion of the first turn of conversation (33), it may not always be possible for a hearer to identify the *s*-meaning of the sequence from this first utterance.

II. Facts about context and the *l*-meanings of the utterances that comprise sequences will conspire to restrict how they are interpreted. We might imagine a hierarchical representation of social actions, with the successive utterances of a sequence directing participants down through the hierarchy until the intended social action is identified.

III. We might imagine that earlier subsequences would address either less sensitive and/or more inclusive preconditions. Thus, a man asking a woman out for a date may try to find out whether or not the woman is able to go out on a particular evening before he asks her whether or not she is willing to do so. How many pre-sequences there might be and the nature of such pre-sequences will be determined by what can and cannot be assumed in the context, among other things. In the sort of commercial exchange we have in (3), the willingness of the clerk to satisfy reasonable commercial requests can be assumed, and all that the speaker needs to do, given principle (20), is determine the ability and willingness of the clerk to satisfy the particular request. That is what T_1 and T_3 are designed to do. Suppose, though, that C wished to carry out the hot chocolate. This might reasonably lead C to engage in more talk. C might ask a willingness question like *Would you mind putting it in a paper cup?* if he or she were uncertain about the availability of a carry out service, or, if C saw carry-out as being quite normal, he or she might continue on with an ability-type question like *Could I have it to go?* The fact that C might have continued in this fashion suggests that it would be quite wrong to say, as Levinson would, that T_3 **is** a request in conversation (3). It is simply the last utterance by the requester in the request routine. In my revised scenario, T_3 would, in Levinson's terms, cease to be a request, becoming, instead, a second pre-request, with *Would you mind putting it in a paper cup?* or *Could I have it to go?* now **being** a request. Clearly, if all we mean by a request is the last utterance in a request routine, then the notion is of no interest to an account of verbal behavior whatever.

IV. There are, I think, two ways in which the two turns that comprise an adjacency pair will normally be related. The second can respond to the *l*-meaning of the first or to the *s*-meaning of the sequence in which the two turns are embedded or to both. In my revisions of turns T_1 and T_2 of (23), I have Russ responding to both the *l*-meaning (respectively, *Yeah* and *No*) of what his mother says and to its suspected social force (*s*-meaning). In (36.a), we have a response that is tied to *l*-meaning in a relatively direct fashion -- to the fact that John is making an assessment. The rest of Mildred's responses are tied to the *s*-meaning of what John has said. *S*-meaning responses may be positive or negative responses, and to understand these, we need a theory of preference (see Levinson 1983 for a discussion and references), or they may speak to felicity conditions on the social action involved, in which case (cf. V immediately below) they may initiate an Insertion Sequence, which is preliminary to a full response to the *s*-meaning of the sequence as a whole.

V. Recognition of Insertion Sequences involves recognition that a response goes to a felicity condition on the suspected *s*-meaning of what has been said, rather than being a direct response to its *l*- or *s*-meaning. Thus, such replies by Mildred in example (36) of *Do you want to go?* and *Aren't you enjoying yourself dear?* are clearly intrusive in that they do not respond to the *s*-intent but to a condition on the social action of making a proposal.

It should be clear that the program I have just outlined is quite preliminary in nature. However, I believe it shows promise in dealing with the very interesting problems posed by the sequencing of utterances in conversation. Certainly, it holds out more promise than the positional approach of Schegloff and Levinson.

64

Footnotes

[1]Jacobs and Jackson (1983a, 1983b) also offer a neoSearlean account of conversational sequences which deserves closer examination than I shall be able to give it here. The principle drawback to their account, in my view, is that they adopt a much too standard theory of speech acts, including, in particular, indirect speech acts.

[2]It is assumed that anyone performing a social action must believe that or ascertain whether or not the conditions on that social action are satisfied.

[3]See Pomerantz (1984) for a discussion and analysis of assessments.

References

Geis, M. L. 1989a. A new theory of speech acts. To appear in the Proceedings of the Sixth Annual Meeting of the Eastern States Conference on Linguistics.

Geis, M. L. mss-a. Speech Acts and Social Actions. Unpublished Inaugural Lecture, delivered January, 1989.

Geis, M. L. mss-b. A Sociolinguistic Theory of Speech Acts. Unpublished lecture, delivered at the University of Kentucky, April, 1989.

Jacobs, S. and Jackson, S. 1983a. Speech act structure in conversation: Rational aspects of pragmatic coherence. In R. T. Craig & K. Tracy, eds., Conversational coherence: Form, structure, and strategy. Beverly Hills: Sage Publications, 47-66.

Levinson, S. C. 1981. The essential inadequacies of speech act models of dialogue. In H. Parret, M. Sbisá, J. Verschueren, eds., Possibilities and limitations of pragmatics. Proceedings of the conference on pragmatics, Urbino, July 8-14, 1979. Amsterdam: John Benjamins.

Levinson, S. C. 1983. Pragmatics. Cambridge, England: Cambridge University Press

Merritt, M. 1976. On questions following questions (in service encounters). Language in Society, 5.3, 315-57.

Pomerantz, A. 1984. Agreeing and disagreeing with assessments: some features of preferred/dispreferred turn shapes. In J. M. Atkinson & J. Heritage, eds., Structures of social action: studies in conversational analysis. Cambridge, England: Cambridge University Press, 57-101.

Schegloff, E. A. 1972. Sequencing in conversational openings. In Gumperz and Hymes, eds., Directions in sociolinguistics. New York: Holt, Rinehart & Winston, 346-80.

Schegloff, E. A. 1984. On questions and ambiguities in conversation. In J. M. Atkinson and J. Heritage, eds., Structures of social action: Studies in Conversational Analysis, 28-52. Cambridge: Cambridge University Press.

Schegloff, Emanuel A. 1988. Presequences and indirection: Applying speech act theory to ordinary conversation. Journal of Pragmatics 12, 55-62.

Schegloff, E. A. & Sacks, H. 1973. Opening up closings. Semiotica, 7.4, 289-387.

REFERENT-TRACKING AND COOPERATION IN CONVERSATION: EVIDENCE FROM REPAIR

Ronald Geluykens
Belgian National Science Foundation (NFWO) & University of Antwerp

1. Introduction[1]

1.1. The tension between pragmatic discourse principles

This paper tries to show that the establishing of discourse anaphora, i.e. the process whereby an element picks up its reference through an item in the previous context, is an interactional process depending on speaker-hearer collaboration. It will also attempt to show that some general conversational principles, originating in Grice's (1975) conversational maxims, can have explanatory value in accounting for the behaviour of discourse anaphors. We will show that there is a tension between two   conversational principles which are, as it were, in competition, and that this tension may result in conversational 'repair' (Schegloff et al. 1977).

Let us start from some of Grice's (1975) maxims, more particularly those which have a direct impact on the linguistic realization of referential elements in discourse, viz. Quantity and Manner. The two quantity maxims are characterized as follows by Grice:

    -Q1: make your contribution as informative as is required for the current
               purposes of the exchange;
    -Q2: do not make your contribution more informative than is required

It is clear that these two maxims make different predictions as to what the speaker should do to effect efficient communication. Whereas Q1 would predict that the speaker has to give as much information as s/he possibly can, Q2 predicts that s/he has to supply information in as economical a manner as s/he possibly can. This apparent contradiction is also present in the Manner maxim ('be perspicuous'):

    -M1: avoid obscurity
    -M2: avoid ambiguity
    -M3: be brief

Whereas M1 and M2 would suggest that, in order to avoid obscurity/ambiguity, the speaker should opt for maximally clear (and thus more complex) linguistic expressions, M3 suggests that economy of expression should be a prime consideration.

We are not the first to note this clash between Gricean principles: Levinson (1987, 1988) has pointed out that there are potential clashes between some of the maxims, and suggests a Quantity principle and a Maxim of Minimization as an alternative for Q- and M-implicatures. Levinson is in turn influenced by Horn (1984), who suggests that all that is necessary to replace Grice's maxims are two different principles:

    -The Q-principle: make your contribution sufficient
        ('say as much as you can')
    -The R-principle: make your contribution necessary
        ('say no more than you must')

Following a similar line of reasoning, we will suggest here that there are indeed two principles which may be in conflict, and which have a direct impact on the realization of referential expressions, more particularly Noun Phrases.

-Informativeness (I-)principle ('say as much as you must to avoid ambiguity')
    i.e. use a full NP whenever you have to
-Economy (E-)principle ('say as little as you can get away with (given I)')
    i.e. use a PRO-form whenever you can

When referring to a particular anaphoric referent, a speaker may thus choose either a pronominal form (i.e. following the E-principle), as in (1), or a full lexical NP (i.e. following the I-principle), as in (2); the choice will depend presumably on the degree to which the antecedent is recoverable (see Geluykens 1988a, 1988b) from the previous context, e.g. easily in (1), not so easily in (2):

    (1)   John came to visit me yesterday; <u>he</u> brought me some wine.
    (2)   John and Bill came to visit me yesterday; <u>John</u> brought me some wine.

The following examples show that violating these principles indeed results in inefficient communication. In instance (3), the speaker, by using a pronoun, violates the I-principle, resulting in ambiguity. Instances (4) and (5) below show that violating the E-principle can be similarly disastrous: whereas opting for Economy results in the perfectly felicitous utterance (4), going for maximal Informativeness results in the awkward (5) utterance, where repetition of the full NP almost forces one into a non-coreferential reading for the two mentions of <u>John</u>.

    (3)   John$_1$ and Bill$_2$ came to dinner. He$_{1/2}$ had to leave early.
    (4)   John$_1$ came in and he$_1$/Ø$_1$ sat down.
    (5)   ?John$_1$ came in and John$_1$ sat down.

Whatever way one looks at it, then, it is important for the speaker to keep a balance between the two principles, making an accurate evaluation of the discourse context.

    There are instances where the choice between Economy and Informativeness is not so clear-cut, the speaker opting first for Economy by picking a pronoun, then realizing this may endanger Informativeness, and thus repairing the pronoun by means of a full NP. This results in a type of repair, not of a real 'error', but of a communicative inefficiency, the kind of repair which Levelt (1983) labels 'appropriateness repairs'. As we will argue in the remainder of this paper, such repair instances show that it is the tension between the two pragmatic principles which results in reprocessing and thus a repair sequence.

1.2. Types of conversational repair

Before looking at the data, let us first consider which types of repair are theoretically possible. Schegloff et al. (1977) distinguish between four main interactional types of repair, depending on who initiates the repair, and who does the actual correcting of the item-to-be-repaired. Both the former and the latter --i.e. initiation and correction-- can be done by either the speaker or another participant, resulting in four logical possibilities.

    First of all, when the speaker himself realizes a repair is in order, initiates the repair process and also provides the 'corrected' version, we can talk about self-initiated self-repair, as in (6) below:

    (6)   She was givin' me all the people that were gone this year
           I mean this quarter (from Schegloff et al. 1977: 364)

Initiation of the repair sequence can also be done by the hearer, in which case we get either other-initiated self-repair --if the repair is carried out by the speaker-- or other-initiated other-repair --if the other participant also does the correcting. These varieties are illustrated by (7) and (8), respectively:

(7) A: she was givin me all the people that were gone this year
     B: What? This year?
     A: This quarter I mean
(8) A: she was givin me all the people that were gone this year
     B: this year? this quarter you mean.

Finally, we can have cases of self-initiated other-repair, as in (9):

(9) A: she was givin me all the people that were gone this year I mean
     B: this quarter you mean
     A: yeah right

As we will see later on, this type of repair is quite rare, for quite straightforward reasons.

Schegloff et al. rightly point out that these four types of repair are not simply alternative possibilities, but that conversation is so organized that self-repair is more likely to occur than other-repair:

"Rather, the organization of repair in conversation provides centrally for self-correction, which can be arrived at by the alternative routes of self-initiation and other-initiation --routes which are themselves so organized as to favor self-initiated self-repair". (Schegloff et al. 1977: 377)

This observation naturally follows if one considers the places in the flow of speech where repair can be initiated, viz. in the reparandum-turn (opportunity 1), in the transition space following this turn (opportunity 2), or in the next other-turn following the TRP (opportunity 3). Levinson (1983: 341) summarizes the preference ranking as follows:

-Preference 1 is for self-initiated self-repair in opportunity 1 (own turn)
-Preference 2 is for self-initiated self-repair in opportunity 2 (transition space)
-Preference 3 is for other-initiation in opportunity 3 (next turn), of self-
    repair (in the turn after that)
-Preference 4 is for other-initiated other-repair in opportunity 3 (next turn)

It will be observed that both opportunity 1 and 2 favor self-initiated self-repair, and that opportunity 3 still may lead to self-repair. It can also be predicted from this that self-initiated other-repair is virtually impossible. In what follows, we will show that the collaborative process of referent-tracking can lead to all the types of repair discussed here, but also that the types are open to refinement.

2. Repair and 'right-dislocation'

In Geluykens (1987), we have already argued that the syntactic construction usually labelled 'right-dislocation' (following Ross 1967; RD for short) is, in fact, often a direct reflection of a repair process whereby a pronominal element is replaced by a full NP. In what follows, we will explore this claim further, and show that RD is only one of the possible outcomes of the repair sequence triggered by the pragmatic principles outlined in section 1.1. RD is exemplified by (10):

(10) He likes Mary, John (does)

RDs are thus concatenations of a complete main clause containing a pronoun (which we will call the Proposition, or PROP), followed by a NP (which we will label the Referent, or REF) which is not the argument of a following verb, and which is coreferential with the preceding pronoun (the latter will be termed the Gap). We are not so much interested here in the precise syntactic characteristics of RDs, or indeed whether a structure which more or less exhibits these characteristics should be labelled a RD or not. Rather, we will attempt to show that RD-like strings are one of the possible reflections of the collaborative process whereby the balance between the E- and the I-principle is restored. In what follows, we will use the REF-PROP terminology introduced here, even for instances where the label RD is perhaps less appropriate.

2.1. Other-initiated self-repair

In our data[2], there are quite a few instances where the hearer explicitly signals the referential trouble-spot and thus initiates a repair. Let us look at one such instance in more detail:

(11)[3] b: what sort of jobs do they get after .
   A: what .
   b: your students -
   A: oh well about half our intake's teachers but less than half the output
      (1.10.153.8)

After b's utterance what sort of jobs do they get, in which he uses the Economical pronominal form they, hearer A explicitly signals that there is a communication problem. This query can be read in a number of ways, one of them being that the reference of the pronoun, which is treated by the speaker as if it were anaphoric, is unclear to the hearer, and that thus, by opting for Economy, the speaker has failed to be sufficiently Informative. Speaker b thus self-repairs his pronoun by means of the full NP your students; this turns out to be exactly the repair the hearer had hoped for, and the clash between the two principles is thereby resolved. This instance clearly shows that the maintaining of unambiguous reference depends crucially on hearer-feedback, and on speaker-hearer collaboration. Let us consider one almost identical example:

(12) A: there was the most [?ə] [ma:] rather marvellous shadow play which
         would [ə:] you the rest of the Senate were in fact in the end
         conspiring to kill him you see *.*
      B: *´mhm
      A: Caligula
      B: yeah (S.7.1.c6.10)

Again, the reference of him in the first turn is explicitly queried by the hearer (note the rising tone on the initiator mhm); in other words, a very overt cooperative process is taking place.

The following example has not only other-initiation of repair, but also an attempt at other-repair. It turns out, however, that the hearer makes the wrong guess as to the reference of it in the speaker's first turn; the speaker thus eventually has to make a self-repair:

(13)   A: I like that one best - the ((tree)) in the middle - but I think it's too [ə:]
            it would dominate the room a bit too much
        C: what the checkerboard .
        A: [ə] no the next one - (S.1.8.40.2)

The fact that the attempt of other-repair fails is clear evidence that there is indeed a referential communication problem here, and that the speaker has overestimated the hearer's ability to identify the intended referent the next one; in other words, the speaker has clearly violated the I-principle. Instance (14) below is similar:

(14)   B: and besides she always comes down in the summer
        c: your sister *. or your mother*
        B: *[ə:] my sister and* my mother . both of them (S.1.12.122.6)

In this exchange, the hearer is almost able to correctly track the intended reference of she in the first turn; however, it turns out his attempt at other-repair is not quite right, as is evidenced by the next speaker-turn.

In the next instance, there is a functional similarity to (11) - (12) above, in that there is other-initiation of repair. Contrary to those two examples however, the speaker in (15) repeats the entire proposition before clarifying the reference of that:

(15)   A: (...) --- hasn't some Canadian recently set up a a foundation you're
            not in fact Canadian though are you
        B: no .
        A: no -
        B: no that's my trouble that was my trouble with applying
            for a Canada Council you see ((and it)).-
        A: what
        B: I say that was my trouble in [plain in tr] in applying for a Canada
            Council - not being a Canadian *-*
        A: *yeah*
        B: citizen you see (S.2.1.64.4)

The string in B's third turn (that was my trouble..., not being a Canadian citizen) is looking very much like a RD here, this time without any intervening hearer-material. It has to be kept in mind, though, that (15) is an instance of other-initiated repair.

The interactional process taking place in the exchanges discussed so far could be schematically represented as follows:

(16)   -Stage 1 (speaker): PROP-utterance violating I-principle
        -Stage 2 (hearer): explicit repair-initiation [+ attempt at other-repair]
        -Stage 3 (speaker): self-repair restoring referent-tracking (REF)

In the following section, we will look at RD-like constructs which are not overtly other-initiated.

70

2.2. Self-initiated self-repair

Most RD-like structures in our data, in contrast to the ones discussed in the previous section, do not have a hearer-turn between REF and PROP; in other words, there is no overt other-initiation of repair involved in the utterances discussed in this section. Nevertheless, we claim that the same interactional repair-process is at work here, the only difference being situated in the way in which repair is initiated. Let us start by considering a few clear examples of referential repair, viz. (17) to (19) below:

(17) A: (...) to know . whether they really surveyed the whole lot themselves or whether they copied it all from --- from . they copied the basic layout from . (. coughs) . the French I mean (...) (S.2.3.2.4)
(18) B: (...) and this was almost news to me . risk . management that is (...) (2.11.b112.4)
(19) C: (...) if this had some more colour in it . [∂:] that is the bottom foreground . *[∂:]*
     A: *yes* (...) (S.1.8.48.9)

These are clear repair-instances, signalled by I mean and that is, respectively, and are interactionally quite similar to the repairs discussed in the previous section. What happens is the following: the speaker utters a PROP with an Economical pronoun, after which he pauses. This pause, from the speaker's point of view, may reflect the re-processing he carries out after he realizes his original utterance is communicatively not ideal. From the hearer's point of view, the pause can be interpreted as a very strong floor-yielding cue on the part of the speaker, especially in combination with the outspoken syntactic TRP (clause-completion). The fact that the hearer does not take up the floor, at a point where he might be reasonably expected to do so, may then be read by the speaker as a tacit signal that there is a trouble-spot which needs repairing. These two interpretations do not necessarily contradict one another, but can be looked upon as complementary sides of the same phenomenon. On the one hand, the speaker-pause may signal that repair is about to be initiated (self-initiation); on the other hand, the absence of positive reaction on the part of the hearer may serve as an additional implicit signal to the speaker (element of other-initiation). The interactional schema can thus be represented as follows:

(20) -Stage 1 (speaker): utterance violating I-principle (PROP)
     -Stage 2 (speaker/hearer): self-initiation + tacit other-initiation (pause)
     -Stage 3 (speaker): self-repair (REF)

In effect, we are thus claiming that in some repairs, there may be a combination of self- and other-initiation, whereby it is difficult to determine the exact contribution speaker and hearer make.

There are plenty of instances of self-initiation combined with tacit other-initiation at TRP in our data; it will suffice here to list a few cases without overt repair-markers, showing pauses of varying lengths:

(21) B: (...) she was old and on her own . my auntie Elsie and .
     (S.1.12.113.2)

(22) C: (...) I'm sure -- ((they've got a way of doing it)) - the authorities
((7 sylls)) (...) (S.2.5.b61.7)
(23) A: (...) he saw somebody . some young lout was digging them up -
the roses (S.4.7.56.6)
(24) B: (...) if you need the income stick it in the building society it may well
come down . the income [i] in in over the coming year (...)
(S.9.4.42.7)

In all these instances, the result of the process is a string which exhibits the formal
characteristics of a RD.
There are a few variant possibilities of this process occurring in our data.
First of all, instead of having a silent pause, repair-initiation may be marked by
other verbal cues, for instance a glottal stop, as in (25):

(25) B: (...) ((it's)) a bit small scale I think [?] Rimini (...)
A: (...) (S.1.2.38.13)

There are also instances of voiced rather than silent pauses, e.g. (26) below:

(26) A: [∂] what [∂:m] - I do know those [∂] the [th th:] [∂] beautiful blooms
or blossoms there (...) (S.4.4.87.8)

Finally, we have to point out that the pause is not a necessary feature of this type of
repair. Irrespective of there being a following pause, the end of the clause
containing the to-be-repaired item is an outspoken TRP by virtue of the fact that it is
syntactically complete; furthermore, it is often prosodically marked by a falling
tone, signalling completeness (we will not go into intonational aspects of repair
here). This TRP is thus in any event a place where self-repair may be self-initiated,
even if the speaker does not get any tacit cues from the hearer. Instance (27) is an
example of such pauseless self-initiated self-repair:

(27) B: well this was the ridiculous thing the ((convergence))
A: yes (S.1.6.88.7)

Once again, the same tension between the Economy and Informativeness principle
lies at the basis of this referential repair.
To finish this section, we have to point out that there might also be non-verbal
cues through which the hearer can signal that a repair is in order. The nature of our
data (tape-recorded conversations) does not allow us to check this; nevertheless, it
would be interesting to investigate to what extent kinetic cues form an integral part
of the process of speaker-hearer collaboration.

3. Other anaphor repairs

3.1. RD-like repairs with Argument-REF

If, as we have argued in the previous section, RDs are, as it were, only an
accidental --albeit interactionally favored-- outcome of an interactional process, one
would expect there to be functionally similar referential repairs which do not take on
the formal characteristics of a RD. There are indeed a variety of instances of this
type in our database.

As an example of a repair which is similar to the ones discussed in section 2.2, in that it is also largely self-initiating and self-correcting, but which does not result in a RD, consider (28):

(28) A: how's the thesis going
  B: [∂] I'm typing it up now . typing up the final
  A: [hm]
  B: copy
  A: [∂] when are you submitting it (S.2.1.1.6)

In this repair, the speaker not only substitutes the full NP the final copy for the pronominal it, but also repeats the main verb typing up. As a result, the REF can no longer be considered to be a bare NP, but is the object of the second mention of the verb to type. This structure thus cannot be labelled a RD anymore; nevertheless, it is functionally very similar to the RDs discussed in the previous section , the only difference being that cases like (28) are what Van Wijk (1987) labels 'backtracking' repairs, i.e. with repetition of part of the reparandum-utterance. Another example of a repair with V-repetition is (29):

(29) [context: about organization of lectures]
  B: he certainly ought to consider that -
  A: well . *you*
  B: *we've* had rather [∂:] - . you know without giving too much
      away to ((3 sylls))
  A: yeah . well he's got a very good bloke doing it now . I mean doing
      this organizing Godfrey Campion . [∂:] (...) (S.5.11.a35.2)

Whether repair processes like (28) and (29) should still be called RDs is really irrelevant from our point of view; it is probably very difficult to delineate which constructions are still RDs, and which are not. Perhaps one could posit a prototype form of what a RD construction should look like, based on (10) above, and describe instances like the one discussed here, and the ones discussed in section 2.1, as non-prototype instances of the RD phenomenon. Our main point here is, however, that those strings which could unequivocally be labelled RDs (cf. section 2.2) are functionally very similar to the other processes described in section 2.1 and the whole of section 3, in that they are reflections of the same collaborative strategy used to resolve a clash between two opposing pragmatic principles.

Backtracking repairs can repeat not only the main verb of the original utterance, but as much as the whole of that utterance; a case in point is (30) below:

(30) B: (...) - . will you feel that you'll do it when it's your own I mean
      [w] when it's your own will you feel sort of you want to do
      a conversion (S.2.10.123.7)

Almost the entire clause in which the reparandum it occurs is repeated here by the speaker. Once again, this repair cannot be reduced to the RD concept, but is functionally very similar to repairs with RD format.

3.2. Other-initiated other-repairs

If our referential repairs follow the normal interactional preference organization of repairs discussed in section 1.2, we might expect the four different preference types of repair to be reflected in our data. Up to now, we have already dealt with possibilities 2 (self-repair at TRP; sections 2.2 and 4.1) and 3 (self-repair after other-initiation; section 2.1). In this section, we will show that possibility 4, i.e. other-repair after other-initiation, indeed also occurs in our corpus, and is due to the same pragmatic factors. Let us look at one example in detail:

> (31) B: and they've done these on groups of undergraduates . ((we don't know what))
> A: *[∂:m]*battery things
> B: *[∂m] -* [∂m] . yes . (...) (S.1.5.31.10)

The interactional schema underlying (31) is the following:

> (32) -Stage 1 (speaker) utterance violating I-principle ('PROP') + TRP
> -Stage 2 (hearer) other-initiation of repair
> -Stage 3 (hearer) other-repair ('REF')
> -Stage 4 (speaker) confirmation of successful other-repair

Stage 4 is an essential step in the collaboration: since the speaker is the one who has the solution as to the real reference of his initial pronoun, he will be obliged to either confirm or reject the referential candidate offered by the hearer. Only then will Informativeness be fully restored. If other-repair is successful, we will get the sequence sketched in (32); if other-repair has failed, we will probably get a sequence like the one represented in (15) above, resulting in eventual self-repair.

Instance (33) below is a very similar additional example of other-initiated other-repair:

> (33) A: (...) we went to dine with Ken and *Carlotta - (-- laughs)*
> B: *((oh)) - ((I)) believe* - James was entertaining Michael
> A: yes that's right . m (. laughs)
> B: he's entertaining us on Friday I think
> A: (--- laughs) hah - everybody individually *. m*
> B: *don't tell* . Ken this but rumour has it that he's . about to go .
> A: Ken is
> B: yeah - (S.7.3.f15.4)

The following instance is a bit special, in that initiation of repair does not occur straight away, but rather after two short intervening turns:

> (34) B: they'll say the unemployed they should be made to do some . some work and not . scrounge off the state
> d: m
> B: [∂:m]
> d: what [?] . sorry Russians
> B: m (S.2.11.b48.7)

3.3. Immediate PRO > NP repairs

Instead of delaying the repair until the end of the clause in which the to-be-repaired item appears, and thus at the first outspoken syntactic TRP, the speaker can of course decide to carry out an immediate repair, and initiate the repair right after the reparandum. What we are dealing with here, of course, is 'preference 1' (self-repair in own turn) in the repair possibilities discussed in section 1.2. Since this is the earliest point at which self-repair could occur, and since self-initiated self-repair is the most favored form of repair at any rate, one might expect this type of repair to be relatively frequent; this is borne out by our data.

Although the linear outcome of such an immediate self-repair process does not look in the least like a RD, from a functional point of view a very similar, if not identical, thing is happening, viz. a clash between the E- and I-principle which is being resolved, the only difference being the point in the production process in which the resolution takes place. An example of such a repair is (35) below:

(35) A: (...) it's just a particular type of stout which the Irish developed
          because of that marvellous water they've got . so you really
          they . the Irishmen say there's no such thing as the true thing in
          England because it's the water . (S.1.7.40.5)

The speaker here once again first opts for an economical pronoun (they), realizes this may cause processing problems for the hearer, and thus repairs the pronoun by means of a more informative NP (the Irishmen). The interactional process underlying (35) is thus the following:

(36) -Stage 1 (speaker): pronominal referent violating I-principle
         -Stage 2 (speaker): self-initiation of repair
         -Stage 3 (speaker): self-repair embedded in complete utterance

In some cases, repair is not initiated until after the main verb has been uttered. Repair is thus not quite immediate, but still occurs in the middle of the speaker-turn, well before the first outspoken TRP. A few examples:

(37) A: and you're [?] . now engaged - in [∂:] . in preparing a book on him .
         B: *((mhm . that's right yes))*
         A: *in the meantime* you're writing on various discrete aspects of
             Piggott in the form of articles and that kind of thing and
             that's been going on for some while
         B: *[∂:] --*
         A: **((1 syll))**
         B: **well** they started the chapters tended to start in the form of
             articles (...) (S.3.6.46.2)
(38) B: (...) I don't know if it was pleurisy or something - but I imagine
             that was because she wasn't heating the house properly [∂:m] -
             oh it it was I mean the house . we used to go over often enough
             to . I mean it wasn't (...) (S.5.8.108.7)

Note that pauses can occur between reparandum and repair-item, the pause (cf. (35)), in these cases, probably reflecting reprocessing and self-initiation of repair.

4. Conclusion

Several things can be concluded from our analysis. First of all, we hope to have shown that the Gricean notion of conversational implicature, given the right type of refinement and operationalization, can be invoked to explain how the system of referent-tracking works in conversational discourse. The clash between the Economy and Informativeness principles has been shown to have a direct impact on the realization of anaphoric NPs.

Secondly, and related to this, we have supplied evidence here that the tracking of referents, and the way they are referred to throughout a stretch of discourse, depends crucially on speaker-hearer interaction. In other words, the maintaining of reference, just like the establishing of new referents in discourse, can be termed a collaborative process. (Clark & Wilkes-Gibbs 1986; Geluykens 1988b). This interactional dimension of referent-tracking has all too often been ignored in the literature on discourse anaphora.

Right-dislocation, we have argued, is nothing more or less than one possible outcome of this interactional process, an outcome which is relatively favored, as it reflects cases of self-initiated self-repair. Insofar as RDs can be labelled syntactic constructions, they should thus be regarded as 'fossilized' interactional processes.

As far as the different interactional types of repair are concerned, we have tried to show that the division proposed by Schegloff et al. into four types could be refined, for there are repairs which are neither totally self-initiated nor totally other-initiated, but which are a mixture of the two.

Several things had to remain undiscussed here. For instance, we did not talk about the intonational aspects of our repairs (see Geluykens 1989). Neither did we go more deeply into the precise reasons why the referential status of the repaired anaphors is problematic. In earlier work (Geluykens 1987), we have already indicated that this might be because of the problematic recoverability status of the reparandum; space does not permit us to go into this more deeply here.

The empirical study of the pragmatics of discourse anaphora is a field of investigation which, despite all the recent literature on anaphora, has up to now not received the attention it deserves. We hope that the present study, however limited, shows that such an investigation has potential relevance for pragmatic theory.

Footnotes

(1)   A preliminary version of this paper was presented in seminar form at the Max Planck Institut für Psycholinguistik, Nijmegen, The Netherlands (February 1989). Thanks are due to the participants in that seminar, more particularly to Willem Levelt, for their comments. Thanks also to Steve Levinson and Mia Vanrespaille for comments on an earlier written version.

(2)   The data are taken from the Survey of English Usage, based at University College London. We are indebted to Sidney Greenbaum for allowing us access to these data.

(3)   Transcription conventions:
      -pauses: brief (.); unit (-); long (--); very long (---)
      -repair: underlined
      -overlapping speech: *...* or **...**
      -speaker identity: A; B; C; ...
      -file number: e.g. 'S.5.6.7.8.' refers to Spoken file 5.6, slip 7, line 8.

References

Clark, H.H. & D. Wilkes-Gibbs (1986). Referring as a collaborative process. Cognition 22: 1-39.

Geluykens, R. (1987). Tails (right-dislocations) as a repair mechanism in English conversation. In: J. Nuyts & G. de Schutter (eds.), Getting one's words into line: On word order and functional grammar, 109-119. Dordrecht: Foris.

Geluykens, R. (1988a). Five types of clefting in English conversation. Linguistics 26 (5): 823-841.

Geluykens, R. (1988b). The interactional nature of referent-introduction. Papers from the 24th Regional Meeting, Chicago Linguistic Society: 141-154.

Geluykens, R. (1989). Anaphora and repair in English conversation. PhD draft, Cambridge University .

Grice, H.P. (1975). Logic and conversation. In: P. Cole & J. Morgan, Speech acts: Syntax and Semantics 3, 41-58. New York: Academic Press.

Horn, L. (1984). Toward a new taxonomy for pragmatic inference: Q-based and R-based implicature. In: D. Schiffrin (ed.), Meaning, form and use in context (GURT 1984).   Washington, D.C.: Georgetown University Press.

Levelt, W.J.M. (1983). Monitoring and self-repair in speech. Cognition 14: 41-104.

Levinson, S.C. (1983). Pragmatics. Cambridge: Cambridge University Press.

Levinson, S. C. (1987). Minimization and conversational inference. In: M. Papi & J. Verschueren (eds.), The pragmatic perspective. Amsterdam: Benjamins.

Levinson, S. C. (1988). Generalized conversational implicature and the semantics/pragmatics interface. Ms., University of Cambridge.

Schegloff, E.A., G. Jefferson and H. Sacks (1977). The preference for self-correction in the organization of repair in conversation. Language 53: 361-382.

Van Wijk, C. H. (1987). Speaking, writing, and sentence form: three psycholinguistic studies. Doctoral dissertation, University of Nijmegen.

Contextualization Cues and Metapragmatics:
The retrieval of cultural knowledge

John J. Gumperz
University of California, Berkeley

If we accept the basic assumption that understanding of situated language always relies on metapragmatic signs (Silverstein in press) – signs which, to use Hanks' words (in press), "define points of articulation between message structure and utterance context," then contextualization cues must count as metapragmatic phenomena. Contextualization cues, as I have argued in previous work (Gumperz 1982, 1989), can be described as a class of verbal signs (having some but not all of the properties of grammatical signs) that serve to relate what is said on any particular time-bound occasion to knowledge acquired through past experience. This knowledge then enters into the process of conversational inference (Gumperz 1982, p.153ff) as part of the background information or ground against which constituent messages can be interpreted. In this paper, rather than attempting an extended theoretical explanation, I will try to document my arguments by means of a series of examples illustrating the workings of such contextualization-based inferential processes.

Many of the phenomena that have been described under the heading of contextualization cues involve signs that are identical in form to those described in the metapragmatic literature. They include, among others, deictic and anaphoric expressions that index extralinguistic reference and assist in reference tracking, choice among lexical or syntactic options, use of certain speech act verbs, and shifts of style or code of the kind which have been shown to play an important role in such signaling functions as managing what folklorists have called "performance," signaling speaker's voice, and distinguishing between such phenomena as direct quotes, reported speech, and indirect quotes, etc.

Consider the following description of a radio broadcast of a religious service in a California Black church analyzed in Gumperz 1982 (pp.190-1). At the end of a musical performance which has evoked prolonged rhythmic prayer and clapping on the part of the congregation, an announcer's voice rises above the shouts of "Amen," "Hallelujah" and "Praise the Lord" to introduce the minister. The minister, instead of waiting for the congregation's shouts to die down or relying on lexicalized requests for silence to announce the coming sermon, merely joins in the group activity as a co-equal. He begins by interpolating his own amens and praise-the-Lord-s, but each time with increasing emphasis and slower tempo, until he has achieved some measure of control. He goes on to repeat the theme of the previous hymn, which is also to be a main theme of his own sermon. His technique once more relies on rhythmic synchrony. Initially, the first two words of the theme "God is" are repeatedly inserted with increasing loudness into the congregation's pattern of shouts until the shouts gradually die down. The minister then completes his theme sentence, *God *is, .. {[lo] standing by//}. The congregation, now quiet, attends to the minister's words and, when his talk shifts to prose genre, goes on to make the responses that conventionally mark the sermon in this type of tradition. In other words, by relying on a combination of cues involving rhythmic, stylistic and lexical shifts, the minister has, solely by the way he talks, achieved what, following Hymes (1983), we might call a "breakthrough" from the group activity of hymn singing into preaching performance in which the minister becomes the protagonist and the congregation follows.

Another early example of contextualization cue analysis comes from Michaels and Collins's (1986) comparative examination of fourth graders' retellings using Chafe's "Pear Story" elicitation techniques (1980). There are two main characters in the story, a pear picker, who has been filling his baskets from a tree and placing them alongside a country lane, and a boy passerby on a bicycle, who is said to have taken some of the pears. In one representative retelling, the pear picker is first introduced as follows,

"This gu:y— ... the *man, was picking pears."

Following that the boy is introduced as,

".. and so:— .. the- .. {[hi] this ~gu:y}

Michaels and Collins comment: "The first and second mentions of 'this guy' are distinguished prosodically. The fall-rise-fall contour on the latter mention ('guy')" (here indicated by contouring and vowel length) "is an implicit cue signaling a new character and a shift in perspective. Additionally, the intonation in the first mention ('guy') is a high level tone followed by a stressed high fall on 'man.' The emphatic high fall indicates that a correction has been made and that 'man' is the more apt descriptor. The second mention of 'this guy' therefore contrasts with 'man' but the clues to this opposition lie solely in the prosodic alternation." Although I would not go so far as to say that coreference is marked only through prosody, clearly prosody here plays a key metapragmatic role.

Yet, apart from the readily apparent similarities between metapragmatic and prosodic signaling mechanisms, there are also some significant differences. To begin with, let us look at the actual processes by which prosody conveys information. No one would argue that prosodic signs are interpretable as meaningful by themselves. Rather, with the exception of just a few conventionalized contours such as have been described by Liberman and Sag (1974), prosodic signaling enters into interpretations only inasmuch as the relevant contours are mapped onto lexical strings and syntactic constructions in such a way as to favor particular interpretations over other options. Furthermore, to the extent that prosody is relevant, information about context is not conveyed by just one type of cue. Typically, participants perceive and respond to a constellation of cues operating at different levels of signaling, and interpretation rests on their assessments of co-occurrences among such distinct levels or channels. Signaling, moreover, functions relationally in the sense that assessments are based on the extent to which what is perceived either confirms or departs from expectations established on the basis of what has previously transpired in the course of the interaction or on the basis of past experience.

Nor is the indexed context describable entirely in terms of known and, for the purpose of an encounter, presumably constant factors such as setting, participants' social characteristics, or even belief or value systems as described in the ethnographic literature. These latter factors are relevant to be sure, but exactly how they enter into interpretation must be determined analytically. Much of this is of course basic also to metapragmatic analysis; metapragmatic notions like genre or perspective shifts, voicing and decentering are designed to deal with just such issues. Contextualization analysis, however, goes one step further in departing from established linguistic practices and adopting procedures that move in the opposite direction from language centered analyses. That is, the move is not outwards from text to context but rather from socially constituted, interactive situations to text, on the one hand, and to extralinguistic micro and macro environments, on the other. To put it in different terms, analysis starts with particular communicative exchanges or time-bound communicative events. The initial aim is to determine how members' knowledge of such events, including the extralinguistic constraints these events entail, enters into members' interpretations at any one point in the proceedings and affects outcomes.

The analysis of contextualization processes, then, focuses on situated conversational exchanges seen as communicative encounters in a broader sense, not just as verbal texts. A basic assumption is that communication by its very nature implies intentionality, and one main analytical goal is to show how communicative intent is cooperatively assessed or negotiated and how assessments affect the management of interaction. Seen in terms of such an interactive perspective, it soon becomes apparent that, apart from the signs discussed so far, signaling mechanisms not ordinarily discussed in the metapragmatic literature can be shown to have signaling value. These include rhythm, tempo and pausing, which have been described in the conversational analytic literature (Atkinson and Heritage 1986), as well as, among others, pitch register and loudness shifts (Gumperz 1989). All these potentially enter into the constellations of cues that affect participants' understanding of what is intended.

One way of integrating the emphasis on participants' understanding with the current metapragmatic literature is to suggest that contextualization-based inferential processes involve several levels of interpretation. My hypothesis is that understanding entails assumptions about what the activity is. "Activity" is here used as a cover term to capture such matters as what communicative outcomes can be expected, what types of interpersonal relations are involved and how they are signaled, what topics are to be discussed, what types of information are to be lexicalized and in what order and what is most appropriately left for indirect inference (Gumperz 1982, 1989). This then is the first and global level of inference. The second level of signaling can be called the local or the sequential level, where what is negotiated are such matters as deictic reference, genre shifts of the kind illustrated in the preceding examples. Contextualization cues on this view can simultaneously act as local level signals and serve as inputs to higher level processes of conversational inference which retrieve the cultural presuppositions about the activity with reference to which interpretations are made and validated.

The recent pragmatic literature on deixis already contains some hints that what is involved in interpretation is more than merely determining the deictic ground for reference. Consider the following quote from Jeffrey Heath's article "Nunggubuyu Deixis, Anaphora and Culture" (CLS 1980, pp.152-3). At the end of his detailed discussion of the referential semantics and pragmatics of the various demonstrative affixes which obligatorily mark directionality of motion, he goes on:

> It should be noted that the correct use of kinetic suffixes, notably centripetal, requires considerable pragmatic sensitivity. The speaker requires not only the ability to perceive but also the ability to interpret the addressee's intention and predict his/her future motion (or to express disapproval thereof). These decisions in turn require both general cultural knowledge (since the addressee is not likely to walk towards certain affines) and fluid situational factors.

Clearly, deictic signaling here and in other native Australian languages (Haviland in press) cannot be explained with reference to the physical setting alone. The suggestion is that interpretation rests on shared, culturally-based knowledge of relevant activities.

In case this seems like an exotic phenomenon, consider the following anecdotal example which involves a college porter in a research office, part of a large urban British university, who calls out half smilingly to a young research officer walking towards her office building after a rather longer than usual lunch break, saying, "*E's UP there." The research officer interprets this utterance to mean, "The professor is in so watch out he doesn't see you coming in late." Note that, since there has been no preceding talk nor other action in this case, the "he" is truly uncoreferenced, that is, there is neither verbal nor nonverbal information, such as would be conveyed by pointing, to show us who the intended referent is. Such uncoreferenced third person pronouns are conventionally used by many British working class speakers not just to refer to the foreman, manager or boss, but primarily to index possible interpersonal situations involving the superior and the addressee. It is the listeners' ability to retrieve such cultural information as to what encounters like this might be about and what interpersonal relations, activities and communicative goals might be involved that enables them to identify utterances of this type as warnings. We might argue, therefore, that in both situations anyone who understands what is intended must rely on culturally specific, but interactively retrievable, typified knowledge which relates what is said to possible interactive situations or activities with predictable interpersonal relations and outcomes, and that it is with respect to such knowledge that participants arrive at their interpretations of what is intended.

The next example comes from a group interview session recorded in the 1960's involving a middle class white university professor, his white research assistant and a group of black teenagers. The professor (in fact, myself), who was just beginning to get interested in Black English discourse, wanted to collect some data involving informal discussions on topics of public interest. In explaining his research to the group, he had mentioned the then current views of educators who attributed school failure among black youth to lack of verbal skills and had said that his goal was to collect information with which to disprove such stereotypes. Active participants are the research assistant (M), two teenagers (W) and (B), and the professor (G). Several other teenagers are listening and join in the group responses.

Example 1.

    1. G: what do we talk about?
    2. W: oh/ you guys pick a subject/ .. *any old subject, {[lo] you know//}
    3. G: *any old subject?
    4. B: *any ol: thang (old thing)//
    5. W: {[hi] are you op*po:sed to,} ... the ˜wa::r?
    6. M: yeah//
    7. W: {[hi] are *you op*posed =to the} .. *dra:ft?=
    8.   =[teenagers laugh]=

9. G: yeah/ well i can afford to be opposed//
10. W: {[hi] tell me about your} *wa:r life? was it *interesting?
    {[hi] i mean your: *military *service *life/} .. was it *interesting?
11. G: oh/ it wasn't very interesting/ no//
12. W: tell me, {[hi] what part of the *service you go *into/} the *ar:my?
13. G: i was in the =army=
14. W: =well,= {[hi] what *war was you *in?}
15. G: second world war//
16. W: second/ ... did you ... how you ... you ... {[hi] where did yo *go?}
17. G: i was in europe//
18. W: that's the {[hi] *only *place?}
19. G: that's the only place//

            ==several turns omitted==

24. W: i mean {[hi] was you *really in *action?}
25. G: oh, once or twice//
26. W: did you {[hi] *kill *any*body?}
27. G: i don't know/ i shot a couple of times//
28. W: you *busy *shootin/ huh?
29. [group laughter]

[After some minutes, the talk shifts to the oncoming presidential elections.]

30. W: did you {[hi] a*gree with the e*lections?}
31. [group laughter]
32. W: did you {[hi] a*gree with the e*lections?}
33. [looks towards M] you first//
34. M: me first// no// .. next question//
35. W: {[singsong] why *do you not agree?}
36. M: why do i like *what?
37. W: why don't you a*gree with the e*lections?
38. M: oh//
39. [group laughter]
40. M: thought it was a joke//
41. G: huh?
42. M: thought it was a joke/ joke// a joke, you know//

With his opening remarks in turns 1 and 3, the researcher had intended to initiate a relatively informal discussion, a free exchange of personal opinions on topics of sufficient interest to elicit a display of the teenagers' persuasive skills. To that end, he was hoping to induce the group to talk about a suitable topic of their own choosing. The actual exchange, however, takes quite a different form. At turn 4, it is the interviewees who begin to take control by questioning the interviewers. On detailed examination we see that their remarks, far from constituting informal argumentation, have a gamelike character which seems to be intended to challenge the addressee to produce similar gamelike retorts, and thus ultimately to "check out," that is, test the researchers. Anyone familiar with the literature on Afro-American verbal games of the last few decades (Labov 1972; Gumperz 1982) will readily see what was going on, but the interviewers clearly did not get the point. Nor did they perceive what close examination of the transcripts reveals to be relatively clear contextualization cues, such as the accenting and the pronounced shift in register, the use of Black English pronunciations of "thang," "ol country," "what war was you in?", "you busy shootin," etc. that mark the teenagers' speech as distinct from everyday conversational style and serve as metapragmatic signs suggesting that the group had indeed turned to a gamelike exchange. Intent as they were on collecting suitable verbal data, the researchers saw the teenagers' speech as normal, unmarked Black dialect, and failed to note the special signaling value of what they heard. They were thus unable to enter into the spirit of the exchange and in effect revealed themselves as lacking in the very types of persuasive skills that their interlocutors had been accused of not having.

The example illustrates a fourth important characteristic of contextualization processes, the fact that knowledge of contextualization cues, although language based, is not distributed along language boundary lines. The researchers and the teenagers were all long-term residents of the same urban community. The differences in their knowledge of verbal strategies suggest significant and long-standing differences in networks of interpersonal relationships and historically-based, background knowledge. Contextualization analysis is particularly sensitive to such intrasocietal distinctions (Gumperz 1988).

Let me now turn to a final, more complex series of examples from more recent field data on institutional encounters collected in the late 1970's. The material is drawn from a body of data from a comparative study of interviews in similar settings where interviewees of different ethnic background were asked similar types of questions. As in the preceding example, we find significant differences in notions of what the activity is about. This time, however, there is no overt cuing of shifts in activity. The ways in which individuals' perceptions differ must be determined indirectly through examination of what transpires in the exchange.

The set of transcripts was recorded in the British Midlands in what is locally called a job center, a publicly financed employment office. Individuals who have lost their jobs must register in such institutions and are interviewed to provide information on their job skills and previous work experience to aid the agency in its effort to place them in a suitable position. The first two examples, where all participants are native British English speakers, will provide an example of what is accomplished in such interviews.

Example 2. Job Center: The machinist

1. Q: tell me a little bit about the job? you know/
2. A: ==ok/
3. Q: ==what you actually did?
4. A: well/ in re- in respect of L [firm's name]/
   i- it was ah:: m- maintaining/ and looking after the machinery/ so that so that the: the: ah-
   ... if any faults cropped up/ you just did a quick repair/ to keep them on the move/
   nothing major/ just minor stuff/
5. Q: mhm/ =yeah/=
6. A: =(   )=
7. Q: ==is it something you did ... a lot of training for?
8. A: no/ no/ i was- i was trained/ more or less/
   for the: ah: ... plumbing side of the industry/ in maintenance/
   where you- you- you do all the radiators/ central heating/ and things like that/ you know/
9. Q: mhm/ yeah/ so did you have any specialized training for your job at L?

Example 3. Job Center: The salesman

1. Q: ehm can you tell me .. what your job actually was?
   you know, a little bit =about what you did?=
2. A: =well, it's a= .. sales representative on the: machine side/
   selling =the:=
3. Q: =hm/=
4. A: ==(   ) photocopying machines/
5. Q: yeah//
6. A: to: industry and commerce/
   ... plus the: relative supplies that go with the- .. with the job//
7. Q: yeah// ... was it-
8. A: =yeah//=
9. Q: =call= kind of thing?
10. A: it was mainly call kind of thing/ yeah//
11. Q: =mhm//=
12. A: =except= on the supply side/ where it was eh.. on-going business with- you know/
   with regular customers/ .. you know?
13. Q: yeah//

14. A: but the machines was: .. (   ) canvass://
15. Q: yeah// so you actually went out to the firm/ .. sold .. you know/ sold the pack of works//
    did you have any part of the: delivery? or: installation? or:?
16. A: eh: well/ i was likely there when the machine went in/ obviously/
    to .. eh brief the staff on how to use the machines/ and-
17. Q: ==yes//
18. A: ==general demonstration of .. what went on//
19. Q: yeah// you said photocopying ehm equipment/
    is that what it was (then)/ it's a photocopying ma=chine?=
20. A: =yeah//= it would mainly be .. photocopiers/
    it's the (   ) photocopiers//
21. Q: =yeah//=
22. A: =although= we did sell the: offsets/
23. Q: mhm// yeah//

The interviewer Q's questioning follows a pattern which is repeated again in all our data. After the initial introduction which is not reproduced here, Q, who already has preliminary information about the applicant in her files, asks questions about the applicant's job and work experience. The goal is to arrive at a description of the applicant's skills which is sufficiently broad to be informative for nonspecialists yet has enough detail to match the applicant's qualifications with descriptions of available positions. Note that the applicants do not produce adequate descriptions of their qualifications entirely on their own. Descriptions are negotiated in the course of the interview by means of the interviewer's queries, comments and backchannel responses which are in large measure indirect. She never explicitly states what it is she needs to hear or what is lacking in a given response. But, judging by the success of her strategy in these two examples, we can assume that both participants agree on what the communicative goals of the interaction are.

In example 2 the initial question, "Tell me a little bit about the job," to which the applicant A replies with "Ok," produces a further probe, "What you actually did," to which A provides a more elaborate response. The response begins with a general descriptive statement which ends in an evaluation, "nothing major, just minor stuff." A subsequent general question, "Is it something you did a lot of training for?" then yields additional information on the applicant's previous training experience.

The mechanics of the negotiating process are more readily apparent in example 3. The opening question is almost identical with that of example 2. There follows a short reply naming the job category and describing some of the work involved. When, after turn 4, Q probes with, "Yeah," more detail is produced in turn 5. By turn 9, Q has enough information to venture a generalization, "Was it a call kind of thing?" whereupon A confirms and follows up by giving still more detail. In turn 13, Q's "Yeah" again evokes more detail. The interaction by now has fallen into a pattern where A produces answers which Q then gradually translates into the accepted terminology of job description. This pattern continues until an adequate description has been cooperatively produced.

The interviewees in the remaining examples are Asian, non-native speakers of English who have worked in local industry for some time and have a good working knowledge of English grammar. The interviewer's questions follow the same pattern as before, but the interactions take a radically different course.

Example 4. Job Center: The threader mechanic

1. Q: yeah// can you just tell me a little bit about your job? what you actually did?
2. A: well/ ... what kind of a job on in this (country)?
   when i were coming in sixty-seven/ or in this country?
3. Q: no/ when you were- when you were at harwood =cash//=
4. A: =harwood= cash/ =(you mean))//=
5. Q: =yeah/ what=
   ... as a threader mechanic?
6. A: yeah/ =(   )=
7. Q: =what-= what does that involve?

8. A: well/ it's a- ... co-ordinating machinery that make a fabric/ and then/ add the fabric//
9. Q: yeah/ and wh-
10. A:a ==and ah ... started on here/ sixty-seven/
11. Q: yeah//
12. A: =so-=
13. Q: =what= did you actually do though?
14. A: well/ i did ehm ... well/ i- ... they started on the thirteen machine/
      and eh ... when i come in this ... country/ i'm ... =(fixed)=
15. Q: =yeah//=
16. A: ==job in (   )/
17. Q: yeah//
18. A: ==eh:: ... foreman at the =(job)/ (   ) [laughs]=
19. Q: =what was your job/ (   )/= as a threader?
      =you know?=
20. A: =it's ehm= ... the fitting machine/ something like that// set- set the kind of quality//
21. Q: mhm//
22. A: ==something like that// (it's all) kind of a job/ you know?
23. Q: yeah//
24. A: =(   )=
25. Q: =did you set= machines/ or?
26. A: yeah// =(   )=
27. Q: =how-= how did you do that? what did you do?
28. A: ... well/ the kind that's bent down here/ so if it's a- ... a type of machine (   )/
      when i was there- .. it's a ... well/ a big roller and m- mortar machine in there//
29. Q: yeah// mhm//

Q's opening question produces a clarification request: "What kind of a job, in this country? when I was coming in '67?" When Q refers to A's previous employer, A again asks for further confirmation. All this uncertainty seems strange behavior for someone who has been in England more than a decade and who presumably has worked in his previous position for several years. In turn 5, it is Q who finally produces the relevant job classification in the form of a question, "Threader mechanic?" The answer is "yes," without any additional information, so that Q must once more ask, "What does that involve?" Instead of then explaining what his work entailed, A describes the machine he presumably worked with. When Q's probes with "Yeah" and with "What did you actually do?", A goes into a personal narrative which reverts to his arrival in England. In turn 18, A finally volunteers that he was a foreman, accompanying his remark with embarrassed laughter. In reply to the next question, he again goes into a description of the machine, and in response to Q's probing, "hm" in turn 21, he says, "something like that, it's all kind of a job, you know." Q then asks more specific questions such as, "Did you set machines, or --." The reply is a simple, "Yeah." Q again asks, "How did you do that? What did you do?" As before, the reply refers to how the machine works, not to what A did. In sum, despite several attempts to obtain the information she needs to deal with the case effectively, the interviewer is unsuccessful. Yet, it is unlikely that the interviewee could have held his job as foreman without knowing more about the work and what it involves than he seems willing to provide here. We ask ourselves, "Is this simply a matter of individual behavior? Was the interviewee unwilling to cooperate?" It turns out that the threader mechanic is far from unique. The same pattern of seeming uncooperativeness is repeated over and over again with Asian interviewees.

Example 5. Job Center: The spinner

1. Q: five years// ... yeah// and what was your job there?
2. A: ... spinning job//
3. Q: it was- you were a spinner?
4. A: yeah//
5. Q: yeah//
6. A: in (essex)//
7. Q: yeah// ... ri:ght// can you just tell me a little bit about the job?

what you actually did? ... you know/ as a spinner/ what were you doing?

8. A: ... well/ eh ... sp- ... with eh spi- spinning job/ machinery job/
9. Q: ... yeah// ... but you =weren't-=
10. A: =so i spun-= i spun from my machine// i have a-
11. Q: =yeah//=
12. A: =head= machine (   )//
13. Q: yeah// i don't know a lot about spinning/ that's all//

----

20. Q: yeah// what did you actually do as a spinner? were you setting machines up?
21. A: ==yes/ i done setting machine/ and i (   ) machine//
22. Q: yeah// you did it all by hand// you didn't use ... knotting- hand knotting machines or anything?
23. A: no::://

Here again the initial question does not elicit sufficient detail. The probe in turn 3 fails to produce more information. When Q, in turn 7, quite specifically asks, "Can you tell me a little bit about
the job, what you actually did, you know, as a spinner, what were you doing?" the answer is, "Well,
with spinning job, machinery job." Q follows with "Yeah, but you weren't-," but is interrupted with
another general statement, "I spun from my machine." Clearly, she is not getting anywhere. After
several turns, she attempts a summary statement of what she has learned, "What did you actually do as
a spinner? Were you setting machines up?" The answer is a mere confirmation, "Yes, I done setting
machine." Finally in turn 22, after the next, more specific question, which suggests some of the
answers Q is looking for, A simply replies, "No."

In the next two examples, the applicants have done various jobs within the same establishment.
They talk about how they moved from task to task but again do not respond to direct queries as to
what skills these tasks involved.

Example 6. Job Center: The relief operator

1. Q: right// now you've put on your form/ you're .. an r and .. d operator//
2. A: yeah/ that's right//
3. Q: can you tell me what that involves? =(   )=
4. A: =well/ it's= .. actually a (laboring) duty/ you know/
5. Q: =mhm//=
6. A: =in a= department where you have latest jobs//
7. Q: yeah//
8. A: ... well/ you know/ a particular department/
    we had a ... sp- spraying/ paint- paint spraying inspection//
9. Q: yeah//
10. A: and repairing//
11. Q: =yeah//=
12. A: =and/= as i've been ... in the company for a long time now/
13. Q: yeah//
14. A: ==i knew all the jobs/
15. Q: yeah//
16. A: so my duty were/ you know/ just (relieve) men/ you know/
    for tea breaks/ and dinner breaks/ and this sort of thing//
17. Q: yeah// a relief operator/
18. A: ==relief operator/ yeah//
19. Q: ==for that s- that sort of thing// yeah//
    ... w- within the department/ what sort of jobs did you do? what did you actually do?
20. A: well/ eh ... it's eh ... television tube (   ) up in the ... company now//
21. Q: mhm// yeah//

Note, despite repeated querying, by turn 17 no new information has been conveyed, apart from
the fact that A was a relief operator and knew all the jobs. The query in turn 19 only produces a
response that refers to the equipment, not specifically to what A did.

Example 7. Job Center: Youth opportunity

1. Q: (   ) that's right/ can you tell me a little bit about it?
     what you- what you're actually doing (on it)?
2. A: well ehm .. you do .. two weeks/
3. Q: .. hmm/
4. A: we change around every two weeks/
5. Q: yeah/
6. A: we're doing ehm .. plastering now/
7. Q: .. yeah/
8. A: it's a work (   ) opportunity/
9. Q: oh yeah/ yeah/
10. A: and then ehm ... we've done some plumbing/
11. Q: yeah/
12. A: and next week/ we'll be going to eh painting/ ... wallpapering/
13. Q: .. oh =yeah/=
14. A: =(   )=
15. Q: yeah/
16. A: (   )
17. Q: ==alright now/ just going back to what you said at first/ the plastering/
18. A: (   )
19. Q: how- .. you know/ what- what do you actually do? how- how involved are you?
20. A: well/ ... he shows us what to do/ and we ... plaster the wall out in plasterboard/
21. Q: yeah/ do you do all the mixing on =that?=
22. A: =yeah/=
23. Q: ==you do all that?
24. A: we mix it by hand/
25. Q: ... mhm/

Here Q's initial question, "Can you tell me a little bit about it? What you are actually doing?" receives the reply, "You do two weeks," and when she probes, A expands by, "We change around every two weeks." With further probing, A provides nothing but general labels, such as "plumbing," "plastering," etc., to list jobs he does. Beginning with turn 17, Q directs her questioning to obtaining information on the specific tasks relevant to the jobs A has listed by focusing on one job at a time, clearly to no avail.

In presenting these examples, I am not just concerned with problems of interethnic communication. I want to argue that the study of communication failures can be used as a starting point for the analysis of inferential processes in much the same way as the analysis of grammatical processes builds on informants' judgments comparing grammatical with ungrammatical sentences. My argument then is that what happens between the native and non-native speakers is due to differences in presuppositions operating at both levels of inferencing referred to in this paper, the global and the local or sequential, and that the case studies I have presented, when interpreted in relationship to other ethnographic findings, can serve as a starting point for generating testable hypotheses of what the inferential processes involved are.

My claim rests on the assumption that what looks like somehow odd and uncooperative behavior on the part of the Asians can be shown to reflect systematic culture based presuppositions. Yet note that, contrary to what was found in the case of the teenagers in example 1, there are no overt contextualization cues that directly mark genre distinctions. We therefore turn to a more detailed, comparative examination of question and response content in the last two sets of examples, that is, of the native/native and non-native/native encounters. Here several points become apparent. (1) When compared to the natives, the Asians' responses to the opening questions seem either evasive, in the sense that they fail to deal with the question as asked, or so general as to be quite uninformative. (2) Non-natives' responses to the interviewer's probes and comments, on the other hand, are often overly specific, seeming to focus on facts which are clearly not relevant to the negotiation of adequate descriptions of their skills and experience. (3) In their speech, the non-natives rarely distinguished between what they themselves did and what the job requires. These patterns occur over and over again, not only in the job center transcripts but also in other, similar ethnographically based studies.

Let me explain what I mean by ethnography. Much of my work on conversational inference in interethnic settings during the last few years has concentrated on what I could call "the comparative analysis of speech events in institutional settings." The research procedure has been as follows. Events for study are selected on the basis of extensive in situ participant observation combined with interviews designed to collect information about members' notions of what their daily work routines are and what kinds of communicative situations they regularly engage in as part of these routines. Such ethnographic enquiry yields what we may call members' or analysts' typifications of speech events and of associated norms. In addition to job center events, training center selection interviews, employment interviews, promotion interviews, advice center sessions, housing office interviews, educational counseling sessions, others have been studied.

In a second stage of the analysis, the goal is to refine these typifications by relying on a series of recursive trial and error procedures to test the extent to which norms and presuppositions discovered through the initial ethnographic procedures explain the participants' inferential processes, and thus gradually to modify the original typifications. The ultimate aim is not to determine what was ultimately meant or intended but to arrive at coherent explanations of communicative outcomes and of verbal strategies employed in achieving them as they are documented through what transpires in the event.

My findings in this area so far are by no means definite, but nevertheless some regularities are beginning to emerge. These have been explained in some detail elsewhere (Gumperz 1989). Here I will merely summarize. Asian English speakers tend to view the activities involved in institutional interviewing as relatively hierarchical in nature in the sense that it is the interviewer who defines the issues to be dealt with on the basis of facts supplied by the interviewee. This has direct interactive consequences. The latter, in making a case, tends to present him or herself as a victim of circumstances, to avoid foregrounding personal abilities and to avoid giving information that she or he has reason to believe the other already knows. Consider also the Asians' recurrent attempts to use personal narration in response to requests to explain job experience, as, for example, in example 4 turns 2 and 10. In several other case studies analyzed, this reflects an interviewee's strategy of going to great length to establish a historical background for whatever claims he or she is making, in order to make sure that these claims are judged within the context of shared frames of reference.

The above perspective goes some way in explaining the seeming oddities in the non-natives' responses. For example, compare the natives' extensive foregrounding of "I" or other markers of agency with the non-natives' use of object-oriented constructions. There is some justification, therefore, for the assumption that the natives and the non-natives have quite different notions of what the activity is about in these examples.

Furthermore, the differences on the global level are compounded at the level of local inferencing by the interviewer's and interviewees' failure to perceive the communicative significance of the metapragmatic mechanisms by which they signal attempts to repair misunderstandings. Thus, native interviewees, as I have noted, readily respond to the interviewer's hints that more information of certain kinds is needed, while non-natives rarely do so. The interviewer, on the other hand, fails to recognize the non-natives' attempts to produce narrative accounts as responding to her request. In fact, she tends to cut off such accounts as irrelevant. In this way she seems to be cutting herself off from being able to obtain the information she needs.

Appendix: Transcription System

Symbol	*Significance*

//	Final fall
/	Slight fall indicating "more is to come"
?	Final rise
,	Slight rise as in listing intonation
-	Truncation (e.g. what ti- what time is it/)

..	Pauses of less than .5 second
...	Pauses greater than .5 second (unless precisely timed)
<2>	Precise units of time (= 2 second pause)
=	To indicate overlap and latching of speakers' utterances

(e.g. R: so you understand =the requirements=

B: =yeah, i under=stand them/

~~~~~~~~~~~~~~~~~~~~~~~~

R: so you understand the requirements?
B: ==yeah, i understand them/
R: ==and the schedule?
B: yeah/

with spacing and single "=" before and after the appropriate portions of the text indicating overlap
and turn initial double "=" indicating latching of the utterance to the preceding one.)

::	Lengthened segments (e.g. wha::t)
~	Fluctuating intonation over one word
*	Accent; normal prominence
CAPS	Extra prominence
{[ ]}	Nonlexical phenomena, both vocal and nonvocal, which overlays the lexical stretch e.g. {[lo] text//}
[ ]	Nonlexical phenomena, both vocal and nonvocal, which interrupts the lexical stretch e.g. text [laugh] text//

( )	Unintelligible speech
di(d)	A good guess at an unclear segment
(did)	A good guess at an unclear word
(xxx)	Unclear word for which a good guess can be made as to how many syllables were uttered with "x" = one syllable
(" ")	Regularization (e.g. i'm gonna ("going to") come soon/)
# #	Use hatchmarks when extratextual information needs to be included within the text (e.g. R: did you ask M #surname# to come?)

Bibliography

Atkinson, J. M. and J. Heritage. 1986. *Structures of Social Action.* Cambridge: Cambridge University Press.

Chafe, W. 1980. *The Pear Stories.* Norwood, NJ: Ablex Publishing Co.

Gumperz, J. J. 1982. *Discourse Strategies.* New York: Cambridge University Press.

—1988. "Linguistic Variability in Interactive Perspective," to be published in a volume on language usage in Mannheim, Germany edited by Werner Kahlmeyer, Institute of German Language, Mannheim.

—1989. "Contextualization and Understanding," in A. Duranti and C. Goodwin (eds.), *Rethinking Context.* New York: Cambridge University Press.

Hanks, W. In press. *Referential Practice.* Chicago: University of Chicago Press.

Haviland, J. In press.

Heath, J. 1980. "Nunggubuyu Deixis, Anaphora and Culture" in *CLS 1980 Papers from the Parasession on Pronouns and Anaphora*, pp.152-3: Chicago Linguistic Society.

Hymes, D. 1983. *"In vain I tried to tell you": Essays in Native American Ethnopoetics.* Philadelphia: University of Pennsylvania Press.

Labov, W. 1973. *Language in the Inner City.* Philadelphia: University of Pennsylvania Press.

Liberman, M. and I. A. Sag. 1974. "Prosodic Form and Discourse Function," in *CLS 10*: Chicago Linguistic Society.

Michaels, S. and J. Collins. 1986. "Speaking and writing: Discourse strategies and the acquisition of literacy," in J. Cook-Gumperz (ed.), *The Social Construction of Literacy.* New York: Cambridge University Press.

Silverstein, M. In press.

Givenness, Implicature and Demonstrative Expressions in English Discourse

Jeanette Gundel, Nancy Hedberg and Ron Zacharski
University of Minnesota

It has long been recognized that the form of natural language expressions correlates with cognitive statuses such as givenness, topic, and presupposition, which depend on the context in which the expression is used. In recent years there has been considerable research and debate regarding the nature of such statuses and their relation to one another. For example, as pointed out in Gundel (1978a), Prince (1981b) and Chafe (1987) there are a number of different senses of givenness, each of which is linguistically relevant. In this paper, we attempt to unify and refine this work as a basis for explaining the use of demonstrative expressions in English discourse.

1. The Givenness Hierarchy

In a previous paper (Gundel, Hedberg, and Zacharski 1988) we proposed that there are five cognitive statuses relevant to the form of referring expressions in natural language and that these are related in the Givenness Hierarchy shown in (1):

(1) Givenness Hierarchy[1]

in focus	>	activated	>	familiar	>	uniquely identifiable	>	type identifiable
$\{it\}$		$\left\{\begin{array}{l}that \\ this \\ this\ \mathrm{N}\end{array}\right\}$		$\{that\ \mathrm{N}\}$		$\{the\ \mathrm{N}\}$		$\left\{\begin{array}{l}a\ \mathrm{N} \\ \mathrm{indefinite}\ this\ \mathrm{N}^2\end{array}\right\}$

type identifiable   In the weakest case, use of a particular referring expression is felicitous if and only if the speaker can justifiably assume that the addressee can identify the type of entity being referred to. We refer to this status as 'type identifiable'. Type identifiability is a necessary condition for use of any referring expression, and it is sufficient for indefinite reference, including the indefinite determiner *this*. Thus, *a dog* or *this dog* in (2) is appropriate only if the addressee can be assumed to understand that the object referred to is a member of the class of dogs.

(2)   I couldn't sleep last night. **A/This dog next door** kept me awake.

uniquely identifiable   Definite descriptions differ from indefinite ones in that their appropriate use requires that the addressee can not only identify the type of entity referred to but can also pick out the particular entity or set of entities that the speaker has in mind. We refer to this status as 'uniquely identifiable'. Unique identifiability is a necessary condition for all definite reference and is both necessary and sufficient for use of the definite article *the*. While identifiability may be based on previous knowledge, this is not necessary, since the basis for identification may be fully encoded in the linguistic form itself. Thus, as Hawkins 1978 points out, the definite description *the dog next door* in (3) is perfectly felicitous even if the addressee has no previous knowledge that the speaker's neighbor has a dog.

(3)   I couldn't sleep last night. **The dog next door** kept me awake.

familiar   Although identifiability does not require previous knowledge of the entity being referred to, it is usually the case that the referent of a uniquely-identifiable noun phrase is identifiable because both speaker and addressee are already familiar with it, and thus have some mental representation of it. The experience which serves as the basis for this shared familiarity may be linguistic or extralinguistic, in current awareness, or in long term memory associated with shared cultural or personal experience. This status, which we refer to as 'familiar,' is a necessary condition for use of all definite demonstratives and a sufficient condition for the demonstrative determiner *that*.[3]   Thus (4) unlike (3) is appropriate only if the addressee already knows that the speaker's neighbor has a dog.

(4)   I couldn't sleep last night. **That dog next door** kept me awake.

activated   The set of familiar entities always includes those which the speech participants are currently aware of due to their presence in the immediate discourse context. We refer to this status as 'activated.' Activated entities may have been linguistically introduced--for example, as referents of nouns and noun phrases, or as events and states of affairs introduced by verb phrases and whole sentences (cf. Davidson 1967, and Hobbs 1985). They also include higher-level discourse topics (cf. "the right frontier" of Webber 1988a, 1988b). Entities may also become activated by virtue of their presence in the immediate extralinguistic context. Thus, activated entities include the speech participants themselves. [4]

Activation is a necessary condition for felicitous use of all pronominal expressions, including pronominal demonstratives. Thus, the form *that* in (5) can appropriately be used to refer to the barking of a dog only if a dog has actually been barking during the speech event or if barking has been introduced in the immediate linguistic context.

(5)   I couldn't sleep last night. **That** kept me awake.

Activation is also a necessary condition for use of determiner *this*. [5]

Both determiner and pronominal *this* have the additional condition that the referent be not only activated, but speaker-activated, by virtue of its inclusion in the speaker's context space (cf. Fillmore 1975, Fillmore 1982, Lakoff 1974). This condition is illustrated in example (6).

(6)   A[6]: Have you seen the neighbor's new dog?
      B: Yes, and **that dog** kept me awake all night.
      B': ?? Yes, and **this dog** kept me awake all night.

in focus   Finally, the most highly activated entities are not only in the speaker and hearer's awareness, but are also at the center of attention at the current point in the discourse. We refer to this status as 'in focus'. In focus is a necessary condition for null anaphora (cf. Gundel 1978b) and for unstressed pronominals, including pronominal *it*. The entities in focus at a given point in the discourse will be that partially-ordered subset of activated entities which are likely to be continued as topics of subsequent utterances (cf. "activated topic" of Gundel 1978a). The status 'in focus' is thus more complex than the other cognitive statuses. It not only involves the assumed status of an entity in memory but also the relative importance or relevance of that entity to the current discourse.

Entities in focus generally include at least the topic of the preceding utterance plus any currently relevant higher-level discourse topics, which may or may not be overtly represented in the sentence itself. To the extent that syntactic and prosodic form of a sentence encodes its topic-comment structure and also the relative importance of its constituents, membership in the in-focus set is partially determined by linguistic form (cf. the centering and focusing algorithms of Dahl 1986, Grosz, Joshi, and Weinstein 1983 and Sidner 1983). Thus, referents of subjects and direct objects of matrix sentences are highly likely to be in focus, whereas referents of elements in subordinate clauses and prepositional phrases are less likely to be in focus. However, the actual inclusion of elements in the set depends ultimately on pragmatic factors, and thus is not uniquely determinable from the syntax.

Consider, for example, (7) and (8). After the utterance of (7a) the referent of the Bull Mastiff is activated. However, it is not in focus, since it is neither the topic of (7a) nor the most important part of what is communicated about the topic. Thus (7b) would be an inappropriate continuation.

(7)　a.　Sears delivered new siding to my neighbors with the Bull Mastiff
　　　b.　# **It's/that's** the dog that bit Mary Ben.

For the same reason, B's question in (8) is interpreted as an interruption; but notice that even here the Bull Mastiff cannot be referenced with *it* since it is not in focus.

(8)　A:　Sears delivered new siding to my neighbors with the Bull Mastiff
　　　B:　Oh, isn't **that** the dog that bit Mary Ben?
　　　B':　#Oh, isn't **it** the dog that bit Mary Ben?
　　　A:　Yeah. Anyway, this siding is real hideous and...

It is not the case, however, that referents of objects of prepositions inside a noun phrase are never in focus. They may be if they are sufficiently relevant in the given context, as illustrated by (9). Note that *a large wind energy project* in (9a) is in a syntactic position similar to that of *the Bull Mastiff* in (7a), but its referent, unlike that of the *Bull Mastiff*, is in focus.

(9)　a.　However, the government of Barbados is looking for a project manager for a large wind energy project.
　　　b.　I'm going to see the man in charge of **it** next week.
　　　　　　　　　　[personal letter]

the Givenness Hierarchy　The hierarchy in (1) encodes the fact that by definition, each status implies all statuses lower on the hierarchy, but not vice-versa. Thus, for example, an entity which is in focus is necessarily also activated, familiar, uniquely identifiable and type identifiable. However, not all identifiable entities are familiar and not all familiar entities are either activated or in focus. Furthermore, as noted above, each status is associated as a necessary and sufficient condition for the use of a form at that point on the hierarchy, with demonstratives being correlated with statuses in the middle.

To test the proposed correlations, we supplemented our previous study of 700 tokens of demonstrative expressions (Gundel, Hedberg, and Zacharski 1988) with a second study of approximately 450 tokens of naturally occurring definite referring expressions. The tokens for both studies were drawn from a variety of spoken and written genres, which varied in degree of formality and preplanning. These included informal conversations, personal letters, televised discussions, mystery novels, newspaper articles, technical articles, and a university planning document[7]. Table 1 shows the distribution of the different forms in our current study according to highest cognitive status met by that form.

Table 1: **Distribution of forms by highest status**

form	in focus	activated	familiar	uniquely identifiable	type identifiable	row totals
it	109 100%					109
this	4 50%	4 50%				8
that	7 27%	60 88%		(1) (2%)		68
this n	5 14%	23 64%			(8) (22%)	36
that n		7 50%	6 43%	(1) (7%)		14
the n	12 5%	55 22%	60 25%	116 48%		243
column totals	137	149	66	118	8	478

As can be seen from the table, all occurrences of definite referring expressions examined met the necessary conditions posited for that expression in the hierarchy.[8]

When the cognitive status necessary for use of a particular form does not obtain, use of that form is infelicitous. Thus a demonstrative determiner is inappropriate when the referent of the noun phrase is uniquely identifiable but cannot be assumed to be previously familiar to the addressee. In (10), for example *the conclusion* cannot be replaced by *that conclusion*.

(10)   I've come to **the conclusion** that I will not extend my contract at the bank.   [Personal letter]

Similarly, a demonstrative pronominal is infelicitous when the referent is unactivated, as in (11).

(11) M: These. Do **these** go in here or there?
K: These?
M: The ones I just got done writing.

[Frederickson tapes]

The requirement that the referent of pronominal and determiner *this* be speaker-activated correctly predicts that both *this* and *that* can be used to comment upon a speaker's own prior remarks, as shown in (12) and (13). Note that *this* in (12) could be replaced by *that* and *those issues* in (13) could be replaced by *these issues*.

(12) K 1: And..So what he DID was ...came in, set up the tree...
2: and then he made wassail, with rum in it?
3: And..made it in coffee cans and heated it on the stove in the graduate lounge.
A 4: Oh, gee.
K 5: And **this** was the solstice tree.

[Frederickson tapes]

(13) John, this speech was a magnificent triumph for the President. He showed he could stay awake for twelve whole minutes. He showed that he could speak every word off of his teleprompter, even the long ones. But the speech doesn't have any chance of putting the scandal behind him, because the scandal is not about mistakes, as he said, and it's not about mismanagement, as the Tower Commission said. It is about a betrayal of principles, it's about lying, and it's about breaking the law. And **those issues** remain. [The McLaughlin Group, 3/6/87].

In general, however, only *that* can be used to comment upon the remarks of another speaker, as illustrated by example (14) where *that* cannot be replaced by *this*:[9]

(14) N: "Bob loves Mary", and someone else wrote "Mary loves Jim" and I wrote "Jim loves Bob"! (laughter). It was three different handwritings, three different people.
K: Yeah, **that**'s good.

[Frederickson tapes]

2. Interaction of Givenness Hierarchy with Gricean Maxim of Quantity

Since each of the cognitive statuses in the Givenness Hierarchy entails all lower statuses, reference with a particular form should imply the possibility of reference with all forms associated with lower statuses. Thus, in (15) *these systems* could felicitously be replaced with *the systems*.

(15) These incredibly small magnetic bubbles are the vanguard of a new generation of ultradense memory-storage systems. **These**

> **systems** are extremely rugged: they are resistant to radiation
> and are nonvolatile.   [Graff 1988:68]

In many instances, however, a form is inappropriate or conveys some special effect even when sufficient conditions for its use have been met. Thus, *it* in (16b) is naturally interpreted as referring to the topic, Simplified English, which is in focus at this point in the discourse. However, if *it* is replaced by *this* as in (16b'), the most natural interpretation is one where *this* refers to the whole statement about Simplified English.

(16)   a.   Simplified English disallows the use of passive, progressive, and
            perfective auxiliary verbs, among other things.
       b.   **It** requires engineers to break up long compound nouns and
            technical expressions into chunks of three or less elements (e.g.
            'liquid crystal display screen' would be illegal in Simplified English).
       b'. **This** requires engineers to break up long compound nouns and
            technical expressions ...
                                         [message from electronic news group]

What is it then that determines the choice among forms when sufficient conditions for more than one form have been met? We will now attempt to demonstrate that such choices follow from the interaction of the Givenness Hierarchy with Grice's maxim of quantity (cf. Grice 1975), stated in (17).

(17)   Q1: Make your contribution as informative as required (for the current
            purposes of the exchange).
       Q2: Do not make your contribution more informative than is required.

The first submaxim, Q1, gives rise to quantity implicatures of the sort we find with *some* versus *all*. Thus, even though *all* entails *some*, *some* conversationally implicates *not all* by Q1. In uttering (18), for example, the speaker implicates that the paper isn't finished yet.

(18)   We've finished some parts of the CLS paper.

The second submaxim, Q2, gives rise to implicatures of the sort associated with *and*, where S1 *and* S2 implicates that the event described by S1 precedes, and where plausible causes, the event described by S2, as in (19).

(19)   His house was robbed, and I lost the speakers and the tape deck.
                                         [personal letter]

Because the statuses in the Givenness Hierarchy are in a unidirectional entailment relation, they form a Horn scale (cf. Horn 1972) and thus would be expected to give rise to quantity implicatures. We do, in fact, find both parts of the quantity maxim interacting with the Givenness Hierarchy.

The frequently noted function of demonstratives to signal a shift in focus (cf. Isard 1975, Linde 1979, Sidner 1983) follows from interaction of the Givenness Hierarchy with Q1--give as much information as required. Since the status 'in focus' entails all the other statuses, use of a form correlated with one of the other statuses implicates by Q1 that the referent is not in focus.[10] This prediction is supported by our data. As Table 1 shows, most elements in focus are referenced by pronominal *it* [11], and demonstratives are generally used when there is a shift in focus. For example, in (12) above, the tree has been activated by its mention in K1 thus licensing the use of a pronominal in K5. However, since the tree is not in focus in K2, K3, and A4, the reference to it in K5 constitutes a focus shift and thus requires a stressed demonstrative form.

Some additional illustrations of the focus shift function of pronominal demonstratives from our data are given in (13) and (15) above, and in (20) and (21).

(20)   When Snepp makes a speech he has to submit a text to CIA censors first. When he wrote a book review for the Los Angeles Times, he had to show it to the agency before he sent it to the newspaper, and when the editor asked for a change, he had to show **that** to the censors too.
[Anthony Lewis. Secrecy policy has no sense. Minneapolis Star and Tribune 4/14/87]

(21)   Anyway going on back from the kitchen then is a little hallway leading to a window, and across from the kitchen is a big walk-through closet. On the other side of **that** is another little hallway leading to a window, and on the other side of **that** is a long bedroom.   [personal letter]

Note that if *that* were replaced by *it* in (20), the referent would most likely be interpreted as the book review since this is already in focus in the previous sentence. Similarly, if *that* were replaced by *it* in (21), the referent would be most likely interpreted as the kitchen.

Use of pronominal *this* and *that* in referring to previous statements (cf. Webber 1988a), as in (14) above, is just a special case of focus shift since the focus of attention at the point after a statement is made is typically not the event or state of affairs described by that statement but rather the entity which is the topic of the statement. Thus, in (16b) above, use of *it* continues the topic and refers to Simplified English. On the other hand, use of *this* in (16b') implicates that the referent is not in focus, and is interpreted as referring to the whole statement about what Simplified English disallows.

The so-called contrastive function of demonstratives may also be just a special case of focus shift. In (22), for example, the speaker could have referred to the currently in-focus travel journal with pronominal *it*. Use of *this* implicates by Q1 that the referent should be viewed in a new way, thus implicitly bringing into focus other travel journals with which it might be contrasted.

(22) N: I've been working some more on my book, on my travel journal from '85. That sounds funny but I have all my notes. However, I want to write a little better than I am, put a little more effort, make **this** a little more quality effort than the last one was.
[Frederickson tapes]

For pronominals, then, it is generally the case that the form associated with the highest possible status is used, and use of such a form implicates by Q1 that necessary conditions for use of a form associated with a higher status do not obtain.[12] In the case of determiners, however, the situation is more complicated. It is true that a high percentage of noun phrases do not meet necessary conditions for use of a demonstrative determiner, since their referents are not familiar but only identifiable, as in (23).

(23)   Harriet gathered herself together to cram her story into the fewest and most telling words. "I am speaking from Darley near Wilvercombe. **The dead body of a man** was found at two o'clock this afternoon."

[Sayers 1986:26]

Most uses of definite article phrases, however, do refer to entities which are familiar, and many of these are not only familiar, but activated, or even in focus. Thus, use of a definite article does not generally implicate by Q1 that the referent is unfamiliar. Rather, it is Q2 --don't give more information than required--which is operating here.

The question that naturally arises is why this should be the case. That is, why should choice of a definite pronominal be primarily dictated by Q1 and choice of a definite determiner by Q2? We believe the answer to this question is related to the fact that in the case of pronominals, the cognitive status of the referent is crucial for identification because the pronominal form itself has little descriptive content. In the case of full noun phrases, however, the descriptive content of the noun and modifiers is often sufficient for identifying the referent. Thus, given that the referent of the phrase must be uniquely identifiable, the more restrictive cognitive statuses associated with demonstrative determiners have little informative value and do not need to be signalled explicitly in such cases.

This is especially true when the referent is already activated or in focus, i.e, when there is a coreferring noun phrase in the immediate discourse context which is at least partially identical in form. As Table 1 shows, many examples of *the* N in our data are, in fact, of this type. Examples of *the* N used for familiar noun phrases are given in (24)-(27). In (25) the referent is not only familiar but activated, and in (26) and (27) it is in focus:[13]

(24)   Then there's Carol Manke, who is a writer -- it's funny because she's the person who writes for, the religious things for the Fargo Forum, and, she also writes uh, anything to do with civil rights or, **the abortion issue women's clinic type thing**.
[Frederickson tapes]

(25)   "How in the world," demanded Harriet, "did *you* get here?" "Car," said Lord Peter, briefly. "Have they produced the body?" "Who told you about **the body**?"
[Sayers 1986:38]

(26)   I am writing you now because (1) I am tired of reading Jung, and (2) you are so incredibly persistent about the damn DIP! I was

going to give you the recipe at the convention, but I'm sure you can't wait until then.

Ron, are you going to cease communicating with me now that you have **the dip recipe**?

[personal letter]

(27)   First, in July I might have a two week consulting job in Egypt working for NASA. I am hoping that **the job** gets approved.

[personal letter]

When determiner *that* is used, it facilitates comprehension by implicating focus-shift, and in many cases serves as an explicit signal to the addressee to search long-term memory for a familiar referent. In such cases, determiner *that* signals that the referent is familiar and implicates by Q1 that the referent is not activated. Examples of such 'reminder *that*'s' are given in (28) - (31).

(28)   The cleanup of **that Alaska oil spill** leads our look at news around America tonight.   [beginning of TV newscast]

(29)   Exxon oil claims it will take several million dollars to clean up **that oil spill off the coast of Alaska**.

[beginning of TV newscast]

(30)   At any rate, at some time in the year 1927 he became acquainted with Harriet Vane. They met in some of **those artistic and literary circles where "advanced" topics are discussed**, and after a time they became very friendly.

[Sayers 1977:7]

(31) K: I realized something that seems significant to me about George. . that in the, in the fall, he . . . as everyone else, he wears. . . .
     N: [Clothes.
     A: [Loafers.
     K: No. [**Those kind of tennis shoes that are expensive**=
     A: [Boots.
     N: Adidas.
     A: [Adidas.
     K: [Adidas, ok.

[Frederickson tapes]

Uses of determiner *this* in our data provide particularly compelling support for our analysis. Most instances of *this* N provide a redescription of an already activated referent, where the noun is not of the same form as that of its coreferent in the discourse context. Determiner *this*, which requires speaker activation, thus becomes crucial in identifying the referent in such cases by serving as an explicit signal that the referent has already been activated by the speaker and implicating by Q1 that the referent is not in focus. Some examples of such uses of *this* N, which appear to be restricted to more formal, written genres, are given in (32) - (34).

(32)   Nearly lost in the polemic was Judge Kennedy himself. That was ironic, because in many ways **this former small-city lawyer**

**with the stable marriage and three attractive children
and the fine reputation** appears to personify just those values
that made the image of Ronald Reagan so attractive after the con-
vulsions of the 1960's and 1970's.

[New York Times, 11/15/87, 4:1]

(33)   <u>Poll Return</u> The attachment feature sends **this inbound tag** to
the series/1 channel controls to indicate a poll capture for interrupt
servicing or nonburst cycle steal servicing. It is not used to signal a burst transfer.

[technical document]

(34) a.   One valuable outcome of these organizational studies was the refinement of our notions of three different approaches that could
be incorporated in an automated message filtering system.
   b.   We refer to **these techniques** as the cognitive, social, and economic approaches to information filtering.

[Malone 1987:391]

To sum up, in the case of pronominals, Q1 predicts use of the strongest
possible form in most cases, and *it* is stronger (gives more information about cognitive status) than *that* or *this*. In the case of determiners it is the weakest possible
form which is most often used, and *the* is weaker (gives less information about
cognitive status) than either *that* or *this*. This is why neither demonstrative determiners nor demonstrative pronominals are used in many instances where both necessary and sufficient conditions for their use have been met. That is, activated entities are often not referenced with a pronominal demonstrative; and familiar entities
are often not referenced with a demonstrative determiner.

3. The Givenness Hierarchy and Prince's Familiarity Scale
We would like to conclude with a comparison between the Givenness Hierarchy
and the Familiarity Scale proposed in Prince (1981b). In her seminal work on this
topic, Prince distinguishes six types of givenness/newness, and suggests, as we
have here, that these are hierarchically related and thus interact with the Gricean
maxim of quantity. Prince's hierarchy is presented in (35) below:

(35)   familiarity scale of Prince 1981b

$$\left\{ \begin{matrix} E \\ E^s \end{matrix} \right\} \quad > \quad U \quad > \quad I \quad > \quad I^c \quad > \quad BN \quad > \quad BN^a$$

E:	Evoked
E^s:	Situationally evoked
U:	Unused
I:	Inferrable
I^c:	Containing inferrable
BN:	Brand new
BN^a:	Brand new anchored

Prince does not provide a rigorous account of how the maxim of quantity actually interacts with the statuses to explain the distribution of different types of referring expressions. Moreover, we believe that our Givenness Hierarchy provides a better basis for such an explanation for a number of reasons.

First, since the relationship between Prince's statuses is not one of logical entailment, quantity implicatures cannot be derived from her scale in a straightforward way.[14] Thus, while her status 'evoked' (including 'situationally evoked') corresponds closely to our 'activated,' some of her statuses correspond to set differences between ours. For example, 'unused' corresponds roughly to our 'familiar' but not 'activated'; 'containing inferrable' corresponds to our 'identifiable' but not 'familiar'; and 'brand new' corresponds to our 'type identifiable' but not 'uniquely identifiable.' Thus, in Prince's system, 'evoked' does not entail 'unused,' and 'unused' does not entail any of the statuses to the right.

Second, Prince's hierarchy includes 'inferrable' as a separate cognitive status. 'Inferrable', however, is not a separate cognitive status. Rather, it is a way in which something can achieve a particular status by association with an entity that has been activated. In fact, inferrables may have any of the statuses in our hierarchy, as illustrated in examples (36)-(39). In (36), for example, *a whole paragraph* is felicitous if and only if its referent is understood as belonging to the class of paragraphs of the activated affidavit. That is, it is type-identifiable but not uniquely identifiable.

(36)   [boss to secretary who just typed an affidavit he is reading]
        Miss Murchison,' said Mr. Urquhart, with an expression of considerable annoyance, 'do you know that you have left out a **whole paragraph**?'

In (37), the referent of *the pulse*, is uniquely identifiable, but this particular patient's pulse does not have to be previously familiar to the addressee.

(37)   Members of the jury - there is no need, I think, for me to recall the course of Philip Boyes'illness in great detail. The nurse was called in on June 21st, and during that day the doctors visited the patient three times. His condition grew steadily worse... On the day after, the 22nd, he was worse still - in great pain,**the pulse** growing weaker, and the skin about the mouth getting dry and peeling off.
                            [Sayers 1977:21]

What must be familiar in order for (37) to be felicitous is the knowledge that patients have pulses, but this is not the same as having a shared representation of the pulse of the particular patient in question. Most instances of inferrables are of the type in (37), that is, uniquely identifiable but not familiar. Thus our analysis predicts correctly that inferrables generally cannot be referenced with a demonstrative determiner (see, for example, Webber 1988a), which, as we have argued, is correlated with familiarity as a necessary condition. *The pulse* in (37) cannot be replaced by *that pulse*, for example.

On the other hand, when the association between the inferrable and its antecedent is strong enough, reference to the antecedent will be sufficient to activate an actual representation of the referent of the inferrable. In such cases, a demonstrative determiner as in (38), or even a pronominal as in (39) may be used.

(38)   My school, New Patty, started a M.T. department.They're trying
         to graduate their first class in June, but **those kids** haven't had
         psych of music yet.   [personal letter]

(39)   There was not a man, woman or child within sight; only a small
         fishing-boat, standing out to sea some distance away. Harriet
         waved wildly in its direction, but **they** either didn't see her or
         supposed that she was merely doing some kind of reducing exer-
         cises.

    Finally, Prince does not distinguish between the statuses 'activated' and 'in
focus' since her status 'evoked' covers both. As we have argued here, the status
'in focus' is crucial in explicating the distribution of referring expressions, and in
particular, demonstrative expressions, in English discourse.

---

[1]As Yael Ziv has pointed out to us, the name 'Givenness Hierarchy' may be
misleading since the term 'given' has generally been used only to refer to entities
that are at least familiar. Our hierarchy, however, includes the whole range of
possible cognitive statuses, from most given to least given.

[2]Demonstratives are typically definite. However, as has frequently been noted (see
Prince 1981a, for example), there is an indefinite use of determiner *this* in colloquial English. Since we are primarily interested in definite reference we will not
discuss indefinite *this* here.

[3]By 'familiar' here we mean mutually familiar (cf. 'mutual knowledge' of Schiffer
1972). We use the term 'familiar' rather than 'known' because what is involved
here is not knowledge or belief in the existence of some entity, but rather that the
existence of that entity has been entertained. This also distinguishes the status
'familiar' from similar notions such as 'presupposed.' See Prince 1981b, Gundel
1985 for further discussion of this point.

[4]Once introduced, entities remain activated as long as they continue to be relevant to
the discourse. After an entity is activated, it enters a permanent set of entities familiar to speaker and addressee (cf. Chafe 1987).

[5]Examples like (i) in which *this* is used to refer to entities which are just about to be
introduced are only apparent exceptions here, since the referent cannot be identified
until the constituent which activates it has been encountered.

    (i)   What should happen when you make a mistake is **this**: you take
         your knocks, you learn your lessons, and then you move on.
                                                    [Ronald Reagan, March 1987].

These cases are analogous to so-called backward anaphora as in (ii).

    (ii)   If you see **him** tell Frank to check his e-mail.

[6] Throughout this paper, lower-case line identifiers indicate consecutive sentences
in a discourse, and upper-case identifiers indicate speaker.

[7]We would like to thank Karen Frederickson for kindly providing us with
transcripts of the casual conversations, and Walling Cyre for providing technical
documents from Control Data Corporation.

[8]The eight occurrences of determiner *this* which were only type-identifiable are cases of indefinite *this*. The two occurrences of pronominal and determiner *that* which are uniquely identifiable but not familiar are cases such as those in (i) and (ii) below, which we believe to be a special 'precision' use of demonstrative *that* :

(i) It has great potential value for **those who must read technical documents**. [message from electronic news group]

(ii) The information sharing problem has to do with disseminating information so that it reaches **those people to whom it is valuable**. [Malone 1987:390]

[9]We do find some instances of *this* used to refer to an entity not activated by the speaker. All of these instances, however, are ones where the speaker-activation condition is being exploited to convey special effects. One such use is in polite interruptions, generally clarification questions, as in (i):

(i) This is Chris you're talking about, right?

[Frederickson tapes]

Another use is in discussions, where discourse topics are treated as part of a shared space that includes all speech participants. Finally, we find uses of *this* in expressions such as *this is true* , where, as Georgia Green has suggested to us, the speaker, by using *this* rather than *that*, appropriates an idea introduced by the addressee.

The speaker-activation condition may also be extendable to uses of *this* for extralinguistic objects relatively close to the speaker and for intervals including speech time, and uses of *that* for objects relatively far away from the speaker and for times prior to speech time (cf. Hanks 1984 for detailed discussion of the relation between deixis and speaker space in Yucatec Maya).

[10]The restriction of *it* to entities that are in focus is no doubt related to the fact that entities whose referents are not currently in focus, i. e. those that represent a focus shift, are necessarily stressed, and pronominal *it* is normally unstressed.

[11]Thus, Schiffman's (1985) finding that *it* unlike *that* occurs frequently in the "subject chaining context" reflects the fact that subjects in such chains refer to topics which are continued and therefore in focus.

[12]We do have some examples in our data where pronominal *that* is used for referents already in focus. These are relatively rare, however, and are used either for emphatic repetition, or in face-to-face interaction where the speaker may have reason to assume the addressee is not attentive.

[13]Notice that Q2 can be invoked here only to explain why the definite article is used instead of a demonstrative determiner. It cannot explain why a full NP rather than a pronominal is used in the activated cases. Some possible reasons for this, including ambiguity resolution and global focus shift, are discussed in Marslen-Wilson, Levy, and Tyler 1982; Fox 1987; Guindon.1985; and Guindon, Stadky, and Brunner 1986.

[14]But see Hirschberg 1985, Ward and Prince 1986; and Levinson 1987 for more recent elaborations of pragmatic scales.

Bibliography

Chafe, Wallace. 1987. Cognitive constraints on information flow. Coherence and grounding in discourse, ed. by R. Tomlin. 21-51. Amsterdam: John Benjamins.

Dahl, Deborah A. 1986. Focusing and reference resolution in Pundit. Proceedings of AAAI-86, Philadelphia.

Davidson, Donald. 1967. The logical form of action sentences. The logic of decision and action, ed. by N. Rescher. 81-95. Pittsburgh: University of Pittsburgh Press.

Fillmore, Charles J. 1975. Santa Cruz lectures on deixis. Bloomington: Indiana University Linguistics Club.

Fillmore, Charles. 1982. Toward a descriptive framework for spatial deixis. Speech, place, and action, ed. by R. J. Jarvella and W. Klein. 31-59. Chichester, NY: John Wiley & Sons.

Fox, Barbara A. 1987. Discourse structure and anaphora: written and conversational English. Cambridge: Cambridge University Press.

Graff, Gordon. 1988. Better bubbles. Popular Science 232:2.68-72.

Grice, H.P. 1975. Logic and conversation. Speech acts, ed. by P. Cole and J. Morgan. 41-58. New York: Academic Press.

Grosz, B.J., A.K. Joshi, and S.Weinstein. 1983. Providing a unified account of definite noun phrases in discourse. Proceedings of the 21st Annual Meeting of the Association for Computational Linguistics, Cambridge, MA, 44-50.

Guindon, Raymonde. 1985. Anaphora resolution: short-term memory and focusing. Proceedings of the 23rd Annual Meeting of the Association for Computational Linguistics, University of Chicago, 218-227.

Guindon, Raymonde, Paul Sladky, and Hans Brunner. 1986. The structure of user-advisor dialogues: is there method in their madness. Proceedings of the 24th Annual Meeting of the Association for Computational Linguistics, Columbia, 224-230.

Gundel, Jeanette K. 1978a. Stress, Pronominalization and the given-new distinction. University of Hawaii working papers in linguistics 10.1-13.

Gundel, Jeanette K. 1978b. A universal constraint on deletion. Proceedings from the XIIth International Congress of Linguists, ed. by W. U. Dressler and W. Meid. 532-536. Innsbrucker Beiträge zur Sprachwissenschaft.

Gundel, Jeanette K. 1985. Shared knowledge and topicality. Journal of Pragmatics 9 : 83-107.

Gundel, Jeanette K., Nancy Hedberg, and Ron Zacharski. 1988. On the generation and interpretation of demonstrative expressions. Proceedings of the 12th International Conference on Computational Linguistics, Budapest, 216-221.

Hanks, William F. 1984. The evidential core of deixis in Yucatec Maya. Papers from the Twentieth Regional Meeting of the Chicago Linguistic Society, ed. by Joseph Drogo, Veena Mishra and David Testen. 154-172. Chicago: Chicago Linguistic Society.

Hawkins, John. 1978. Definiteness and indefiniteness: a study in reference and grammaticality prediction. Atlantic Highlands, NJ: Humanities Press.

Hirschberg, Julia. 1985. A theory of scalar implicature. Dissertation, University of Pennsylvania.

Hobbs, Jerry R. 1985. Ontological promiscuity. Proceedings of the 23rd Annual Meeting of the Association for Computational Linguistics, Chicago, 61-69.

Horn, Larry. 1972. On the semantic properties of logical operators in English. Dissertation, UCLA.

Isard, Stephen. 1975. Changing the context. Formal semantics of natural language, ed. by E. L. Keenan. 287-296. Cambridge: Cambridge University Press.

Lakoff, Robin. 1974. Remarks on this and that. Papers from the Tenth Regional Meeting of the Chicago Linguistic Society, ed. by M. LeGaly, R. Fox and A. Bruck. 345-356. Chicago: Chicago Linguistic Society.

Levinson, Stephen C. 1987. Minimization and conversational inference. The pragmatic perspective, ed. by J. Verschueren and M. Bertuccelli-Papi. 61-129. Amsterdam: John Benjamins.

Linde, Charlotte. 1979. Focus of attention and the choice of pronouns in discourse. Discourse and syntax, ed. by T. Givon. 337-354. New York: Academic Press.

Malone, T. W., K. R. Grant, F. A. Turbak, S. A. Brobst, and M. D. Cohen. 1987. Intelligent information-sharing systems. Communications of the ACM 30.390-402.

Marslen-Wilson, William, Elena Levy, and Lorraine Komisarjevsky Tyler. 1982. Producing interpretable discourse: the establishment and maintenance of reference. Speech, place, and action, ed. by R. J. Jarvella and W. Klein. 339-378. Chichester: John Wiley & Sons.

Prince, Ellen. 1981a. On the referencing of indefinite-this NPs. Elements of discourse understanding, ed. by A. Joshi, B. Webber and I. Sag. 231-250. Cambridge: Cambridge University Press.

Prince, Ellen F. 1981b. Toward a taxonomy of given-new information. Edited by P. Cole. Radical Pragmatics. New York: Academic Press.

Sayers, Dorothy L. 1986. Have his carcase. New York: Harper & Row, Publishers.

Sayers, Dorothy L. 1977. Strong poison. Sevenoaks, Kent: New English Library.

Schiffer, S.R. 1972. Meaning. Oxford: Clarendon Press.

Schiffman, Rebecca J. 1985. Discourse constraints on 'it' and 'that': a study of language use in career-counseling interviews. Dissertation, University of Chicago.

Sidner, Candace L. 1983. Focusing in the comprehension of definite anaphora. Berwick, R.C., ed. by M. Brady. 267-330. Cambridge, MA: MIT Press.

Ward, Gregory L., and Ellen F. Prince. 1986. On the topicalization of indefinite NPs. Paper presented at the annual meeting of the Linguistic Society of America, New York,

Webber, Bonnie Lynn. 1988a. Discourse deixis and discourse processing. University of Pennsylvania Department of Computer and Information Science technical report.

Webber, Bonnie Lynn. 1988b. Discourse deixis: reference to discourse segments. Proceedings of the 26th Annual Meeting of the Association of Computational Linguistics, Buffalo, NY, 113-122.

The indexical ground of deictic reference

William F. Hanks
University of Chicago

INTRODUCTION
        When viewed as transcriptions of typical American English utterances, the sentences in (1-5)
illustrate what is commonly called verbal "deixis," and the underlined items belong to the class of
linguistic forms called "deictics."

        1. You and I could meet here Tuesday.
        2. Now you tell me this?
        3. Here , take it.
        4. He told her about it over there.
        5. There, does that make you happy?

There is widespread agreement in the literature that deixis and the linguistic forms that subserve it play a
central role in the routine use and understanding of language. Levinson (1983:54) described it as " . . .
[the] single most obvious way in which the relationship between language and context is reflected in the
structures of languages themselves . . ." In a similar vein, Horn (1988:116) notes that "the interaction
between the context of utterance of an expression and the formal interpretation of elements within that
expression constitutes a central domain of pragmatics, variously labelled deixis, indexicality or token-
reflexivity."
        Whereas both Levinson and Horn define deixis in such a way as to encompass an entire range
of referential and non-referential functions of speech, from pronouns to regional accents, this paper
focuses on the more restricted class of referential usages of lexical deictics, such as the ones in (1-5). To
see the difference, imagine that any of (1-5) is pronounced in an accent that identifies its speaker as
being from a certain region or social stratum, or that (2) is rendered with prosody appropriate to an
angry response, or that (1) were coded for deference to addressee as it might be in Javanese. All of these
codings are indexical, but none is deictic for the purposes of this paper. Rather, "deixis" designates a
special variety of reference, sometimes called "demonstrative reference," which is limited both formally
and functionally.
        Formally, whereas Levinson's (1983) "social deixis" can be signalled by any aspect of utterance
form whatsoever, deictics in the present sense are morphemes (or strings of morphemes) that in most
languages make up closed paradigmatic sets. Standard examples include pronouns (1-5),
demonstratives and articles (2, 4, 5), spatial (1, 4-5), temporal (2) and presentative (3) adverbs. In
functional terms, these are what Jespersen (1965:219) and Jakobson (1957) called "shifters," and
Silverstein (1976) defined as "referential indexicals." Their basic communicative function is to
individuate or single out objects of reference or address in terms of their relation to the current
interactive context in which the utterance occurs. So a shifter like "here" denotes a region of space by
indicating that this region is proximal (or otherwise immediate) to the place in which the form is uttered.
For Silverstein (1976) this relational correspondence was to be accounted for through rules of use
linking contextual variables with deictic tokens, a formulation consistent with Horn's (1988:116) " . . .
shifters or indexicals, [are] expressions whose meaning can best be viewed as a function from context to
individual by assigning values to variables for speaker, hearer, time and place of utterance, style or
register, purpose of speech act, etc."
        But what are these contextual variables and how exactly are they related to the denotata picked
out in deictic usage? If deictic context is segmentable in this way, how does it hang together as a whole?
How is interactive context linguistically structured in acts of reference? It is noteworthy that Horn's list
ends in an "etc," suggesting that there might be an open-ended list of such variables. In similar fashion,
ethnographies of speaking as in Hymes (1974) and Silverstein (1976) have long proposed that speech
events be decomposed into a number of segmentable components, typically symbolized as $Es \rightarrow \{Spkr,$
$Adr, Loc, Time, Key, . . .\}$. The problem is that such open ended lists suggest that the components are
coordinate and independent, and they leave us with the nagging uncertainty of never knowing whether
the list is complete or whether yet more components are needed (cf. for instance Levinson's 1987
expansion of the set of participant roles, and decomposition of roles into features along the lines of
distinctive features in phonology). Do components differ from utterance to utterance, context to context,

104

language to language, or all of these? In examining individual utterances, how should one think of the relations between the components? A good description of deixis could help answer these questions.

It is widely recognized that all natural languages have deictics (Anderson and Keenan 1985, Benveniste 1972, Kurylowicz 1972, Weinreich 1980), and that these forms constitute key points of juncture between grammar and context. Yet there has been relatively little in depth description of actual usage, and available descriptive frameworks are partial and relatively coarse (cf. Levinson 1983). One result of this is that it is difficult if not impossible to do comparative research on deixis. As Irvine (1985:574) observed in relation to studies of honorifics, indexical features tend to be erratically handled in standard descriptions, with inconsistencies and lack of appropriate data getting in the way of systematic comparison between languages (or even contexts in a single language).

In this paper I try to show that deictics (under the present definition) share a distinctive semantic structure, which sets them apart from non-referential indexicals (like status indicators) and also from other kinds of expressions that do combine reference with indexicality, but are nonetheless not deictics.[1] My aim is to get a clearer picture of the semantic and pragmatic mechanisms of deixis, and to contribute to a better metalanguage for pragmatic description and cross-linguistic comparison. Because deixis links language to context in distinguishable ways, the better we understand it, the more we know about context. In effect, the study of deixis provides privileged evidence for the ways that natural languages define interactive context by encoding pragmatic categories and forms of interaction in the grammar itself.

Functional heterogeneity of deixis

It is helpful by way of starting to summarize the kinds of information encoded in deictic forms. The first fact one confronts in trying to describe the conventional meanings of these forms is their functional heterogeneity. Table 1 displays in rough outline what I take to be the main types of information encoded in standard deictics.[2]

Table 1. Functional components of deixis

TYPE	ROLE	TYPICAL EXEMPLAR
Communicative	signal speech act value	Presentative, Directive, Referential, Phatic, Expressive
Characterizing	describe referent	Human, Animate, Regional/Extended, Punctual/Restricted
Relational	signal relation referent-to-origo	Proximal, Distal, Visible, Tactual, Inclusive, Exclusive, Discourse
Index	ground reference to origo in speech event	Speaker, Addressee, Speaker & Addressee, Anaphoric

In saying that the information in Table 1 is *encoded*, I do not wish to assert that for any form it is possible to state a set of invariant features that remains constant across all of its uses. The features are not necessary and sufficient conditions on the proper usage of forms. Rather, they are defeasible aspects that conjointly characterize the range within which proper usage varies, and therefore the conventional *potential* of forms. Consider the different uses of "here" in (6-10).

6. Oh, it's just beautiful here! (sweeping arm gesture to countryside)
7. Here's a good one for ya', (embarking on narrative)
8. John lives over here, but we live here (pointing to small map)
9. Oh doctor, it hurts here (hand on abdomen)
10. I'm over here! (hollered to companion through the woods)

Notice that whatever else is going on in these utterances, the word "here" in each contributes to an act of reference, and yet these acts seem quite different. The region referred to in (6) is of broad extent and includes both interlocutors, whereas the one in (10) is restricted to the speaker's place and excludes that of the addressee. (9) refers to a small segment of the body of its speaker, whereas (8) is a deferred ostension using a map in the common perceptual field of the interactants. Notice that (8) could well be used to refer to a spatial region that actually excludes both interlocutors at the time of utterance, and the two regions contrasted could be actually very close together or very far apart depending on the scale of the map.

Rather than attempting to reduce all of these to a single abstract feature bundle, a revealing description of deixis must maintain these distinctions and try to explain why they fall within the range of a single lexical form in English, whereas the paraphrase equivalents in another language might require distinct forms.[3] For instance, in Yucatec Maya, examples (6) and (10) require what I have called the Egocentric Inclusive locative adverb *way e?* 'here', whereas (7) requires the Presentative Evidential *hé?el a?* 'here it is', as in *hé?el ump'eél a?* 'here's one (take it)' and (8-9) correspond to yet a third form, the Sociocentric Restricted locative adverb *té?el a?* 'right here (where we can perceive)' (see Table 3). The descriptive challenge for a comparative theory of deixis is to provide a sufficiently delicate vocabulary to give a consistent account of such a range of pragmatic effects.

The Communicative functions of deictic types are speech act values that specify what kinds of act are performed in routine proper usage of the deictic. Presentative designates the kind of act illustrated in (3). Directive designates the act performed when one speaker points out a referent, as in "There it is (look!)." The Referential function is the contribution of deictics to acts in which referential objects are individuated, as in (1-10) (with the possible exception of (7)). The term Phatic is the standard label for what speakers do in managing their contact with interlocutors, including what (Yngve 1970) called backchannel, as well as the participation procedures described by Goodwin (1981). In Maya the adverbial deictic *b'èey* 'thus, so, like (that)' is commonly uttered *sotto voce* by addressees listening to a speaker, as a way of signalling attentiveness and comprehension (not necessarily agreement). This is a Phatic use. Expressivity is the foregrounding of a speaker's own involvement in an utterance, including subjective evaluation, special emphasis, surprise, admiration, etc. Expressive functions of deictics in Maya include these and others signalled by special foregrounded constructions in which only deictics occur (Hanks 1984, Forthcoming).

It is occasionally observed that deictics differ from semantic descriptions in that they denote referents without actually describing them, as in (11) versus (12):

11. I work here.
12. I work at my desk in my office on Wilton Avenue in the shadow of Wrigley Field.

While this observation captures what is indeed a different blend of information in the semantics of deictic and non-deictic expressions, it is not strictly accurate. Deictics regularly encode features such as Human, Animate, Regional/Extended vs. Punctate/Restricted, Concrete vs. Abstract, and Static vs. Kinetic. These do describe aspects of the objects to which they refer, and they therefore make up a dimension of Characterizing features. Contrast these with the true Relational features, which specify the relation between the object of reference and the current utterance framework in which the act takes place. Typical ones include Proximal vs. Distal, Immediate vs. non-Immediate, Visible, Inclusive vs. Exclusive, Up vs. Down, Centripetal vs. Centrifugal. The distinctive property of these is that they all presuppose an origo relative to which they are computed. That is, they describe not the referent itself, but the relation between the utterance framework and the referent.

If the Relational features specify the deictic relation, the Indexical ones specify the origo to which the relation attaches. In (6) the Indexical function is what grounds the reference to the interlocutors in the countryside at the time of utterance. In (7) it includes the state of the discourse and interaction leading up to the utterance, and in (8) it includes both the proximity of the interactants to each other and to the map, as well as the fact that this is a deferred or transposed deictic reference. Although all of these examples are cited as single utterances, for the sake of brevity, they should all be understood as interactive moves in a chain of moves, and this too is an aspect of the indexical ground of reference.

It is this plurality of features that I point to in saying that deictics are functionally heterogeneous. While studies may focus on one or another subset of the functions, a general account must provide a way of integrating them. What is the organization of all this information in the semantics of individual utterances, deictic types, given classes of deictics, and deixis in general? Where do gestures fit in the semantics of deixis? As diacritics of Communicative functions? As special constraints, as aspects of the indexical ground, or as independent signs with their own semantic structures? How do the different features bundle in languages? Are there patterns of cooccurrence that would allow us to predict likely combinations? The first step towards answering such questions is to clarify the relational structure of indexical reference.

RELATIONAL STRUCTURE OF DEICTIC REFERENCE
Consider the paraphrases in (13-17), which are alternative attempts at defining what I call the relational structure of deictic reference.

13. "This" is equivalent to "what I-now notice" (Russell 1940:114)
14. "I" means the person who utters ↓this token↓" (Reichenbach 1947:284)
15. "The [substitution] types of this, here, now, and that represent relations of distance from the speaker or from the speaker and the hearer." (Bloomfield 1933:248)
16. "This book" is equivalent to "the book which is near the speaker" (Lyons 1977:646)
17. "This" indicates that its object is nearest to the present communication, dominant in the field of perception or attention, focused in the center. (Collinson 1937:43ff)

Russell's treatment of egocentric particulars was an attempt to reduce deixis to the experience of the speaking subject, whereas Reichenbach sought to reduce it to the token reflexivity of deictic form (hence the diacritic arrows in [14]). Bloomfield states the classic proximity-based gloss recapitulated by Lyons, whereas Collinson combines proximity with perception and cognitive focus. What they all share is that they posit as fundamental to deixis a relation between some part of the speech event and the object of reference.

This basic observation can be rephrased by saying that each deictic category encodes a Relation between the Referent and the Indexical framework in which the act of reference takes place. Thus, a single deictic word stands for minimally two objects: the referent is the thing, individual, event, spatial or temporal location denoted; and the indexical framework is the origo ('pivot' or zero-point) relative to which the referent is identified (the speech event in which the act of reference is performed, or some part of this event). We can see that where (13-17) differ is on the nature of the origo (the speaker, the token sign, the present communication) and the quality of the relation (proximity, perceptibility, cognitive focus). Table 2 shows an array of hypothetical paraphrases for English usages.

Notice that the column labelled DENOTATUM TYPE, shows distinctions between objects, regions, persons and times. This list (surely incomplete) reflects the differences among the classes of referents typically individuated by different categories of deictic. This portion of the gloss incorporates what was called Characterizing features in Table 1, since regionality, individuality and so forth are taken to be inherent features of the referent, like shape, animacy and other more familiar features.

The Relational Types in the middle column localize the referent relative to the origo. The most important point regarding these at this stage in the discussion is that they may be multiple. That is, we need not assume that any of the glosses in (13-17) is correct to the exclusion of the others. Any language contains more than one type of relational feature, and languages differ significantly on which ones they encode. The standard assumption that space is always foundational in deixis is an inconvenient fiction not borne out comparatively (Frei 1944, Levinson 1983, Anderson and Keenan 1985).

Table 2. Some relational structures of deictic reference

FORM		DENOTATUM TYPE	RELATIONAL TYPE	INDEXICAL TYPE [a]
this	=	'the one	Proximal to	me'
that	=	'the one	Distal to	you '
that	=	'the one	Distal to	you and me'
this	=	'the one	Visible to	me'
that	=	'the one	Visible to	you and me'
here	=	'the region	Immediate to	you'
there	=	'the region	non-Immediate to	you and me'
I	=	'the person	Speaker of	this utterance'
You	=	'the person	Addressee of	this utterance'
now	=	'the time	Immediate to	this utterance'

a. Indexical types are abbreviated and stand for participation configurations realized in the utterance and actually occupied in the interactive situation.

Whereas Table 2 shows only a few possible indexical types, this portion of the relational structure is susceptible to significant variation as well. The problem is that it is simply not known which aspects of interactive events can serve as the ground of reference. In clear cases one or another of the participants serves as origo, as assumed in (13, 15, 17). Instances of speaker-grounded reference appear to be what justifies Russell (1940) and Lyons (1977:646, 1981:121) when they assert that deixis is egocentric, and others when they assert that it is "subjective". But as Bühler (1982:105) pointed out, this subjectivity is based in the fact that all indictors require an origo in order to be interpreted, whether or not the origo is the speaking subject. It may be that the location, knowledge and orientation of participants are inherently more central to reference than other aspects of the situation, but Reichenbach (14) and Collinson (17) pose a challenge to this assumption. In theory at least, one could imagine any number of alternative indexical pivots, logocentric, person-centric, event-centric and so forth. Given that acts of reference are interactively accomplished, a sociocentric approach is certain to be more productive than an egocentric one, even when the speaker is the primary ground of reference.

The paraphrases in Table 2 incorporate the Characterizing, Relational and Indexical features from Table 1, but they leave out the extra-referential Communicative functions. These could be represented heuristically as predicative elements in paraphrases like (18-19).

> 18. 'Take the one Tactually available to me right now' (Presentative)
> 19. 'Look at the one Visible to you and me right now' (Directive)

As incomplete as these paraphrases are, they allow us to sketch out an important part of the referential apparatus encoded in deictic systems. As a heuristic device, they are productive in two ways. They can be read off as mini-descriptions of interactive contexts in which deixis occurs, thus setting a direction for pragmatic research. And, by varying the three components independently, one can raise questions regarding how features from each component combine. Do certain Relational features require certain types of Indexical context, or occur only in certain grammatical categories?

Table 3 presents a sketch of part of the deictic system in Yucatec Maya, a native American language spoken in Mexico. The first three forms are labelled Ostensive Evidential. OSTEVs form a special series of adverbs whose Communicative functions range from Presentative to Directive, while the Deictic Modal *hé?el e?* 'Indeed, for sure' is an Expressive indexing speaker certainty. The modal is not a referring item at all, while the OSTEVs subsume reference within a complex communicative act. The remaining five forms are locative adverbs (DLOCs) which share the primary function of reference, but differ in terms of their Relational and Indexical features.

Table 3. Synopsis of Maya deictics (partial)

FORM	GLOSS	PARAPHRASE	FEATURES
hé?ela?	'Here it is'	'Take the one in my hand'	Pres,Tactual/ Spr
hé?elo?	'There it is'	'Look at the one visible to us'	Dir, Vis/ Spr&Adr
hé?eb'e?	'There it is'	'Listen to the one audible to us'	Dir, Aud/ Spr&Adr
hé?ele?	'Indeed'	'for sure, affirmative'	Expr,Certain
té?ela?	'There, here'	'at this very place immediate to us'	Ref, Imm/ Spr&Adr
té?elo?	'There'	'at that place non-immed to us'	Ref, ØImm/ Spr&Adr
way e?	'Here'	'at this place including me'	Ref,Incl/Spr
tolo?	'There'	'at that place excluding me'	Ref,Excl/Spr
tf?i?	'There'	'at that place known to us'	Ref, Anaph/ Disc

Transformations of the Indexical ground

A basic property of the indexical context of interaction is that it is dynamic. As interactants move through space, shift topics, exchange information, coordinate their respective orientations, and establish common grounds as well as non-commonalities, the indexical framework of reference changes.

Patterns of deictic usage reflect these changes, and thereby provide us with a powerful tool for investigating them. Consider a situation in which two Maya interactants are physically separated from each other in the forest, looking for a misplaced tool. One speaker calls out to the other, asking whether he has found it, and the other responds that he has.

20.	A	tí'an wá tol o' ?	'Is it over there ?!'
	B	hàah, way yan e' !	'Yeah, It's here (where I am)'

Notice that A codes B's location with the Exclusive DLOC *tol o'*, which always refers to a place removed from its speaker, whereas B makes reference to the same place by using the Inclusive DLOC *way e'*, which always refers to a region that includes its speaker. Wherever B is, the tool is with him, and A can simply follow the voice to find it. Schematically, the two deictic references can be contrasted as in Figure 1.

Figure 1. Relational schemas for way e' 'here' and tol o' 'there'

tol o' 'there (excluding me now)'

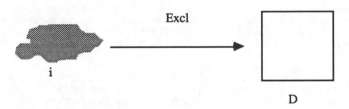

way e' 'here (including me now)'

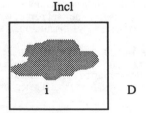

Excl, Incl	Relational types
i	Indexical origo, always entails Spr
D	Denotatum

The inversion in their positions is a canonical case of an Indexical difference: A and B stand in different actual relations to the object (the location of the tool) at the moment of the exchange, and they must therefore code it differently. The same phenomenon arises in the exchange of participant deictics and nominal demonstratives: A and B are both "I" to themselves but "you" to each other; A's "this" is B's "that" (more or less). If in (20) B follows the voice and goes to A, then he too would refer to the tool with the Inclusive form *way e?* 'here'. Once he has joined A at the tool site, he can no longer describe its location as *tol o?* 'out there', any more than he could switch the participant roles at his pleasure, describing himself in the second person and his interlocutor in the first.[4] These rudimentary details of usage make up what might be called an implicit playing field for interaction -- a set of positions in deictic space, along with expectations about how actors occupy these positions over the course of talk. In their deictic systems, languages provide irreplaceable resources for this process.

Consider now a slightly less simple but equally mundane example, in which an interactant uses quoted speech. A and B are working in a corn field, squatting down, weeding nearby sections. The two are loosely engaged in talk, but separated by 10 feet or so, each paying attention to his own work. A recounts a strip of interaction he had with C, a mutual friend, in the market the day before, and says at one point,

21. . . . ká tuún tuyá?alah ten, <u>kó?oten way e?</u> kih, ká hb'inen i?
. . . . so then he says to me, "<u>Come here (to me)</u>" he says, so I went to him."

Notice that the underlined portion of (21) is quoted speech. Although A utters the standard directive for summoning an addressee in Maya, B understands immediately that A is not calling him to his side. He also understands that the referent of *way e?* does not refer to A's current locus, but to C's locus at the time of the original utterance. Thus, if either A or B makes reference to C's locus in the subsequent discourse, as A does in the final clause of (21), then they do so using distal or anaphoric deictics *tɨ?i* 'there (where we said)' or perhaps *té?el o?* 'there (where we both know)'.

Thus one and the same place is referred to with the Inclusive deictic in quoted discourse but with the Distal or Anaphoric one in direct talk. This shift is well-known and typical of all deictic categories. It is what motivated Jespersen's original description of these forms as 'shifters'. It follows that one and the same deictic is interpreted in one way in quoted discourse, but quite differently in direct. This does not mean that the Relational values reverse from use to use, however. *way e?* encodes Inclusive in (21) just as it does in (20). Rather, the shift can be accounted for by saying that quotation involves a transposition of the indexical ground of reference. The Relational features of the forms remain constant in both types of discourse, but the *origo* is projected in quoted speech from the actual utterance framework into a narrated one. This projection is an important part of what is signalled in the phrases that often mark quotation, 'he said, she said' (for extensive discussion of this, see M. Goodwin 1988, Hanks Forthcoming, Lucy In Press).

The information status of referents changes over discourse even when the interactants sit still and speak entirely in direct talk. This change is a third example of the dynamic character of the indexical framework, and it is reflected systematically in the distribution of deictics in text. To take another very simple example, consider (22), in which Francisco explained to me that his nephew teaches English in a nearby town called Yotholim.

22. yàan untuúl insobrino *té? yot'olim a?* , yohe ?íŋgles [. . .]
I have a nephew   right here in Yotholim (who) knows English [. . .]

té? yot'olim o? k u ¢'ik klàases
There in Yotholim he gives classes [BB.5.56]

At the time of this utterance, we were sitting in Francisco's store some 20 miles from the place to which the underlined phrases refer, and in uttering both phrases, he made vague pointing motions in the direction of the town. Notice that he has shifted from the DLOC *té?el a?* '(right) here' in the first reference to *té?el o?* 'there' in the second.[5] Extensive research on Maya usage confirms that this shift is a standard one, motivated by the fact that in the first case, Francisco is introducing a new referent into the discourse (compare Leonard 1985). He knows that I am familiar with Yotholim, and that it is generally considered to be a neighboring town, but he is introducing it into the talk for the first time. In the second case he is maintaining a reference already established. This difference pertains to the indexical ground, in particular to the state of knowledge and attention focus of the interactants.

In general, because indexical frameworks change more or less constantly in talk, the deictic forms that make for proper reference to objects change as well. Thus whereas the Relational features associated with deictics may remain relatively consistent across uses, the indexical framework of interaction is in constant flux. This may be due to a variety of factors, including the adjustments in bodily orientation of the participants, any motion they may be engaged in, the arrival of new participants on the scene, as well as background frames that may be activated. Because of its relational structure, deixis is perhaps the clearest linguistic indicator of the interactive transformations involved in producing context. General statements about indexical centering can only be evaluated in relation to distinct tokens and distinct types, not to the entire phenomenon of deixis as a whole.

The focality of the referent

The referential and indexical poles in the deictic relation are not coordinate, but are actually in a foreground-background relation. The referent (denotatum) is the figure and the indexical origo is the ground. This disparity is evident both in the grammatical structures of deixis, and in its interactive production.

Regarding grammaticalization, recall the Characterizing and Relational features from Table 1. It is the denotatum that these features describe, as illustrated in (23-37).

23. wuna:-'ga:-'=garan^{g}ga:-'   nu:-'ba-gi-yun^g
    3Pl/3MSg-Rdp-Ben=look-Pa2   M-Anaph-MSg-Abs
    'They looked for that one' (Heath 1980:18)
24. ma-na-ri
    NClass-NonProx-Immed
    'that' (Heath 1978:59)
25. ni-na-ri-tu   narguni-ga-bidič-yaw
    MaSg-that-Imm-Erg   3MSg/2Pl-Sub-nearly-spear
    'That one almost spears you' (Heath 1978:227)
26. les voi-ci
    ArtMascPl Adv-Prox
    'Here they are'
27. hé?el-6?ob-a?
    OSTEV-Pl-Tact
    'Here they are (take them!)'

Example (23) is from a collection of Nunggubuyu texts. It illustrates a nominal deictic composed of four morphemes which encode masculine gender (M), Anaphoric function, singular number and absolutive case. Gender, noun class and number categories subcategorize the denotatum of the deictic, whereas what Heath labels the Anaphoric function is, by my reckoning, a Relational feature. It encodes the fact that the denotatum is in a relation of being known (cognitively accessible) to the interactants. Similarly, (24-25) are from Ngandi, another Australian language in which deictics are composed of morphemes signalling noun class, number and case (among other things). Insofar as case markers specify the role of the denotatum in the event described, they too apply to the denotational pole of the deictic relation, rather than to the indexical one.

The Ngandi deictic stems (24-25) are composed of two morphemes which conjointly specify the Relational value of the expression: -na- encodes non-Proximal (in opposition to -ni- Proximal), and -ri encodes Immediate (in opposition to -? 'non-Immediate'). While the precise nuances of these features are not clear from Heath's description, it is clear that they have to do with distinct kinds of relations to the indexical origo. In (26), Characterizing information is encoded primarily in the article (Masculine, Plural), while the adverbial deictic encodes the Immediate relation and Presentative/Directive Communicative function. In (27) the Yucatec Ostensive Evidential encodes the Tactual relation with Presentative function. The only Characterizing feature is the plurality encoded in the suffix. These are all instances of grammaticalized information bearing primarily on the denotatum.

Relational features function in deictic reference to foreground the denotatum, but they do so in a way different from the Characterizing features. The latter apply directly to the denotatum, describing it or its role in the proposition. Relational features, by contrast, subcategorize the link between the denotatum and the indexical origo. Thus relations such as Proximal and Distal may appear to offer no evidence for the focality of the referent over the ground. After all, proximity is reversible: if A is close to B, then B is close to A, and the two poles of the relation are coordinate. However, in deictic systems, the relation to ground is heavily weighted toward the referent, even when the link is spatial proximity. The referent is essentially a target rather than a mere end point.

Consider (28), in which A asks B where he left the hammer they had been working with, and B tells him it is at the worksite (several kilometers from the location of the exchange).

28.   A: túʔuš yàan martiyòo
              'Where's (the) hammer?'
          B: toloʔ
              there   (vague point towards worksite)

B's response encodes that the place referred to is Exclusive relative to the location of utterance (see Figure 1). That is, it is outside the boundaries of the current interactive field, however broadly or narrowly this is conceived. In order to successfully interpret the reference, A must have sufficient background knowledge to infer which place B has in mind. Both the location of the exchange and the background knowledge A and B share are part of the indexical origo of the reference. It would be clearly incorrect to say that B's utterance *refers to* his own location or to the shared background knowledge, yet the reference cannot be computed without these factors. The correct description is that the shared spatial and cognitive field of interaction is the background relative to which the worksite is individuated as a referential foreground.

Predicative and so called 'modifying' uses of deictics provide further indications of the salience of the referential component. Consider (29-32).

29.   tíʔ an tol oʔ   'It's (out) there'
30.   way yan eʔ   'It's here'
31.   to nukuč k'aáš oʔ   '(Out) there (in the) old forest'
32.   le pak'b'i nah oʔ   'That cement-construction house'

The underlined element in (29-30) is the locative existential verb 'to be (in a place)'. This is the standard way of deriving a predicate from a spatial deictic in Yucatec. Both sentences would make appropriate responses to A's question in (28), conditions permitting, since both assert the location of the object (in this case the hammer). Thus (29) might be paraphrased roughly 'it is located in the place Exclusive in relation to me' and (30) 'it is located in the place Inclusive in relation to me'. Notice that they could not be paraphrased even roughly as 'it is in relation to me that its location is Exclusive' or 'it is relative to me that it is close at hand'. The problem with these would-be paraphrases is that they reverse the Figure-Ground relation encoded in the deictics, focalizing the indexical ground rather than the denotatum. Predicative uses of deictics retain the Figure-Ground structure of referential uses. They assert the Relational feature, not the Indexical one.

Similarly, phrases in which deictics function as modifiers to lexical descriptions, like (31-32) usually elaborate the Relational or Characterizing features, not the Indexical ones. So in (31) the place referred to by the Exclusive deictic is described as 'high forest' and in (32) the referent is described as a cement-construction house. In other words, lexical description combines very productively with deictics to individuate the denotata more precisely. By contrast, attempts to further specify or make explicit the indexical origo of the reference in the same phrase with the deictic are usually odd or require special interactive contexts for proper use: ?'Out there relative to me', ?'This in relation to us right now', ?'that relative to our visual field', ?'over there from me', and so forth.

Thus the Characterizing and Relational features of deictics serve to focalize the referential pole in the deictic relation. Lexical descriptions and predicative derivations preserve the Figure-Ground asymmetry between the two poles. This is of course related to the fact that in referential usage, it is the denotatum and not the indexical ground that is uniquely identified. Languages provide sometimes elaborate semantic resources for deictic reference in the form of large inventories of Relational and Characterizing features, as in Yucatec Maya (Hanks Forthcoming), Malagasy (Dez 1980), Santali (Zide 1972) and Inuktitut Eskimo (Denny 1982). We summarize this information with cover labels like 'relative proximity', but it is clear that this proximity is not a matter of reversible spatial contiguity. Instead, what is basic to deixis is the access (cognitive, perceptual, spatiotemporal) that participants have to objects of reference in the current speech event. Access, like awareness, is an intensional arc from participants to objects, and this inherently orients deixis towards the denotatum.

So far as can be determined from published descriptions, most languages encode more distinctions among types of referents than among types of indexical origos. Elaborate inventories of Characterizing or Relational features are offset by minimal and often vague indexical grounds. This holds even for many 'person oriented' languages (Anderson and Keenan 1985), in which the origo is subcategorized by distinct speaker-grounded vs. addressee-grounded vs. other-grounded deictic types. A possible counter-example is Japanese, for which Anderson and Keenan (1985) cite the three-way distinction: *kono* 'near speaker' vs. *ano* 'far from speaker and addressee' vs. *sono* 'near addressee'. Note that the three terms have three distinct indexical grounds, but only two relational features. According to Boas (1917:113), Tlingit has only a single Relational feature, 'Near', paired with several distinct indexical grounds (relative to me, to you, to him), while Lower Chinook has an analogous three way split (Boas 1911: section 44).[6] If these descriptions are accurate, then Japanese, Tlingit and Lower Chinook are atypical in that the indexical ground is more finely subcategorized than the referential focus. Usually, the inverse is the case, in accord with the greater salience of the referent.[7]

FIGURE AND GROUND IN THE SEMANTICS OF DEIXIS

The discreteness, individuation, definiteness, and singularity that are the hallmarks of deictic reference are all typical figure characteristics. The diffuseness, variability, and backgrounded character of the indexical origo is due to its being, in fact, the ground upon which the referential figure is defined. The Figure/Ground relation, as invoked here, organizes visual perception. Deictic reference is by no means limited to visual, or even perceptual access to referents, but perceptual distinctions are encoded in deictics in a variety of languages, including Yucatec (Hanks 1984), Crow (Graczyk 1986), Malagasy (Dez 1980) and Santali (Bodding 1929, Zide 1972). Even in languages like German and English, in which apparently no perceptual distinctions are encoded in deictics, the perceptual corollaries of spatial or cognitive immediacy may still be fundamental to the actual use of the forms (Bühler 1982, Lakoff 1985). One advantage of the analogy to Figure/Ground is exactly that it focuses our attention on the fact that deixis is a framework for organizing the actor's ACCESS to the context of speech at the moment of utterance. Deictic reference organizes the field of interaction into a foreground upon a background, as figure and ground organize the visual field.

Figure and ground in linguistic systems

A number of linguists have proposed applications of the Figure/Ground concept to linguistic categories. Starting from examination of spatial prepositions, as in 'the pen rolled off the table', Talmy (1978) distinguished the figure object (the pen) from the ground (the table). The figure is conceptually movable and localized relative to the ground, which is stationary within a frame. Talmy noted that such 'relative referencing' functions in a broad range of linguistic contexts, including non-locational sentences (X resembles Y, where X is figure and Y is ground), equational sentences (X is Y, cf. figure is ground), temporal reference, assertion (figure) as opposed to presupposition (ground), cause (figure) as opposed to result (ground) and temporal sequence of events (ground is prior). More recently, Talmy (1983) investigated verbal descriptions of spatial scenes and considerably refined the Figure/Ground analysis. Starting from the selectivity of linguistic representation, he argues that language imposes a primary-secondary division among portions of spatial scenes, thereby laying the basis for a Figure/Ground relation in speech. The corollaries of the primary/secondary division are consistent with this correspondence, and include: movable/more permanently located; smaller/larger; geometrically simpler (point-like)/more geometrically complex (with extent, shape, dimensionality); more salient/more backgrounded; and more recently in awareness/earlier in scene or memory (Talmy 1983: 231). To these can be added another, anticipated (forward path)/recalled (behind, path already covered) (Hanks 1983). Hence, in linguistic systems, and particularly in spatial reference, a broad variety of asymmetric oppositions among objects are encoded according to a consistent division between figure and ground.

Recent linguistic research on discourse has contained further applications of the distinction, to explain the relations among a still broader spectrum of grammatical categories. Summarizing work by a number of scholars, Wallace (1982:212) organized categories of nouns, verbs, clauses and sentences into paradigmatic oppositions, as in {human, animate, proper, singular, definite, and referential}, which are salient, as opposed to their non-salient counterparts {non-human, inanimate, common, nonsingular, indefinite, and nonreferential}. Similarly, {perfective, present-immediate tense} are the more salient counterparts of {nonperfective, nonpresent-remote tense} within the verb.

It is important to bear in mind that the proposals summarized by Wallace are focused on the paradigmatic relations among different grammatical categories, assigning each category a single coefficient of relative salience. Hence, when linked to an analysis of information structure in narrative, the salience coefficients of each category condition its distribution in foregrounded versus backgrounded portions of the discourse. In this kind of system, a speaker selects either the more or less focal term for use at a specific point in discourse.

The basic proposal of this paper is different in that I am applying the Figure/Ground dichotomy to the internal semantic structure of individual grammatical forms. A term like "this" incorporates within its own relational structure both figure (denotatum) and ground (indexical origo). Whereas a speaker must choose between perfective and imperfective aspect, or proper versus common nouns, one does not choose between an indexical and a referential object. Rather, one identifies the referential in relation to the indexical. Whereas the asymmetric relations among categories that Wallace treats can be described in terms of markedness oppositions, the linkage between relational and indexical components of reference is a matter of combination, not opposition. The difference becomes quite obvious in light of the different generalizations about deixis that arise from the two perspectives. Consider first the classification of distinct deictic categories by their relative salience coefficients.

Relative salience of distinct deictic categories. In a number of languages, including Yucatec and Malagasy, there are lexical distinctions among the Communicative functions in Table 1. Presentative-directive adverbial deictics make up a distinct series from merely referential ones. The former are typically associated with actual gestural presentation of the referent, as opposed to merely indicating it, and may be used as the sole predicate in 'minor' sentences, as opposed to a modifier within a noun or adverbial phrase. In Yucatec, presentative and directive forms (top three in Table 3) are all subject to a number of special grammatical constraints (Hanks 1984). Most of the remaining forms, by contrast, are typically used to make reference, not to assert the presence of the referent. In Yucatec, these other deictics do not encode perceptual distinctions, nor are they typically used to actually present a referent, nor are they predicative unless derived grammatically, nor, finally, are they subject to the same set of grammatical constraints (Hanks 1984). The presentative and directive forms are relatively more salient and figure-like than the others, and their grammatical and pragmatic features reflect this.

The distinction between categories that encode perceptual features and those that do not could be viewed as another relation of relative figure-like as opposed to ground-like forms. Perceptual deictics single out the referent according to the mode of perceptual access by which it is available to interactants. In Yucatec, perceptual individuation combines presentative force (Table 3) to make a series of deictics whose central interactive function is to direct the addressee's perceptual focus to the referent. Figure-like values cluster together in this case. In Malagasy by contrast, nominal, adverbial and presentative bases all encode perception (Dez 1980), while Crow deictics distinguish visible from invisible in the nominal series, but lack a distinct presentative (Graczyk 1986).

It is intuitively obvious that proximal deictics like *way e?* 'here' and *té?el a?* 'right here' in Yucatec are more figure-like than distal ones such as *tol o?* 'out there' and *té?el o?* 'there' (Table 3). As such they tend to be more punctual (as opposed to regional), more canonically referential (as opposed to anaphoric or non-referential), more likely to take on presentative or directive force and to be used in reference to concrete as opposed to abstract objects. Some tokens of deictics are non-referential in that they fail to individuate any existent object, "referring" instead to some vague or hypothetical object. The forms in question tend to be non-proximal and non-punctate. The Exclusive locative *tolo?* may be used to convey that the speaker does not know where something is located, as in *tinsatah wá tú'uš tolo?* 'I lost it somewhere out there'. Compare (33-35).

33. W má tawáal ten yàan abin?
      'Didn't you tell me you're going?'
   E n iŋ ká?a→ pero máa č im bin <u>to naáč o?</u>
      'I'm going, but I'm not going <u>way out there</u>'   [BB.5.48]

34.   un-ani   'there, somewhere down there' (Extended, Subord, AT)
                           (Denny 1982:361)
35.   n-ɔ-kɔ+e   'this' (Prox, Inan, Intensive) (Zide 1972:268).

In (33), taken from my field notes, E was explaining to me that she goes to collect firewood only at the edge of the planted fields by her house, never straying into the forest. The underlined spatial expression refers vaguely to the out back of the woods. (34) is taken from Denny's (1982) discussion of Inuktitut Eskimo where he reports that the distal extended deictic is used to indicate the speaker does not know the precise whereabouts of the object. Canonically referential usages are more figure-like than such non-specific, only marginally referential ones. In Santali, the inverse case arises. According to Zide (1972) and Bodding (1929:125), there is an 'intensive' or 'particularizing' infix -*Vk'*+ that restricts deictic reference, glossable roughly as 'the very one'. This infix occurs only on Proximal bases. These divisions are summarized in Table 4.

Table 4. Relative salience of opposed deictic categories (partial)

HIGHER SALIENCE	LOWER SALIENCE
Presentative	non-Presentative
Directive	non-Directive
Predicative	non-Predicative
Perceptual	non-Perceptual
Proximal	Remote
Anticipated	Recalled
Punctual	Regional
Concrete	Abstract
Referential	non-Referential

The hierarchy summarized in Table 4 can help answer the question of how information is linguistically organized in the encoded structures of deixis. On the assumption that figural properties tend to cluster, Table 4 generates a number of interesting predictions that can help motivate facts of structure and use that appear otherwise arbitrary. For instance,

- If a language has both Presentative and Perceptual features in the deictics, they will tend to be lumped in the same forms.
- Directives are more likely to individuate points than regions of broad extent.
- Proximal forms lend themselves readily to anticipatory reference (as in 'this one [coming up]') whereas Remote ones do not.
- Remote forms tend to be used for anaphora and reference to discourse.
- Forms used for non-specific reference to vague zones will be the same ones used for non-punctate, remote, and recalled referents.

Relative salience of simultaneous components. These uses of the Figure-Ground relation as a way of classifying grammatical categories necessarily involve a logical transposition. Whereas the members of a paradigm are opposed according to their respective salience coefficients, figure and ground elements of perception are syntagmatically combined in the organization of the visual field. The syntactic combination of elements in discourse corresponds more directly to the Figure/Ground concept than does the assignment of coefficients inherent in individual categories. What actually makes a member of a paradigm figure-like is that it tends to be used in reference to figural objects in discourse. The considerable generality of this approach derives partly from its linking up of discourse with grammar. We would expect such a linkage to interact in detailed ways with markedness oppositions which account for many of the same distributional facts.

In applying figure and ground to the internal structure of deictics, on the other hand, there is also a linking together of discourse with grammar, but there is no transposition. The two simultaneous components of deictic reference combine in just the way the two components of perception do: as asymmetric parts of a single event. When a speaker utters (36), he creates BOTH a figure (the one moving) and the ground upon which it is individuated (the shared perceptual and orientational field).[8]

36. "hé? kubin o? "   '(Look!) There he goes (pointing)'

The duality of the referential focus as against the indexical background in deictic usage fits into a larger series of Figure/Ground relations among components in a single utterance. Consider the routine Maya utterance in (37).

37. hé?el a? p'o? a k'ab' i? i?
    'Here! Wash your hands here' [BB.4.80]

Margot was filling a water basin with a hose in the back yard when I walked towards her, looking for a place to wash my hands. Although we were not engaged in talk, she was aware of my intention. Holding the running hose out to me, she uttered (37). The underscored deictic is Presentative, and individuates the running hose as a maximal figure. This entails a Directive to me to focus on the referent, walk to it and touch it. Observe that in (36) the directivity was also in force (hence the finger pointing gesture), but there was no presentation, since the object was not available in the tactual field. Presentative and Directive further entail the distinct act of singular definite Reference to the object. While the three functions are laminated in (37), there are clearly cases of deictic reference that are neither Directive nor Presentative (20, 22, 28). Reference in turn entails the indexical origo.

The Presentative, Directive, Referential and Indexical components of (37) are scaled from the most figural to the most backgrounded. Presentative is maximally focal and entails all of the other functions. The indexical origo is the interactive ground on which the all of the others rest. The focality of the Presentative is well reflected in native speaker metalinguistic glosses of this form, which consistently associate it with acts of manually handing the referent to the addressee (Hanks 1984, In press). In general, those components of deictic acts which are new in context (Leonard 1985), or which effect a change in the orientations of participants, are the most figural. These generalizations are summarized in Table 5.[9]

Table 5. Relative salience of simultaneous components of deictic utterances

FIGURAL	BACKGROUNDED
Presentative	Directive
Directive	Referential
Referential	Expressive
Expressive	Phatic
Relation-to-referent	Indexical origo
Characterizing features	Indexical features
Newly introduced	Already part of common ground

j
Interactive emergence of the indexical ground

Insofar as it alters discourse context, deixis has a creative or 'constitutive' function. Even when interlocutors can presuppose a common context rich with shared information, the individuation of the referent may be new (cf. 33, 36, 37). To point out or present an object to an interlocutor is to orient his attention. In some situations, the change may be relatively radical, as in (38), a quote taken from a personal narrative told by DC, a Maya speaker. When he was just a boy, DC once locked his grandfather out of his house, by accident. The old man returned at night wanting to get in, and had to guide DC, who was inside, disoriented in the pitch darkness. DC groped along the inner wall towards the door as the old man rapped his cane, saying

> 38. hé?el a? hé?el a? way a tàal e?
> 'Here it is! Here it is! Come here (to me)'   [BB.4.87]

This utterance alters its own context by localizing the door for DC, and summoning him to it (cf. Bühler 1982:109 on importance of voice as an auditory signal of the origo).

Locative deictics in Maya are commonly used in utterances that initiate interactions. This is another case of constitutive reference, in which a participant relation is created and the parties to it arrive at mutual orientation. For instance, (39) is a standard greeting that Maya speakers call out to announce their arrival at the home of another.

> 39. tàa téeloóo 'Coming in theere!'   [BB.4.66]

In this example a woman arrived at DC's gate and called out before slowly entering, waiting for a response of acknowledgment from within the house. DC's daughter-in-law (his neighbor within the homestead) responded with (36), an equally routine utterance.

> 40. ?òoken i?   'Enter there!'   [BB.4.66]

Occurring without prior interaction, from a perceptually and spatially remote location, from outside the boundaries of the homestead, (40) rests on a relatively lean indexical framework. Rather, it creates a framework, producing an interactive relation that did not exist prior to the utterance.

Speakers routinely interact across boundaries of various kinds, talking from one room to another in the homestead, one corner to another at a work site, through the vegetation in the woods, orchards and fields. In such situations, deictic reference has the potential to reorient participants to a relatively great degree, creating a reciprocal or common focus of attention and bringing about physical proximity (see Kendon 1985). These uses are what Collinson (1937:17ff) called "points," as opposed to "markers," and more recent studies have called "creative" as opposed to "presupposing" (Errington 1988, Friedrich 1979: 96, Hanks 1984, Silverstein 1976). Creative deixis significantly alters its own indexical origo. Thus (39) creates the engagement that functions as indexical ground from which the speaker "points" into the homestead, while the response in (40) presupposes the ground and "marks" the spatial referent relative to it (anaphorically).

The play between creative and presupposing aspects of usage is an ongoing one, which means that the indexical origo is a dynamic ground, rather than a fixed object. In many deictic acts, an already constituted indexical framework is presupposed, in which interlocutors share certain relevant knowledge, immediate experience and engagement (22, 28,37, 40). The origo is already in place. For instance, a Directive utterance like "There he goes (pointing)" is most likely to be used when interactants are already mutually oriented, close together, and perhaps awaiting the motion of a particular individual. Even in highly creative uses, the object may recede to the status of a given, being introduced as a referential figure, and thereafter presupposed as common indexical ground.

Indexical symmetry and referential salience

A central aspect of the indexical origo is the degree to which the interactants share, or fail to share, a common framework. It is convenient to distinguish between the specific fields of participant access (spatial, perceptual, cognitive), and the participant domains relative to which reference is made. Typical participant domains are the Common ground (sociocentric), Spr (egocentric), Adr (altercentric) and Other (non-Participant in current speech event). Ego- and altercentric grounds are pragmatically asymmetric because they split the Spr from the Adr, while the common ground is pragmatically symmetric, because it joins the two and puts them on roughly equal footing relative to the referent. This use of 'symmetry' is consistent with its use by Brown and Gillman (1960) and Friedrich (1966) in their classic studies of address, and is analogous to Labov's (1972: 299ff) A vs. B vs. AB events in discourse. The participant relation is negotiated in an ongoing fashion, and the relative symmetry of context is gradient rather than all or nothing (cf. Clark and Wilkes-Gibbs 1986, Goffman 1981, Goodwin 1981, 1984).

The indexical origo of deictic reference is bound up crucially in the interaction between participants, and relative symmetry provides a limited way to talk about this interaction. By lumping together many different aspects of the interactive origo into the single dimension of symmetry, it provides a unifying framework in which interactive contexts can be compared and scaled. Examples, (28, 37) illustrate relatively symmetric indexical grounds, whereas (20) was relatively asymmetric. Other aspects of social symmetry and asymmetry have been shown to play a fundamental role in the use of 'pronouns of address' (Brown and Gillman 1960, Friedrich 1966, Silverstein 1976), as well as verbal etiquette (Errington 1988) and forms of conversational inference (Gumperz 1982). What we see in deixis is the same social relation among participants, this time as a backgrounded origo for reference and presentation.

A more concrete view of symmetry focuses on the specific parameters in which the interactive origo is embodied. As Friedrich (1979 [1966]) showed for Russian pronoun usage, the indexical ground consists in a number of distinct dimensions, not just an abstract dichotomy (or continuum). Participants can be separated spatially and perceptually, but share highly determinate knowledge of the referent based on experience prior to the speech event. Hence two indexical contexts could be equally asymmetric, but qualitatively distinct in terms of WHAT is shared and unshared. This is significant because different deictic forms rely on different aspects of the indexical field. Whether or not interactants share background knowledge of a referent is largely irrelevant to the usage of Presentatives, which require immediate sensory access (cf. 18, 27, 37). On the other hand, reference to a place empirically remote requires proportionately more background knowledge (28, 31). Given a sufficiently rich common knowledge of a place, even reference to it from a great distance can be accomplished with normally punctate, proximal forms (22).

The overall symmetry of a speech context, therefore, has a central impact on deictic usage. There are relatively few deictic forms that can be used appropriately in highly asymmetric contexts, when interactants fail to share basic information and orientation.[10] Presentatives, punctual immediate reference and manual demonstration for instance, mean little to an addressee who cannot see the speaker and share in his perceptual field. Thus while creative reference can transform indexical context, indexical context also constrains reference. There is a simple proportion between the two, which says that the greater the symmetry of the indexical ground, the greater the possibilities for individuated reference. This is equivalent to saying that the more information participants already share in the indexical origo, the more precisely they can individuate referents. When they are face to face, engaged, mutually oriented, and share detailed background knowledge of referents, they can mobilize potentially any shifter in the language. Proper and successful reference can be based on the presupposition that the interlocutor will accurately identify the object (even a remote one), given only the relational description. The less they share, on the other hand, the leaner the indexical origo and the fewer the referential oppositions available to individuate objects. Under very asymmetric circumstances, it is more difficult to succeed at deictic reference without further lexical description or collaborative work of the sort analyzed by Clark and Wilkes-Gibbs (1985). This proportion can be summarized in a principle of relative symmetry, which says simply:

The more symmetric the indexical origo (the more fully constituted the ground), the greater the range of deictic oppositions available for making reference (the more differentiated the possibilities for denoting figures).

This principle has among its interactive corollaries two which I will state here in the form of generalizations for further research. Relatively symmetric indexical frameworks, where interactants share a current orientation, experiential field, and background knowledge, can be treated in reference as though they were asymmetric. Interlocutors can and routinely do 'distance' themselves from one another, and from aspects of their immediate situation, through their choices of deictic forms. What is commonly called the "proximal" zone of interaction is not merely contiguous, but is maximally available to participants for subdivision by distinct deictic acts. The more richly defined the origo, the more possibilities there are for deictic use.

Under asymmetric circumstances, where interactants fail to share a common experiential field, less can be presupposed and relatively fewer alternative deictic acts can be performed. Asymmetric frameworks are not typically treated in reference as though they were symmetric. That is, it is relatively difficult for interlocutors who are in fact separated to successfully use deictics whose interpretation requires a common ground. Non-deictic lexical description becomes necessary in the absence of a common ground.[11]

The principal of relative symmetry also has structural concomitants that may help motivate the observed configurations of deictic categories in the world's languages. Relatively more focal deictic categories, which are used to individuate maximally figural referents, require a symmetric indexical ground in order to be fully interpretable. The more focal the deictic reference, the more likely it is that the act requires a symmetric origo in relation to which the object is identified. Hence, 'proximal' deictic categories tend to presuppose indexical frameworks in which mutual access among participants is already established. Furthermore, deictic systems should tend to be skewed towards symmetric contexts. That is, they should tend to have a greater number of relatively figural forms than background ones (Table 4).

CONCLUSION

Verbal deixis is a central aspect of the social matrix of orientation and perception through which speakers produce context. Many communicative effects are fused with or achieved through indexical reference as shown in Table 1. At the heart of deixis is the unique relational structure whereby the referent is identified through its relation to the indexical origo.

Although part of grammar, Relational features are inherently embodied in communicative contexts and cannot be reduced to any set of would be objective dimensions, like spatial contiguity. Each relation is paired with indexical conditions that link modes of access to actual sets of actors under concrete conditions. The indexical component of deixis is the processual background of interaction within which the act of reference takes place. Hence, the generalized structure of shifters conjoins the two poles of practical action in an interactive 'conjuncture', which we might call the 'conjuncture of indexical reference'.

Deixis entails at least three further kinds of relations. The first are the paradigmatic oppositions between categories, of which some are inherently more figural than others. This leads to a classification of functions by relative figurality, analogous to markedness, although not identical to it (Table 4). Presentatives, for example, are inherently more focal than merely Referential deictics, as Proximate, Punctate forms are inherently more focal than Remote, Regional ones. The second relation is the syntagmatic contrasts between different components of discourse, in terms of their being interactively focal or backgrounded (Table 5). The third relation is the relative symmetry of the indexical origo. The origo consists of the social relation between participants, and symmetry is a way of describing the degree to which their respective orientations overlap. The greater the mutuality, reciprocity and commonality between participants, the more symmetric the origo. The more symmetric the origo, the greater the range of paradigmatic selections available to a speaker for the purpose of reference.

By joining together these different orders of context in the semantics of individual linguistic forms, deixis illustrates a special case of a more general phenomenon in natural language, whereby the meanings of individual lexical items may be of the same order of complexity as those of sentences. The indexical-referential structure of 'this' or 'here' is a formally condensed case of the more global interplay between grammar and discourse, which is central to communication as an interactive phenomenon.

Acknowledgments. The research and writing of this paper were made possible in part by a grant from the Division of Research Programs of the National Endowment for the Humanities. I am grateful for this support. Earlier versions of the paper were presented at the 1986 Annual Meeting of the American Anthropological Association (Philadelphia), the Conference on Discourse in Sociocultural Context at University of Texas, Austin in April, 1987, and at the December 1988 monthly meeting of the Chicago Linguistic Society. I am grateful to the other participants in these meetings for their questions and critical remarks. In particular thanks to Chuck Goodwin for extensive and very helpful written comments, as well as to Joe Errington for written comments. Thanks to Lynn MacLeod for editorial assistance.

ENDNOTES

[1] Indexicals are traditionally defined as signs that stand in a relation of contiguity with their objects (Morris 1971:31, Peirce 1940:107). In more recent works, this contiguity may be more or less abstract, depending on the theorist. In a framework like Putnam's in which the extension of terms is fixed by local standards, even natural kind terms like 'lemon' and 'gold' have indexical components (1975:233ff), just as Searle's (1979) treatment of literal meaning generalizes indexicality to virtually all of language. Schutz (1967), Cicourel (1972), Garfinkel (1972) and Schegloff (1982) are among sociologists who have noted the pervasiveness of indexicality in everyday language use. One consequence of the progressive indexicalization of semantics is that deictics can no longer be called merely "indexicals," as they have been in the past. We must look elsewhere for their distinctive features.

[2] In this paper I concentrate exclusively on the referential-pragmatic aspects of deixis, and there are several kinds of information conspicuously missing from Table 1 that would need to be specified in a fuller treatment. These include *Major category features* (e.g. NP, ADV, PARTICIPANT); *Semantic roles* (e.g. Agent, Object, Location, Path, etc.); and *Special constraints* on distribution (e.g. main clauses only, restrictions on derivation, inflection, cooccurrence).

[3] It would be possible to claim that these are all different lexical forms that happen to be homophonous, but the problem of variable usage of a single form would arise ultimately anyway.

[4] This is oversimplified for brevity. The Exclusive zone may be quite close physically, and there are usually more deictic alternatives available to speakers than the ones I cite. Transpositions are also common, particularly in status asymmetric exchanges. See Errington (1988:160ff) on the transposed speech style in Javanese known as *mbasakaké.*

[5] The deictic is split into discontinuous portions that circumfix the place name, according to the standard grammatical pattern (Hanks Forthcoming).

[6] Although see Swanton (1911:172) and Story and Naish (1973:387), both of whom cite more standard glosses for the Tlingit, with three distinct Relational features and the standard range of grounds.

[7] This statement is abbreviated for purposes of brevity. I do not discuss here the linguistic resources that languages do provide for transforming the indexical ground by way of transposition, quotation (see above) and special foregrounding constructions (Hanks 1984). Languages with elaborate speech levels, like Javanese (Errington 1988) or honorifics, like Japanese, also subcategorize the indexical origo by signalling aspects of the social relations among participants and referents. Moreover, bundles of Relational and Characterizing features can function as indexes of social relations within the origo, as in the usage of Tu and Vous forms (and their analogs) in address and person reference systems (Errington 1988, Friedrich 1966, Silverstein 1976). These facts notwithstanding, the origo of the referential relation is typically less differentiated than the figural object.

[8] Taking into account the combination of utterance, directed gaze and manual indication, the example actually illustrates creation of three focal objects, one by each signal. Speakers assume that the three objects coincide, and they typically do, but examples are easy enough to imagine in which they would not, in Maya as well as English. The speaker could be intently observing the addressee or some other portion of the immediate field other than the referent, or the pointing gesture could be omitted, or

shrugged off. In canonical events of ostensive reference with *hé?*, all signals reinforce the individuation of a single focal referent.

⁹ The hierarchy in Table 5 can be rearranged through foregrounding. For instance, the Expressive force of a Maya presentative utterance can be boosted into focus through reduplication of the deictic base, yielding *hé? yàan hé?el a?* 'Here it is (Take it!!)' from simple *hé?el a?* 'here it is (take it).' Such foregrounded constructions are fairly elaborate in Maya (Hanks Forthcoming) and cannot be treated here.

¹⁰ This generalization does not apply to other types of social asymmetry, such as the status differences coded in honorifics and address forms. A language like Javanese elaborately codes status asymmetry, especially in the deictic paradigms (Errington 1988:96, 205ff). The kind of symmetry I am most concerned with is the commonalities of participant access to referents distinct from the participants themselves. The emphasis I place on shared access is motivated by the requirement that, for interactively successful reference to take place, both participants must identify what counts as the same object.

¹¹ These generalizations all assume that no major status asymmetry exists between interactants which licenses one of them to make exceptional presuppositions that the other must be able to fill in.

REFERENCES

Anderson, S. R. and Keenan, E. L. 1985. Deixis. In T. Shopen, ed., Language typology and syntactic description, volume III: Grammatical categories and the lexicon. Cambridge: Cambridge University Press, pp. 259-308.

Bauman, R. 1977. Verbal art as performance. Prospect Heights, IL: Waveland Press.

Bauman, R. and Sherzer, J., eds. 1974. Explorations in the ethnography of speaking. Cambridge: Cambridge University Press.

Benveniste, E. 1966 [1956]. La nature des pronoms. In Problèmes de Linguistique Générale. Paris: Editions Gallimard, pp. 251-58.

Benveniste, E. 1966 [1958]. De la subjectivité dans le langage. In Problèmes de Linguistique Générale. Paris: Editions Gallimard, pp. 258-66.

Bloomfield, L. 1933. Language. New York: Holt.

Boas, F. 1911. Chinook. In F. Boas, ed., Handbook of American Indian Languages. BAE Bulletin 40 part 1, pp. 559-677.

Boas, F. 1917. Grammatical notes on the language of the Tlingit indians. Anthropological Publications, volume VIII.1. Philadelphia: University of Pennsylvania Museum.

Bodding, P. O. 1929. Materials for a Santali Grammar II, mostly morphological. Dumka. Bengaria: The Santal Mission Press.

Brown, R. and Gillman, A. 1960. The pronouns of power and solidarity. In T. Sebeok, ed., Style in language. Cambridge, MA: MIT Press, pp. 253-76.

Bühler, K. 1982 [1934]. Sprachtheorie, die Darstellungsfunktion der Sprache. Stuttgart: Gustav Fischer Verlag.

Cicourel, A. 1972. Basic and normative rules in the negotiation of status and role. In Sudnow, pp. 229-259.

Clark, H. and Wilkes-Gibbs, D. 1986. Referring as a collaborative process. Cognition 22(1): 1-39.

Collinson, W. 1937. Indication, a study of demonstratives, articles and other 'indicators'. Language monographs #17, April-June.

Dez, J. 1980. Structures de la langue malgache. Éléments de grammaire à l'usage des francophones. Publications des orientalistes de France. Paris: Institut national des langues et civilisations orientales de l'Université de Paris VII.

Errington, J. J. 1988. Structure and style in Javanese, a semiotic view of linguistic etiquette. Philadelphia: University of Pennsylvania Press.

Fillmore, C. 1982. Towards a descriptive framework for spatial deixis. In R. Jarvella and W. Klein, eds., Speech, place and action, studies in deixis and related topics. New York: John Wiley, pp. 31-59.

Frei, H. 1944. Systèmes de déictiques. Acta Linguistica 4:111-29.

Friedrich, P. 1979. Language, context and the imagination, essays by Paul Friedrich. Stanford: Stanford University Press.

Garfinkel, H. 1972. Studies of the routine grounds of everyday activities. In Sudnow, pp. 1-30.
Goffman, E. 1981. Forms of talk. Philadelphia: University of Pennsylvania Press.
Goodwin, C. 1981. Conversational organization: interaction between speakers and hearers. New York: Academic Press.
Goodwin, M. H. 1988. Retellings, pretellings and hypothetical stories. Paper presented at the 87th Annual Meeting of the American Anthropological Association, Phoenix.
Graczyk, R. 1986. Crow Deixis. Unpublished ms., Dept. of Linguistics, University of Chicago.
Gumperz, J. 1982. Discourse strategies. Cambridge: Cambridge University Press.
Hanks, W. F. 1983. Deixis and the organization of interactive context in Yucatec Maya. Unpublished PhD thesis, Dept. of Anthropology, Dept. of Linguistics, University of Chicago.
Hanks, W. F. 1984. The evidential core of deixis in Yucatec Maya. In J. Drogo et.al, eds., Papers from the Twentieth Regional Meeting of the Chicago Linguistic Society. Chicago: Chicago Linguistic Society, pp. 154-72.
Hanks, W. F. 1987. Markedness and category interactions in the Malagasy deictic system. University of Chicago Working Papers in Ling. 3:109-36.
Hanks, W. F. In Press. Metalanguage and pragmatics of deixis. In Lucy (in press).
Hanks, W. F. Forthcoming. Referential practice, language and lived space among the Maya. Chicago: University of Chicago Press.
Heath, J. 1978. Ngandi grammar, texts and dictionary. Canberra: Australian Institute of Aboriginal Studies.
Heath, J. 1980. Nunggubuyu myths and ethnographic texts. Canberra: Australian Institute of Aboriginal Studies.
Hopper, P. J. 1982. Tense-aspect: between semantics and pragmatics. Amsterdam/Philadelphia: John Benjamins Publishing Company.
Jakobson, R. 1971 [1957]. Shifters, verbal categories and the Russian verb. In Selected writings of Roman Jakobson, vol. 2. The Hague: Mouton.
Jespersen, O. 1965 [1924]. The philosophy of grammar. New York: W. Norton.
Kendon, A. 1985. Behavioural foundations for the process of frame attunement in face-to-face interaction. In Discovery strategies in the psychology of action. London: Academic Press, pp. 229-53.
Labov, W. 1972 [1970]. The study of language in its social context. In P. P. Gigliolo, ed., Language and social context. New York: Penguin, pp. 283-308.
Lakoff, G. 1984. There constructions: a case study in grammatical construction theory and prototype theory. Berkeley Cognitive Science Report no. 18.
Leonard, R. A. 1985. Swahili demonstratives: evaluating the validity of competing semantic hypotheses. Studies in African Linguistics 16(3):281-95.
Levinson, S. 1983. Pragmatics. Cambridge: Cambridge University Press.
Lucy, J., ed. In Press. Reflexive language: Reported speech and metapragmatics. Cambridge: Cambridge University Press.
Lyons, J. 1977. Semantics, vols. 1 and 2. Cambridge: Cambridge University Press.
Lyons, J. 1982. Deixis and subjectivity: Loquor, ergo sum? In R. Jarvella and W. Klein, eds., Speech, place and action, studies in deixis and related topics. New York: John Wiley, pp. 101-24.
Morris, C. W. 1971. Writings on the general theory of signs. The Hague: Mouton.
Peirce, C. S. 1955 [1940]. Philosophical writings of Peirce. J. Buchler, ed. New York: Dover Publications.
Putnam, H. 1975. The meaning of meaning. In Mind, language and reality, philosophical papers II. Cambridge: Cambridge University Press, pp. 215-71.
Reichenbach, H. 1947. Elements of symbolic logic. New York: Macmillan.
Russell, B. 1940. An inquiry into meaning and truth. London: Allen and Unwin.
Searle, J. 1969. Speech acts, an essay in the philosophy of language. Cambridge: Cambridge University Press.
Searle, J. 1979. Expression and meaning. Cambridge:Cambridge University Press.
Schegloff, E. A. 1982. Discourse as an interactive achievement. In D. Tannen, ed., Analyzing discourse: text and talk. 1981 Georgetown University Round Table on Languages and Linguistics. Washington, DC: Georgetown University Press, pp. 71-94.
Schutz, A. 1967. The phenomenology of the social world. G.Walsh and F. Lehnert, trans. Evanston: Northwestern University Press.

Silverstein, M. 1976. Shifters, verbal categories and cultural description. In K. Basso and H. Selby, eds., Meaning in Anthropology. Albuquerque: School of American Research, pp. 11-55.

Story, G. L. and Naish, C. M. 1973. Tlingit verb dictionary. Fairbanks: University of Alaska, Alaska Native Language Center.

Sudnow, D., ed. 1972. Studies in social interaction. New York: The Free Press.

Swanton, J. R. 1911. Tlingit. In F. Boas ed., Handbook of American Indian Languages. BAE Bulletin 40, part 1, pp. 159-204.

Talmy, L. 1978. Figure and ground in complex sentences. In J. Greenberg et. al, eds., Universals of Human Language, vol. 4. Stanford: Stanford University Press.

Talmy, L. 1983. How language structures space. In H. L. Pick and L. P. Acredolo, eds., Spatial orientation, theory, research and application. New York and London: Plenum Press, pp. 225-82.

Timberlake, A. 1982. Invariance and the syntax of Russian aspect. In Hopper, pp. 305-34.

Vološinov, V.N. 1986 [1929]. Marxism and the philosophy of language. L. Matejka and I.R. Titunik, trans. Cambridge, MA: Harvard University Press.

Wallace, S. 1982. Figure and Ground: the interrelationships of linguistic categories. In Hopper, pp. 201-26.

Weinreich, U. 1980. On semantics. W. Labov and B. Weinreich, eds. Philadelphia: University of Pennsylvania Press.

Zide, N. 1972. A Munda demonstrative system: Santali. In J. M. C. Thomas and L. Bernot, eds., Melanges Haudricourt, vol. 1. Paris: Editions Klincksieck, pp. 267-72.

Verbless Presentation and the Discourse Basis of Ergativity

Susan C. Herring
University of California, Berkeley

1.0 Introduction.

This paper is concerned with the use, in oral discourse, of verbless 'presentational' utterances. I define a verbless presentational utterance as a bare noun or noun phrase, often preceded by an adverbial element, which stands alone as an intonationally-defined unit, and which functions to 'present' a referent in natural discourse. In English, such utterances tend to have an informal flavor,[1] as in the following examples:

(1) And so then this..then this..young guy,
   who is...the guy who's supposed to go through your suitcases, you know.
   He looks at me and he goes uh- "Why don't you open up that suitcase?"

(2) A: Boy, that burrito the other day?
   B: Mm
   A: She said, "Do you want it with salsa?"

In these examples, the NP presented verblessly in the first utterance (*this young guy; that burrito*) is resumed pronominally in the following utterance (*he; it*). The first utterance introduces the referent into the world of the discourse, and the second utterance predicates something new of it.

This device, while rather restricted in occurrence in English, is exploited much more systematically in other languages. One such language is Tamil. Examples of verbless presentations in spoken Tamil are given in (3) - (5) below:

(3) Aṅkiṭṭē iruntu, oru kuṇa   keḷavi.
   there from   one hunchbacked old.lady

   Anta keḷavi   taṇṇi eṭuttukiṭṭe varrā.
   that old.lady water carrying   come-Pr-3fs

   'From the other direction, *a hunchbacked old lady*.
   That old lady comes carrying water'.

(4) Aṅkē...araca kuṭumpattinarkku..nakai   ellām ceyyaravaṇ.
   there king's family-DAT   jewelry all   one.who.makes

   Avaṇ Kōvalaṇ koṇṭu-pōra cilampai pārttāṇ.
   he   Kovalan hold-go   anklet-ACC look-P-3ms

   'There, *the royal family's jeweler*.
   He looked at the anklet Kovalan was holding'.

(5) Namma āḷ irukkāṉ pārunka, turiyōtaṉaṉ. Avaṉuṭaiya koṭi.
    our man be-Pr3ms TAG Duryodhanan. He-GEN flag.
    Koṭiyile uḷḷa ciṉṉam...
    flag-LOC be-AjP insignia...

'There's our man Duryodhanan, right? *His flag.*
The insignia on his flag...'

The use of the verbless constuction in Tamil is pragmatically conditioned. It correlates strongly with the introduction of *new* referents — that
is, referents which have not yet been activated or which are otherwise
inaccessible in the context of the immediate discourse — and thus functions as a device to monitor information flow. Moreover, the verbless
presentational construction specializes in introducing new information, in
a way that other devices in the language do not. This makes it of particular relevance to studies of information flow, especially those which make
claims regarding grammatical structure on the basis of observed patterns
in the encoding of new and given information.

A recent study of this type is Du Bois (1987), which advances two original and potentially important hypotheses. The first hypothesis is that
there exists in all languages a Preferred Argument Structure (PAS),
according to which speakers tend to introduce new nominal referents
either as the *subject* of an intransitive clause, or as the *object* of a transitive clause, but rarely if ever as the subject (semantic *agent*) of a transitive clause. The restriction against encoding new information in the
'agentive' role follows from the pragmatic fact that agents are typically
human protagonists who tend to be thematic (and hence treated as
'given') in the discourse, and a cognitive principle, elaborated in Chafe
(1980, 1987) and Pawley & Syder (1977, 1983), which imposes a limit of
one new piece of information per utterance unit. Du Bois' second
hypothesis follows from the first: the tendency for intransitive subject (S)
and transitive object (O) to group together in discourse, in contrast with
transitive subject (A), constitutes a functional motivation for the grammaticalization of ergative morphology, which treats S and O similarly.
Since Preferred Argument Structure (PAS) is claimed to be universal, the
question naturally arises as to why *all* languages are not then ergative. Du
Bois accounts for this in terms of competing motivations, pointing out
ways in which S and A group together naturally as well (as in accusative
languages): *pragmatically*, in that both are natural 'topics', and *semantically*, in that subjects of both transitive and intransitive clauses tend to be
animate, while transitive objects are frequently inanimate.

In essence, then, Du Bois would have us believe that grammatical
ergativity is the result of the specialization of two case roles (which
together make up the 'absolutive' category) in the discourse function of
introducing new nominal referents. He states:

[T]he absolutive position...bear[s] a special relationship to new information, by allowing for the speaker's processing which is associated with this status. ...[T]he absolutive syntactic position constitutes a sort of grammatically defined 'staging area' — reserved for accomodating the process...of activating a previously inactive entity concept (p.834).

In Tamil, as stated above, the device which 'bears a special relationship to new information' is the verbless presentational clause. Since the grammatical roles S, A, and O are defined relative to a verb, NPs presented via the verbless construction cannot be said to occupy any of these roles; they are not 'arguments' in any usual sense of the word. Moreover, although Tamil is a case-marking language, verblessly presented NPs are almost always in the ambiguous zero-marked ('nominative' or 'citation') form. What, then, is the significance of a language like Tamil for Du Bois' analysis? Specifically, does Tamil discourse exhibit Preferred Argument Structure, and if so, what place does the verbless construction occupy in the system? I will address these questions in what follows.

2.0 Information flow in Tamil.

Tamil is a Dravidian language spoken by about 70 million people in South India, Sri Lanka, and parts of Malaysia. Three features of Tamil grammar are relevant to the present discussion. First, it has nominative-accusative morphology, and inflects nouns for nominative (but see above), accusative, dative, genitive, locative, ablative, sociative, and instrumental cases. This is in contrast with Sacapultec (Mayan), the language on which Du Bois' claims are primarily based, which is ergative-absolutive. Second, Tamil is verb-final, with no more than one finite verb typically allowed per sentence. Third, Tamil tolerates verblessness in a wide range of constructions, from equational sentences (e.g. *John ___ a nurse*), to a variety of construction types which lack any surface predication whatsoever (cf. Herring, in progress). Of the latter, the 'presentational' variety is by far the most frequent in oral narrative, the type of discourse analyzed by Du Bois for Sacapultec, and also in the present study.

My findings are based on a corpus of 30 oral narratives, collected several years ago in Tamil Nadu, India. The narratives represent a range of genres: personal (and other 'non-fictional') narratives, informal retellings of folk tales, and professional or semi-professional performances of epic and mythological tales. Out of a judgement sample of 1507 utterances,[2] the verbless presentational construction was found to occur 36 times, or 2.4% of all finite clauses. In order to expand the data base, I then turned to the larger corpus, weeding out all texts in which no verbless presentation was used. In this way, I produced a 'saturated sample' of 20 narratives, each containing at least one instance of the construction. This brought the total number of tokens up to 55, distributed over 1686 finite utterances, for a percentage of 3.4%.

At first glance, the incidence of verbless presentation may seem rather unimpressive. I have stated that the device is specialized for the introduction of new nominal referents in Tamil. Yet surely this percentage represents only a portion of the 'new' NPs available in the corpus; by means of what devices are the others introduced?

In order to answer this question, I identified first mentions of all nominal participants in the saturated sample, noting the grammatical role in which each appears.[3] Separating out 'new' mentions from those which are 'accessible' from context[4] resulted in a total of 207 new mentions. Verbless presentations account for only about one-quarter of these; the remainder are introduced in predicate constructions in a variety of case roles.

Following Du Bois, I grouped the oblique cases (predominantly locatives and datives) together, and distinguished between S and A roles, despite the fact that in Tamil, both are morphologically 'nominative'. The distribution of first mentions across case roles is compared with new mentions in verbless constructions in figure 1 below.

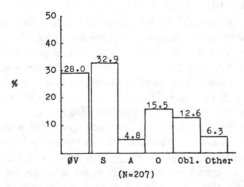

Fig. 1: <u>New mentions (combined) by grammatical type</u>

It will immediately be noted that the A (subject of transitive clause) role ranks lowest for the introduction of new NPs in narrative discourse, in keeping with Du Bois' first pragmatic principle, to wit:

"Avoid new A's" (p.827).

However, there are also problems. Once we have excluded accessible mentions (which are especially common in O and oblique roles), it becomes apparent that the O role does *not* group together naturally with S in Tamil, as per the predictions of PAS. Rather it falls out approximately half-way between S and A, and if anything, is slightly closer to A.

The relationship of O to S is even more problematic when we consider animate and inanimate referents separately, as shown in figures 2 and 3.

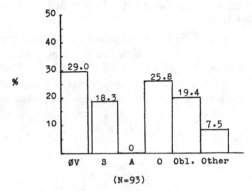

Fig. 2: New mentions (inanimate) by grammatical type

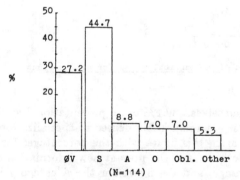

Fig. 3 : New mentions (animate) by grammatical type

Inanimate participants tend to be introduced for the first time either verblessly, or in the O role; following that, S and obliques are about equally preferred. When we turn to the animates, however, a completely different picture emerges. The preferred position for the introduction of new animate protagonists is as the subject of an intransitive clause; verbless clauses hold steady; but both O and obliques have dropped down below A.

The radically divergent statuses of O in animate and inanimate introductions give rise to a number of questions. The first and most important of these is whether they can legitimately be grouped together to support the claim of a functional similarity between S and O, when in the case of animates — which we might reasonably take to be the more central of the two classes of narrative participants — S and O are in fact functionally opposed. Methodologically, this does not seem entirely justified, and I will have more to say on this point later.

From the general distribution of first mentions across various grammatical roles, we now turn to the extent to which each role specializes in introducing new referents — that is, the percentage of all nominal referents in each role which are new. Figure 4 below shows the relative degrees of specialization of the verbless construction and of the major argument roles in Tamil.[5]

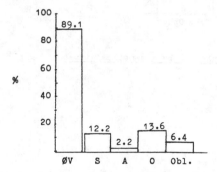

Fig. 4: Specialization of grammatical roles for new mentions

The figures speak for themselves. 89.1% of all presentational verbless utterances present 'new' NPs — a remarkable degree of specialization, as can readily be seen by comparing this figure with the percentages for the major argument positions. Both S's and O's present new information only 13% of the time, on the average, and the figure for the A category is so low as to be insignificant. If we exclude verbless presentation, we may discern a pattern which is reminiscent of PAS; yet the actual values of S and O are so low that it is highly improbable that a speaker of Tamil would be motivated to perceive of them as functionally similar in bearing 'a special relationship to new information'. Given, moreover, the high degree of specialization of the verbless construction, we may conclude that there is no support in the Tamil data for the notion of a functionally specialized S and O category.

At this point, one might be tempted to conclude that the specialization of the verbless construction in introducing new information in Tamil has somehow "interfered" with Preferred Argument Structure. The hypothesis could be advanced that first mentions are diverted into the verbless construction which might otherwise be expressed as S's or O's, and hence that in languages which have not developed such a device, we should expect to find stronger evidence of PAS. Since Tamil is after all *not* an ergative language, the lack of pronounced ergative patterning in information flow is at least consistent; there may even be a relationship of cause and effect.

I will argue, however, that such is not the case. Rather, I assert that the problems pointed out here for Tamil are problems for PAS and for the proposed discourse basis of ergativity in general. In order to demonstrate this claim, let us reconsider Du Bois' analysis of Sacapultec.

3.0 Sacapultec revisited.

I will first address the problem of the semantically-based 'split' patterning of the O argument role. In Tamil, the O role was found to favor new mentions when the referent was inanimate, but to disfavor new mentions of animate referents. In fact, a similar pattern exists in Sacapultec, as Du Bois himself notes: "When speakers have a human protagonist to introduce, it seems they frequently select the S role to do this" (p.830). In contrast, "in the O position, ...we tend to find inanimate patient arguments in much greater variety" (p.829). Later, in describing 'competing motivations' which relate S to A *as opposed to O*, he makes the same observation in more precise terms:

> In the S role, a substantial majority of mentions are of human referents (69.8%). But in the O role, far less than half the mentions are of human referents (10%).

Despite these figures, Du Bois chooses to down-play the implications of this discrepancy for his claims — his graphs show only a single O, with the categories of animate and inanimate conflated — and it is not difficult to understand why. He himself states that "human protagonists tend to be the central participants in most narratives" (p.829); they have a privileged status over inanimate objects, both linguistically and cognitively. This being so, statistical results which widely separate S from O in this important area of reference could potentially undermine the hypothesized "functional unity" of S and O, which in turn is the very cornerstone of PAS. This is not to say that animacy is *necessarily* bound to the pragmatic notion of 'new' information; in theory, speakers might overlook distinctions of animacy in favor of making a broader generalization regarding favored grammatical roles for introducing new referents *of any type*. However, this is a separate question which would need to be independently demonstrated.

The second point to be addressed is the degree of specialization of the S and O roles in presenting new information. We have seen that in Tamil, evidence for this claim is lacking. Tamil S and O roles introduce new referents only about 13% of the time (cf. figure 4); the

130

remaining 87% of their uses are associated with given and accessible NPs. How specialized is the 'absolutive' case in introducing new referents in Sacapultec?

The answer, I submit, is "not very" — or at least, the evidence is weak enough to invite us to reconsider how "powerful" a motivating force PAS really is. The structure of my argument will be to point out two methodological choices — one large and conscious, the other small, and probably unconscious — made by Du Bois in his analysis, and to show the extent to which his conclusions hinge on these choices.

The varying degree of specialization of each case role for new mentions is illustrated graphically in Du Bois (1987:828), and I reproduce that graph as figure 5 below:

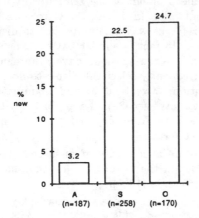

Fig. 5: Specialization of major argument roles for new mentions
(Sacapultec; Du Bois 1987, p.828, figure 7)

Du Bois restricts his sample of case roles to A, S, and O, an important methodological choice which he justifies as follows:

> Given the centrality of grammatical relations for this study, it is necessary to attend consistently to the distinction between elements which bear a direct grammatical relation *to the verb*, and those which do not... Argument nominals (A, S, O) bear this relation, and thus participate in the *ergative/absolutive structural opposition*. Obliques, not bearing such a relation, remain outside the structural system. Thus, in relating discourse patterns in the texts, I distinguish 'core' or 'direct' arguments (i.e. A, S, and O) from non-arguments (primarily obliques and possessives, but also various minor roles...) (p.815; italics mine).

However, this choice can be objected to in the context of Du Bois' larger analysis. It is true that the A, S, and O roles enjoy a privileged status in the grammars of ergative languages, and (to the extent that the thematic roles 'agent', 'patient', and 'experiencer' are preferentially grammatically encoded cross-linguistically), in language in general. What is not clear, however, is that they are similarly privileged with respect to the pragmatic principle of information flow. According to Du Bois' argument, the functional distribution of new nominal mentions in discourse gives rise to a recognizable pattern, or PAS. This pattern, in turn, motivates the grammaticalization of ergative morpho-syntax, particularly in those languages where there are few competing forces. Given that PAS logically precedes ergativity in this scheme, it is circular, at best, to select in advance the case roles for analysis, on the basis of their known correlation with ergativity.

Again, however, it is easy to see why this choice was made. The specialization levels of 22.5% (for S) and 24.7% (for O) seem high when contrasted with 3.2% for the A role, as in figure 5 above. When contrasted with the higher degrees of specialization of the oblique (38.7%) and the 'other' (36.1%) categories — which Du Bois does not depict graphically — S and O do not look as specialized. This is represented in figure 6 below (Du Bois' graph, plus the 'oblique', 'possessor', and 'other' categories).

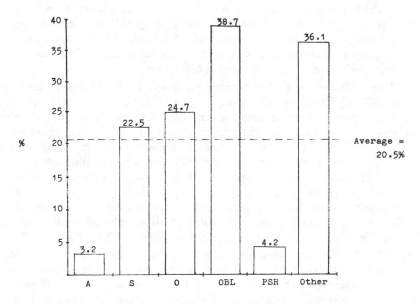

Fig. 6: Specialization of grammatical roles for new mentions
(Sacapultec)

This impression is borne out statistically as well. Du Bois notes that the average percentage of new mentions in the corpus as a whole (cf. Du Bois 1987; table 6, p.826) is 20.5%. Applying this figure back to each case role, we find that the greatest deviation from the average is evidenced by the A role (and secondly, the human 'possessor' category), which falls short of average by a factor of more than six. This of course bears out Du Bois' principle of avoiding new mentions in A role; it is also the finding which is most strongly supported by the Tamil data. At the other extreme, the oblique[6] and the 'other' categories are nearly two times more specialized than the average. *The categories which most closely approach the average or predictably random distribution of new mentions are S and O.* In other words, far from being "reserved" for the introduction of new information in Sacapultec as Du Bois claims, the absolutive case is the *least* marked for this function, according to his data. Thus, unless it can be demonstrated that there is something inherently salient about new mentions in S and O roles that makes them stand out even in relatively small proportions, the claim that S and O are "specialized" in this task stands on shaky empirical ground.

The second, smaller methodological point concerns the category labelled 'other' in Du Bois' study. In a footnote on p.814, he lists the phenomena included in 'other':

> ...*vocatives* (proper names used in address); *marked topics* (NP's which are topicalized and set off in a separate intonation unit without a verb, and usually precede a predication about the same referent in the immediately following clausal intonation unit); and *predicate nominals* (non-referential nouns functioning as predicates in an equational construction).

Of the 36 instances of this assorted category, a surprisingly high percentage (36.1%) introduce new narrative participants. Why this should be so is a question of some interest, given that the description of the second phenomenon — what Du Bois calls the 'marked topic' — sounds strangely like what I have been calling 'verbless presentation' for Tamil. Unfortunately, the 'marked topic' construction is nowhere illustrated in the paper, and since it accounts for only 19 instances of nominal reference, Du Bois relegates it to the grab-bag category, concluding early on that "it was not possible to arrive at a significant characterization of [its] distinctive role" (p.814, fn.11). By piecing together figures and comments from various parts of the paper, however, we can reconstruct the following:

1) The 19 instances account for 4.3% of all clauses in the Sacapultec corpus (19/443)[7]. Comparing this with the figure (2.4%, or 3.4% in the saturated sample) for Tamil, we can see that the 'marked topic' construction is actually *more* frequent in Sacapultec than its counterpart in Tamil.

2) The 'predicate nominal' construction, of which 13 instances are noted, only introduces a new referent once.[8] This means that out of the 13 new mentions in "other" roles, as many as 12, and no fewer than 8, are associated with the 'marked topic' construction. (The indeterminacy here is due to not knowing whether any new mentions were introduced for the first time as vocatives. On the basis of the Tamil corpus, where a vocative never constitutes a first mention, we might predict that it is unlikely; however, I cannot be certain that it does not occur in Sacapultec).

3) Thus, the percentage of specialization of the 'marked topic' construction for new mentions is between 63% (if no vocatives are 'new') and 42% (if all vocatives are 'new'). That is, it is by far the most specialized construction for this function in Sacapultec, as indeed the verbless construction is in Tamil. This is represented in figure 7.

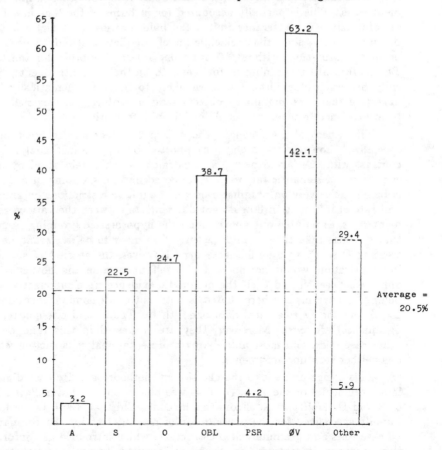

Fig. 7: Specialization of grammatical roles for new mentions, with 'marked topics' (ØV) separated from 'other' (Sacapultec)

Whether the 'marked topic' construction in Sacapultec is comparable in every detail with the Tamil verbless construction remains, of course, to be demonstrated. In the meantime, however, the evidence is highly suggestive of a functional, as well a structural, parallel between the two.

4.0 Conclusion.

The conclusions to be drawn from this are, I believe, two-fold. First we must evaluate, in light of the critique presented here, the validity of Du Bois' claims regarding PAS and the discourse basis of ergativity. In addition — and in some sense largely independent of the above — there is the issue of the relationship between methodology and results which my (re)analysis raises.

Regarding PAS, it is certain that the A argument role is pragmatically constrained, in a way which sets it apart from the other major argument roles. This is partially accounted for in terms of the 'one new piece of information per utterance unit' (cf. Chafe; Pawley & Syder) principle, but not entirely, since that principle merely predicts that only A or O can be new information, without selecting one role or the other for the task. The additional determining factor seems to be that semantic agents, typically human protagonists, are more likely to function thematically in a narrative than are inanimate objects, and accordingly are carried over from utterance to utterance as old or 'given' information.

The aspect of PAS which groups S and O together as functionally specialized, however, is largely unsupported by the present analysis. In contrast with the 'avoid new A's' constraint, which is reinforced by both cognitive and semantic factors, the supposed natural grouping of S and O is based exclusively on pragmatic usage. Cognitive restrictions on amount and rate of information flow do not differentiate between the various argument roles, as pointed out above. And the hypothesized grouping assumes that speakers take the semantic feature of animacy to be *irrelevant*, i.e. by treating O as a single unified category. However, the absence of supporting motivation would not in and of itself undermine the notion of an affinity between S and O, if the pragmatic evidence were sufficiently compelling. I have argued here that it is not: out of all nominal mentions in the S and the O roles, less than one-fifth (in Tamil) and one-quarter (in Sacapultec) are new. Moreover, they are surpassed in this function by other case roles, and most notably, by a presentational construction which has neither verb nor arguments.

This brings us back to the question of methodology. By excluding all 'non-arguments' of the verb, Du Bois was able to infer a natural grouping of S and O *relative to A*. From this he concluded that S and O are functionally specialized for the presentation of new information. By comparing *all* case roles and grammatical constructions which introduce new information, however, it emerges that S and O are virtually neutral with respect to this function. Thus a very different interpretation arises when a less restricted methodology is employed. The alternative interpretation in this case is that PAS — broadly defined as a cross-linguistic pattern in natural language use according to which speakers avoid introducing new referents in A role, but exhibit no such avoidance in S and O roles — is not the powerfully motivating force for the grammaticalization of ergativity that Du Bois claims. This does not of course rule out the possibility that PAS may be one of a larger set of factors which, taken together, results in the grammaticalization over time of the ergative pattern in any given language. It seems unlikely, however, that it is the sole, or even the most influential, factor in this process.

As regards verblessness and information flow, a different methodological problem arises. Given the relatively infrequent use of 'marked topics', Du Bois can hardly be faulted for having excluded them from his analysis — part of the rigor of linguistic analysis is that one avoids drawing conclusions from insufficient data. However the fact that he did exclude them, and long before approaching the analysis of first mentions, belies a methodological bias of the same sort noted above. That is, rather than taking the investigation of information flow to be primary, and demonstrating how the ergative pattern falls out naturally from that, Du Bois takes the phenomenon of ergativity to be primary, then looks for a way in which to account for it functionally.

One consequence of this approach is that devices which genuinely *do* specialize in introducing new information in Sacapultec are entirely overlooked. Although I have had little to say here regarding the role of obliques in this function, it is a phenomenon which I feel is worthy of further investigation. Of more immediate relevance is the confirmation which the Sacapultec data provide of the cross-linguistic validity of verbless presentation, a strategy with important implications for the theory of cognitive processing and information flow (cf. Herring, in progress).

In spite of its bias, Du Bois' article is commendable in many respects. The insights it contains are original, and clearly presented. Moreover, if it were not for the fairly complete statistical representation of the data provided, it would not have been possible to reinterpret it and evaluate the methodology employed. One shudders to imagine how many influential works, equally ingenious but not as responsibly presented, couch significant biases which even the most scrupulous reader is in no position to evaluate. The moral of the story is perhaps that it is not enough to be faithful to one's data; even the best-intentioned fall prey to investigative bias.

ENDNOTES

1.   Verbless sentences are also found in written literary genres in English
      and in numerous contemporary languages; a classic example is the
      opening of novels with sentences such as *A dark and stormy night. A
      lone freighter off the coast of Madagascar*, etc. Highly stylized literary
      uses of this type will not be considered here, both because of the
      emphasis I wish to place on functional motivations in spontaneous
      discourse, and because of space limitations.

2.   A judgement sample made up of 16 of the best (i.e. most successful in
      performance) and most typical of the narratives, representing each of
      the three types, had already been selected prior to this investigation,
      and I used this sample to determine the overall frequency and distri-
      bution of verbless presentational utterances.

3.   Here, and in the analysis that follows, I do not continue to distinguish
      between the three narrative genres, in that they pattern roughly
      alike. The only exception is that longer narratives (e.g. epics) tend to
      have more nomimal participants, but a somewhat lower 'information
      pressure quotient' (Du Bois 1987:834) — that is, new mentions are
      spread out over larger portions of the text. The information pressure
      is not low enough, however, to affect the distributional pattern of new
      mentions across grammatical type.

4.   While it is possible to rate degrees of accessibility along a continuum
      (cf. for example Gundel, Hedberg, and Zacharski, this volume), for
      the purposes of this paper I follow the 3-way system employed by
      Chafe (1987), who distinguishes between 'active', 'inactive', and
      'semi-active' concepts, and Du Bois (1987), who applies the terms
      'given', 'new', and 'accessible' to the same categories. Examples of
      accessible mentions include a participants' body part, when the parti-
      cipant has already been introduced, and stock characters within an
      established genre (e.g. if it is a 'Tenaliraman story', it will necessarily
      involve the comic hero Tenaliraman and the king he works for).
      Around 30% of first mentions in the Tamil corpus were classified as
      'accessible' according to this system.

          In contrast, Du Bois notes that in his study, "accessible mentions
      were by far the least common" (816). The discrepancy between this
      statement, and the relatively high incidence of accessible mentions
      identified in my data, may well be an artifact of the differing metho-
      dologies used in the two studies. The Sacapultec subjects described a
      film — Chafe's 'Pear Film' — which contains a relatively restricted set
      of focused participants, in contrast with some of the Tamil folk tales,
      which are highly complex in this respect. Second, the artificialness of
      the Sacapultec narrative context — speakers (some of whom, as Du
      Bois himself observes, had never seen a film before) being asked to
      describe a film, made in a culture other than their own, to an

interviewer who had *not* seen it — may have militated against the notion that any information was mutually 'accessible'.

5. The percentage indicated for verbless presentations is based on the entirety of the corpus; out of 55 instances previously identified as 'presentational', 49, or 89.1%, were found to be first mentions. (An additional 7 first mentions are verbless but not 'presentational'; most of these are instances of elipsis). However, daunted by the task of identifying all nominal mentions in S, A, O, and oblique roles in a corpus of 1686 utterances, I based my analysis of these roles on 8 representative narratives, or approximately one-third of the sample (541 utterances).

6. One possible explanation for this is the tendency for temporally and spatially-orienting NPs to be introduced in oblique (especially locative and dative) cases in numerous languages; e.g. *The king lived | for twenty years | in a cave | in the forest.*

7. This calculation is based on the total clause number given in Figure 1, p.818 of Du Bois 1987.

8. Cf. Du Bois 1987, p.826, Table 5.

9. A number of Mayan languages — for example, Chuj and Chol — are known to make use of 'verbless presentational sentences' (Judith Maxwell, personal communication). It would not be surprising to discover that Du Bois' 'marked topics' are an instance of this more general phenomenon.

REFERENCES

Chafe, Wallace L. 1980. "The deployment of consciousness in the production of a narrative". In W. Chafe (ed.), **The Pear Stories: Cognitive, Cultural and Linguistic Aspects of Narrative Production;** 9-50. Norwood, New Jersey: Ablex.

Chafe, Wallace L. 1987. "Cognitive constraints on information flow". In R. Tomlin (ed.), **Cohesion and Grounding in Discourse;** 21-51. Amsterdam: Benjamins.

Du Bois, John W. 1987. "The discourse basis of ergativity". **Language** 63,4:805-55.

Herring, Susan C. In progress. "Verbless 'sentences' in Tamil narrative: cognitive, pragmatic, and typological implications".

Pawley, Andrew & Frances Hodgetts Syder. 1977. "The One Clause at a Time Hypothesis". University of Auckland, MS.

Pawley, Andrew & Frances Hodgetts Syder. 1983. "Natural selection in syntax: notes on adaptive variation and change in vernacular and literary grammar". **Journal of Pragmatics** 5:551-579.

The Cultural (?) Context of Narrative Involvement

Jane H. Hill
University of Arizona

1. INTRODUCTION. "Involvement" is significant for students of vernacular oral
narrative, since involvement-oriented strategies constitute a preferred research site for the interactional, mutually-constructed, negotiated, and "dialogic" properties of the genre. Discourse analysts generally attend more to
the local micro-interactional contexts of involvement than to the larger
socio-cultural contexts in which narrative events are embedded. But, as I hope
to show here, the construction of involvement is constrained by such broader
contexts, specifically by the understandings about self and other that anthropologists have called "cultural." As a first step in untangling the complex
interrelationships of cultural knowledge and locally-driven interactional constraints in the study of oral narrative, I propose that two important rhetorical devices for constructing involvement, direct-discourse reported speech
or "constructed dialogue" (Tannen 1988) and interactional-world evaluation,
are associated with different ethnopsychological perspectives.[1] Specifically,
constructed dialogue is the preferred involvement strategy among most speakers of Mexicano, who manifest a "sociocentric" view of selfhood and personhood. Interactional world evaluation is the preferred strategy among middle-
class Euro-Americans, who manifest an "egocentric" perspective.

The materials for this study include 22 narratives of personal experience: stories in which the narrator figures as a central character. Eighteen
narratives are told by 8 male and 4 female speakers of Mexicano (modern Nahuatl), a Uto-Aztecan language of Mexico (some Spanish also appears in these
narratives). The Mexicano narratives include 800 T-units.[2] The other four
narratives were collected from five middle-class Anglo American women; they
appear in Polanyi (1989).[3] They include 465 T-units.

All of the Mexicano narratives and one of the Polanyi narratives were
collected during the course of sociolinguistic interviews. Most of the Mexicano narratives were responses to the "danger of death" question developed
by William Labov. All the stories are about misfortunes--illnesses, getting
arrested, being abandoned, or bewitched, or threatened by contact with an
outsider. The Polanyi stories are also about misfortunes, including being
served bad food in a restaurant, being robbed, being in the hospital after a
difficult labor and delivery, and fainting on the subway. Thus, the 22 stories
share a common theme: a narrator confronts a hostile world.

The Mexicano narratives are not precisely "conversational," since they
were collected during sociolinguistic interviews. Every effort, however, was
made to keep a relaxed, conversational tone to these interviews; during most
of them, several speakers of Mexicano were present, and I believe that the
stories that speakers told were similar to those that occur in ordinary conversation in their communities. But since several of them occur in answer to
questions, they don't begin with negotiations about the right to tell a story.
Instead, sequences requesting clarification ("Does witchcraft count?") appear,
or else they open with an affirmative, "Yes, that sort of thing happened to
me. It was when ...."

Three of the Polanyi narratives occurred in conversations among
friends. While Polanyi chose each narrative to represent a different type of

138

story structure, the three "friendly conversations" are not dissimilar to "Fainting on the Subway," a text elicited in an interview with a group of women, at least for the discourse systems that I'll examine here.

2. PERSON, SELF AND SOCIAL RELATIONS IN MODERN MEXICANO AND MIDDLE-CLASS EURO-AMERICAN CULTURE. Speakers in the two narrative samples represent groups which anthropologists find to be quite different in their understandings of selfhood and personhood. Mexicano speakers generally share a set of themes that Shweder and Bourne (1984) have labelled "sociocentric," while middle-class Euro-Americans share an "egocentric" perspective. The brief sketches of the relevant themes given here cannot surpass stereotypy, but will serve to suggest the relevant distinctions.

Members of Mexicano communities consider themselves to be neither highly differentiated one from another nor autonomous of one another or of the influence of sacred beings or "powers." There is hierarchy in the communities, but relationships between insiders should manifest mutual trust and interdependence, exemplified in relationships (of which every member has literally hundreds) of ritual kinship or *compadrazgo*. People should labor for the good of all, without attention to personal advantage; a repeated theme is that of "sacrifice" for one's family and community.

A principal cultural theme is the distinction between people inside the community, and those outside. Outsiders, especially outsiders who do not speak Mexicano, are considered to be dangerous representatives of a disorderly and peripheral realm, where people are cruel, irrational, and self-seeking. Involvement with outsiders is inevitable (it is usually done as a "sacrifice"); in conducting such involvement, one behaves so as to "defend oneself." But such contact usually yields unhappy results or "suffering."

Mexicano people attend closely to the sacred, considering human beings to be simply one type of inhabitant of a realm that also includes "powers," including the saints, Mary and Jesus, God, and autochthonous powers such as the Malinche and the Cuatlapanga (Nutini 1988). The souls of the dead inhabit a moral sphere intermediate between that of the living and the domain of the powers, and intercede with the latter for the good of the former. To live a moral life is essential, and is part of the propitiation of "powers," who can send both good and evil to human beings. People who are punished with bad fortune--"suffering"--often do not know why they have offended; they only know that they must have done something, and strive anew to behave appropriately and give lavish attention to the needs of the dead and the powers through offerings, prayers, and proper ritual conduct. "Suffering," however, cannot be avoided. It is central to the human condition, which is dominated by forces of destiny that are essentially beyond rational human control.

The thematic underpinnings of self-concept among middle-class Euro-Americans could hardly be more different from those found among Mexicano speakers. The ethnopsychologies of this community have been discussed by many scholars. Since texts analyzed by Polanyi (1989) form part of the present study, I summarize her thematic analysis. For middle-class Euro-Americans, central to human nature is choice and the right to satisfy needs, with the constraint on this goal being that one should not hurt others or inhibit their own autonomous drive to self-satisfaction. The central goal of work is to permit this satisfaction (middle-class Euro-Americans, like Mexicano speakers, find work hard, but the goal of work is self-fulfillment, not "sacrifice" and community service). People are highly differentiated from one another, having "true feelings" and a "true self." Instead of the structured universe of the community and the powers, a shifting, egocentric network of "friends," people with whom one can be most truly one's self, are one's most important relations. Friends should be changed if they no longer meet the self's needs. If these requirements for choice, satisfying work, and relationships which nurture the "true self" are satisfied, people will be happy, brave, strong, and rational. Pain and ill fortune result from failure to meet these requirements (nowhere do supernatural powers or "destiny" appear in the thematic repertoire of middle-class Euro-Americans[4]). In summary, in contrast to the low interpersonal differentiation and attention to interdependence, sacrifice, and suffering of Mexicano speakers, middle-class Euro-americans emphasize high interpersonal differentiation, autonomy, success, and well-being.

3. THE DISTRIBUTION OF SELF-REFERENCE IN THE PRONOMINAL SYSTEM. Mexicano is a nominative-accusative language. Case is marked only on pronominal elements, distinguishing nominative, accusative, and possessive. The independent person pronouns in Mexicano are used for discourse foregrounding only, and occur only in addition to a pronominal prefix. They are not counted in the present paper. Thus the counts include only the Mexicano nominative and accusative pronominal elements, and the English pronouns.[5]

The following possibilities are available for self-reference in personal narrative:[6] 1. As "I" (M. ni-); 2. as object, 'me', (M. nēch-, also both accusative and dative object); 3. as part of a collective, 'we', (M. ti-... plural suffix -h present, -queh non-present); 4. as part of a collective object, 'us', (M. tēch-); 5,6. as subject or object 'you' (M. ti- subject, mitz- object), mentioned in constructed dialogue of a third-person figure; 7. as a third person, mentioned in the constructed dialogue of a figure; 8. as a member (presumably with the addressee) in an impersonal reference, such as impersonal 'they, one' (M. cē 'one') or 'you' (M. ti-, mitz-). One can also, of course refer to oneself as a possessor or oblique object; in Mexicano the possessive prefixes indicate both possession and the object of a postposition. While these pronominal usages merit study, the present sample does not offer enough examples. I have also ignored reciprocal "self," a last possibility for self-reference.

The eight types of pronominal self-reference must be distributed by speakers across narrative structure. I distinguish five structural contexts. The first three are all in the "story world," the time and place in which the events recounted occurred. These include 1. the "orientation" section of narratives, 2. the main event line, 3. "story-world evaluation." The notion of "story-world evaluation" is derived from Labov and Waletzky (1967) and Labov (1972), who include in evaluation all durative-descriptive clauses not in the orientation, any clause departing from the event-line sequence, such as flash clauses, negatives, irrealis clauses of various types, modifiers such as relative clauses, and several other categories. I include also repetition, often of main-line clauses; this is especially common in the Mexicano narratives.[7]

Constructed dialogue is included with "evaluation" in Labov's original work, and constitutes an important type of what he calls "internal evaluation," evaluation constituted within the narrative. I distinguish it here from "story-world evaluation," since analysis of deixis shift and possibilities for anaphoric co-reference between clauses in constructed dialogue and other narrative clauses shows that constructed dialogue constitutes a "world line," separate from the event line and evaluative and background information clauses located in the story world.

"Interactional world evaluation" (IWE) is distinguished from story-world evaluation, following the distinction between story world and interactional world made by Chafe (1980); this is identical to Polanyi's "non-story-world clauses." Some cases of IWE parallel what Labov (1972) called "external evaluation," evaluation that departs from the narrative context. However, some examples of "external evaluation" given by Labov would not be considered IWE in this analysis. An example is seen in (1):

(1)   And it was the strangest feeling because you couldn't tell if they were really gonna make it, if they didn't make it, it was such a small little plane, there was no chance for anybody. But it was really quite terrific, it was only a half-hour's ride to Mexico City... But it was quite an experience (Labov 1972:371)

In this excerpt, the speaker seems to be reflecting on thoughts that she had during the events recounted, and does not actually depart from the story world with reference to her present state of mind. The "you" in the first line is "impersonal you," and does not constitute a direct address to the interlocutor. Included here in IWE are English expressions like "I mean" and "I guess," or Mexicano expressions like (2) and (3). Also included are cases of coda evaluations that refer to the current state of affairs, as shown in (8).

(2)   niquilnāmiqui "I remember" (a very rare rhetorical strategy)
(3)   Para tlen niquihtōz? "Why would I say it?" (meaning, "Why would I lie to you?"; this is a fairly common rhetorical strategy.)

The data on pronominal self-reference frequency and distribution across clause types are given in Tables I and II (next page).

Tables I and II reveal several differences between the two samples. In the IWE column of Table I, the Polanyi sample shows a concentration of "I," 30% of all occurrences (contrasted to 13% for Mexicano). Table I also shows differences in the distribution of "we." In the Polanyi texts this is four times more frequent in orientation than in the Mexicano sample. While Mexicano shows high "we" in IWE, this occurs mainly in the usage of a single speaker, RC, who will be discussed below. Thus no conclusions can be drawn from this latter differential.

Table II shows that the two samples are generally similar in the frequency of the different types of pronominal self-reference in each discourse component, with "I" being the most common representation across all discourse categories. The exception is the Mexicano use of second person representation of the speaker in constructed dialogue, where it surpasses "I" as by far the highest-ranking pronoun.

The right-hand column of Table II shows that the relative ranks of the most frequent pronouns are identical for the two samples; all these narrators prefer "I" for self-reference. However, while the preference is very strong in the Polanyi sample, it is very weak in Mexicano. This occurs because Mexicano speakers use "me" and "we" at twice the frequency of Polanyi's Euro-Americans, and because of the very high percentage of "you" in Mexicano constructed dialogue.

TABLE I. PERCENT OF EACH PRONOMINAL TYPE ACROSS FIVE DISCOURSE CATEGORIES

		ORIENTATION	EVENT LINE	S-WORLD EV	CONSTR.DIAL.	I-WORLD	TOTAL N
I	M	10 (21)	25 (51)	42 (84)	10 (20)	13 (27)	(203)
	P	7 (10)	14 (20)	43 (61)	6 (9)	30 (43)	(143)
ME	M	14.5 (16)	24 (26)	44 (48)	13 (14)	4.5 (6)	(110)
	P	9 (2)	35 (8)	43 (10)	13 (3)	/	(23)
WE	M	6 (3)	37 (18)	20 (10)	10 (5)	27 (13)	(49)
	P	25 (3)	25 (3)	33 (4)	8 (1)	8 (1)	(12)
US	M	13 (2)	33 (5)	47 (7)	7 (1)	/	(15)
	P	14 (1)	13 (1)	57 (4)	14 (1)	/	(7)
YOU	M				100 (55)		(55)
	P				100 (3)		(3)
YOUob	M				100 (15)		(15)
	P				/		
P3	M				100 (7)		(7)
	P				100 (3)		(3)
IMP	M					100 (5)	(5)
	P					100 (13)	(13)

N in parentheses; total N in parentheses in right-hand column. M = Mexicano, P = Polanyi, YOUob = P2object, IMP = Impersonal

TABLE II. PERCENT OF SELF-REFERENCE IN EACH PRONOMINAL TYPES IN EACH DISCOURSE CATEGORY

	ORIENTATION		EVENT LINE		S-WORLD EV		CONSTR.DIAL.		I-WORLD EVAL.		TOTAL	
	Me	Po	Me	Po	Me	Po	Me	Po	Me	Po	Me	Po
I	50	63	51	63	56	74	17	53	53	77	44	70
ME	38	13	26	25	32	12	12	18	12	2	24	11
WE	7	19	18	9	7	5	4	6	25	2	11	6
US	5	6	5	3	5	5	1	6			3	3
YOU							47	18			12	1
YOUob								13			3	/
P3							4	6			2	1
IMP							10	25	1	7		

(% only; See Table 1 for N)

Lutz (1988, pp. 88-90) noted a strong preference for "we" among speakers of the Micronesian language Ifaluk, and associated this with Ifaluk ethnopsychology. Like Mexicano speakers, Ifaluk people emphasize connections and relationships between people. The differential "we" frequency here is not a product of micro-interactional context; to the contrary. In three of the Polanyi texts we would expect high "we," since speakers are discussing specific experiences shared with one or more of the conversationalists present. None of the Mexicano narrators are discussing experiences that were shared with their interlocutors (except in a general sense—almost everyone has been sick, for instance) yet they use "we" and "us" frequently. I have previously pointed out that Mexicano speakers are prone to use a sort of "royal we"; expressions such as "Drink has destroyed our (= "my") stomach" occur in these data. If there is an opportunity to include others in recounting an experience, this will be exploited, even though the "others" are not present. The tendency to use "we" in conversation is strongest among people who define themselves as full-time cultivators, the most communally-oriented sectors of the Mexicano population (Hill 1988a). Thus "we" usage when no obvious experience-sharers are present may offer a rough index of sociocentric orientation of a speaker, and may differentiate between more and less sociocentric sectors in communities where some members are developing a more egocentric perspective, which may occur under pressures from an encroaching capitalist marketplace.

The high frequency of self-reference as "you" in the constructed dialogue of others by Mexicano speakers may be associated with an emphasis on seeing oneself as essentially embedded in social relationships, and may hint at low differentiation between self and other. The striking difference between this usage in Mexicano and middle-class Euro-American constructed dialogue suggests the different functions of this rhetorical device in the two communities, a point to which I will return. The Mexicano frequencies of "me" might be taken to suggest a sort of "objectification." I suspect, however, that they mainly appear because of certain characteristic Mexicano ways of talking, especially expressions like "a disease caught me" (in contrast to American English "I caught a disease"), and I'm uncertain about the cultural significance of these.

4. INTERACTIONAL-WORLD EVALUATION VS. CONSTRUCTED DIALOGUE AS STRATEGIES FOR NARRATIVE INVOLVEMENT. The most striking difference between the Mexicano and Euro-American personal narrative samples is the differential frequency of self-reference in two important narrative-involvement strategies, constructed dialogue and interactional-world evaluation. This distribution of self reference reflects a broader difference in frequency of use of the two rhetorical strategies, but the self-reference difference is somewhat larger than the gross difference in number of T-units in each discourse category, as shown in Table III.

TABLE III. CONSTRUCTED DIALOGUE VS. INTERACTIONAL WORLD EVALUATION

	MEXICANO		POLANYI	
	SELF-REF	TOTAL	SELF-REF	TOTAL
CONSTRUCTED DIAL.	118 (26%)	190 (24%)	17 (8%)	52 (11%)
I- WORLD EV.	51 (11%)	122 (15%)	56 (27%)	90 (19%)
OTHER	291 (63%)	488 (61%)	132 (61%)	323 (70%)
TOTAL	460*	800	205	465

* There is a discrepancy of 1 between this total and that in Table I. I have given up trying to find out where it came from!

The figures given for the Mexicano sample reflect a highly-developed use of constructed dialogue that Ken Hill and I have observed in previous studies of two very long narratives of personal experience from Mexicano speakers that are not part of the present analysis, since they would simply swamp the remainder of the data. Ken Hill identified 32 "figures" represented through constructed dialogue in a 45-minute narrative by a middle-aged woman from San Isidro, Tlaxcala (K. Hill 1985). In the analysis of a seventeen-minute narrative by an elderly man from San Lorenzo Almecata, Puebla, I found twelve such figurative voices (along with a number of other "voices" in the larger, Bakhtinian, sense) (Hill 1988b).

In Mexicano stories, an instance of constructed dialogue often constitutes an "event." For instance, MP's story consists simply of background, a first event--her late husband was stoned when he carried ballots to the city for counting--, a second event, her "speech" about the first (scolding her husband for getting involved), and a coda. JR's story includes an orientation, a report of her own speech, and a second event constituted by the failure of a represented participant to understand what she said. This failure is then

evaluated--young people don't speak Mexicano any more. Such texts apparently satisfy the requirement proposed by Polanyi (1989), that a "story" include
at least two events. Most Mexicano narratives, however, exhibit constructed
dialogue involving at least two speakers, and often have several episodes of
such exchanges. Typical episodes include time-place orientation, a brief
conversation between two speakers, and a coda evaluating the conversation.

Not only do Mexicano narrators use a great deal of constructed dialogue, but the distribution of pronominal self-reference within it is distinct
from that found in the usage of middle-class Euro-Americans. A high percentage of constructed dialogue in middle-class Euro-American narratives reports
the speech of the narrator, who says "I....." In contrast, Mexicano speakers use
a great deal of the constructed dialogue of other figures, who refer to the
narrator as "you." An example is given in (4); here a foreman (a dangerous
outsider) orders EZ to continue work in a hailstorm; he catches the *gripa*
(influenza) and nearly dies.

(4)   Huān ōquihtoh in nēca maestro, "Debe de ticcolarōz nicānca castillo,
        huān tlāmo ticcolarōz, āmo tictlānīz in ocho peso." "And the foreman
        said, 'You must set this rebar, and if you don't set it, you won't earn
        the eight pesos.'"

Pronominal self-reference in constructed dialogue coded as "you" very frequently takes the form of commands, as in (5), where jailers order the narrator and his fellow prisoners:

(5)   "Ándale, ximotlaquihquīxtilicah, xpatzacan namotilmah, huan nēpa
        xzoacan, ma tōna!" "Get along, take off your clothes, wring out your
        blankets, and hang 'em up there, so the sun will dry 'em!"

A very common form of self-reference as "you" in these texts occurs in the
constructed dialogue of doctors who are summoned to treat illnesses, as in (6):

(6)   Ōquihtoh in nēca doctōr, "In tlā quēmah este nimitzpahtīz, pero mitz-
        costarōz." That doctor said, "Certainly I will cure you, but it will cost
        you."

The presence of self-reference through "you" in the constructed
dialogue of non-narrator figures was noted by Labov (1972) as an important
feature of working-class Euro-american narrative style. He suggested that
such usage constituted a "step inward" (Labov 1972:373), a more deeply
embedded form of his "internal evaluation" than constructed dialogue by the
figure of the narrator.

Constructed dialogue is, of course, a universal rhetorical strategy (cf.
Longacre (1976) and Larson (1978)), and the preferred story form for middle-
class Euro-Americans demands some constructed dialogue; even "Eating on the
New York Thruway," which of the Polanyi texts has the least constructed dialogue, includes a brief line. Constructed dialogue can be used by middle-class
Euro-Americans at high frequencies. For instance, Tannen (1988) gives a narrative of 65 T-units in which 31 are in constructed dialogue. This narrative
has only nine T-units of interactional-world evaluation. But this narrator, a
resident physician in an emergency room, does not clearly figure as a central

character; Tannen notes that in the voice representation he is merged with other figures to constitute the voice of "the staff." There is no pronominal self-reference in the narrative except through the use of impersonal "you." In the same paper, Tannen published a personal-experience narrative by a middle-class teenage girl. In this narrative, with 33 T-units, nine are in constructed dialogue. However, eight T-units include interactional-world evaluation; only two of the twelve Mexicano speakers shown in Table IV below exhibit a comparable ratio. While the Tannen sample shows that the long speeches and conversations that are very characteristic of Mexicano narrative are not unthinkable in middle-class Euro-american personal narrative, they are absent from the sample given by Polanyi, who, unlike Tannen, presumably did not have constructed dialogue especially in mind when she selected her illustrations.

While Mexicano speakers are virtuoso users of constructed dialogue, the speakers in the Polanyi texts exhibit an equally striking emphasis on interactional-world evaluation, especially a type that represents attention to their own current, interactional-world-relevant, feelings and thoughts about what happened in the narrative. Many examples include the pronoun "I": "I mean, I guess, I don't know, I think, I'm happy to say, I know quite a lot" etc. Tag questions like "Right?" and appeals to interlocutors like "You know" also occur with high frequency. Polanyi notes that people who have read these texts often ask if they are "normal," and I certainly don't dispute her claim that they are, for Euro-Americans. But they would be odd, to the point of unthinkability, for Mexicano speakers.

Mexicano speakers do use interactional-world evaluation, but it is both less frequent and different in content and interactional impact from that found in the Polanyi stories. This will be illustrated through a more detailed examination of the Mexicano sample. The use of interactional-world evaluation is distributed very unevenly across the 12 Mexicano speakers. I note, however, that it is not associated with narrative length; the two very long narratives mentioned above have very little IWE. Table IV gives the breakdown for total T-units in interactional-world evaluation and constructed dialogue for the twelve Mexicano speakers.

TABLE IV. INTERACTIONAL-WORLD EVALUATION AND CONSTRUCTED DIALOGUE FOR MEXICANO SPEAKERS

		INTERACTIONAL-WORLD EVAL.		CONSTRUCTED DIALOGUE	
		TOTAL	SELF-REF	TOTAL	SELF-REF
RCV (S56)	(1 narrative)	7	3	0	
RC (S65)	(2 narratives)	28	20	22	17
MPP(S37)	(1 narrative)	15	6	13	6
GA (S12)	(1 narrative)	16	1	3	4*
SP (S55)	(1 narrative)	12	1	5	2
FM (S38)	(3 narratives)	30	10	50	26
AT (S77)	(2 narratives)	9	9	31	14
MP(F,S14)	(1 narrative)	1	0	1	0
JR(F,S58)	(1 narrative)	2	0	6	0
RS(F,S75)	(3 narratives)	2	1	45	29
EZ (S5)	(1 narrative)	0	0	3	3
DX(F,S53)	(1 narrative)	0	0	11	16

* The "Total" column is number of T-units. The "Self-reference" column is for number of pronominal self-references. Note that it is possible to have more than one instance of pronominal self-reference in each T-unit in Mexicano. "F" means "female speaker". Subject numbers from Hill and Hill (1986) are also given.

Two male speakers, RCV and RC, exhibit a higher rate of self-reference in interactional-world evaluation than in constructed dialogue. RCV, 80 years old, told about a time in the 1910 revolution when federal troops burned his stored fodder and fed all of his corn and beans to their animals, and then threatened to hang him if he did not produce more supplies for them. RCV represents his plea to the federal officer in indirect-discourse reported speech, but uses no constructed dialogue. This is the main reason that he shows up as aberrant, since his IWE is not exceptionally elaborated. Two instances of IWE in his story are a mere murmur, "Mhm." He also uses sentence-final *āmo* "no" twice, as in (7):

(7)   Pero āmo ōnēchpilohqueh, āmo. "But they did not hang me, no."

I have counted this type of usage as IWE. He uses one "Why would I lie to you?" rhetorical question. The other two self-references appear in the coda to his narrative, where he reports that he suffers illness to this day from the fear that he felt. This coda, in (8), contains one of the five impersonal usages in the sample, in *cē mococoa* "one is ill."

(8)   Hasta āxān huān por nōnīc quēmaniān nimococoa [mhm]. Porque nochi nōn sufrimiento de, de mocayotl, huān [mhm] nochi nōn. Siempre, cē mococoa. "And today, I am still ill, because of all the suffering from, from the fear, and all that. Always, one is ill."

Had RCV used constructed dialogue instead of indirect discourse, no doubt his constructed dialogue self reference would have exceeded the small IWE number.

The second speaker in the table, RC, a factory worker 47 years old, especially stands out. First, he has all the IWE self-reference as "we" in the entire Mexicano sample. This occurs in the coda and "exit talk" from his first sub-narrative. This subnarrative is about the first time he ever spoke Spanish, to a peddler who came to his village, and how difficult it was for him. In his coda, he remarks that today "we have no trouble speaking Spanish as we are drinking together." He elaborates this theme for several sentences. These instances of "we" are almost certainly a product of micro-interactional context, since RC, the Hills, the interviewer, and several local men are, in fact, sharing a liter or two of *pulque*, a mildly alcoholic drink distilled from the juice of agaves. Second, of the 51 cases of interactional-world evaluation containing self-reference, 20 occur in his two narratives, about meeting out-siders and having to speak Spanish. Third, of the five cases of self-reference as an impersonal in the Mexicano sample, four occur in RC's usage (the fifth is in (8) above); impersonal self-reference appears 13 times in the Polanyi texts.

The most notable feature of RC's IWE usage is his reference to his own intellectual attitude toward his narrative material. He uses "I remember" twice and "I don't know" once to introduce background material; these are the only instances of such usage in the Mexicano narratives (contrasted to five cases of "I remember" in "Fainting on the Subway," and 16 additional cases with " I know, mean, guess, think" in other the Polanyi narratives.) The only other example of "I don't know" in the Mexicano sample does not mark an intellectual stance toward narrative material, as do RC's usages. Instead, it appears in a sort of aside at the beginning of AT's first narrative, about the time when he was arrested in town even though he had been no more than an innocent bystander in a fight. He remarks:

(9)   Huăn con ser ămo nicmah nihuinti. "And it's a fact that I don't even know how to get drunk."

(One further apparent "intellectual attitude" IWE expression appears in GA's usage, and is discussed below.)

While we should not put too much weight on the usage of a single speaker, it is worth speculating about the possible sources of RC's unusual style. RC has shown up in other studies (e.g. Hill and Hill 1978, 1981, 1986) as an especially extreme case of a "narrow-honorific" speaker, one who makes minimal use of the complex Mexicano honorific system in third-person usage, where "broad-honorific" speakers make complex distinctions. We have a substantial sample of RC's usage, and he simply does not use third-person honorifics except when he is talking about God. Especially notable was his usage in reference to the death of his own mother; he used the verb ŏmic "she died," instead of the respectful ŏmomiquilih (a reflexive form, sometimes suffixed with honorifics) preferred by most Mexicano speakers in referring to the death of any human being, let alone a senior kinsperson.

RC is a factory worker, an economic situation that is highly correlated with narrow-honorific style. We have proposed that through narrow-honorific usage people whose central commitment is to the wage labor market and to individual advancement try to assert that they are full members in their communities. Narrow-honorific usage, which is "egalitarian" in the sense that it does not make traditional fine-grained rank distinctions among third-persons, challenges the traditional hierarchy that men ascend through community service. Factory workers lack time for community service, so their communitarian commitment may be in doubt. This is especially the case since, with their cash wages, they are perceived as being wealthier than cultivators. They are also more "exposed" to the outside world, spending more time in it, so that their "insider" status is not precisely delineated. I speculate that RC is sufficiently exposed to the capitalist market-place that he has in fact begun to develop a sort of individualism, which is showing up in his IWE self-reference usage. That this "egocentric" style occurs together with a coding strategy that manifests "egalitarianism" is quite interesting, and shows the complexity of intersecting coding phenomena that must be untangled.

MPP, aged 56, has equal numbers for self-reference in IWE and constructed dialogue. MPP is very wealthy by local standards, owner of a fine house and a tractor, and a leader in the civil government of his community. In spite of his wealth, he lives in a rather traditional way; his household sleeps on *petates,* straw mats, not on modern beds with mattresses, and his beautiful (and much younger) wife spoke no Spanish when we first knew her. His story is about an illness that he and his doctors traced to too much *copa,* "hard liquor." The story emphasizes how many doctors MP saw and how much money he spent on his cure. It is not appropriate in these communities to boast about one's wealth; the self-reference in IWE occurs in a passage in which he justifies this display of his wealth in terms of the community norms of sacrifice for others:[8]

148

(10)   Siquiera in novida, ma, ma nicsalvarō, huān siquiera in novida, ma, ma
         ye contento. Que orita, que gracias a Dios orita niquincāhtehua in
         nofamiliahhuān, ihquĭn tlayoatoc, huān āmo tlen cmatih, non tlenōn
         [mhm]. Bueno, neh āmo nēchtlacōltia in tlālticpac, nēchtlacōltiah in
         nopilhuān [mhm]. ¿Qué es más grande? "As for my life, let, let me save
         it, and as for my life, let it be happy. For now, thanks be to god I
         would have left my family thus in darkness, and they don't know any-
         thing about that. Well, as for me I don't regret earthly things, I am
         concerned for my children. What is more important?"

         Two speakers, GA and SP, exhibit high rates of IWE, but very low self-
reference in this context. GA, with the second-highest frequency of interactional-world evaluation, is a prominent elder in his community, who happened
to be a compadre (ritual kinsman) of the interviewer, a 16-year-old youth. He
uses one self-reference to intellectual attitude. This occurs when, in trying
to remember when the incident he recounts happened, he begins his narrative
with an attempt to place the exact date, opening with *ticadivinaroah* "we
infer." The "we" is used even though the interviewer would have been a little
child at the time of the events narrated, 11 years before. GA continues to be
concerned with the exact time with two IWE T-units, *Pos, nēci...* "Well, it
seems..." He addresses the interviewer twice during the narrative as *compadrito*. Nine of the T-units of IWE occur when he pulls up his trouser leg and
invites the interviewer to feel the bump on his shin where his leg was broken
in an accident; these include a combination of instructions to the interviewer
(*ma cmottil nĭn* "see this"; *ma cmomachililĭ* "feel this"), and third-person
references to the topography of his shin. GA manifests a type of usage that
we have elsewhere seen ritual kin display for one another, which seems to
require close attention to the interlocutor's presence.
         SP, over the objections of his current companion, tells about how his
first wife left him, taking his fortune with her. The IWE in his heavily-
evaluated narrative includes only one first-person reference, in a rhetorical
question addressing the situation of being alone with his father, without a
woman to cook:

(11)   Āquin tēchmocuitlahuĭz? "Who would take care of us?"

         Table IV shows that the female speakers in this small sample are con-
centrated in the lower part of the table, with very little IWE of any type.
Since the interviewer was a male, even though he was very young, we must
consider the possibility that the very low frequency of usage of IWE by these
speakers occurs because of a difference in solidarity and hence appropriateness of involvement in opposite-sex dyads, compared to same-sex dyads. However, the distribution could equally occur because women feel themselves to
be less autonomous of others than do men, and have far less contact with the
world outside their communities; while women trade in regional markets, none
of these women had ever worked for wages.
         Mexicano IWE is made up mainly of relatively few usage types. Ref-
erence to intellectual attitude toward narrative material is very rare in
Mexicano IWE, while it is extremely common in Euro-American usage. Rhetorical
questions are very common and are a preferred site for self-reference in IWE;
11 instances occur in the sample. These are illustrated by the "Why would I

lie to you?" type illustrated in (3) above, in the expression *¿Qué es más grande?* "What is more important?" that concludes MPP's speech in (10), and in SP's question in (11). Another example is given in (12). RS tells how she asked to be permitted to go to school as a child, but her father wouldn't let her go. I give the full context:

(12) Quihtoa, "Āmo, āmo cah āquin quinpiāz in ichcameh. In tlā tnequi tiāz
in escuela, xiquinhuica in ichcameh, ōmpa ma quicuacan plátano
yehuatl." [mm]
Pos āmo ōniah, porque ōnicrespetaroh in nopapacito.
Pos quen niāz in āmo nēch-, in āmo nēchcāhua in nopapá? [Amo cah.]
"He says, "No, there's nobody to take care of the sheep. If you want
to go to school, take the sheep, let them eat banana peels there."
Well I didn't go, because I respected my father.
Well how would I go, when my father doesn't permit me? [It's impossi-
ble].

Note that the interviewer's reply to the question shows clearly that it is part of the interactional world.

In a second preferred site for pronominal self-reference, the speaker's current condition is traced to, or contrasted with, events in the past, as in (8) above. Such instances are always found in "codas" at the end of narratives or sub-narratives. Another example of this type is found in the humorous coda in (13), where an old man observes that he is perfectly healthy now, even though his relatives had been so convinced that he was dying that they bought clothes for him to be buried in:

(13) Hasta in notecachuān ōmpa cateh hasta orita, h-h-h-h. Nēchiliah quil
ma niquimaquitih, uh! Tēpīnāhtih. Niquimpia occēqui tecactin, huān yeh
zan de ichtli [mm], toz hasta āxān ōmpa pilcatoqueh. [General laugh-
ter]. "My shoes are still there to this day, h-h-h-h. They tell me that
I should wear them, uh! I have other shoes, and they're just hemp fiber
[mm], so they're just still hanging over there."

RC's exit-talk, where he uses several instances of "we," also exemplifies this type, since it contrasts the ease with which he speaks Spanish today, compared to the old days in which so few Spanish speakers visited his community that he felt very awkward when he had to speak it.

Examination of the differential frequency of self-reference in IWE compared to total IWE in Table III shows that, while in Mexicano less than 50% of all IWE T-units contain self-reference, in the Polanyi sample at least 50% must contain self-reference (recall that a single T-unit can contain more than one pronominal self-reference). The difference in "tone" between Mexicano and middle-class Euro-American IWE is, however, much more biased toward self-reference in the latter than these numbers reveal, since so much IWE in the Polanyi sample is made up of that shibboleth of grammarians, compulsive "you know." The Polanyi sample includes 22 instances of "you know," 24% of the total IWE sample.

Schiffrin (1987) finds replies to "you know" when it accompanies a direct question to the interlocutor, so she argues that when "you know" appears in other contexts, as a sort of focus marker, it also addresses the hearer. "Y'know," concludes Schiffrin, "displays the speaker as one whose role as information provider is contingent on hearer reception" (Schiffrin 1987:295). In a sense, then, one of the jobs of "you know" in English is to construct the interlocutor's role as audience.

While Schiffrin has shown that "you know" can receive a reply, no instances of replies to it appear in the Polanyi materials (although it appears several times at turn transitions). Schiffrin, while she discusses the difficulty of assigning social characteristics to speakers, describes her sample as living in a "lower middle class urban area" (Schiffrin 1987:45). It may be that the frequency of replies to "you know" reflects a class differ-ence between these speakers and those in the Polanyi sample. Similar Mexicano usages are very likely to be followed by a reply: of 13 cases of usages that translate "you see?", "you know?", "you understand?", 7 received direct replies from the interviewer, as in (14), from SP's story. He is recounting the time when his first wife abandoned him and stole all his money; upon concluding his first sub-narrative, he has the following exchange with the young interviewer:

(14) Ye tmati? "Do you know/understand?"
      [Mhm, quēmah. "Mhm, yes."]
      Bueno. "Good."

Tags like "Right?" appear in both samples. Mexicano speakers use tags at relatively low frequency in personal narrative, but their function seems to be quite similar to that of Euro-American tags. The most common is *¿verdad?* "right?" Like *ye tmatih?*, this often seems to require an answer, which will be greeted with *ándale* "there you go."

In summary, Mexicano speakers and Euro-American English speakers prefer different strategies for the creation of conversational involvement. A general Mexicano preference for constructed dialogue is even more striking when self-reference is considered; in contrast, middle-class Euro-Americans use far more IWE, and prefer to make self-reference within it.

5. DISCUSSION. In light of these data, I propose that, while both constructed dialogue and interactional-world evaluation create "involvement," they reflect distinct underlying ethnopsychological understandings about the relationship of self to other. We might argue that this occurs because the two strategies are inherently distinct in their semiotic potential. Constructed dialogue seems to take very seriously the preexistence of a social order, while interaction-al-world evaluation makes visible the creation of that order.

Students of constructed dialogue have universally noted that what is represented is a sort of ideal, trimmed of the disfluencies and infelicities of actual talk. Unlike ordinary talk, which is often trivial, constructed dia-logue appears only at moments of high narrative significance, both in terms of thematic content and plot dynamic. Urban (1986) pointed out the signifi-cance for cultural semiotics of pronominal reference in constructed dialogue, where the anaphoric trace of referential-indexical "I" is projected onto a world line that represents memory and the continuity of the social order. Ur-ban finds this use of "I" to be central to the project of self construction. Such "anaphoric" and "dequotative" instances of "I" will occur at moments of heightened plot tension (Longacre 1976); Urban finds that they often index a breakthrough into "performance" and heightened audience involvement as an "icon" of reality is constructed. But the world-line on which the iconicity is constructed is deeply embedded, two world-lines removed from, and barely accessible to, the interactional world in which the discourse takes place.

In Mexicano personal-experience narrative, constructed dialogue contains as high frequencies of self-reference with "you" as it contains "I" in reference to the self and to the other. The concern is thus not only to connect an "I" with previous "I's" and with the "I's" that stand for other people, but to connect the "I" with the "you" that is constructed by the other.

Mexicano attention to constructed dialogue, in contrast to their low level of IWE usage, can be examined in terms proposed by Roy Wagner (1981). Mexicano speakers seem to vigorously "do" the self, the center of morality and appropriate behavior, while "being" in a social order that is "discovered"; seemingly trivial conversational contributions such as greetings, which index this order (Mexicano greetings specifically index the community hierarchy through honorific markers), are thus an important part of Mexicano constructed dialogue. The semantic content of these narratives reveals such a "discovered" social order. A narrator suffers because of some deed which would clearly lead to misfortune. He washes his blanket at the direction of a prison guard and spends the whole night shivering when it does not dry, sets rebar in a hailstorm and catches the flu, starves by the stove in his house because his wife, who cooks, has left him. A woman trembles in terror unto death because a witch has buried bones of the dead in her garden. These actions are represented "presentatively," as self-evident, and not requiring explanation, reflection or negotiation.

Interactional-world evaluation is of quite a different order. While IWE, like constructed dialogue, appears at moments of heightened thematic and plot relevance, it is entirely located in the immediate interactional context. Interestingly, interlocutors seldom raise questions about either type--they seem to be both, in their context, "indexical" (the semiotic mechanics of this require investigation). In IWE self-reference, what is indexed is the validity of the speaker's immediate presence in the participant structure of the interaction and her intellectual or emotional relationship to the memory constituted through explicit narrative reference, not the indexical connection of the speaker to memory and cultural continuity constructed through self-reference in constructed dialogue. In middle-class Euro-American usage, the "valid presence" of the speaker has as its center the manifestation of "mind" (D'Andrade (1987)), shown through compulsive attention of speakers to guessing, thinking, meaning, and knowing. Again, borrowing from Wagner, Euro-American narrators seem to be taking themselves "absolutely seriously," "being" selves, a taken-for-granted "tool" that can establish through reflection "what really happened" in the negotiation of events that are not taken for granted. In contrast, they "do" society in compulsive on-line negotiation in the interactional world. "You know" usage where interlocutors do not reply may manifest an appeal to the "knowledge" of audiences that is itself presentative, so that no reply is needed, in contrast to the full and formal answers Mexicano audiences give to rhetorical and "you know" questions.

An analogy, from another kind of self-representational moment, may help to capture the point. Ethnographers are expected to compile a photographic record of what goes on in their study area. In order to do this in Mexicano communities, the Hill family had to acquire a zoom lens so expensive that we are nervous about having it in the field. For as soon as Mexicano people become aware that they are being photographed, they drop what they are doing, stand up very straight, and form an unsmiling line. We reveal our own ethnocentric conception of human being through our judgement that the "natural" is thereby lost (they, of course, feel themselves at their most human in a line in front of the family altar, where life's most significant relationships are consummated). Mexicano narratives of personal experience have a similar quality. They are delivered with high formality and few offers to negotiate, and the audience is taken for granted. Listeners attend with signal respect, and seldom interrupt with question and challenge.

In contrast, middle-class Euro-Americans like to be photographed "doing" social interaction--barbecuing, picnicking, schmoozing at a reception. That most characteristic artifact of Euro-American anthropological (and other professional) life, a photograph of two or three worthies, drinks in hand, chatting it up at the annual meeting, is perhaps the photographic analogy to the Polanyi personal experience narratives. Middle-class Euro-American narrators are constantly "creating" an audience, which in turn compulsively "creates" itself through very active verbal engagement in the negotiation of "what happened."

RC, the Mexicano narrator who is most like a Euro-American, is also the person in my sample who is most involved in the capitalist marketplace. I am convinced (along with many other people) that there is a connection, that such involvement creates "individuals," fundamentally altering the self-other relationship. If my speculations about RC are correct, this occurs in spite of what must be the foundations of his cultural knowledge about the nature of persons, since, as he notes, he grew up in a Mexicano-speaking community and remembers that the first time he ever spoke Spanish, he was twelve years old. The existence of speakers like RC suggests that "culture," whatever it may be (presumably it is a manifestation with some permanence), is not the locus of sociocentric vs. egocentric understandings of persons. There is some evidence that among Euro-americans, narrative style is associated with class; Labov (1972) pointed out the tendency of middle-class narrators to use "external" evaluation, in contrast to the "internal evaluation" techniques used by working-class speakers.[9] "Class" is probably not a sufficiently well-conceptualized variable either; in fact Tannen (personal communication) states that she would consider the narrator of "Fainting on the Subway," a narrative in the Polanyi sample that she collected, to be "working class." It may be that what is at issue is something like the sort of network variables that have recently been proposed by Milroy (1980) and Eckert (1988). I hypothesize that emphasis on constructed dialogue vs. interactional-world evaluation will be distributed cross-culturally in accordance with some complex continuum of combinations of political economic, cultural, and social-organizational properties of speakers.

This is a speculative paper, with far-reaching proposals built on rather slender foundations. But the results, albeit tentative, suggest some important points. First, "culture" may be oversimplified as a locus to which self-concept differences should be referred. Second, socio-cultural anthropologists might profit from close attention to language use, which can index forms of social differentiation between people within communities that are otherwise too subtle to distinguish. Third, linguistic discourse analysts should attend to the precise characterization of the sociocultural and interactional contexts in which they gather their materials, in spite of the dangers of reification thereby presented.[10] Finally, the current "practice theory," interactionalist, social-constructionist orientation of much linguistic anthropology may be as deeply ideological as the "structuralism" that preceded it. As Ortner (1984) pointed out, such theory is traced to the work of Weber, analyst par excellence of the European bourgeois tradition that our lives inherit and develop. This is not to say that Mexicano structuration is not "practice," since in its realm it is as much "invention" in Wagner's (1981) sense as what is accomplished by Euro-Americans. It is, however, important to note that practice theory is peculiarly appropriate for theoreticians who may conduct conversational narrative, an important moment of cultural reproduction, self-consciously "on line."

NOTES

1. Most of the field data discussed in the present paper was collected with funding from the National Endowment for the Humanities, the American Philosophical Society, the American Council of Learned Societies, and sabbatical leave funding from Wayne State University.

2. For this count, the following elements count as T-units:
A sentence including a main verb and its arguments, including sentential complements. Clauses with "if" and "when" are counted as complements, while clauses with "because" are counted as separate T-units. For constructed dialogue, the first sentence is counted as a single T-unit with the locutionary verb; succeeding sentences, if present, are counted separately. For English, sentence-initial "you know" and "I mean" are counted with the sentence; "you know" following a sentence is counted separately. The discourse particles "Well," "Yeah," and "See" are counted separately, as are tags like "right?". Invocations such as "God" are counted separately. "Yes" and "No" are counted separately, as is "Mm."
For Mexicano, the discourse particles *pos* "well" and *bueno* "OK, well," and *vaya* "I mean" (initial--this one is rare in these texts, and can't be easily distinguished from the final one, which means roughly "right" are counted separately, as is the tag *¿verdad?* Sentence final instances of negatives *amo*, *aic* are counted separately. Sentence-final repetitions of words or expressions are counted separately even if there is no verb included. An example is seen in (15):

(15) Huān occē nicān īpan noma nīn señas, todavía. Señas. "And again here on my hand there are these scars, still. Scars."

One example of this type in the English materials is counted similarly.
Finally, terms of address such as *compadrito, hija,* and *papa* are counted separately in the Mexicano texts, as are addresses by names in the English texts.

3. The stories include "Eating on the New York Thruway" (lines 32–87), "The Robbery" (entire text), "Kate's Triumph" (including only Kate's part of the sections, "The Interlude," "The Walk," and "Hospital Hierarchy," and "Fainting on the Subway." In "The Robbery" the contributions of both Nancy and Susan are counted; this seems to be an inseparably dialogic performance. In "Eating

on the New York Thruway" only Carol's contribution is counted. In the Mexi-cano stories, the contributions of listeners are minor, and are not counted.

4. There is, of course, a minority counter-current in middle-class Euro-American thought, that one should live a life of public service, and of course many people claim adherence to religions that give sacred beings a prominent role in the shaping of human destiny. But material reflecting such beliefs does not appear in the stories in the Polanyi sample.

5. Mexicano permits no "empty categories;" all verbs are marked for person. In order to avoid a substantial bias, tenseless verbs in the English sample are counted as if they had a pronominal argument. For instance, "I wanted to come" would be counted as "I wanted to I come," parallel to Mexicano *nicnequi nihuāllāz* "I want it I will come." This is a somewhat ad hoc solution, since there are other grammatical differences between the two languages, but this is the only one that would massively affect the frequency of self-reference if I did not somehow compensate for it.

6. As Goffman (1974, 1979) pointed out, the use of "I" (or of any other type of pronominal self-reference) can index several types of participant roles. This "lamination" of personal reference is to some degree accounted for in the distribution of pronominal self-reference across the world lines of the interactional world, the story world, and constructed dialogue.

7. Mexicano speakers use far more repetition than do the speakers in the Polanyi sample. Repeated clauses are often in the perfective aspect, like event-line clauses, but I take repetition to be "evaluative." Thus, in the following example, the first instance of the verb *ōnēchquīxtilih* "she took from me" is in an event-line T-unit, while the second is counted as a T-unit in story-world evaluation.

(16)   Ōnēchquīxtilih cuatro mil pesos [mm], nahui mil peso ōnēchquīxtilih. [Aah]. "She took from me four thousand pesos, four thousand pesos she took from me."

8. This passage immediately follows a passage of constructed dialogue in MPP's voice, where he tells his doctor that he will pay him any amount, if only he will cure him. It is possible that the first line of what I have taken to be IWE, up to the word *contento*, is in fact in constructed dialogue; I do not adequately control the contextualization cues that would permit clear differentiation (and of course we can expect ambiguity).

9. In discussion following presentation of the present paper, Labov noted that he did not think that "culture" was at issue, since the Mexicano narrators reminded him of working-class American English speakers.

10. Hymes (1974) pointed out the problems with the refusal by ethno-methodological conversational analysts to locate their speakers, even roughly, in some sociocultural realm. As phenomenologists, they of course argue that all such realms are constructed within the interactional context, and refuse on principle to (in their view) hypostatize "sociocultural" variables.

155

BIBLIOGRAPHY

3391

Chafe, Wallace A. 1980. "The deployment of consciousness in the production of a narrative." In *The Pear Stories*. Norwood, NJ: Ablex Publishing Corporation.
D'Andrade, Roy. 1987. "A folk model of the mind." In D. Holland and N. Quinn (eds.) *Cultural Models in Language and Thought*. New York: Cambridge University Press.
Eckert, Penelope. 1988. "Adolescent social structure and the spread of linguistic change." *Language in Society* 17:183-207.
Goffman, Erving. 1974. *Frame Analysis*. New York: Harper and Row.
-----. 1979. "Footing." *Semiotica* 25:1-29.
Hill, Jane H. 1988a. "Language, genuine and spurious." In P. V. Kroskrity (ed.) *On the Ethnography of Communication: The Legacy of Sapir. Essays in Honor of Harry Hoijer, 1984 (Other Realities 8)*. Los Angeles: UCLA Department of Anthropology.
-----. 1988b. "The voices of Don Gabriel." To appear in B. Mannheim and D. Tedlock (eds.) *Dialogical Anthropology*. Philadelphia: University of Pennsylvania Press.
-----. 1980. "Mixed grammar, purist grammar, and language attitudes in modern Nahuatl." *Language in Society* 9:321-348.
-----. 1986. *Speaking Mexicano*. Tucson: University of Arizona Press.
----- and Kenneth C. Hill. 1978. "Honorific usage in modern Nahuatl: The expression of social distance and respect in the Nahuatl of the Malinche Volcano area. *Language* 54:123-155.
Hill, Kenneth C. 1985. "Las penurias de Doña María." *Tlalocan* 10:33-115.
Hymes, Dell H. 1974. *Foundations of Sociolinguistics*. Philadelphia: University of Pennsylvania Press.
Labov, William. 1972. "The transformation of experience in narrative syntax." In *Language in the Inner City*. Philadelphia: University of Pennsylvania Press.
----- and Joshua Waletzky. 1967. "Narrative analysis." In J. Helm (ed.) *Essays on the Verbal and Visual Arts*. Seattle: University of Washington Press.
Larson, Mildred. 1978. *The Functions of Reported Speech in Discourse*. Dallas: Summer Institute of Linguistics.
Longacre, Robert E. 1976. *An Anatomy of Speech Notions*. Lisse: The Peter de Ridder Press.
Lutz, Catherine A. 1988. *Unnatural Emotions*. Chicago: The University of Chicago Press.
Milroy, Leslie. 1980. *Language and Social Networks*. Oxford: Basil Blackwell.
Nutini, Hugo G. 1988. *Todos Santos in Rural Tlaxcala*. Princeton: Princeton University Press.
Ortner, Sherry. 1984. "Theory in anthropology since the Sixties." *Comparative Studies in Society and History* 26:126-166.
Polanyi, Livia. 1989. *Telling the American Story*. Cambridge, MA: The MIT Press.
Schiffrin, Deborah. 1987. *Discourse Markers*. New York: Cambridge University Press.
Shweder, Richard A. and Edmund J. Bourne. 1984. "Does the concept of the person vary cross-culturally?" In R. A. Shweder and R. A. Levine (eds.) *Culture Theory*. New York: Cambridge University Press.

Tannen, Deborah. 1988. "Hearing voices in conversation, fiction, and mixed genres." In D. Tannen (ed.) *Linguistics in Context* (*Advances in Discourse Processes* XXIX, R. A. Freedle, ed.). Norwood, NJ: Ablex Publishing Corporation.

Urban, Greg. 1986. "The I of discourse." Paper presented at the 85th Annual Meeting of the American Anthropological Association, Philadelphia, PA.

Wagner, Roy. 1981. *The Invention of Culture.* Chicago: University of Chicago Press.

OME MORPHOSYNTACTIC ASPECTS OF FRENCH/ENGLISH-BANTU CODE-MIXING:
Evidence for Universal Constraints

Nkonko Mudipanu Kamwangamalu
University of Illinois at Urbana-Champaign

1. Introduction

Syntactic studies of code-mixing (CM) in the past ten years have been concerned mostly with two basic issues: (1) Explaining whether CM is random or rule-governed; and (2) determining whether there exist universal constraints on CM. In response to the first issue a number of constraints have been proposed which show that CM is rule-governed (e.g. Timm 1975, Pfaff 1976, Poplack 1978, Nartey 1982, Kachru 1983). However, due in part to the paucity of cross-linguistic studies, no significant generalizations have been made yet regarding the issue of universal constraints (Goke-Pariola 1983, Bentahila and Davies 1983, Berk-Seligson 1986, Clyne 1987, Bokamba 1988, Vallduvi 1988).

In this paper I present preliminary results of an on-going cross-linguistic study of CM, with a focus on the issue of universal constraints. I shall discuss this issue in light of data on CM in French/English with selected Bantu languages, e.g. Ciluba, Lingala, and Swahili. Based on these data, I argue that bilingual CM, at least in the African context, is almost exclusively governed by the morphosyntactic structure rules of the African language that is code-mixed with French or English. This I shall call the 'Matrix Code Principle.' In essense, the Matrix Code Principle says that in every code-mixed discourse (D) involving language 1 (L1) and language 2 (L2), where L1 is identified as the matrix code (i.e. host code) and L2 as the embedded code (i.e. guest code), the grammar of L2 must conform to the morphosyntactic structure rules of L1, the language of the discourse.

The evidence for the Matrix Code Principle comes from four sources. The first is the omission of the French article before French nouns used in French-Bantu CM. I shall demonstrate that this is dictated by the syntactic structure of Bantu languages. Second, I shall show that in French/English-Bantu CM French/English adjectives are postposed rather than preposed to the noun they modify, as is required in Bantu languages. Third, I shall present data which indicate that French/English infinitive verbs used in French/English-Bantu CM undergo 're-infinitivization', a process whereby they take on a Bantu infinitive marker so as to fit Bantu verbal morphology. Finally, I shall discuss data on tense/aspect marking in the code-mixed variety under consideration, the French/English-Bantu variety. I show that French/English verbs used in this variety are inflected with Bantu rather than French/English inflectional morphology. I argue that this also follows from the Matrix Code Principle.

In earlier studies of the syntactic aspects of CM (e.g. Joshi 1984, Klavans 1983), the matrix code seems to be defined strictly in terms of the linguistic structures of the languages that are code-mixed. In this paper, however, I argue that in addition to linguistic structure the matrix code can also be determined by the sociolinguistic context in which the process of mixing takes place. For CM involving African languages and European languages such as French and English, for example, it is not surprising that the European language is usually the guest/embedded code, while the African language is the host/matrix code. I claim that this has to do with the fact that for some reasons, such as prestige associated with European languages, bilingual Africans tend to use words from European languages when they speak an African language, whereas the reverse, though not impossible, is not a common trend. What this claim means is that context is as important as linguistic structure in determining the matrix code. Following Klavans (1983), this study assumes that each code-mixed sentence has a matrix code and that CM is asymmetrical. That is, constraints on CM hold depending on whether mixing in a given discourse is from code A to code B, or from code B to code A.

2.0 Current issues on the syntax of CM

Some of the issues that recur in most studies of syntactic aspects of CM include the following, among others: (1) Is there a difference between CM and other language contact phenomena such as code-switching and borrowing? (2) Is CM predictable? (3) Is there a grammar from which CM is generated? (4) Are there constraints on CM? And if there are, are these constraints language-specific or language-universal? In the discussion that follows I shall present a review of the basic assumptions that have been made in the literature regarding these issues.

2.1 Defining code-mixing, code-switching, and borrowing

Code-mixing (CM), code-switching (CS) and borrowing are often lumped together, though I shall argue that they are different from one another in many respects. For example, Di Pietro (1977:1) defines CS, *and this is supposed to include CM*, as the use of more than one language by communicants in the execution of a speech act (emphasis added). Hartular (1982:1) rejects this definition on the grounds that it is too restricted. She argues that the term 'code-switching' may also be used to refer to the switching of, say, dialects, registers or styles within language. But even in her own study, Hartular does not seem to distinguish code-switching from code-mixing. One notes that many of the examples of English-Romanian mixing she refers to as code-switching are rather cases of code-mixing (e.g. am avut eu apartment la upstairs si u room..'we had an apartment upstairs and a room..' (Hartular 1982:2).

Baker (1980:1) has also observed that there is confusion in the overlapping terminologies employed to describe the phenomena under consideration, especially with respect to Hispanic communities in the United States. However, recent studies have shed considerable light on this topic (e.g. Sridhar and Sridhar 1980, Kachru 1983, Bentahilla and Davies 1983, Ewing 1984, to list a few). These studies have shown that structurally, for example, in code-mixing the alternation of linguistic units (e.g. words, phrases) is intrasentential, while in code-switching the alternation is intersentential. On the other hand, borrowing involves integration of the linguistic unit borrowed from one language into the grammatical system of the borrowing language (Kachru 1983). This, however, is not the case with the other two language contact phenomena discussed above, code-switching and code-mixing. Finally, borrowing can occur in the speech of both monolinguals and bilinguals, while code-mixing and code-switching are uniquely a product of bilingual competence.

2.2 Predictability/Unpredictability of a code-mix

Some investigators (e.g. Beardsley and Eastman 1978) have suggested that CM is predictable, while others (e.g. Hatch 1976, Goke-Pariolla 1983) argue that it is not. Beardsley and Eastman (1978) suggest that CM is triggered by discourse markers such as pause, interjection, false start, etc. Similarly, Clyne (1987) proposes the notion of triggering, where an item of ambiguous affiliation (that is, one belonging to the speaker's two systems) triggers off a switch from one language to another. Like Eastman and Beardsley, Clyne (1987) maintains also that the trigger word (in German-English CM) is frequently preceded by a hesitation or a pause, where an attempt is made to find a standard L1 word for an English transfer.

2.3 Code-mixing/bilingual's grammar

The fact that bilinguals can alternate codes in a given speech event has led CM investigators to postulate that there exists a CM grammar, or what has come to be known as the 'bilingual's grammar' (e.g. Poplack and Sankoff 1980, Joshi 1984). The assumption in these studies is that the linguistic repertoire of a bilingual includes three separate underlying linguistic systems, two monolingual grammars plus the grammar from which CM is generated, the CM/bilingual's grammar. For some (e.g. Lance 1975, Lipski 1978, Sridhar and Sridhar 1980), this assumption is based on factors such as bilingual's judgments of grammaticality/acceptability of various types of mixed elements, normalization of mixed sentences in repetition tasks, and self-corrections in spontaneous speech. This assumption is rejected by Pfaff 1979, Klavans 1983, for example and others, who argue that elicitation techniques such as acceptability and sentence repetition tasks often represent stereotypes about verbal behavior rather than reflecting the behavior itself.

For others (e.g. Poplack and Sankoff 1980), the assumption that there exists a CM grammar is based on Chomsky's definition of grammar as a system of rules that iterate to produce an infinite number of sentences. Building on this definition, Sankoff and Poplack (1980:10) argue that any finite sets of rules and procedures for generating an infinite set of sentences is a grammar, so that any set of rules for constructing the set of sentences containing code-switches is a grammar. In my view, however, it seems that when Chomsky speaks of grammar, he refers to an 'independent system' of rules that a speaker-hearer has internalized. The question, then, is whether the proposed CM grammar can be treated as an independent linguistic system. There is a growing body of literature which rejects the idea that in addition to his/her two monolingual grammars, the bilingual has a separate CM grammar (Pfaff 1979, Lederberg & Morales 1985, Berk-Seligson 1986, Bokamba 1988, Vallduvi 1988, Kamwangamalu, forthcoming).

3.0 On constraints on code-mixing

The question of whether there exist constraints on CM has been brought up several times in earlier studies of the syntactic aspects of CM (e.g. Lance 1975, Mkilifi 1978). While studies such as these suggested that CM is random, recent studies of the phenomenon have shown that CM is rule-governed (e.g. Timm 1975, Pfaff 1979). The literature on this topic suggests that two categories of constraints be distinguished: language-specific constraints on the one hand, and the proposed language-universal constraints on the other.

3.1 Language specific-constraints

Language-specific constraints include constraints that hold for CM in a given bilingual community. For example, An (1985) identified one such constraint which applies to Chinese-English CM: the Morpheme Constraint. According to An, in Chinese-English CM no code-mix is allowed at the morpheme level. This explains why in the Chinese-English variety one does not encounter code-mixes such as the Lingala-French ba-chances 'chances', ba-cahiers 'notebooks', nor the Navajo-English shi-pants 'my pants', shi-sisters 'my sisters' (Hatch 1976), where the prefix is Lingala/ Navajo, and the noun it is attached to French/English.

Along the same lines, Timm (1975) identified a number of language-specific constraints which apply to Spanish-English CM, including the Determiner Constraints and the Pronominal Subject-Verb constraint, to list just a few. Regarding the Determiner Constraint, for example, Timm (1975) suggests that in Spanish-English CM no code-mix is allowed within NPs containing one or more adjectives and a determiner. Therefore, the Determiner Constraint disallows phrases such as

(1) *su favorite lugar/ * His favorite lugar

because they each include a determiner and an adjective which are from two different languages, Spanish and English. But compare the sentences in (1) with the Spanish-English sentence in (2). According to Poplack (1978:175), the sentence in (2) shows that contrary to Timm's claim, in Spanish-English CM even a lone determiner can be code-mixed.

(2) Where are they, los (the) language things?

A similar language-specific constraint is proposed by Gumperz (1982:88): The Conjunction Constraint. This constraint says that the conjunction used in a Spanish-English sentence must be in the same code as the conjoined linguistic unit (phrase, clause, sentence). However, Poplack (1978:174) found that in Spanish-English CM the conjoining conjunction does not necessarily have to be in the same code as the conjoined clause. This view is corroborated by Timm (1978:242) for Russian-French CM, Bentahila and Davies (1983:310) for French-Arabic CM, and by Ewing (1984:52) for Polish-English CM.

3.2 The proposed language-universal constraints

The search for universals in CM seems to have been motivated by the commonly accepted fact that all languages are cut from the same pattern. This is the idea that although there may be differences among languages, linguists believe that there are things that are common to all languages of the world. Building on this idea, many studies of the syntax of CM have proposed implicitly or explicitly that there exist universal constraints on CM. Some such constraints are the Free Morpheme Constraint (Poplack 1978), the Bicodal Word Constraint (Wentz 1977), and the Equivalence Constraint (Pfaff 1979).

3.2.1 The Free Morpheme Constraint

This constraint stipulates that no switch is allowed between a bound morpheme and a lexical form unless the latter has been phonologically integrated into the language of the former (Poplack 1978:175). The Free Morpheme Constraint allows structures such as (3a), in which mixing can occur at any of the boundaries indicated by the slant line, but not at the structure in (3b), unless one of the morphemes, either the English eat or the Spanish -iendo, is integrated phonologically into the language of the other.

(3) [Spanish-English] (Poplack 1980:586)
    a. I/told him/that/ pa que la trajero ligero
       'I told him that so that he would bring it fast'
    b. *eat-iendo.

The Free Morpheme Constraint is corroborated in An 's (1985) study of Chinese-English CM. As pointed out earlier, Chinese-English code-mixes may occur at all linguistic levels, except the morpheme level. However, unlike Poplack (1978), An does not say whether there ought to be phonological adaptation for Chinese-English CM to be allowed at the morpheme level. In spite of the support it has received from CM involving languages such as Chinese and English, the Free Morpheme Constraint has not remained unchallenged. Several studies of CM in other bilingual communities around the world have presented data which cast doubt on the universality of the Free Morpheme Constraint, such as Nartey (1982:186) for Andanme-English CM, Bentahila & Davis (1983:315) for Arabic-French CM, Sridhar (1978:110) for Kannada-English CM, Berk-Seligson (1986:325) for Hebrew-Spanish CM, and Clyne (1987:752) for German-English CM.

3.2.2 The Bicodal Word Constraint

This constraint suggests that no word can exist in natural languages which contains morphemes from two codes identified as distinct by the speaker (Wentz 1977:237). The Bicodal Word Constraint would prevent words such as *eat-iendo, which are also disallowed by Poplack's Free Morpheme constraint. However, it would erroneously rule out code-mixed items such as the Navajo-English shi-pants 'my pants', the Lingala-French ba-cahiers 'notebooks', or the Kannada-English broadminded-u 'broadminded' (Sridhar 1978:110), all of which are considered as perfect code-mixes in their respective varieties. Thus the Bicodal Word Constraint appears to be too powerful to account for the morphological structure of CM because it rules out even those code-mixed patterns that are known to occur in code-mixed varieties worldwide.

3.2.3 The Equivalence Constraint

Stated in simple terms, the Equivalence constraint proposes that for a code-mixed sentence to be acceptable, no syntactic rule of either language involved in CM should be violated (Lipski 1978:258). Sridhar and Sridhar (1980) counter that the Equivalence Contraint is flawed because it does not specify the degree of correspondence that must obtain for two structures to be equivalent. In addition, quite a number of other studies, including Goke-Pariola (1983), Nartey (1982), Berk-Seligson (1986), have cast doubt on the universality of the Equivalence Constraint. For example, Berk-Seligson (1986:328) points out that one of the main pieces of evidence used to support the Equivalence Constraint has been the rarity of 'code-mixing errors', i.e. ungrammatical combinations of L1 and L2. However, she found that the speech of her Hebrew-Spanish informants was predominantly filled with violations of Spanish syntax, in total 186 violations. One such violation was the omission of the Spanish determiner, either the definite article (el, la) or the indefinite article (un, una) before a noun or noun phrase, as in (4). Both (4a) and (4b) demonstrate the absence of an indefinite Spanish article before a Hebrew noun.

(4) [Spanish-Hebrew] (Berk-Seligson 1986:328)
    a. Izitis taut
       'You made (a) mistake'
    b. Aki ay misrad abaso
       'Here is (an) office down below'

The review presented here shows that the proposed constraints seem not to be as universal as they have been claimed to be. What this means is that if there are universal constraints on CM, then such constraints are as yet to be determined. In the remainder of this paper I shall investigate the possibility of there being a general constraint, the Matrix Code Principle, which governs CM in African languages and European languages, and French/English-Bantu CM in particular. The claim I am defending is that bilingual CM, at least in the African context, is governed by the morphosyntactic structure rules of the African language (e.g. Ciluba, Lingala, Swahili) that is code-mixed with a European language, French, English, or others. The evidence for this claim comes from sources such as the omission of the French article in French-Bantu CM, the re-infinitivization of French/English verbs in accordance with Bantu morphology, the imposition of Bantu inflectional morphology on French/English verbs used in French/English-Bantu CM, and the ordering of elements in French/English adjectival phrases in conformity with Bantu rather than French/English word order.

4.0 The French/English-Bantu data

The data of this paper is drawn from CM in Swahili-English on the one hand, and from Ciluba/Lingala-French CM on the other. The Swahili-English data was collected from an article by Mkilifi (1978) on triglossia in Tanzania. A large body of similar data can also be found in Scotton 1982, who has done extensive investigations on Swahili-English CM in East Africa. The Ciluba/Lingala-French data was gathered from popular songs in Ciluba/Lingala, and from notes of CM in spontaneous conversations between Ciluba/Lingala-French bilinguals in the United States.

Like other European languages (e.g. Portuguese), French and English were introduced in Africa as a result of colonization. In Africa every European language is used as the official language of its former colonies. For example, French is the official language in Senegal, Gabon and in many other Central and West African countries. English is the official language in many East/ West African countries including Tanzania, Kenya/Nigeria, Liberia, to list a few. French and English also each function as the language of the media, instruction, government and administration, diplomacy, international business transactions, etc. It should be noted, however, that in Africa French and English are spoken by a minority of the population, viz. the elite group. Consequently, these languages have been forced to live in permanent contact with the native languages of their former colonies. One product of this contact is code-mixing. In the remaining sections of this paper I shall discuss the morphosyntactic characteristics of CM involving French/English with three Bantu languages, Ciluba, Lingala, and Swahili. The main objective of this discussion is to determine the morphosyntactic rules that govern this kind of code-mixing. Again, my working hypothesis is that French/English-Bantu CM is governed by the Matrix Code Principle, which says that for a code-mixed structure to be acceptable the morphosyntactic structure of the guest code must conform to the morphosyntactic structure rules of the host code. The evidence for this hypothesis is presented below. Note that although this hypothesis is based on data drawn from French/English-Bantu CM, one can easily find parallels in code-mixed varieties involving French/English with non-Bantu languages (e.g. Berk-Seligson 1986, Gibbons 1987, Vallduvi 1988).

4.1 Omission of the French article

One of the things that one notes in French-Bantu CM is that French nouns used in a Bantu-based code-mixed discourse are generally not accompanied by a determiner, though they would be if they were used in exclusively French sentences. Compare the Lingala-French code-mixed sentences in (5) with their French counterparts in (6).

> (5) Lingala-French
>   a. Kindumba ezali <u>punition</u> te
>   'prostitution is not punishment'

    b. *Kindumba ezali la punition te.
    c. Ezali probleme monene 'it a big problem'.
    d. *Ezali un probleme monene.

(6) French
    a. La prostitution n'est pas une punition.
    b. *La prostitution n'est pas punition
    c. C'est un grand probleme.
    d. *C'est grand probleme.

In (6a) and 6c) the noun punition and probleme are preceded by an article, une for the former and un for the latter. Otherwise, structures (6a) and (6c) would be unacceptable by French standards, as (6b) and (6d) show. By contrast, Lingala requires that the article be omitted before a French noun used in a Lingala-based sentence, as in (5a) and (5c). This is done to fit the grammar of Lingala, the matrix code. Similarly, if a French article is retained in a Lingala-French structure, as in (5b) and (5d), then the structure is unacceptable. The omission of the French article is observed in CM involving French with other Bantu languages, e.g. Ciluba, Kikongo, Swahili. It seems that the French article is omitted in French-Bantu CM because unlike French Bantu languages have no concept of article per se. In French the article is used to express gender and number, while in Bantu languages these notions are determined by the noun and the noun prefix, respectively. Also, it seems to be the case that from a Bantu speaker's point of view the article does not convey any extra information in addition to the information conveyed by the noun it accompanies. These conclusions accord well with the findings of Berk-Seligson (1986) about Hebrew-Spanish CM. Berk-Seligson (1986:328) notes that in her study 66 percent of violations of Spanish syntax consisted of the omission of the Spanish determiner, either the definite article (el, la) or the indefinte article (un, una) before a noun or noun phrase. She explains that the Spanish determiner is omitted in Hebrew-Spanish CM because in Hebrew the determiner does not exist as a grammatical category. That is, like Bantu languages, the meaning of the determiner in Hebrew is implicitly understood, but not overtly represented. In either case, whether Hebrew-Spanish or Bantu-French CM, it seems that the syntactic rules of the matrix code override the syntactic rules of the embedded code.

4.2 Word order in a French/Bantu adjectival phrase

In French, an adjective may precede or follow the noun it modifies depending on the adjective involved. For example, in (7) the adjective serieux 'serious' may precede the noun femme 'woman' as in (7b) or follow it as in (7a). In (8), however, the adjective grande 'big' can only precede the noun femme, as in (8a). English also follows the latter pattern. Thus postposing grande to femme would result in an unacceptable adjectival phrase, as (8b) and (8c) show.

(7) a. C'est une femme serieuse
    b. C'est une serieuse femme
    c. She is a serious woman.

(8) a. C'est une grande femme 'she is a big woman'
    b. *C'est une femme grande
    c. *She is a woman big

Note that while in French some adjectives may be preposed (7b) or postposed (7a) to the noun they modify, in English adjectives usually precede the noun (7c). Contrastively, in Bantu languages the adjective must always follow, not precede, the noun it modifies, as in (9). The adjectival phrases in (9) show that the adjective -nene 'big' follows the noun -tu 'person'.

(9) a. [Swahili] Mtu mnene
    b. [Ciluba] Muntu munene
    c. [Lingala] Moto monene
       'person big'

Now, consider the French-Lingala structures in (10). Like Lingala, the code-mixed structures in (10) show that in French-Bantu CM the adjective must also follow the noun it modifies.

(10) a. Zaire ezali mboka propre.
        'Zaire is a clean country'
     b. *Zaire ezali propre mboka.

In (10a) the adjective propre 'clean' follows the noun mboka 'country' in accordance with Bantu syntax, as predicted by the 'Matrix Code Principle'. If the adjective were made to precede the noun so as to fit French syntax, as in (10b), then the resulting structure would be unacceptable in French-Bantu CM. Similarly, if two adjectives, one French and the other Bantu occur in the same adjectival phrase, Bantu syntax requires that both adjectives follow the noun in conformity with the constituent structure of adjectival phrases in Bantu, and by extension, with the constituent structure of adjectival phrases in French/English-Bantu CM. The structure in (11) is illustrative. It shows that both the Lingala adjective monene 'big' and the French adjective revolutionnaire 'revolutionary' follow the noun pays 'country', as required by the Matrix Code Principle. What this means is that the order of constituents in a French/English-Bantu adjectival phrase must conform to Bantu syntax, regardless of whether the modified noun is Bantu or French/English.

(11) Zaire ezali pays   monene revolutionnaire
     Zaire is   country big   revolutionary
     'Zaire is a big revolutionary country'

4.3 Re-infinitivization
In Bantu languages infinitive verbs are marked by the presence of the infinitive prefix ko-/ku-, which must be attached to a verb stem, as in (12).

(12) a. [Ciluba] Ndi muswe ku-lamba.
           'I want to cook'
     b. [Lingala] Na-lingi ko-lamba
           'I want to cook'

As can be seen here, infinitive verbs in Bantu are marked the same way as in English. However, the difference between English and Bantu languages is that in English the infinitive marker, to, is a free morpheme, while the Bantu infinitive marker, ko-/ku-, is a bound morpheme. Unlike Bantu languages and English, French infinitive verbs are marked by a verb ending, which may be -re (e.g. vendre 'to sell'), -ir (e.g. servir 'to serve'), or -er (e.g. colorer 'to color').

Compare the structures in (12) with the code-mixed structures in (13). The structures in (13) show that French/English infinitive verbs used in French/English-Bantu CM keep their original form. However, they take on an additional infinitive marker, the Bantu infinitive prefix ko-/ku-, resulting in what I have termed 're-infinitivization'. French/English infinitive verbs are re-infinitivized, that is they take on an additional infinitive marker, ko-/ku-, so that they will conform to Bantu verbal morphology.

(13) a. [Ciluba-French] Tudi amu comme tu nous avais
   laisses, tu-essayer amu bwa ku-survivre.
   'We are as you left us (i.e. nothing has changed),
   doing the best we can to survive.'

   b. [Lingala-French] L'heure ya kala trois quarts ya
   ba-jeunes bazaka ko-comprendre l'avenir te,...
   'In the past three fourths of young men did not
   understand [i.e. care for] the future. (Mobutu SS.)

   c. [Swahili-English] Inakuwa maana yake they go against
   their own wishes ku-standardize...matatizo haya
   wameweze ku-ya-solve kwa kutumia dictionary mpia...
   'This is because they go against their own wishes to
   standardize...They can solve this problem by using
   the new dictionary.... (Mkilifi 1978:140).

The relevant items for our discussion include the Ciluba-French infinitive verb ku-survivre 'to survive', the Lingala-French ko-comprendre 'to understand', and the Swahili-English ku-standardize 'to standardize' and ku-ya-solve 'to solve it'. The question that is worth raising here is why the French/English infinitive verbs listed are each prefixed with the Bantu infinitive marker ko-/ku-. Earlier in this section it was pointed out that Bantu infinitive verbs are marked by the presence of the prefix ku-/ko-, which must be attached to a verb stem. Also, it was observed that according to the Matrix Code Principle, French/English items used in French/English-Bantu CM must conform to the morphosyntactic structure of Bantu languages. Thus for verbs such as the French survivre (13a), comprendre (13b) and the English standardize and solve (13c) to be considered as infinitive verbs in French/English-Bantu CM, they must be re-infinitivized, that is, they must be prefixed with the Bantu infinivitive marker ko-/ku-. A morphological consequence of the process of re-infinitivization is that French/English-Bantu CM is characterized by a double-marking of the infinitive, a feature which does not exist in either English/French or Bantu languages. This feature is found in all French/English-Bantu code-mixed varieties (e.g. Bokamba 1988), and it is also reported to occur in CM involving English or French with non-Bantu languages (e.g. Nartey 1982, Goke-Pariola 1983).

4.4 Bantu Tense/Aspect

The last characteristic of French/English-Bantu CM I would like to consider has to do with tense/aspect marking in Bantu languages. In Bantu languages tense is

166

expressed by the verb suffix. Depending on the language the suffix may precede or follow the verb stem. In Swahili and Ciluba, for example, the tense marker (TM) suffix precedes the verb stem (14), whereas in Lingala it follows it (15).

(14) a. [Swahili] a-   li-   u-   a
     b. [Ciluba] u-   aka-   ship-   a
                  Sbj   TM/past   Vstem   FV
                  'He killed'

(15) [Lingala]   a- bom- aki
                  Sbj-Stem-TM/past
                  'He killed'

Next, consider the data in (16). These data demonstrate that when a French/English verb is used in a French/English-Bantu sentence, it must be inflected with Bantu rather than French/English inflectional morphology.

(16) a. [Swahili-English] Ile accident ilitokea alipolose
        control na akaoverturn and landed into a ditch.
        'The accident occurred when he lost control and
        overturned and landed into...(Mkilifi 1978:141).

     b. [Ciluba-French] Ba-aka-rendr-angana visites ya
        bungi quand elle etait ici.
        'They visited each other a lot when she was here.'

The items of interest to this paper include those underlined in (16), viz. alipolose, akaoverturn (16a) and barendrangana (16b). First, I shall discuss the first two. In a-li-po-lose 'he lost', a- is a subject prefix, -li- is a past tense marker, -po- is a narrative temporal marker, and lose is an English verb. Similarly, in a-ka-overturn a- is a subject prefix, -ka- is also a past tense marker, and overturn is an English verb. The question that needs to be raised here is why the verbs lose and overturn are not inflected with the English past tense morpheme -ed, as they should be since alipolose and akaoverturn translate as 'he lost' and 'he overturned', respectively. The answer to this question can be found in the Matrix Code Principle, which requires that the grammar of the guest/embedded code conform to the grammar of the host/ matrix code. Thus the English verbs lose and overturn in (16a), for example, cannot take the past tense inflectional morpheme -ed not only because the tense information conveyed by -ed is already provided by the Swahili tense marker -ka-/-li-, but also because in this case and many similar others Swahili requires that English conform to Swahili morphosyntactic structure.

A similar argument also holds for the Ciluba-French phrase in (16b), viz. ba-rendr-angan-a (visites) 'they visited each other'. In ba-rendr-angan-a ba- is a plural prefix referring to the subject of the sentence, -angan- is a reciprocal suffix, and -a is a final vowel. Sandwiched between the prefix ba- and the reciprocal suffix -angan- is the French verb rendre 'return'. Note that as a result of this sandwiching the verb rendre has lost its ending, -e. Note also that if the verb rendre were used in an exclusively French sentence, it would have the present perfect form rendus, as in ils se sont rendus visites 'they visited each other'. But since rendre is used in a French-Bantu sentence it must, by the Matrix Code Principle, obey the inflectional morphology of the Bantu language involved, Ciluba.

The facts described here are not unique to Bantu languages. Similar cases can be found in other code-mixed varieties, though they have not yet been described in detail as I have done in this paper. For example, Vallduvi (1988:371) cites examples such as the Spanish-English in (17a), the Arabic-French in (17b), the Yiddish-English and English-Yiddish in (18) which show that the root of the verb is inflected with the host language inflectional morphology, much as we have seen for the French/English-Bantu data presented in (16) above.

(17) a. [Spanish-English] los hombres me TRUSTearon
                                              +tns
            'The men trusted me'

     b. [Arabic-French] Ana GUESS-t-h-a
                                 +tns+it
            'I guessed it'

(18) a. [Yiddish-English] er WATCHt   nor andere zoln arbeten
                          he   +tns only other Aux   to-work
            'but he only sees to other people working'

     b. [English-Yiddish] PATSHed 'slapped' (3sg pret)
            KHALISHed 'fainted' (3pl pret)

In (17a) the English verb TRUST is inflected with the Spanish tense affix earon, and the verb GUESS is inflected with the Arabic tense affix -t-. The data in (18) show that in Yiddish sentences English verbs take on Yiddish inflection, as in WATCHt (18a), while in English sentences Yiddish verbs show English inflection, as in PATSHed and KHALISHed (18b).

5. Conclusion

In this paper I have argued for the existence of a general constraint, the Matrix Code Principle, which governs French/English-Bantu CM. This constraint holds for the linguistic structures of the languages involved and for the context in which the process of mixing takes place. In essence, the Matrix Code Principle says that if a European language (e.g. French, English) is involved in CM with an African language, the former must conform to the morphosyntactic structure rules of the latter, the host language. Four pieces of evidence have been presented which support the Matrix Code Principle. One is that following Bantu rather than French syntactic structure a French article is omitted before a French noun used in French-Bantu CM. Second, I have shown that in accordance with Bantu syntax French/English adjectives used in French/English-Bantu variety are postposed rather than preposed to the noun they modify. Third, I have demonstrated that French/English verbs used in the variety under consideration are inflected with Bantu rather than French/English inflectional morphology, as required by the Matrix Code Principle. The final piece of evidence for the Matrix Code Principle is that in French/English-Bantu CM French/English infinitive verbs undergo 're-infinitivization', a process whereby they take on an additional infinitive marker so as to fit Bantu verbal morphology. I have shown that the principle advocated here seems not to be unique to Bantu languages. Further evidence for it can also be found in CM involving French/English with non-Bantu languages, as can be concluded from the work of, for example, Agheysi (1977) on CM in English with Nigerian languages, Annamalai (1978) on CM in English with Indian languages such as Tamil, Bentahila and Davies (1983) on Arabic-French CM, Gibbons (1987) on Cantonese-English CM in Hong Kong, Vallduvi (1988) on Yiddish-English CM, to list a few.

For example, Agheyisi (1977:107) notes that *at the grammatical level, rules of inflection governing the surface forms of English nouns and verbs used in CM involving English with Nigerian languages are typically frozen and superceded by those of Nigerian languages.* She concludes that *this prevalence of the rules of Nigerian languages over English explains why a code-mixed variety which involves English and a Nigerian language is usually perceived as a variety of the Nigerian language rather than of English.* Annamalai (1978:240) reached a similar conclusion about CM in English with Indian languages. He observes that *the mixed variety involving an Indian language with English is considered by the participants in the speech act as a variety of their mother tongue, and not as a variety of English.*

Along the same lines, Bentahila and Davies (1983) discuss morphosyntactic aspects of Arabic-French CM which provide support for the principle I have advocated in this paper, the Matrix Code Principle. For example, they point out that *in Arabic-French CM it is always the Arabic adjective or pronoun which is made to agree not with its French antecedent, as one would expect, but with the Arabic antecedent* (Bentahili & Davis 1983: 328). More importantly, the authors conclude that *this tendency to use forms which accord with the grammar of Arabic rather than French could perhaps also be thought to suggest that the Arabic rules are somehow more dominant.* As it turns out, this conclusion is corroborated by the principle proposed in this paper, the Matrix Code Principle.

Like the investigators referred to above, Gibbons (1987) also shows that the grammar of the guest code must conform to the grammar of the host code, much as I have suggested in this paper. Speaking of the use of single words in Cantonese-English CM, Gibbons (1987:59) notes that *on occasion one finds English verbs or adjectives which have been repeated and/or divided in conformity with Cantonese syntax,* i.e. in conformity with the syntax of the matrix code, Cantonese, emphasis added. Here, the phrase 'in conformity with' is of value in itself since it spells out which language dictates its rules over the other in a code-mixed variety such as Cantonese-English. Gibbons (1987:59) notes further that *in the great majority of cases where the fragment of English consists of two words or more, it retains English grammar internally, while not disrupting the surrounding Cantonese grammar: That is, the fragment of English is fitted into the overall Cantonese syntax at the same point as the equivalent Cantonese element.* Conclusions such as these as well as those presented above accord well with the principle suggested in this paper, the Matrix Code Principle. These conclusions, therefore, are a sign of good development in the search for universal constraints on CM. However, more cross-linguistic studies are needed before the principle advocated here can be generalizable to code-mixed varieties across cultures.

REFERENCES

AGHEYISI, R. 1977. Language interlarding in the speech of Nigerians. Language and linguistic problems in Africa, ed. by P.F.A. Kotey & H. Der-Houssikian. Columbia, S.C.: Hornbeam Press, 99-110.

AN, Wu Y. 1985. Code-mixing by English-Chinese bilingual teachers of the People's Republic of China. World Englishes 3.303-317.

ANNAMALAI, E. 1978. The Anglicized Indian languages: A case study of code-mixing. International Journal of Dravidian Linguistics 7.239-247.

BAKER, Opal R. 1980. Categories of code-switching in Hispanic communities: Untangling the terminology. Working Papers in Sociolinguistics 74-80.

BENTAHILA, Abdelali and Eirlys E. Davies. 1983. The syntax of Arabic-French code-switching. Lingua 59.4.301-330.

BEARDSLEY, B. & C.M. Eastman 1978. Markers, pauses and code-switching in bilingual Tanzanian speech. General linguistics 11.1.17-27.

BERK-SELIGSON, Susan. 1986. Linguistic constraints on intra-sentential code-switching: A study of Spanish-Hebrew bilingualism. Language in Society 15.313-348.

BOKAMBA, E. 1988. Code-mixing, language variation, and linguistic theory: Evidence from Bantu languages. Lingua 76, 21-62.

CLYNE, Michael G. 1987. Constraints on code-switching: How universal are they? Linguistics 25.739-764.

DI-PIETRO, R. 1977. Code-switching as a verbal strategy among bilinguals. Current themes in linguistics, ed. by F.R. Eckman. Washington: Hemisphere Publishing Company.

EWING, Anny. 1984. Polish-English code-switching: A clue to constituent structure and processing mechanisms. Chicago Linguistic Society 20, 54-64.

GIBBONS, J. 1987. Code-mixing and code choice: A Hong Kong case study. Clevedon, England: Multilingual Matters Ltd.

GOKE-PARIOLA, Abiodun. 1983. Code-mixing among Yoruba-English bilinguals. Anthropological linguistics 25.1.39-46.

GUMPERZ, J.J. 1982. Conversational code-switching. Discourse strategies, ed. by J.J. Gumperz, London: Cambridge University Press, 55-99.

HARTULAR, A. 1983. On defining code-switching. Revue Roumaine de linguistique 28.3.239-244.

HATCH, E. 1976. Studies in language switching and mixing. In W.C. McCormark and S.A. Wurm, ed., pp. 201-214.

JOSHI, A. 1984. Processing of sentences with intrasentential code-switching. In D. Dowty et al., eds., pp. 109-204.

KACHRU, Braj B. 1983. On mixing. The Indianization of English: The English language in India, ed. by B.B. Kachru, 193-207. New Delhi, India: Oxford University Press.

KAMWANGAMALU, Nkonko M. Forthcoming. Theory and method of code-mixing: A cross-linguistic study. Doctoral dissertation, University of Illinois, Urbana-Champaign.

KLAVANS, J.L. 1983. The syntax of code-switching: Spanish and English. Proceedings of the Linguistic Symposium on Romance Languages 18. Amsterdam: Benjamins.

LANCE, D. 1975. Spanish-English code-switching. In C. Hernandez-Chavez, ed., pp. 138-153.

LEDERBERG, A. & C. Morales. 1985. Code-switching by bilinguals: Evidence against a third grammar. Journal of Psycholinguistic Research 14.2.113-136.

LIPSKI, J. 1978. Code-switching and the problem of bilingual competence. Aspects of bilingualism, ed. by M. Paradis. Columbia, S.C.: Hornbeam Press, 250-264.

MKILIFI, A.M. 1978. Triglossia and Swahili-English bilingualism in Tanzania. In J.A. Fishman, ed., pp. 129-149.

NARTEY, J.S. 1982. Code-switching, Interference or Faddism? Language use among educated Ghanaians. Anthropological Linguistics 24.2-183-192.

PFAFF, C. 1976. Functional and structural constraints on syntactic variation in code-switching. Papers from the parasession on diachronic syntax. Chicago Linguistic

Society, 248-259.

PFAFF, C. 1979. Constraints on language mixing. Language 55.291-318.

POPLACK, S. 1978. Syntactic structure and the social function of code-switching. Latino discourse and communicative behavior, ed. by R. Duran. New Jersey: Ablex Publishing Company.

POPLACK, S. 1981. Sometimes I'll start a sentence in Spanish y termino en Espanol: Toward a typology of code-switching. Linguistics 18.581-618.

SANKOFF, D. & S. Poplack. 1980. A formal grammar for code-switching. Working Papers in the Center for Puerto Rican Studies 8. CUNY, New York.

SCOTTON, C.M. 1982. The possibility of code-switching: Motivation for maintaining multilingualism. Anthropological linguistics 24.4.432-444.

SRIDHAR, S. 1978. On the function of code-mixing in Kannada. IJSL 16, 109-117.

SRIDHAR, S. & K. Sridhar. 1980. The syntax and psycholinguistics of bilingual code-mixing. SLS 10.1.203-215.

TIMM, L. 1975. Spanish-English code-switching: El porque y how-not-to. Romance Philology 28.4.473-482.

TIMM, L. 1978. Code-switching in WAR AND PEACE. In M. Paradis, ed. pp. 302-315.

VALLDUVI, Enric. 1988. On lexical and grammatical language mixing. Linguistic change and contact. NWAV 16.368-377.

WENTZ, J. 1977. Some considerations in the development of a syntactic description of code-switching. Doctoral dissertation, Department of Linguistics, University of Illinois at Urbana-Champaign.

THE LIMITATIONS OF CONTEXT:
Evidence from Misunderstandings in Chicago

William Labov, University of Pennsylvania

1. Introduction: limited and unlimited views of context.

In one way or another, every linguistic analysis is concerned with the effect of context on linguistic form.[1] No analysis is needed if the linguistic element always occurs in the same form, in the same location, with the same meaning and unaffected by its surroundings, but this is true only of a few isolated words. The vast majority of the phonemes, morphemes, and syntactic constructions are variable, and in the search for the regular patterns that determine their use and form, we take various kinds of context into account. Many of these contextual effects are the straightforward constraints of the physical system, and no one would question the influence of articulatory and acoustic context on phonological or morphological form. Others are more abstract aspects of the organization of forms, and again, no one would question the relevance of noun classes to the selection of derivational suffixes.

The *context* of discourse analysis, ranging beyond the boundaries of the sentence, is more problematic. In some cases, the need for extra-sentential context is obvious from the particular demands of a sentential element, like anaphors, elliptical responses or sentential adverbs like *furthermore* or *nevertheless*. No one would question our right to search the immediately preceding context for well defined linguistic elements that permit the interpretation of these sentential units. But in other types of discourse analysis, the relevant context is allowed to expand without limit. Many analysts of discourse would account for the choice of one form rather than another by calling into play the unlimited context that includes the semantic, pragmatic, cultural and social domains that surround the speech act. Behind this analytical activity there seems to be the concept of the informed homunculus, seated at the controls of the speech apparatus, who acts in a purposive way to maximize the fit of an utterance and its social context before turning language into speech.[2]

This context is not mechanical, like the phonetic context of the phoneme, nor constrained, like syntactic context. It is on the contrary unconstrained and unlimited, and overrides the mechanical limitations of sentence structure and phonology. A discourse grammar that is sensitive to such a larger context is not likely to be finite or measurable.

The view that I will present here is that of a language faculty somewhat more constrained by its structure and more mechanical in its operation.

2. Some mechanical effects on language choice.

Recent studies of linguistic variation have explored and compared the various types of forces that bear on language choice and language change. The most extensive investigations have concerned the interface between phonology and morphology, where the variable realization of a segment sometimes coincides with the variable realization of a morpheme. In her studies of the aspiration and deletion of Spanish (s), Poplack was the first to take into account the effect of syntactic, semantic, cultural and pragmatic factors, alongside phonetic and other mechanical forces (1979,1980,1981). The assumption that Poplack was testing was that speakers' linguistic choices are sensitive to the amount of information in the context, and realize the /s/ of the plural more often when it is needed to convey information. Thus it is a syntactic fact of Spanish that object noun phrases without articles must be plural, so that *hablan con muerto* does not require a final /s/ to be heard as meaning 'they talk with dead people.' It is a cultural fact that we usually eat more than one bean, so that in most contexts, *arroz con habichuela* does not require a final /s/ to mean 'rice and beans.' It is a fact of nature that we usually have two eyes, a fact of social life that a certain person has more than one child, and so on. Poplack's variable rule analysis was designed to test the proposition that /s/ would appear less often in such contexts, and more often when no supporting information was available.

At first glance, the results seemed to favor this idea. But closer examination showed that there was an inevitable tendency to overestimate such contextual effects. It was found in studies of both Spanish and Portuguese that the less supporting context available, the more likely it was for the plural production to be misinterpreted as a singular (Guy 1981, Poplack 1981). Furthermore, it was found that the strongest effects on the choice of /s/ or zero were purely mechanical: a preceding /s/ favored another /s/, a preceding zero favored another zero (Poplack 1981).

Similar mechanical effects were found in studies of the choice between the agentless passive and the generalized active (*The liquor closet was broken into/They broke into the liquor closet*), where the tendency to preserve parallelism in subjects proved to be a stronger constraint than the tendency to keep the given referent in subject position (Weiner and Labov 1983). Furthermore, the strongest constraint favoring the passive is the previous use of another passive. Estival 1985 found that this "priming" effect was powerful and sensitive enough to distinguish transformationally derived from lexical passives. Bock and Kroch 1989 present a variety of evidence to demonstrate that linguistic production is controlled by "processes that are directly governed not by communicative functions, but by syntactic categories operating to some extent independently of those functions."

These variable syntactic processes may show the effect of a context that goes beyond the sentence, but it is not the kind of purposive or goal-oriented context that is often proposed in discourse analysis. These are mechanical effects that facilitate the production of speech; they are comparable to the mechanical effects that determine the phonetic shape of phonemes or morphemes. In fact, the study of sound change offers a useful background in evaluating the contribution of two opposing types of contexts. The neogrammarians saw sound change as an essentially mechanical context, which proceeds without regard to the meaningful context of the sentence or the discourse. Studies of sound change in progress confirm this model for the vast majority of cases (Labov 1981), and even in the detailed distributions of dialect geography, long considered to be the repository of lexical irregularities, it can be shown that sound changes are distributed across the landscape in a regular and mechanical fashion, under the control of phonetic conditions (Labov in press). Though sporadic changes occasionally preserve a distinction between two words, these are rare events: the overwhelming majority of mergers override important lexical distinctions.

3. The problem of cross-dialectal comprehension

All of the discussions of the effect of context considered so far are concerned with the effect of context on the process of sentence production, and the purported tendencies of a speaker to avoid confusion by taking the point of view of the listener. This paper will consider the converse situation: the use of context by the listener to understand what has been produced. The work to be reported here is drawn from a series of experiments carried out in a project funded by NSF on "The study of cross-dialectal comprehension."

3.1. Patterns of increasing linguistic diversity.

The questions raised here are in response to the results of research on linguistic change in progress in contemporary speech communities, as reflected in the production of spontaneous speech. In a series of earlier studies, we have found that sound change is continuing at a rapid pace in all the major cities of the United States, primarily in the form of systematic chain shifts of vowels, so that the dialects of Buffalo, Boston, Chicago, Atlanta, San Francisco and Los Angeles are more different from each other than they were 50 or 100 years ago (Labov, Yaeger & Steiner 1972; Labov 1980; Ash 1982, Labov in press). Research by others using both instrumental and impressionistic measures have confirmed and extended our knowledge of these chain shifts (Boston: Laferriere 1977; Detroit area: Eckert 1988; Northern Illinois: Callary 1975; Central Illinois: Habick 1980; San Francisco area: Luthin 1987, Moonwoman 1987). These findings run counter to the common sense expectation that massive exposure to the mass media would produce linguistic convergence and that local dialects would give way to a national network standard. Instead, we find an increasing divergence of the sound system led by the highest status members of the local community (Labov 1980).

The major sources of the linguistic diversification that we are studying are chain shifts of vowels. Two major patterns of chain shifting in English have been identified: the **Northern Cities Shift** and the **Southern Shift** (Labov in press). Both operate across vast territories and both follow the general principles that govern chain shifts across languages:

(1) In chain shifts,   I. tense nuclei rise.
                          II. lax nuclei fall.
                          III. back vowels move to the front.

However, these principles are implemented in patterns that move in opposite directions. Figure 1 shows the Northern Cities shift as realized in Chicago, one of our target cities. The earliest shift affects the entire word class of short *a*, which is tensed as a whole to /æh/³ and is raised along a front, peripheral track to high upgliding position [iᵊ]. Secondly, short open /o/ is tensed and moves forward occupying the former place of /æ/. Third, open /oh/ is laxed, and falls to a fronted, shortened, non-peripheral position. Short /e/ falls towards /æ/, but it also moves to the back, to the position of *cud*, which in turn moves back towards the former position of /oh/. Finally, short /i/ falls to mid position, where short /e/ was located.[4]

The Northern Cities Shift, as exemplified in Chicago, will be the major focus of this discussion. But in order to grasp the full nature of the problem of cross-dialectal comprehension, it will be necessary to examine the other major pattern of chain shifting, the Southern Shift. Figure 2 shows the mechanism of the Southern Shift, including two distinct patterns. The back vowels participate in the well-known raising and fronting pattern that is one of the most common types of chain shifts in Western Europe (Haudricourt and Juilland 1949). In the most common American implementation of this shift, (a) the low vowel /o/ moves up and back along a peripheral track, while (b) the mid ingliding vowel /oh/ rises to high position; at the same time, the nuclei of the upgliding vowels /uw/ and /ow/ are fronted (c,d). A different pattern affects the front vowels. First, the diphthong /ay/ is either backed or monophthongized and fronted (1). The nuclei of /iy/ and /ey/ become laxed and centralized (2,3), and fall along a non-peripheral track until the nucleus of /ey/ becomes the most open vowel in the system. Finally, the original short vowels /i/, /e/ and /æ/ become tensed and shift to peripheral position until they reach the positions originally occupied by the nuclei of /iy/ and /ey/. In American Southern States they develop an inglide, so that *kid* is [ki< ᵊd], *ked* is [ke< ᵊd], and *cad* is [kɛ< ᵊd] (4,5,6).

In general, the full extent of these sound shifts is not evident to speakers of the language, not even to active local participants in the most advanced stages of the shifts. Sound changes in progress take place well below the level of social awareness, and it is only completed changes that receive public attention, when they often are stigmatized and undergo some irregular correction. Phoneticians and dialectologists are not immune from these limitations on the perception of sound changes. The impressionistic transcriptions of dialect geography focus on the most conser–

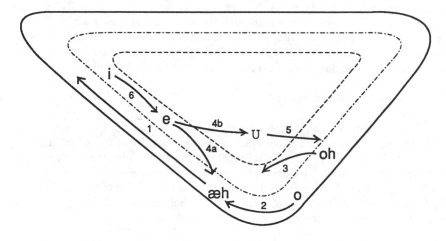

Figure 1. The Northern Cities Shift (Chicago)

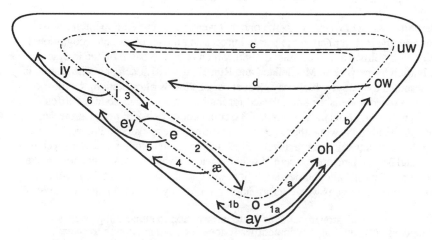

Figure 2. The Southern Shift (Birmingham)

vative forms of rural dialects, and consistently understate the phonetic diversity of urban dialects.[5] Only those phoneticians who work with the spontaneous productions of the speech community are likely to be aware of the nature of the shifts taking place. A full recognition of the extent of sound changes is usually achieved only by a long process of interaction between instrumental measurements and auditory comparison, as exemplified by the edited tape recordings of spontaneous speech that are the working tools of the experiments to be described below.[6]

3.2. How do we understand Chicago?

In our approach to the systematic study of cross-dialectal comprehension, we selected three target cities: Chicago, the largest representative of the Northern Cities Shift; Birmingham, the corresponding metropolis representing the Southern Shift; and Philadelphia, our base city with a system that combines elements of both of these basic patterns. In the light of these radically opposed directions of rotation, we asked the question "How do people from Birmingham understand Chicagoans?" There are several possible answers :

1. They may have already built a pan-dialectal phonology that includes the Chicago realizations of English vowels; *or*
2. they may deduce the systems by observing several correlated changes; *or*
3. failing to decode the vowels in an appropriate way, they may discard the vowel information and use morphological, syntactic, semantic and pragmatic information to deduce the meaning.

The third PARALLEL strategy is the one that we expected to find operating most consistently. It is implicit in the parallel processing model of speech recognition developed by Elman and McClelland 1986, which is in turn based on the interactive activation framework of McClelland and Rumelhart 1981. Each phonetic feature is represented by a node which may exist at various levels of excitation; the most highly excited node is the one selected for interpretation. Other nodes at different levels represent phonemes or words. The connections between nodes at the same level are inhibitory, while those connecting different levels are excitatory. Thus a high level of activation at one level will excite a node at a higher or lower level. Elman and McClelland are concerned with the way in which node connections make use of the "lawful" allophonic variability built into the system. But they also note that there are situations where information provided by one level is inadequate.

(2)   The speech stream contains more information than most approaches successfully exploit, but sometimes it does not contain enough to specify the correct sequence of phonemes uniquely. In these cases, the model's ability to exploit top-down input from the word level to the phoneme level causes the model to prefer lexically acceptable alternatives consistent with the input to lexically unacceptable alternatives (p. 379).

This is what we would originally have expected to happen when a person from one dialect hears a word from another dialect with a vowel that does not fit semantic or pragmatic expectations. The other information in the system will have excited the higher level nodes representing the most plausible interpretation, and a word will be selected in spite of the bad fit with the phonetic information. This is the view that Chomsky and Halle (1968) seem to have adopted in their response to Stockwell's criticism of their exchange rules for the representation of the Great Vowel Shift, where speakers with different rules would have opposite interpretations of [bo:t] and [bu:t], [bi:t] and [be:t].

(3)   One may reasonably doubt, however, that intelligibility between dialects would be impaired, for it is well known that intelligibility is only moderately affected in normal everyday speech even when all vowel contrasts are eliminated and a single vowel is made to stand in their place. A change like the one described would have very striking effects if subjects speaking a dialect that had not undergone the change in question had to identify correctly words in a randomly selected list. But word identification tests of this type, though valuable for testing the quality of telephone lines, are of only marginal value in determining the effects of a phonological change on intelligibility (p. 256).

In other words, vowels do not count for very much. Chomsky and Halle obviously feel that information contained at a higher level of organization would override anomalous phonetic input. Given the great mobility of English vowels, this is a comforting point of view, and it is one that I had adopted myself before beginning the current research.

3.3. Pilot studies of decoding: persistent misunderstandings.

When we began a pilot study of cross-dialectal comprehension in 1985, our first results suggested that we may have been asking the wrong question. The evidence that we gathered indicated that people from outside Chicago often did not succeed with any of the three strategies outlined above.

The first experiments used a technique of **Extended Decoding** to assess the extent of listeners' comprehension of advanced sound changes, heard in spontaneous speech under best possible conditions. In these experiments, individual subjects hear passages from narratives presenting the most advanced examples of the sound shifts described above. The example (4) below was spoken by a 13 year old Chicago girl recorded in 1973. Each line was played separately, together with that part of the preceding line following the / mark, so that the listener was always fully aware of the context.

(4) (Did you ever do ouija boards?)
    a   No, we have seances.
    b   And so, at this one party, we had a seance an'--
    c   Well, my ma said we shouldn't be in 'em 'cause they're dangerous
    d   I just watched/ what everybody did
    e   An' so then they were callin' [kɔˇn] this one person
    f   And they said, "If you're here, /knock on the wall."
    g   So all of a sudden /they hear a knock and they
    h   And they all come screamin', /run into the bedroom [bE>drum] ,
    i   And turn all the lights on.
    j   /But then they did this other thing
    k   That [ðiᵊt] they would ask the candle a question
    l   an' if it was yes, /they would tell the candles to move
    m   and if it was no, they would have [heᵊv] it stand still.
    n   And so, nobody really got scared of that [ði:ᵊt].

    This individually administered experiment was designed to make the task of comprehension as easy as possible. Subjects from Philadelphia and Chicago were recruited in Philadelphia, and were simply asked to repeat what they heard, and allowed to hear the passage as many times as they wanted. If they did not understand a passage, or misunderstood it, they were asked to try to make sense of it. The words with bracketed transcriptions show advanced tokens of the Northern Cities Shift that presented difficulties to subjects. Figure 3 shows the location of these nuclei in a two-formant display of the word classes involved. Some of the striking results of these preliminary studies showed the following frequent errors:

    •The phrase *They were callin'* in line **e** was very often heard as *Here comes*; the intervocalic /l/ is vocalized and the long open /oh/ vowel is shortened and fronted, a consequence of shift 5 in Figure 1.
    •The word *bedroom* in line **h** was heard as *budgeroom* or other nonsense words with a /ʌ/ nucleus, a reflection of shift 4a in Figure 1.
    •The word *that* in line **k** was frequently heard as *yet*, showing a shift of syllabicity not uncommon for advanced tokens of /æh/ which are raised following shift 1 in Figure 1.
    •The word *have* in line **n** was often heard as *hear*.
    •The word *that* in line **o** was frequently heard as two words such as *the act* or *the fact*.

    To understand the pattern of errors in the last three items, it is important to note that Philadelphia has a parallel tensing and raising of /æh/, but it affects only a selected subset of the short *a* word class (Labov 1989). Philadelphians never tense and raise short *a* words before voiced fricatives or voiceless stops. 41 individual subjects tested in this preliminary assessment of the *Seance* passage showed a sig-

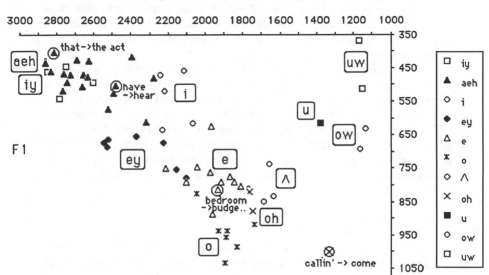

Figure 3. Words commonly misunderstood in the vowel system of
Debbie S, 13, Chicago, in the Extended Decoding SEANCE passage.

nificant local advantage for all four of these words: that is, subjects born and raised[7]
in the Northern Cities understood them much better than other subjects. For
example, *that* in line **n** was persistently misunderstood by half of the 12 subjects
from outside of the Northern Cities, but by none of the 9 Northern Cities listeners.
The *that* in line **k** was more difficult: all of the subjects from outside the Northern
Cities misunderstood it, and 60% of the Northern Cities subjects. This pattern of a
significant but limited local advantage repeats throughout our research.

A second pattern that emerged in this pilot study was the fact that the PAR-
ALLEL strategy did not appear to be available to many subjects. They did not seem
able to use the full context of the Seance passage, which they had available, to
overcome the effects of an unexpected phone. The word *bedroom,* for example,
was misunderstood by only a minority, and none from Chicago; but of those who
did misunderstand, and heard the backed /e/ as /ʌ/, many could not free themselves
from this perception. From the preliminary studies, we have the following record of
misunderstandings of *bedroom* in the phrase *runnin' to the bedroom.* The ortho-
graphic transcription is the experimenter's record of what the subject said.

(5) Repetition No.	1	2	3	4
Phillip B., 30, Phila area	?	budgemen	budgemen	bedroom
James P., 18, Alabama:	?	budgemen	budgement	budgement
Carol C., 51, Phila area	?	budgemen	budgepen	budgepen
Ilana L., 20, Cleveland Hts	?	budgjim	budgim	budgim

Only the first subject was able to use his pragmatic understanding of the situation to find the word *bedroom*. One might ask, where indeed could a young girl at a seance party run but into a room. But given the slight affrication of the /r/ by the release of the preceding /d/, these subjects heard the first syllable as [bʌdʒ] and came up with a word that made no sense. No matter how the experimenter probed, they seemed to have no idea of what this word could mean.

It did of course occur to us that the subjects were balking at the task, refusing to try to understand an accent that was so far from their own phonetic norms. Perhaps they were delivering the message, *one should not try to understand speech of this kind*. So far, we have not been able to find any support for this explanation, either in the remarks of the subjects, or the observations of the experimenter. It seemed that they did not understand the passage, no matter how often they listened to it. In other words, something in the stimulus had interfered with their ability to use the syntactic, semantic and pragmatic information that was available.

4. The Gating Experiments.

The main design of the research on Cross-Dialectal Comprehension [CDC] involved four experiments carried out in the target cities. The over-all design is displayed in (6):

(6)

		CONTEXT	
		Full	Minimal
STIMULUS			
	Fixed	Experiment 1: Extended decoding	Experiment 2: Vowel identification
	Variable	Experiment 3: Contextual gating	Experiment 4: Vowel alteration

Experiment 1 was a systematic extension of the Extended Decoding technique that we had used in the preliminary laboratory experiments, using advanced tokens of sound changes in spontaneous speech, with full context and multiple re-playings. Experiment 2 was a dialect-controlled replication of the Peterson-Barney experiment on vowel identification (1952). Subjects were asked to identify words containing 14 different vowels pronounced by two speakers of a given dialect in the /k__d/ frame: *keyed, kid, cade*, etc. The realization of the sound changes involved was the formal and conservative style of word lists. This is the type of experiment on context-free identification that Chomsky and Halle referred to; while it may not seem to be directly related to the contextual interpretation of spontaneous speech, it tests the primary linguistic function of a phoneme: its capacity to differentiate and identify words without any contextual support. Phonemes must function in this way in proper names, new vocabulary, and citation contexts.

Experiment 3, the **Gating Experiment,** will be the main focus of attention in the discussion to follow. Here the tokens were drawn from the most advanced tokens of sound changes in spontaneous speech, and the context varied systematically. Subjects first heard an isolated word or syllable, and were asked to transcribe it in ordinary spelling. Subjects were told that some of the items were words, and others might be only parts of words. After the series of 18 items was completed, they then heard the same items expanded to a phrase, and transcribed them again on the opposite side of the page. Finally, they were given a new transcription form where all 18 sentences were fully transcribed except for the phrase they had last heard. They then heard the full sentences, and were asked to fill in the blanks. These are referred to as Gating Experiments, since the context is enlarged by opening a gate to expand the information available to subjects.

Our experiments were carried out in three cities : Chicago, representing the Northern Cities Shift; Birmingham, representing the diametrically opposed Southern Shift; and Philadelphia, representing the Middle Atlantic States with distinct patterns of its own and elements of the other two. The major subjects for these experiments were native residents of the target cities.[8] We looked for sites where we could obtain moderate numbers of local, upwardly mobile subjects, fully integrated into the community, who were themselves characteristic of the advanced wave of sound change. For this purpose, we chose large urban universities in the three cities, and drew our subject groups from undergraduate classes. Here we had the help of two linguists : Ed Batistella, at the University of Alabama, Birmingham, and Penny Eckert, at the University of Illinois, Chicago Circle.

To prepare the stimuli, we needed new recordings in the target cities, with a sound quality that went beyond the field recordings that I had made in previous years. Ash carried out a new series of interviews in the target cities, from the same population as the subject groups. She used a Nagra IVS tape recorder at 7 1/2" per second, and a Sennheiser 415 directional microphone. With these recordings, we were able to preserve good sound quality as we digitized the speech signals, prepared experimental tapes, re-recorded them, analyzed the formant values, and in the final experiment, re-synthesized them in different forms.

The experiments themselves were carried out by Ash in the target cities. Three different series of Gating experiments were done, so that 54 items were tested. In Chicago, there were a total of 69 native subjects; in Birmingham 121, including 83 white subjects and 38 black; in Philadelphia, 54 overall. The number of subjects for each item varies from 15 to 34, depending on the sizes of the groups involved in each series of 18.

In the report of the results to follow, I will concentrate entirely on the interpretation of the Chicago gating items. We will first consider two sets of gating items: those that involve the fronting of short /o/ to the position occupied by short

/æ/ in other dialects, and the backing of short /e/ towards the position of /ʌ/ in other dialects.

The fronting of short /o/ is the second element of the Northern Cities chain shift. It moves into the gap created by the raising and tensing of the entire short /æ/ class. Figure 3, from a recording made in 1973, showed /o/ shifted into low central position, becoming the most open vowel of the system. In the most recent recordings made in Chicago, we frequently find forms of short /o/ that are perceived phonetically as [æ] by everyone. One such token appears in the tripartite format of the Gating Experiment as:

(7)   The SOCKS Gating item:
            Word: [sæks]
            Phrase: [yɛdəwɚsæks]
            Sentence: You had to [wɚrsæks]. No sandals.

The 15 Chicago subjects were no different from anyone else in their response to [sæks] at the Word level. The great majority identified it as a member of the /æ/ phoneme. Ten subjects heard a low front vowel, 3 heard a lower mid-front vowel, and only one identified it as the word intended. Birmingham and Philadelphia whites showed identical patterns.

(8) Responses to SOCKS at word level:

/o/	socks	1				
/æ/:	sax, sacks	8	sass	1	ants	1
/e/:	sex	3				
?		1				

Figure 4 shows the cumulative pattern of recognition of Chicago [sæks] as *socks* for Chicago, Birmingham and Philadelphia subjects. A sizeable difference between Chicagoans and others appears in the phrase context, where one third of the Chicagoans were able to reproduce the intended reading, but only two of 15 Philadelphia subjects and only one of the 24 from Birmingham. When the disambiguating phrase "No sandals" was added, all but two of the Chicagoans produced the correct response, but from 30 to 50% of the subjects from other cities continued to be puzzled. 8 of the 24 Birmingham subjects, for example, continued to record forms like *wear sack*, even though this made very little pragmatic or cultural sense in the context of "No sandals."

The same pattern is reproduced throughout the results of the Gating Experiments. Whenever the advanced token moves into the position occupied by another phoneme in a conservative dialect, and there is a lexical realization of the conservative option, the great majority of subjects choose the conservative form in isolation, even when the advanced token corresponds to their own spontaneous speech. The local advantage in such cases appears when there is some disambigu–

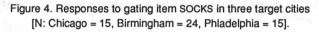

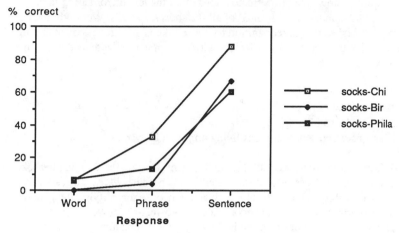

Figure 4. Responses to gating item SOCKS in three target cities [N: Chicago = 15, Birmingham = 24, Phladelphia = 15].

Figure 5. Phonetic positions of /e/ and /o/ items in the Gating experiment.

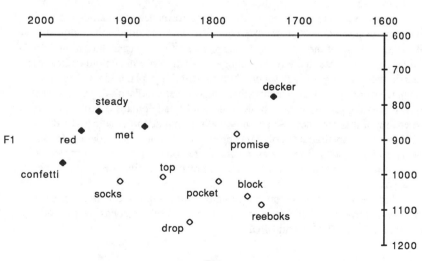

ating context: the local subjects are quicker to envisage the possibility that this is an advanced token of another phoneme.

Figure 5 shows the phonetic positions of all the /e/ and /o/ gating items. Note that SOCKS is in the most fronted of all the short /o/ words. We might then expect to get a higher rate of recognition for those tokens that are less fronted. Let us now consider another item that displays a lexical opposition with a conservative token: BLOCK

(9) The BLOCK Gating item:
      Word: [blæ:ˀk]
      Phrase: [wʌn blæ:ˀk]
      Sentence: Old senior citizens living on [wʌn blæ:ˀk].

Figure 6 shows the responses of subjects to this item. Despite the fact that the token [blæ:k] is considerably less fronted than [sæks], it is heard as *black* almost universally. Part of the effect is the unusual length and tension, exemplifying the general tendency for Northern cities /o/ to become a tense vowel as it moves forward. Again, subjects from all cities hear the isolated syllable as containing /æ/ in the word *black*. But here there is very little improvement in the phrase context. It may be true that *one black* is less likely that *one block*, but the push it gives towards the correct reading is somewhat less than in the case of *y'hadda wear socks.* of Figure 4. With the full sentence, almost all the Chicago subjects produce the right reading, and Birmingham white subjects do almost as well. But the Philadelphia subjects continue to respond *black* , even though it makes no sense at all in the full context.

One possible explanation for the poor performance of Philadelphia subjects is that the vowel in *black* is pronounced quite far back in Philadelphia, almost identical to the position of the advanced Chicago *block*.[9] In any case, the fronted vowel heard here is very close to the typical phonetic position of Philadelphia *black*, more so than in the case of Birmingham or Chicago. But this explanation makes little sense in terms of the model of contextual support that we discussed at the outset. How is it possible that only three of the nineteen Philadelphians could   figure out the meaning of this sentence? Apparently, their semantic, pragmatic and cultural faculties were not available to solve this problem. We must conclude that for some subjects, under some circumstances, an aberrant phonetic form may completely block access to other sources of information relevant to the interpretation of the sentence as a whole.

Figure 6 also shows responses to the word *drop*. For this item, the sentence form incorporates three items that are presented separately as words and phrases: POCKET, STEADY and DROP.

185

Figure 6. Responses to DROP and BLOCK in the Gating Experiment.
[N: Chicago = 19; Birmingham = 24; Philadelphia = 19]]

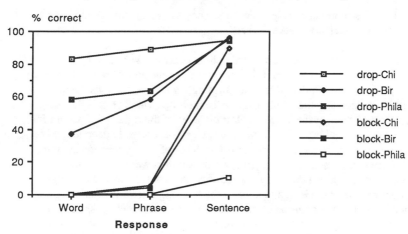

(10) The DROP Gating item
Word: [draᶜp]
Phrase: [mɛsɪv draᶜp]
Sentence: [And I didn't know there was such a thing as an [ɛr paᶜkɪt]. And
we kept going up and down in the air and uh you get to a point where
you're [stʌᶜdi fər ə mɪnɪt]. All of a sudden you just take this [mɛsɪv
draᶜp].

Even though *drop* is considerably fronter than *black*, comparatively few subjects respond to the isolated word   as containing an /æ/ nucleus. The local advantage
for Chicagoans is quite evident, however. They have little difficulty in identifying
this word as containing a short /o/ without any context, and with context proceed to
100% identification. The Birmingham subjects register only about 40% correct responses at the Word level. The most common mishearing was to identify it as a
word like *dry*, and to perceive the [æˀ] as a form of monophthongized /ay/. The
differences between the responses to *drop* and to the preceding types are clearly due
to the fact that there is no lexical opposition between an advanced token of /o/ in this
frame, and the neighboring phoneme /æ/: that is, there is no word *drap*. Thus the
existence of a lexical opposition is more important in determining recognition than
the phonetic position of the nucleus.
        It is particularly interesting to note, however, that the addition of the word
massive in the Phrase context does not necessarily improve the recognition of
drop. This is surprising, since one way that outsiders might reconstitute a chain
shift is by recognizing that if Vowel A has moved to A', then Vowel B may have

moved to A. A sixteen-year-old woman from Detroit with no linguistic background made this observation in the early 1970's:

(11) You know, it's funny about New Yorkers. They say [bɑɾḷ] for 'bottle' [bæɾḷ] and they say [bæɾḷ] for 'battle' [bɪᵊɾḷ]!

      Nevertheless, the tensed and raised /æh/ in *massive* was more of an obstacle than a help to outsiders. Only the full context yielded the correct reading for the majority of subjects from Philadelphia and Birmingham. Table 1 shows the individual patterns in decoding the combination *massive drop* . On the left is the pattern for the decoding of *drop* at the Word and Phrase level; at the right is the pattern for decoding *massive* at the Phrase level. When *massive* was correctly decoded, there was some improvement in the treatment of *drop:* 8 out of 11 right responses at the word level were maintained, and 5 out of 7 wrong answers were corrected. But when *massive* was not heard correctly, the damage was considerable: 5 of 7 right interpretations of *drop* were lost, and none of the 8 wrong interpretations were corrected. In other words, the addition of the second element of the chain shift interfered with interpretation more than it helped.

TABLE 1
INDIVIDUAL PATTERNS IN THE DECODING OF *MASSIVE DROP*

Decoding of *drop*		Decoding of *massive*		
Word	Phrase	right	wrong	Total
right	right	8	2	10
right	wrong	3	5	8
wrong	right	5	0	5
wrong	wrong	2	8	10
				33

      Turning to the short /e/ items in the Gating experiments, the item STEADY shows a pattern similar to BLOCK.

(12) The STEADY Gating item.
   Word: [stʌdi]
   Prase: [stʌdi fər əmɪnɪt]
     Sentence: [same as (10) above] And I didn't know there was such a thing as an [ɛr paˁkɪt]. And we kept going up and down in the air and uh you get to a point where you're [stʌˁdi fər ə mɪnɪt]. All of a sudden you just take this [mɛsɪv draˁp].

Steady participates in a lexical opposition with *study*, in the same way that *block* is opposed to *black,* and as Figure 7 shows, all but two of the subjects transcribe the Word level item as *study*. It is not accidental that those two are Chicagoans, how—

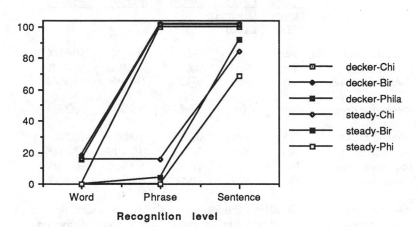

Figure 7. Responses to DECKER and STEADY in the Gating Experiment.
[N: Chicago = 19; Birmingham = 24; Philadelphia = 19]

ever: there is a small advantage for Chicagoans at the Word level. The same advantage is maintained at the Phrase level, where there is little disambiguating information. At the Sentence level, the majority of the subjects apply the contextual information correctly: the full sentence yields a context that make sense only with *steady*, since *study* is completely irrelevant here. The item DECKER, on the other hand, shows a pattern more similar to DROP.

(13) The DECKER Gating item:
   Word: [dʌˁk]
   Phrase: [dʌbl dʌˁkər]
   Sentence: They have a [dʌbl dʌˁkər] bus.

The short /e/ heard in *deck* is phonetically a wedge in the isolated syllable, and as Figure 7 shows, it is transcribed as such by almost all subjects (including all of the Chicagoans). In the Phrase context of *double decker*, it is instantly recognized by everyone as a form of short /e/. Thus the lexical information of *double decker* is much more effective in interpretation than the contextual information that is provided for *steady*. This pattern is repeated throughout the Gating experiment. Table 2 adds two additional short /o/ Gating items to those discussed so far, and arranges them according to whether or not there is a lexical opposition with the conservative phoneme that is overlapped, and whether or not the Phrase context provides clear lexical disambiguation.

TABLE 2
GATING RESPONSES BY LEXICAL OPPOSITION AND DISAMBIGUATION

	Lexical Opposition	Lexical Disambiguation	Word	Phrase	Sentence
[sæks]>Y'hadda wear socks	Yes	No	0-10%	0-15%	50-90%
[blæ:ˀk]-> one block	Yes	No	0%	0-5%%	10-90%
[stʌdi]->steady for a while	Yes	No	0-15%	0-15%	65-90%
[dræˁp]->massive drop	No	No	37-83%	55-90%	100%
[dʌˁk]->double decker	No	Yes	0-20%	100%	100%
[pæˀk]->air pocket	No	Yes	5-25%	75-90%	95-100%
[præˀm]->promise ring	No	Yes	10-20%	80%	80-85%
[bæˀks]-> Reeboks	No	Yes	10-20%	65-90%	85-90%

These data show the decisive role of lexical information, which across all dialects is effective in overriding unexpected phonetic information. There is no indication that the information derived from the larger linguistic framework — syntactic, semantic and pragmatic — is as effective in the process of understanding sentences.

5. Is the information present in the context?

The results of these experiments conform to the findings of the pilot project described in section 3. Under certain circumstances, an undecipherable phonetic form can effectively block semantic interpretation. When a segment is clearly identified as a member of a given phoneme, and the result does not fit any reasonable semantic interpretation, it appears to be difficult for many listeners to discard that information. But one might ask whether there is enough information in the context of our experimental design to provide that reasonable interpretation. It is possible that the experimental setting, removed from the context of every-day life, does not give the subject the full support that is needed to solve the puzzle. This problem was investigated in a series of experiments carried out by Roberts at the conclusion of the major series described above. In order to see if the information in the Sentence phase of the Gating Experiment was sufficient for decoding, one set of subjects was given the sentence orally, with a blank space to transcribe the critical phonetic elements that had been misunderstood by others; another set of subjects were given the sentences in written form only, and asked to fill in the blank from the context. Three of the items tested were:

(14) Philadelphia vocalization of intervocalic /l/:
she took a r [ʊɚr] and smacked my hands [10]

(15) Chicago backing of /ʌ/ to [ɔ].
I can remember vaguely when we had [ðəbɔsɪz] with the uh- like the
antennas on the top that were attached to um--like, some kind of like a
wire. From, like, street pole to like, you know, like from street lamp
to street lamp.

(16) Chicago fronting of /o/ to [æ]:
Y'hadda wear [sæks]. No sandals.

In (14), the vocalization of intervocalic /l/ in Philadelphia yields a single syllable
[rʊər], which is an uninterpretable chunk of sound for those who are not familiar
with this process. Nevertheless, the sentential context, from a story about a nun in
Catholic school, is reasonably clear: it is generally known that teachers used to hit
children on the hands with a ruler. In (15), the vowel is fully backed and the production is homonymous with the conservative form of *bosses*. The full context
should be quite clear to anyone who knows that some busses have poles to contact
with an overhead cable. (16) is the familiar Gating item SOCKS, with results presented in Figure 4.

In all three cases, there was a sizeable increase in comprehension when the
phonetic information was not present, as shown in Table 3.

TABLE 3
RESPONSES TO PRESENCE AND ABSENCE OF PHONETIC FORMS
IN THE SENTENCE FORM OF THE GATING EXPERIMENT

| | Phonetic form heard | | No phonetic form heard | |
	% right	N	% right	N
ruler	0	5	89	38
busses	57	75	100	38
socks	64	72	87	38

Thus it is clear that uninterpreted phonetic material can block further semantic interpretation, since for all but a very few subjects, the information needed could
be found in the context.

190

6. The study of natural misunderstandings.

No matter how well one experiment correlates with another, the question remains as to whether any of the experimental results correspond with the way that people understand language in everyday life. In addition to the amount of information provided in the experiment, there may be differences in the reference grid for interpreting the sounds heard, in the understanding of what responses are requested, and in the motivations for responding. Though these problems cannot be perfectly controlled, there are points of comparison that can be made with observations made in daily life. Here our main source of evidence is an auxiliary study of naturally occurring misunderstandings, which now total 556 reports gathered over the past several years by members of the research group and their acquaintances. These reports are collected on standardized forms, which register the dialect background of the speakers and listeners, how the misunderstanding came to light, how long it took for it to be corrected (if at all), and as much of the contextual situation as is needed to understand what was said. More than a quarter of these are correlated with regional dialect differences or sound change in progress. All elements of the Northern Cities chain shift were involved in these naturally occurring misunderstandings.

(17) /æh/ → [iːə]
Lynelle M. : Alice is almost 6.
Ruth H. : Who's Ellis? [at potluck supper with several small children present, none named Alice or Ellis, but some unknown, Ruth H. heard "Ellis" and thought he might be the little boy she'd seen.]

(18) /æh/ → [iːə]
Labov asked a Rochester speaker : "Where did your father work?" She responded "[kodiˀək]." A transcriber persistently heard this as 'coding', adding the nasal quality of the vowel to the final velar, and not until several repetitions did she understand "Kodak."

(19) /e/ → [æ]
A telephone surveyor from Chicago asked Brian T. [No. NJ], "Do you have any [pæɪts] in the house?" Brian T. reported his efforts to interpret this as follows: he can't be asking me about *pots* -- everybody has pots in the house -- and he can't be asking me about *pot* - that would be too personal. On the third repetition, he understood the question as directed to *pets*.

(20) /o/ → /æ/
A Chicago speaker referred to [kulads] which was heard first as *cool ads* and finally deciphered as *culottes*.

(21) /oh/ → [ʌ]

    Franz S. [Chicago] sitting in O'Hare airport heard, " Will lucky passenger
Arnold Stein report to the Eastern Airlines Counter?" He wondered what
was so lucky about Arnold Stein. Five minutes later he heard "Will Mil-
waukee passenger Arnold Stein. . ." The laxing and centralization of /oh/
from [ɔ] to [ʌ] is largely responsible for this misunderstanding.

        These observations increase our confidence that the results of the CDC ex-
periments are not unrelated to the events of everyday life. Yet the observation of
natural misunderstandings is biased in many ways. Our observers can only report
those misunderstandings that rise to conscious attention, and attract the notice of the
observer, and the phonetic character of the original utterance is often uncertain.
Nevertheless, we can use this data base to draw a number of inferences about the
nature of the relations between the larger social and cultural context, and the process
of decoding phonemes and words.

        In the pilot studies discussed in section 3.2, the backing of short /e/ led to
persistent misunderstandings. But this sound change did not produce the mis–
understanding alone: the affrication of the following /d/ was also involved. This
suggests that such persistent misunderstanding may require the joint failure of two
phonetic elements in the stream of speech. If Elman and McClelland's connection–
ist model applied here, we would predict that two segments that did not fit the tem–
plate of *bedroom* would have twice the inhibitory effect of one segment, and that
the activation of *bedroom* at the word level would be twice as difficult. If more than
two segments were involved, the task of activating the correct word would be even
more difficult. We can look for some confirmation of this possibility by examining
the collection of natural misunderstandings, the information on how the misunderstanding was detected (if at all), and how long it took for the problem to be corrected by speaker and listener. For those misunderstandings where we can trace a
clear phonetic relation between the production and the interpretation, we can examine the relationship between the number of segments involved and the difficulty of
noticing and correcting the misunderstanding. The categories that register how the
misunderstanding was brought to attention are shown as (22):

(22) **1**   before utterance was over
     2   by speaker's response to look or query
     3   by inference from further utterances
     4   by accidental events that followed
     5   not at all by the participants

These are also closely correlated with the amount of time involved; categories **1-2**
require less than 5 seconds, while **3-5** involve much more time.

In our 556 recorded cases, more than a third involve differences in only a single phonetic segment: a single feature or the deletion of a segment, as in (17-21) above and in (23).

(23)   Lynn B. (Utah).: She doesn't have any fillings.
        Ruth H. (CT).: Oh, because she hit her head so hard?
        Lynn B.: Fillings in her teeth.

Here the misunderstanding involved a confusion of tense /iy/ for lax /i/: Ruth H. thought that the speaker meant 'feelings.' It was corrected by her query within several seconds.[11]
        A smaller proportion of the data, about one sixth, involve two segments as in (24):

(24)   Lavinia B. [Phila]: I'll get you a red and green sticker for Christmas.
        Sherry M. [Northern Pa.]: Just one SLIPPER?
        Lavinia B.: Sticker, not Slipper.
        Sherry M.: I'll have to get an amputation [as Lavinia walked out of the room]

Though Sherry M. pretended not to understand, the misunderstanding was in fact corrected within a few seconds.
        In another sixth of the data, more than two segments are involved:

(25)   Elke K. [No. NJ]: We got two *Towntalks*?
        [two local newspapers, "Towntalk" had been delivered instead of one.]
        Mark K. [No. NJ]: => two tampax?

Here the listener corrected his own misunderstanding before a whole second had gone by. On the other hand, there are many misunderstandings that are not corrected for many hours, or days, until some new event brings them to light. I was instructed to go to a bakery named *Barallo's* at a certain address in South Philadelphia, but it was not until I got quite near that I realized it was *Varallo's*. Robin Sabino of our Linguistics Laboratory received a recommendation for a new dentist named *Lynn* from her roommate, who happens to come from Virginia. It was not until a week later, when she got the address straight and the spelling of the name that she realized she was going to a male dentist named *Len*. In (26), a misunderstanding involving multiple segments persisted for some time:

(26)   Otto S. [N.M.]: Hit carriage return. [hitting the key marked ENTER].
        Elise M. [W. Mass]: [to herself] How odd, he calls it *caricature*.
        Several hours later, Otto S.repeated the same sentence and she understood.

These data will allow us to examine the relationship between errors involving single segments and those involving more than one. Figure 8 shows the relationship between the number of segments involved and the way in which misunderstanding was recognized and corrected.[12] It is immediately evident that the single-segment errors do not enjoy a privileged status. For the first three categories, they march in lock-step with 2-segment errors, and the small differentiation for "later events" is not in the least significant. This view of natural misunderstandings conforms to the results of the Gating Experiments, which show that single phonetic forms can effectively block decoding.

The only significant differences between the segment types in Figure 8 concern those words where more than two segments were involved. These show a higher total in the "look or query" category [$\chi2 = 3.66, P < .05$] . This is quite understandable. If the listener did not understand three or more segments in the utterance, it is likely to have been quite unclear from a phonetic standpoint, and the listener would be more likely to ask for clarification.

A more significant difference is found in the "later events" category. These are the cases where the misunderstanding was only accidentally discovered, and nothing in the verbal context clarified the situation. Together with the last category, these represent true misunderstandings from the overall communicative point of view. This result is the contrary of what would have been predicted from a parallel processing model. Errors with a larger number of segmental errors are less likely to produce confusion than errors with one or two segments involved. In other words, phonetically unclear utterances are actually easier to decipher than clear ones that

Figure 8. Mode of recognition by number of segments involved

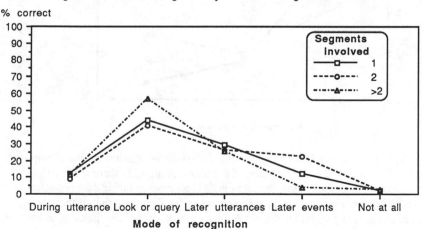

contain unexpected phonetic forms. Words with more than two problematic segments appear to permit the activation of higher level information more easily than misunderstandings based on phonetically clear utterances.

In most of the cases involving one segment, there is no question of phonetic unclarity at all. The stressed nuclei are usually identified correctly from a phonetic point of view; the difficulty lies in the lack of fit to a recognizable word. It is therefore interesting to look at the errors that are motivated by dialect differences, like (17-21), as compared to all others. Of the 346 errors showing clear segmental phonetic motivation, 128 or 37% were motivated by such dialect differences. Of these, 62% involved only one segment, as compared to 41% for those errors that showed no clear dialect motivation. Figure 9 shows the radical difference between the two sets of data. Dialect motivated errors are most clearly associated with single segments, and rarely involve multiple segments. It follows that there is no clear association between the errors produced by sound change and difficulty in hearing. On the contrary, the reason that such errors may be difficult to decipher is that they are utterances heard as clearly as any other, and heard as phonetic forms that are not clearly what they are expected to be.

Figure 9. Dialect-motivated vs. other errors by number of segments involved.

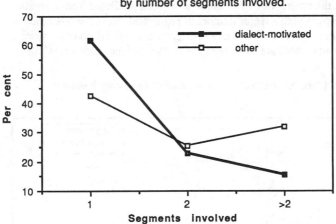

Thus the effects of sound change and dialect differentiation are sharply opposed to the effects of the degeneration of the phonetic input. In natural misunderstanding as well as in the Gating Experiment, it is phonology rather than phonetics that presents the major problem for comprehension. To the extent that the advanced tokens of changes in progress in dialect A overlap the expected distributions of another phoneme in dialect B, the phonologies of these dialects are mutually unintelligible.

7. Conclusion

Weinreich, Labov and Herzog (1968) pointed out that linguists' increasing concern with structure made the facts of language change appear even more mysterious.

(27)   After all, if a language has to be structured in order to function efficiently, how do people continue to talk while the language changes, that is, while it passes through periods of lessened systematicity? Alternatively, if overriding pressures do force a language to change, and if communication is less efficient in the interim... why have such inefficiencies not been observed in practice? (p. 100-1).

We have now observed such inefficiencies in practice and we must correct our appreciation of the effects of change. Sound change does interfere with the communicative function of language, in a serious way, reducing the capacity of phonemes to function effectively in their primary role, that is, to distinguish words through the opposition of distinctive features. If this incapacity were confined to outsiders, we might be content to analyze this effect as an instance of the centrifugal pattern that underlies all linguistic diversification and the pattern that led to the fragmentation of the Indo-European languages. If it were confined to cross-class or cross-ethnic comprehension within a community, we could attribute the effect to the unfortunate fragmentation and segregation of our own society. But we have now observed lessened efficiency of the system within the most narrowly defined speech community: people of the same age, and the same social class who associate every day within the same institution.

One might say, and linguists have said, that vowels do not count for very much after all. Within this framework, one expects that the great redundancy of the linguistic system along with pragmatic information drawn from the context will effectively solve problems of communication. We too thought at the outset that listeners carried on many lines of analysis in parallel, and were free to switch to other sources of information when one was blocked. Our preliminary tests with extended coding surprised us: many subjects failed to understand utterances, even where many avenues of common sense reasoning pointed towards a solution. Experiment 3 was designed to examine this effect in a controlled way, by opening the gate for contextual information one piece at a time. The results clearly showed that advanced tokens of sound changes in progress can effectively block the process of comprehension. This is particularly true where the advanced tokens enter into a lexical opposition with the neighboring phoneme whose margin of security is overlapped.

These results are drawn from the first empirical investigations of the consequences of linguistic change for perception and comprehension of speech. They lend confirmation to the view that much of language processing occurs in a step-by-step, deterministic manner, and that the output of one component of speech recognition process is not easily overriden by another. Bock and Kroch demonstrate that during sentence processing, communicative intention gives way to a system sensitive to abstract structural features (1989). Research on cross-dialectal comprehension brings us to the similar conclusion that the processing of phonological elements shows a considerable degree of independence of contextual controls.

At the same time, a good percentage of the listeners do manage to decipher utterances with advanced tokens, and it is important to account for the difference between those who succeed and those who fail. Our current research aims to isolate the conditions that favor comprehension by controlling more closely the subjects' underlying assumptions about the nature of the stimuli. One reasonable goal is to establish conditions where those who use the most advanced forms will recognize them uniformly in the speech of others. We hope to orient the subjects towards the reference grid that they use in every-day life. Further, we hope to improve comprehension by increasing the subjects' tendency to search for alternate interpretations. Though contextual information may not be available at all stages of comprehension, it will be interesting to know how and when it can be put to work.

BIBLIOGRAPHY

Ash, Sharon 1982. The vocalization of /l/ in Philadelphia. University of Pennsylvania dissertation.
Bock, Kay and Anthony S. Kroch 1989. The isolability of syntactic processing. In G. N. Carlson and M. K. Tannenhaus (eds.), *Linguistic Structure in Language Processing*. Kluwer Academic Publishers. Pp. 157-196.
Callary, R. E. 1975. Phonological change and the development of an urban dialect in Illinois. *Language in Society* 4:155-170.
Chomsky, Noam and Morris Halle 1968. *The Sound Pattern of English*. New York: Harper & Row.
Di Paolo, Marianna 1988. Pronunciation and categorization in sound change. In K. Ferrara et al. (eds), *Linguistic Change and Contact: NWAV XVI*. Austin, TE: Dept of Linguistics, U. of Texas. Pp. 84-92.
Eckert, Penelope 1988. Adolescent social structure and the spread of linguistic change. *Language in Society* 17:183-208.
Elman, Jeffrey L. and James L. McClelland 1986. Exploiting lawful variability in the speech wave. In J. S. Perkell and D. Klatt (eds.), *Invariance and Variability in Speech Process*. Hillsdale, NJ: Erlbaum. Pp. 360-385.
Garcia, Erica C. 1979. Discourse without syntax. In T. Givón (ed.), *Syntax and Semantics: Vol 12. Discourse and Syntax*. NY: Academic Press. Pp. 23-49.
Givón, Talmy 1979. From discourse to syntax: grammar as a processing strategy. In T. Givón (ed.), *Syntax and Semantics: Vol 12. Discourse and Syntax*. New York: Academic Press. Pp. 81-114.
Guy, Gregory 1981. Syntactic and phonetic variation in Carioca Portuguese. University of Pennsylvania dissertation.
Habick, Timothy 1980. Sound change in Farmer City: A sociolinguistic study based on acoustic data. University of Illinois at Urbana-Champaign dissertation.

Haudricourt, A. G. and A. G. Juilland 1949. *Essai pour une histoire structurale du phonétisme français*. Paris: C. Klincksieck.

Hubbell, Allan F. 1950. *The Pronunciation of English in New York City. Consonants and Vowels*. New York: King's Crown Press, Columbia University.

Kuno, Susumu 1987. *Functional Syntax*. Chicago: U. of Chicago Press.

Kurath, Hans & Raven I. McDavid, Jr. 1961. *The Pronunciation of English in the Atlantic States*. Ann Arbor: U. of Michigan Press.

Labov, William 1966. *The Social Stratification of English in New York City*. Washington D.C.: Center for Applied Linguistics.

Labov, William 1975. On the use of the present to explain the past. In L. Heilmann (ed.), *Proc. of 11th Int. Congr. of Linguists*. Bologna: Il Mulino. Pp. 825-851.

Labov, William 1980. The social origins of sound change. In W. Labov (ed.), *Locating Language in Time and Space*. NY: Academic Press. Pp.251-266.

Labov, William 1981. Resolving the Neogrammarian controversy. *Language* 57:267-309.

Labov, William in press. *The Use of the Present to Explain the Past.*.

Labov, William, Malcah Yaeger & Richard Steiner 1972. *A Quantitative Study of Sound Change in Progress*. Philadelphia: U. S. Regional Survey.

Laferriere, Martha 1977. Consideration of the vowel space in sound change: Boston /æ/. Paper given at the LSA.

Luthin, Herbert W. 1987. The story of California (ow): the coming-of-age of English in California. In Keith M. Denning et al. (eds.) *Variation in Language: NWAV-XV at Stanford*. Stanford: Department of Linguistics, Stanford University. Pp. 312-324.

McClelland, James L. and D. E. Rumelhart 1981. An interactive activation model of context effects in letter perception. Part i: An account of basic findings. *Psychological Review* 88:375-407.

Moonwoman, Birch 1987. Truly awesome: (O) in California English. In Keith Denning et al. (eds.), *Variation in Language. NWAV-XV at Stanford*. Stanford, CA: Department of Linguistics, Stanford University. Pp. 325-336.

Payne, Arvilla. 1980. Factors controlling the acquisition of the Philadelphia dialect by out-of-state children. In W. Labov (ed.), *Locating Language in Time and Space* .New York: Academic Press . Pp. 143-178.

Peterson, Gordon E. and Harold L. Barney 1952. Control methods used in a study of the vowels *JASA* 24:175-184.

Poplack, Shana 1979. Function and process in a variable phonology. University of Pennsylvania dissertation.

Poplack, Shana 1980. The notion of the plural in Puerto Rican Spanish: competing constraints on /s/ deletion. In W. Labov (ed.), *Locating Language in Time and Space*. New York: Academic Press. Pp. 55-68.

Poplack, Shana 1981. Mortal phonemes as plural morphemes. In D. Sankoff & H. Cedergren (eds.), *Variation Omnibus*. Alberta: Linguistic Research. Pp. 59-72.

Weiner, E. Judith and William Labov 1983. Constraints on the agentless passive. *Journal of Linguistics* 19:29-58.

Weinreich, Uriel, William Labov and Marvin Herzog 1968. Empirical foundations for a theory of language change. In W. Lehmann and Y. Malkiel (eds.), *Directions for Historical Linguistics*. Austin: U. of Texas Press.

APPENDIX A: LCD Notation for English Vowel Patterns

The LCD [lowest common denominator] notation is an inventory of symbols for representing the phonemic and broad phonetic structure of a wide range of English dialects which share a common recent history. It is designed to register the surface realizations of phonemes that are the common point of departure for most American English dialects at stages preceding the major vowel shifts that are the subject of research on sound changes in progress. *Italics* are used to represent a segment that occurs in the designated historical word classes: that is the entire set of lexical occurrences of a given segment that show a common history (normally from Middle English to the present). E.g., the short *a* word class is the vowel that occurs in *bat, bad, man, at,* etc.: words that show a uniform development of this nucleus in the great majority of modern dialects.

The slash notation / / represents phonemic status, and brackets [ ] phonetic notation as usual. The phonemes designated here are those units whose lexical membership is not predictable by any general rule, including phonetic or grammatical conditioning. In various dialects, historical word classes may be split or merged. For example, short *a* is split into tense /æh/ and lax /æ/ in the Middle Atlantic States, but remains intact as /æh/ in the Northern Cities dialects.

The vowels of English then fall into two major classes according to a fundamental distributional criterion: checked vs. free. The checked vowels occur in LCD notation with simple nuclei, always followed by consonants, while the free vowels, where the nucleus is combined with upgliding or ingliding semivowels, occur with and without following consonants.

		FRONT		**BACK**
CHECKED	/i/	bit, bill, sister	/u/	put, pull, book
	/e/	bet, bell, very	/ʌ/	but, dull, Murray
	/æ/	pat, man, marry	/o/	cot, doll, apology

FREE FRONT UPGLIDING
	/iy/	beet, free		
	/ey/	bait, bay	/oy/	quoit, boy
	/ay/	bite, buy		

BACK UPGLIDING
	/iw/	fruit, true	/uw/	boot, do
			/ow/	boat, dough
			/aw/	about, cow

INGLIDING
	/ih/	idea		
	/eh/	yeah	/oh/	bought, law
			/ah/	pa, father, llama

The inglide notation /h/ represents either [ə] or lengthening of the nucleus (most characteristic of low and low back nuclei). Before /r/, the same phonetic element occurs allophonically. When postvocalic /r/ is vocalized, the system of ingliding phonemes is expanded to free and checked position:

/ih/	beer, beard, idea		/uh/	moor, moored
/eh/	bare, bared, yeah		/oh/	core, cord, bought, law
			/ah/	bar, bard, pa, father, llama

The wholesale tensing or splitting of short *a* adds the phoneme /æh/ to this inventory. For those dialects that maintain the distinction of *four* and *for*, the older contrast of /oh/ and /ɔh/ must be maintained.

Notes

[1]The work reported here was supported by a National Science Foundation grant to the University of Pennsylvania on "The study of cross-dialectal comprehension." The results reported here are the work of the research group as a whole: Sharon Ash, Julie Roberts, Robin Sabino and Tom Veatch. I am indebted to them for their contributions to both field work and analysis.

[2]Bock and Kroch 1989 review the variety of functional approaches that emphasize that "the central importance of meaning and communication is the understanding and creating of sentences," and that "comprehension is influenced by contextual, conceptual and semantic factors". Perhaps the clearest exposition of this approach is to be found in the contributions to discourse analysis in Givón 1979, in particular, those of Givón and Garcia. Both put into question "whether syntax has any independent existence apart from discourse structure" (Givón p. 81). Garcia concludes that "there is no need for 'autonomous syntax', 'discourse structure', 'rules' or 'constraints' once one takes seriously the proposition that language is a device of communication manipulated by human beings" (p. 47). The direction taken by Kuno 1987 is a somewhat more constrained attack on formal sentence grammar, but argues for an even wider extension of context: "The linguist must always be examining his target phenomenon in a larger perspective than is immediately called for by the phenomenon itself. Furthermore, that larger perspective might involve nonlinguistic cognitive processes as well." (p 8.) The contextual effects that Kuno calls for include whatever the "speaker/experiencer/thinker/feeler/knower/hearer" knows about the referent (p. 29).

[3]The notation used here to describe chain shifts is presented more systematically with lexical exemplifications in Appendix A.

[4]The complete view of the Northern Cities Shift owes a great deal to Eckert, who discovered the completion of this rotation of short vowels in the backing of /e/ and /U/ in her work in Livonia, Michigan (1988).

[5]See for example the Atlas records for New York City compared to actual recordings (Hubbell 1950). Atlas transcriptions of the Southern Shift (Kurath and McDavid 1961) consistently show the short vowels with lax nuclei , e.g., [ɪə] in *bit*, though instrumental studies of the short ingliding vowels show that many speakers have tense nuclei in these words, [iə]. The IPA itself is quite limited in the expression of fronting and backing, and the differentiation of the peripheral and non-peripheral routes that are followed in chain shifting.

[6]A cassette entitled "Demonstration tape for Cross-Dialectal Comprehension" is available from the Linguistics Laboratory, University of Pennsylvania, 418 Service Drive, Philadelphia, PA 19104.

[7]The criteria that we follow for classifying geographic backgrounds focus on the formative years 4-13 years old. Subjects who came to the community before the age of 9, and spent more than half of their formative years in the community, were grouped with other native subjects. This cutting point conforms to the findings of the New York and Philadelphia studies (Labov 1966, Payne 1980).

[8]See footnote 7 for the definition of native status.

[9]The initial /bl/ cluster and the following /k/ combine to give the least favoring position for fronting and the most favoring for backing. Strangely enough, the

same allophonic influence is not exerted on the short /o/ phoneme, which is comparatively front, so that the Philadelphia *black* and *block* are quite similar.

[10]Since all subjects heard the initial /r/ correctly in the original gating experiments, the /r/ was supplied in the graphic form, and the rest of the word left blank.

[11]This is one of the many misunderstandings motivated by dialect differences that reflect change in progress. The neutralization of /iy/ and /i/ before /l/ is an ongoing change affecting many regions of the United States, but is particularly advanced in Utah. It was first detected in exploratory field work in Utah in 1973 (LYS Ch. 6) and has been the particular focus of work by di Paolo in Salt Lake City.

[12]The total of 346 items represented here does not include reanalyzed cases, where word boundaries were changed, metatheses, errors where the crucial change involved deletion or insertion of segments, or semantic and syntactic differences of interpretation involving no phonetic differences at all. N for each category is as follows:

Segments involved:	1	2	≥ 2
Mode of recognition			
During utterance	22	7	9
Look or query	79	41	44
Later utterances	53	26	20
Later events	22	11	3
Not at all	4	2	2

Turning the Talk: Ku Waru "Bent Speech" as Social Action

Francesca Merlan

University of Sydney

Most works on figures of speech, or tropes, treat them as parts of cultural systems, and accordingly describe their meaningfulness in ways that focus on them as types rather than upon their situated use (see e.g., Fernandez 1974, Sapir and Crocker 1977, Wagner 1978). In this paper, by contrast, I shall mainly try to illustrate what, for Papua New Guinea Highlanders of the Nebilyer Valley in the Western Highlands Province, constitutes the efficacy of their recognized category of figurative speech. To explore the perspective of their appreciation, as I will show, is to locate the effectiveness of tropes precisely in their allusiveness and suggestiveness in particular contexts, rather than in their properties as cultural types.[1]

People of this area recognize a genre of speaking which they call ung eke, literally "bent speech", contrasting with ung kuni or "straight speech". (See Strathern 1975 for discussion of the equivalent figurative speech style among the Melpa, called by the cognate term ik ek). A necessary characteristic of bent speech is the use of tropes, and this, while valued in both public and private settings, tends to be most keenly valued in speech-making of the public domain, where in fact there is a strong association between the occurrence of tropes and a special, prosodically and paralinguistically marked oratorical style called el ung, literally "arrow/fight talk", which derives its name from one of its salient contexts of use: the intoning of taunts and insults directed at the enemy battleline in warfare. In this and other contexts, the use of el ung keys speech as of heightened relevance for inter-group political affairs (see also Strathern 1975).

In studying speeches of the public domain from which most of our examples come, we relied entirely on our informants' judgments about the identification of passages as "bent", since not everything that we as analysts might regard as figurative is considered by them to be ung eke. (For example, the common use of images of "roads", "bridges" etc. to express notions of social relationship is generally not seen by them as ung eke, but is simply taken as common usage). Finding considerable agreement among them in the identification of passages as ung eke, we were able to draw some conclusions about them as cultural types, and I will briefly describe some of these properties first.

One thing that became clear from our interviews with people about ung eke passages (from events which most of

them, along with ourselves, had attended) is that there is a
large stock of more-or-less standard figures which we can
call ung eke commonplaces. In most cases, what is fixed
about them is not their precise wording---these are not
"proverbial" in that sense---but the image conveyed. Let me
illustrate some of the "stock" images drawn from transcripts
of the warfare compensation payment cycle we attended and
recorded in 1983, which all of the people we consulted
agreed to be "bent speech". The main form of action at these
events was the public presentation of compensation payments
by members of segmentary groupings or "tribes" to others who
had acted as their allies in recent episodes of warfare.

Speakers frequently use images of slippery things:
logs, vegetation, and mud. Most are understood to be located in the forest. Slipperiness stands for precariousness,
and so such figures are taken to suggest imminent mishap and
the need for caution.

There is imagery of man as tree, usually making use of
tree types which are especially sturdy or tall. This identification is generally taken to express the value and
irreplaceability of the (especially male) person, the person
as a todul "strong" thing of enduring value. Such images
must be seen in relation to a system of social exchanges,
including life cycle payments of various kinds, which "stand
for" aspects of the person, but also largely occur in the
context of rhetorical assertions that the value of a
man/person is not fully substitutable by that of any valuable or payment (cf. Wagner 1975:92). There is also constant
use of imagery relating to the size and strength of segmentary ("tribal" and lower-level) groupings. Inadequacy and
weakness are expressed by imagery of small or dwarfed body
size, or by shortness or inadequate size in other objects.
This contrasts with metaphors of substantial body size.

There is standard imagery of alliance and dependence.
A transparent example of the former is the stock image of
ally as wife, or dependent female; a related turn of phrase
is that of "taking a wife", meaning "to gain as ally". In
talking about inter-group alliance and its renewal, speakers
talk of "taking a wife", "getting her back", etc., so that
their implicit identification is with the male role and the
ally is female, bargainable as is a wife concerning whom one
makes and debates bridewealth offers. A standard image of
dependence is that of getting others to help one apply
paint, the elaborate headdresses and other body decoration
of the kinds these people use. Here again, the implicit
identification of the speaker is usually with the perspective of male tribesman preparing for a display, but requiring assistance.

There are many stock images of harmony and disharmony.
Many of the former are at least cryptically female, such as
the stock image of "sleeping in the netbag" to express

living in accord with others: the basic image seems to be that of the child sleeping in the netbag or womb (for which the same term, wal, is used). But there is considerable additional development of netbag imagery, and so for instance, the image of a netbag splitting is taken to suggest trouble or the outbreak of warfare, and often, mention of where it breaks (top, bottom, side etc.) is understood as spatial homology for the territorial locations of segmentary groupings.

Imagery of "looking after" or "watching over" is common in the speeches of so-called "big men", usually as they attempt to depict themselves as having mediatory roles in regional relations. For example, in one speech a big man expressed his guardianship of the region through an analogy of parts of the Nebilyer Valley to parts of his own body. Another used an image of himself as snake, saying that his head and tail were at opposite ends of the valley and if anything happened in between, he would sense it. It is also common for speakers to use images of themselves as birds of the air who can watch over regional relations, a figure supported (for example, in the giving of personal names) by structural identifications of maleness with the air and (particularly predatory and/or splendid) birds of the air, femaleness with the ground and the typically more humble and defenceless birds of the ground (see also Strathern and Strathern 1968).

In final illustration, there are several sets of common images, often constructed in parallel form, which derive their significance from belonging to the range of events or signs that are commonly understood as temal "omens". Such images involve contrasts of "rain versus shine" (for example, actual occurrence of rain on the occasion of inter-group events is taken as an unfavorable omen for political relations); or "light and dark" ("red and black"), "hot and cold, damp", or equivalently, "cultivated area versus forest". For example, at the end of one payment event a speaker said: As you return home and come to the confluence of the Lupi and Ukulu rivers, if you see a red lake, take notice; or if you see a black lake, take notice. "Black" connotes peace, and "red", turbulence or hostility, and most people interpret such images as having to do with future peace or war. The more general significance of such omen images is that they underscore and express the notion that the future is unclear, holds options, may either be this way or that way; and thus they are part of a wider pattern, (involving both speech and other concurrent aspects of action such as material exchange), of suspecting and attempting to probe as-yet unrevealed significance.

These examples illustrate the point that most "bent" images are commonplaces and so perhaps it is no surprise to find, as this discussion has implied, that there is usually

considerable agreement on the part of the audience concerning the general sense of tropes deployed by speakers, for
example, that the contrast between red and black has to do
with options of war or peace. And also, given the standard
nature of tropes, it is perhaps not surprising to find that
there is no indigenous emphasis on their novelty or speaker
creativity in an absolute sense, that is, on speakers'
coining of new tropes. But there is much less consensus
about their possible and intended reference in context, and
for people of this area, it is in the question of reference
that most of the action lies, including the appreciation of
skilful speaking for its allusiveness and suggestiveness. I
will try to illustrate the audience interest in questions of
reference in context by talking about a couple of figures in
an excerpt from a speech which comes from the warfare compensation payment cycle of 1983 (see Appendix below, before
the Endnotes). The part excerpted was intoned in el ung.
While the example illustrates the indigenous interest in
reference, it also illustrates how people can operate without explicit agreement on it.

The examples I will discuss are the image of the
rotting tree at line 1047 of the speech, and the suggestions
concerning the payment being given, in the parallel lines
1049-52, and the relation between these two. However, to
understand the example to which the speech excerpt relates,
the reader needs some background illustrating the kind of
"context" against which appositeness and suggestiveness are
judged.

In an outbreak of warfare in our part of the Nebilyer
Valley in 1982, people of a "tribe" called Laulku aided the
people among whom we were living, of a tribe-pair called
Kopia-Kubuka. There is much intermarriage between Laulku
and Kopia-Kubuka, and this certainly was important motivation for their assistance. In 1983, a large-scale payment
event was staged of which a central focus was a compensation
payment by Kopia-Kubuka to Laulku for their help. However,
there was an issue about how this payment should be made, a
typical one in terms of the usual conduct of segmentary
politics in this area (for which see Merlan and Rumsey
forthcoming). The tribe-pair, or paired formation of especially closely allied tribes, is usual is this region, and
it happens that Laulku is paired with a segmentary grouping
called Mujika, and in fact some Mujika had fought alongside
the Laulku in helping the Kopia-Kubuka in 1982. Should the
Mujika, between whom and Kopia-Kubuka---to illustrate their
difference from Laulku---there is not as significant a
number of intermarriages, also be compensated? This was
something on which the Kopia-Kubuka evidently did not agree
among themselves. When, at the payment event, money was
placed on decorated display boards in typical fashion by the
Kopia-Kubuka, none was specially allotted to Mujika. It was

going to be left up to the Laulku recipients to make an
allotment to them. But as speeches got going, and in the
speech exchanges which, as usual, accompanied and explored
the nature and social significance of the material exchange,
a Laulku speaker suggested that the Kopia-Kubuka might
increase the amount to be given, since two Mujika men from a
particular (Mujika) sub-clan were married to Kopia women,
and the Laulku would have to give them money from the payment they were about to receive. The Kopia-Kubuka heard
this as an attempt to get them to increase the compensation
payment. But it was also generally heard as an expression
of the possibility that the Laulku were only going to make
payment to some of their Mujika allies as individuals, and
not to the entire Mujika grouping, to be shared more generally within it. However, this possible construction was
contravened by a leading man of one of the Kopia sub-clans,
Kopia Noma, the speaker of the el ung speech excerpted in
the Appendix. At the end of that speech, as can be seen at
line 1056, he expresses the idea that the Mujika will feel
badly if not recognized and compensated as a group, and he
calls out the name of a leading Mujika bigman, Kasipa, and
presents 200 kina ("one hundred pounds") to him. In accept-
ing the money, this bigman reaffirmed publicly "you are
giving money to Mujika", and praised Noma for being sufficiently sensitive to make an allocation to them himself,
instead of leaving it up to the Laulku to do: "You see with
flea-eyes", he said, meaning, you see from close up the
condition of our skin (an important indicator of psycho-
bodily condition).

What did the audience, and Noma himself (with whom we
discussed this speech later) take to be especially significant about it? One feature was the image at lines 1047-8 of
the rotting tree; the other was the interpretation, especially linked to lines 1049-52 (which express in parallel
form[2] a sense of option concerning what the recipients might
do with the money), that here he was making a bid to have
this compensation payment interpreted as an initiatory
payment, to be followed later in the usual fashion of this
area by a major return payment back to Kopia-Kubuka, from
what Noma is here working to possibly constitute as the
wider donor pair, Mujika-Laulku. (In this region, warfare
compensation is the prototypic form of exchange from which
major ceremonial exchange is seen to arise; see also Strathern 1971:94). In other words, one thing regarded as suggestive was Noma's understood bid for a following round of
major, inter-group exchanges.

The tree image illustrates the earlier point that
skill in this genre does not depend upon the use of original
tropes. Not only is the "tree as man" image standard, but
it had been used in a speech shortly before this by a Kubuka
big man in what had been taken as a less pointed but nonethe-

less specific reference. He had spoken of _sunga_ _kare_ "some
logs" of nothofagus beech, referring to the location of a
spirit-cult place (of Kilkai and Maip, also echoed in Noma's
speech at 1043-5 and 1049-52) where the money is to be
"baked" (the analogy is to the baking of food in an earth
oven, for further distribution to an assembled public).
But Noma rings a change upon this image, speaking of _karaip_
puruyl-te "_a_ rotting trunk" of nothofagus, on which there is
danger of slipping (line 1047-48). Members of the audience
we spoke with all interpreted the sense of this figure in
terms of the tree-as-man image, and further its being rotten
and the cause of imminent mishap as alluding to a lingering
or unrequited grievance or debt, related to standard practices of making compensatory payments which stand for aspects of the person. Though we asked many people about
their interpretation of this aspect of Noma's speech we
found that no one was aware of the details that he had had
in mind. But everyone thought that he did indeed have
something specific in mind, as suggested by his form of
words, which turned the Kubuka bigman's earlier reference to
place through the mention of "some logs", to a specific
unidentified "log" at that place, through use of the still
indefinite but individuating -_te_ "a".

Our later conversations with Noma revealed that a
"man" did indeed lie behind his image, but not in just the
expected way. He said his grievance concerned a mission his
father had performed as an assassin for the Mujika-Laulku,
during a war fought at least fifty years before. His father's sister had been married to a Mujika man, and his
father had been led to believe by them that he would be
rewarded for his services. However, he had never been
compensated for his help. Noma said that nothofagus beech
takes a long time to decompose, remaining firm and slippery
on the inside long after it appears rotten on the outside.
Hence its aptness to allude to an "old" grievance, which the
Laulku might have thought had been put aside.

Though nobody else appears to have had these details
in mind, nearly everyone realized that he was expressing a
grievance, and also understood him to be making a bid to
have this compensation payment interpreted as an initiatory
or first minor payment to induce a main payment to follow
from Mujika and/or Laulku to Kopia-Kubuka later on. The
link is that everyone takes the image of fallen tree as a
reference to a fallen man, or death, now a "rotten log"
which renders dangerous the path in the forest. It is
understood to be so because compensation payment should be
made for a death, and apparently has not been: the log is
slippery and precarious, hence the debt unrequited. By
taking up the reference in line 1045 to a Maip spirit-cult
place (which as noted had been mentioned by the Kubuka big
man in a previous speech), Noma locates the rotting tree in

the dense forest between the territories of Kopia-Kubuka and
Mujika-Laulku, hence metaphorically locating the debt as one
between them. From our interviews with members of the audience, the most likely inference would seem to be that the
fallen tree/man was a Kopia-Kubuka ancestor, for whose death
the Mujika and/or Laulku are being held responsible, and for
which they have never paid compensation. These as noted are
standard grounds for initiating a major exchange cycle. And
if this were to happen in future, Noma's speech will be
taken as a significant portent and influence in the matter,
given the fact that no major exchange cycle has ever been
transacted between Kopia-Kubuka and Mujika-Laulku. But as
Noma and others no doubt realize, the conditions for it were
favorable: at this time, Kopia-Kubuka's other main exchange
obligations were about to be discharged, and Kopia and
Kubuka each had far more affinal links to Laulku, at least,
than to any other tribal grouping, a factor invariably
positively correlated with major exchange in this area.

The effectiveness of Noma's remarks, and especially
his tropes, was obvious, in that nearly every following
Laulku and Mujika speaker took up his figures in some way.
One kind of response was to deny any outstanding debt. One
Laulku speaker said that the log had been burnt already,
i.e. the debt disposed of. Another literalized his interpretation of the log image and said, "I don't hear [=under-
stand, accept] those things you have been saying about your
ancestor". Others took up the possibility of major exchange
to which Noma was understood to have alluded. "You did not
give any cooked pork", one said, "that was a mistake". This
suggests that while money might be adequate for lesser
compensation, only pork would do if this were a matter of a
death, the kind of matter on which major exchange is typically based. He thus takes the occasion to try to shift the
blame Noma is attempting to locate, from himself and
Mujika-Laulku, back to Kopia-Kubuka for attempting to build
major exchange on an inadequate form of gift, while still
appearing to leave open the possibility that a debt may
exist, and that there may thus be grounds for future exchange.

These interventions by Mujika and Laulku speakers
showed how they could operate within the general sense of
the "rotting log"/"man" trope without agreement upon or
exposition of its precise reference. Here, it is sufficient
that they understand Noma to be suggesting their indebtedness, and that he is making a bid to establish further
exchange relations---on the strength of what all take to be
a specific reference to which his figures of speech allude.
It is this allusive and suggestive quality of bent speech,
and the dialectical, often (as here) multi-party working
between general sense and specific reference, in the light
of shared assumptions about the implications for social and

political relations of allowing particular sense-reference matchings to be made and to stand, that constitutes for people of this area the special interest and potential effectiveness of bent speech.

As this paper has suggested, we (Merlan and Rumsey forthcoming) find that this particular valuation of speech resources is part of a broader pattern of indigenous emphases in the constitution and valuation of social action---that is, speech here does not have what some ethnographers of speaking have claimed for their material, a patterning "all its own" (cf. Sherzer 1983). Here, in speech as in other forms of social action, indigenous emphasis and interest is not focused upon its conformity to structural "types", nor, consequently, on the instantiation of new types (that is, neither upon tropes as metaphor, nor upon the coinage of novel ones), but upon "event" as that which offers the possibility for revelation of potential meaningfulness in context, and exploration of the difference this makes. The indigenous category of "bent speech" might be characterized somewhat more closely as a set of formally diverse, but indigenously accessible[3] speech resources for alluding as a central way of making meaning.

To return to the beginning of this paper and the theme stated there: the local appreciation of bent speech backgrounds its general figurative and systemic properties, and focuses upon the deployment of familiar images of known general sense, within contexts such that possibilities for future social relations and political action are understood to be suggestively formulated.

APPENDIX

Transcript of Speech made by Kopia Noma at Compensation Payment by Kopia-Kubuka to (Mujika-) Laulku, July 24, 1983

KOPIA NOMA [pause lengths in seconds shown after each line]

i yi-ma-oooo [last two syllables 3.5 seconds long; pause 2.17]
men!

1030 i-yi-ma-oooo [.37]
men!

kunutapiya peng kera pelka-ja-o [.43]
if there were a feather on the shield

el adi-yl tekir nyib pilyilyka-o [.40]
I would really think I'm fighting

kera mek bulumingi-na telka-ja-o [.44]
If I fought on the back of the Princess Stephanie's bird of paradise

el adi-yl tekir nyib pilyilyka-o [.37]
I would really think I'm fighting

1035 yunu laimkangi lyip tekir-o [.37]
as it is I'm just going around quietly

kaspis-kiyl tekir-o [.35]
I'm just giving [money] for Irish potatoes

po pubu-kiyl tekir-o [2.1; falling pitch over last three syls.]
I'm just giving it for sugar cane

na-nga yiyl-a [0.00]
my 'man'

mensik pukun pukun-a [1.23]
you (sg.) take it for him

1040 tikiyl kang-ayl-a [0.00]
the Tikiyl man

tikiyl sokudu pukun-a [0.00]
you (sg.) go into to Tikiyl

idi kani-na-a [0.00]
there, where, as you know

kilkai lelym-kiyl-a [0.00]
there is a Kilkai spirit-cult place

idi kani-na-a [0.00]
there, where, as you know

1045 maip lelym-kiyl-a [1.47]
there is a Maip spirit-cult place

idi manya suku kalya-na-a [.30]
and there, half sunk into the ground

karaip puruyl-te pelym-kiyl-a [0.00]
there's the rotting trunk of a nothofagus beech tree

siyl-topa toba kanakun-a [0.00]
watch out, lest you (sg.) slip and fall on it

mekin pukun kilkai-ne kuyini kanapa [0.00]
if you (sg.) want to take this [payment] and sacrifice to Kilkai

1050 kilkai-na kuyui [0.00]
     then go ahead and sacrifice (sg.) to Kilkai

     maip-ne kuyini kanapa [0.00]
     if you (sg.) want to take it and sacrifice to Maip

     maip-ne kuyui [1.30]
     then go ahead and sacrifice (sg.) to Maip

     moni ilyi lepa nyim kanap-o [.97]
     this money which is here

     nu lyin kanapa-a [.96]
     you (sg.) take it

1055 nu tid kanapa [0.00]
     I gave it to you (sg.)

     mudika kit pilyiba [2.20]
     the Mujika (sg.) will feel badly about it

     mudika kasipa [0.00]
     Mujika Kasipa [man's name]

     okun ilyi-nga ena lyirin kanarud kanilyi [0.00]
     I saw you (sg.) come here and stay in the sun [on the battlefield]

     handet ilyi koma lensikir-o [0.00]
     I'm carrying this hundred ['pounds', i.e., 200 kina] for [you]

1060 ilyi-nga ok-lyi
     come and get (sg.) it

Endnotes

1. Fieldwork conducted jointly by my husband, Alan Rumsey, and myself in this area over sixteen months between 1981 and 1983 was funded in some part by the Australian Research Grants Council, and for the most part by a National Science Foundation Research Grant (No. BNS-8024174). We feel continuing commitment and indebtedness to many people in the Nebilyer Valley who helped us during our time there. See Merlan and Rumsey (forthcoming) for further details concerning Nebilyer oratory, and its place as an aspect of social action.

2. Du Bois (1986:326-7 and citations there) has recently argued that the parallelism of "ritual speech" centrally serves to project an image of inevitability, and otherwise may have an "elusive semantic effect" comparable to binocu-

lar vision. Though there is no space here for extended
examination of the use of parallelism in speech of public
and private domains in this area of the Highlands, it may be
said in summary that parallel linguistic structure often
appears to constitute a simplest formal basis for the projection of option and uncertainty, something that links it
importantly to local structures of social agency.

3. Accessible as compared, for example, to the special use
of pronominal categories we have called "segmentary person"
(Merlan and Rumsey forthcoming), which speakers deploy in
the public domain, and which contributes to the effacing of
possible distinctions as between the social actorhood of
"individuals" and the segmentary groupings with which they
are identified. In our extensive discussions of speeches of
the public domain with informants, none clearly identified
instances of segmentary person as a kind of speech resource,
at the same time that many of them were at pains to attempt
to clarify the often difficult and allusive references of
passages involving such pronominal usage. Thus it appears
that "segmentary person" alludes and is felt by local people
to be allusive, but resists indigenous identification as a
formal device or set of devices.

References

Du Bois, J. W. 1986. "Self-evidence and ritual
speech". Pp. 313-36 in Evidentiality: The linguistic coding
of epistemology, W. Chafe and J. Nichols eds. Series: Advances in Discourse Processes, v. 20. Norwood, N.J.: Ablex
Publishing Corporation.
Fernandez, J. 1974. "The mission of metaphor in expressive culture". Current Anthropology 15(2):119-45.
Merlan, F. and A. Rumsey (forthcoming) Ku Waru: Language and segmentary politics in the Western Nebilyer Valley. Papua New Guinea. Cambridge: Cambridge University
Press.
Sapir, J.D. and J. Christopher Crocker 1977. The
social use of metaphor: Essays on the anthropology of rheto-
ric. Philadelphia: University of Pennsylvania.
Sherzer, J. 1983. Kuna ways of speaking: An ethnographic perspective. Austin: University of Texas Press.
Strathern A.J. 1971. The rope of moka: Big men and
ceremonial exchange in Mt. Hagen. New Guinea. Cambridge:
Cambridge University Press.
-----1975. "Veiled speech in Mt. Hagen". Pp. 185-203
in M. Bloch (ed.), Political language and oratory in traditional society. London, New York and San Francisco: Academic Press.
Strathern, A.J. and A.M. Strathern 1968. "Marsupials

and magic: A study of spell symbolism among the Mbowamb".
Pp. 179-202 in E.R. Leach (ed.), Cambridge Papers in Social
Anthropology.

    Wagner, R. 1975. The invention of culture. Englewood
Cliffs, N.J.: Prentice-Hall.

    -----1978. Lethal speech: Daribi myth as symbolic
obviation. Ithaca: Cornell University Press.

Hao: A Chinese Discourse Marker[1]

W. Charles Miracle
The Ohio State University

1.0   Introduction

In the traditional approach to Chinese syntax, the scope of investigation has been limited to linguistic phenomena which are no larger than a sentence. Following the lead of Chao Yuen Ren and his now famous statement, "The sentence is the largest language unit that is important for grammatical analysis" (Chao 1968:57), linguists studying the Chinese language have largely ignored in their analysis the impact of such language units as speech act, discourse, etc.   In the past decade more and more Chinese linguists have begun to direct their attention to these larger language units and their influence on Chinese as it is spoken in everyday conversation (Tsao 1979 and Biq 1984 and 1988). Building on the work of the syntacticians, they have attempted to explain phenomena which cannot be explained when the sentence is taken as the largest significant unit of linguistic analysis. This paper is an effort to extend this extra-sentential inquiry by analyzing in some depth the use of hao in spoken Chinese discourse.

The lexical item hao in Mandarin Chinese has a variety of related functions and meanings as a review of several dictionaries will reveal. A Concise Chinese-English Dictionary, compiled for the use of foreigners learning Chinese, defines hao as follows:

Adjective: 1) good, well, having the desired quality;
        2) friendly; 3) of a high level; 4) beneficial,
        useful, efficient; 5) healthy, sound;
Used as a resultative complement: 1) indicates that
        something is ready to be used; 2) in proper order;
Indicates approval or agreement;
That's enough, stop;
Adverb: 1) used with an exclamatory sense before an
        adjective to indicate high degree; 2) quite; 3) used
        before certain verbs to indicate that sth. is easy;
        4)used before the predicate of the second clause of
        a compound sentence to introduce the purpose for
        which one does something. (BLI 1982:224[2])

This investigation will focus on the use of hao as described in the portion of the definition highlighted above. Other reference works designed for the use of Chinese also recognize these uses of hao. The Gwoyeu Ryhbaw Tsyrdean, compiled in Taiwan, states that hao is a "word which expresses approval and permission; expresses conclusion or stopping; contrary to expectation" (He 1974:198-99). Xiandai Hanyu Cidian, published in the People's Republic of China, states that hao "expresses a tone of approval, agreement or conclusion; used ironically, expresses dissatisfaction" (Linguistics Research Institute 1984:445). Finally, Lu Shuxiang in his Xiandai

Hanyu Babai Ci comes closest to capturing the use of _hao_ as I see
it.

> Expresses several moods. When used alone, it resembles
> an interjection.
>   a) expresses agreement
>   b) expresses conclusion
>   c) irony: expresses taking pleasure in or gloating
>   over others' misfortune (Lu 1980:226)

While the above definitions do capture the essence of the meaning
of _hao_ they do not begin to explain the function of this lexical
item.

The syntactic analyses also fail to explain the discourse usage
of _hao_. Consider the following utterance:

> 1) ZT1: _Hao_ ba, Wang xiansheng, zhei zhen buhaoyisi.
>   HAO PART Wang   Mr.   this real embarrassing
>   Fine, Mr. Wang, this is really embarrassing.
>
>   B2: Hao le, hao le, bu yong   keqi   le.
>   good ASP good ASP NEG use politeness PART
>   Fine, fine, no need to be polite.

In Chao's (1968) analysis, B2 in the above exchange would consist of
three "minor sentences."   Regarding this type of sentence Chao
states the following:

> A minor sentence is not in the subject predicate form.
> It occurs more frequently in two-way conversation and in
> speech interposed or accompanied by action than it does
> in connected discourse. (Chao 1968:60)

The above example then would consist of the "minor sentences," a)
Hao le., b) _Hao le.,_ and c) _Bu yong keqi le._ In each of these
sentences the subject or topic NP would be missing and would have
to be recovered from the surrounding discourse. Li and Thompson
(1981), while not using Chao's term "minor sentence," would probably
also adhere to the above analysis. While most people would readily
agree that the "lost" subject NP for c) above is _ni_ 'you,' the
hearer, the "missing" NPs in a) and b) are not nearly so apparent.
I would argue that there is no "missing" subject in these sentences
but rather that _hao_ here is a discourse marker and as such is not
amenable to internal syntactic analysis.

Based upon the inspection of a small body of data, I will show
that the above instances of _hao_ can be more adequately explained by
a method of analysis which goes beyond syntactic evidence and
utilizes the surrounding discourse as a primary source of information. Because this investigation is my first real foray into the
arena of discourse/conversational analysis (I use this nomenclature
because my theoretical framework draws from the theory and

methodology of both conversational and discourse analysis in an attempt to overcome the inherent weaknesses of each approach), my attention will be focussed largely on the model for analysis. The small body of data and this focus on methodology will not allow me to draw any strong conclusions, rather I will be restricted to suggestions of possible tendencies.

2.0 Theoretical Framework

The theoretical framework and methodology for this work will draw primarily from Schiffrin's (1987) work on discourse markers and her theory of discourse coherence. I will utilize this framework in my analysis of the discourse structure and the role of the discourse marker hao in that structure. My definition of discourse particle draws upon the work of Ostman (1982) as modified by Bourgerie (1987) and Schiffrin (1987). The method of discourse parsing utilized here is drawn primarily from the theory of speech acts and social actions proposed by Geis (1989a and 1989b).

2.1 Discourse Marker — Definition

The first issue to be addressed here is one of terminology. Ostman (1982) discusses "pragmatic particles," yet these same phenomena are called "discourse particles" by Bourgerie (1987) in his investigation of Cantonese particles and "discourse markers" by Schiffrin (1987). In this paper I will adopt the terminology of Schiffrin first because I have adopted her model of discourse investigation and secondly because the term "particle" seems too restrictive for the linguistic units under investigation. While some discourse markers are clearly included in this category of linguistic units, items like jiushi, keshi, you know, OK, and others, being polysyllabic and containing significant phonetic content, do not easily fit the label "particle."

Schiffrin (1987:31) defines discourse markers as "sequentially dependent elements which bracket units of talk." The key terms in this definition are "sequentially dependent" and "units of talk." "Sequentially dependent" is used to indicate that discourse markers operate on an extra-sentential level and are not dependent on the smaller units which make up a discourse. "Units of talk" is a broad term used to include speech acts, sentences and smaller units, thus discourse markers can occur sentence initially, sentence finally and sentence internally. Ostman (1982:149) approaches the definition of pragmatic particles in a rather different manner. He defines the pragmatic particle in prototypical terms as follows:

> Typically, a pragmatic particle would be (a) short, and
> (b) prosodically subordinated to another word. It would
> (c) resist clear lexical specification and be proposition-
> ally empty (i.e., it would not be part of the proposition-
> al content of the sentence). Furthermore it (d) would
> tend to occur in some sense cut off from, or on a higher
> level than, the rest of the utterance, at the same time
> as it tends to modify the utterance as a whole.

As Bourgerie (1987:43) points out regarding discourse particles in Cantonese, the criteria regarding prosodic dependence does not necessarily hold across languages. One should also note that this is a definition of the prototypical discourse marker and as such deviations from this ideal should be expected. In the case of hao one would clearly wish to argue that it is one of the discourse markers that Ostman would want to classify as "PERIPHERAL members of the class of pragmatic particles" (Ostman 1982:153). Hao clearly has some propositional content although it arguably does not add to the propositional content of the sentence with which it is associated. Again as Bourgerie (1987) has noted for Cantonese, the final criteria, (d), appears to be the crucial test for discourse markers. I will argue that hao does indeed operate at a "higher level" than the rest of the utterance.

2.2 Discourse Parsing — Geis' Model of Speech Acts and Social Actions

Geis (1989a and 1989b) has proposed a new theory of speech acts in which it is argued that what have been called speech acts are, in fact, fundamentally social, rather than linguistic in nature. He argues that there are three basic constructions, Declaratives, Interrogatives and Directives, each of which has a social action potential, and that utterances are "meant to be taken literally in conversation" with the social force of an utterance being calculable given

- the literal meaning (*l*-meaning) of the sentences (which includes truth-conditional aspects of meaning, presuppositions, conventional implicature, and most aspects of deixis)
- contextual information (including what has preceded conversationally, aspects of the social context, and epistemic context)
- shared background knowledge
- a set of conditions on social actions
- common sense reasoning of the Gricean sort
- principles governing the conduct of conversation, e.g., turn taking rules. (Geis 1989a)

Each of the three basic constructions is subject to a sincerity condition namely:

- A. Declaratives: for S asserts P to H: S must have a warranted belief that P is true.
- B. Interrogatives: for S asks H whether or not P: S must have a warranted belief that P is true or P is false. for S asks H an Interrogative of the form "WH-X, ...X...": S must have a warranted belief that there is an instantiation of "...X..." which is true.

C. Directives: If S directs that H do A. under a description
    of P, then S must have a warranted belief that A is
    performable action. (Geis 1989a)

One or more of these basic constructions then comprise a social
action. The social actions (traditionally called **speech acts**) we
use these constructions to perform are not necessarily or even
normally accomplished in a single speaker turn but are rather
accomplished over a series of S turns and H responses. The various
turns that comprise a single social action typically involve
negotiation concerning satisfaction of the conditions associated
with that social action. These conditions are essentially what
Searle (1969) called "felicity conditions."   The individual
utterances which comprise a social action sequence are typically
meant literally and normally make covert or overt reference to the
preparatory conditions of the social action.   When all of the
preparatory conditions are met, either implicitly through inference
from the speech situation, the social relationship of the interlocutors, etc., or explicitly through the basic utterances, then the
social action is completed.

2.2.1 Commissive/Requestive Social Actions

    Searle (1979:14 from Austin (1962)) describes commissive
illocutionary acts as those which commit the speaker to a course of
action. Directive illocutionary acts, including commands, requests,
and invitations, on the other hand, are an attempt to commit the
hearer to a course of action (Searle 1979:13). These two types of
illocutionary acts share an important property in Searle's clas-
sificatory framework; they have the same "direction of fit between
words and the world" (Searle 1979:3). They both are attempts to
cause "the world to fit the words," i.e., to cause a change in the
world.   Hancher (1979), in his review of Searle's taxonomy of
illocutionary acts, faults Searle for inadequately dealing with the
group of illocutionary acts which he calls "commissive directives"
(Hancher 1979:6). These acts, including offers and invitations, at
the same time commit the speaker to a course of action and attempt
to move the hearer to action.

    In this study I will focus on the social actions which I will
label Command, Request, Suggestion, Offer, and Invitation. These
social actions all share the characteristic that they are attempts
to change the world to fit the words. They differ, however, on
several important variables:

    1- Benefit   Speaker--------Mutual---------Hearer
                       command   suggestion   suggestion
                       request   invitation   offer

2⁻	Commitment to Action	Speaker————Mutual————Hearer

```
2⁻   Commitment      Speaker---------Mutual---------Hearer
     to Action                       offer          command
                                     invitation     request
                                     suggestion     suggestion

3⁻   Speaker         Total---------------------------No Control
     Control         command         request        suggestion
                                   (invitation)
                                     (offer)
```

The issue of speaker control above may need some explanation. With regard to commands, requests and suggestions, this issue is fairly clear. The speaker control comes from the extra linguistic situation. A mother has the authority to command her children while friends can only make requests and suggestions to one another. The control involved in invitations and offers is one of control over outcome. The speaker can only control his actions relative to the invitation or offer (I should note that this parameter is not crucial to invitations and offers). These different social actions can then be defined in terms of these variables. Note in this case that a suggestion can be for either hearer action or joint action and thus would involve hearer or mutual benefit respectively.

The felicity conditions of these social actions can also be seen to derive from these three variables;

Command
1. S wants H to do A or bring about P (benefit to S).
2. S believes that H is willing and able to do A or bring about P.
3. S has authority over H.

Request
1. S wants H to do A or bring about P (benefit to S).
2. S believes that H is willing and able to do A or bring about P.
3. S has limited authority over H.

Suggestion
1. S wants H to do A or bring about P (benefit to S).

   or

2. S believes A to be in H's interest.
3. S believes H is willing and able to do A or bring about P.
4. S has no authority over H (or is not exercising it).

Offer
1. S is willing and able to do A.
2. S believes A to be in the interest of H.
3. If H agrees, S will do A.

Invitation	1.	S is willing and able to do A (benefit to S).
	2.	S believes H wants A (benefit to H).
	3.	If H agrees, S will do A and H will participate.

While the benefit to the parties and the speaker control is made explicit in these felicity conditions, the commitment to action, because it necessarily is involved in the outcome of the social action, is not always explicitly stated.

2.3 Discourse Structure - Schiffrin's Model of Discourse Coherence

Schiffrin (1987) describes coherence in discourse as deriving from the interaction of different structures, frameworks and states in which the persons involved in a discourse participate. The Action Structure is that structure in which speech acts (social actions in the framework used in this paper) are situated. She defines this structure as

> ...the management of oneself and others so as not to violate appropriate standards regarding either one's own demeanor or deference for another. (Schiffrin 1987:25)

The Exchange Structure is the turn structure which the conversational analysts attend to. Schiffrin defines this structure as

> ...the outcome of the decision procedures by which speakers alternate sequential roles and define those alternations in relation to each other. (Schiffrin 1987:24)

The Ideational Structure involves the organization of semantic units, propositions and ideas within the discourse. This structure includes the relationship between old information and new information, descriptive background and the main point, specific instances and a generalization based on them, etc. The Participation Framework includes the relationship between the speaker and hearer deriving from their respective social status, the speech situation, etc., and the relationship between the interlocutors and their utterances. This aspect of the Participation Framework includes a speaker's commitment to his utterance, his willingness to fight for or relinquish a turn, etc. Finally, the Information State is used to describe the speaker/hearer interactions regarding their respective cognitive states and their organization and management of knowledge and meta-knowledge. Knowledge here is what the speaker/hearer knows while meta-knowledge is what they know or believe about their shared knowledge, i.e. the other's knowledge. Schiffrin (1987:28) points out that "information states are constantly evolving over the course of a conversation." Discourse markers operate in one or more of these structures, frameworks or states at the same time and in this manner tie together these different levels of discourse structure and thereby participate in the creation of discourse coherence.

3.0 The Data and Analysis
3.1 Data

The following conversational excerpts come from a series of radio plays broadcast by the Jingcha Guangbo Diantai (Police Radio Network of Taiwan) in Taipei, Taiwan. Each broadcast consists of a short moral play regarding the perils of life in contemporary Taiwan. These plays are scripted but still contain a very colloquial and natural style of conversational Chinese. In transcribing these plays I have been helped immeasurably by the text of the plays prepared by the staff of the Inter-University Program for Chinese Language Studies (IUP 1984). They are currently using these transcripts and audio tapes for teaching purposes. I have edited them liberally and provided my own gloss and translation.

The data to be analyzed is taken from four different broadcasts involving eight different speakers. Additional instances of hao were found in these plays but were not transcribed due to time limitations. These other instances are generally similar to the instances transcribed here. There were, however, several instances of hao used to convey the propositional content of `that's enough' or `stop' described earlier. While these instances would no doubt be worth analyzing, that task is beyond the scope of this investigation.

3.2 Analysis

From a close analysis of the data it appears that the discourse marker hao operates primarily in the Action Structure of the discourse to mark the closure of Commissive/Requestive social actions. Secondarily hao can function in the Exchange Structure as an answer to a question, an appreciation of a statement, and an assent to a command. The Action Structure is identified as the primary operating arena of hao because it appears that hao can operate either in the Action Structure alone or in the Action Structure and the Exchange Structure simultaneously. Further, it appears that the discourse marker hao is used exclusively in Commissive/Requestive social actions. This exclusive use may be tied to the requirement of this type of social action for the commitment on the part of one or both of the interlocutors to a course of action.

A cursory examination of the data reveals that hao is found only in the Commissive/Requestive type social action. Within this body of data there are four distinct types of Commissive/Requestive social actions; commands, requests, suggestions, and offers. Of the different types of social actions which appear in this category as outlined above, only invitations fail to appear. I would argue that this fact is due to the small size of the data rather than any incompatibility of hao with invitations. I should also note here that these different types of Commissive/Requestive social actions are not always clearly distinguishable from one another.

The command social action below is straightforward and very revealing of the role of _hao_;

2) X3: Mingjian, ma   yijing ba   damen suoshang le. Ni
       Mingjian mother already PART door lock   ASP you
       Mingjian, mother has already locked the door. You

       dai   meimei   zai   fujin   war a.   Ma
       take little sister in neighborhood play PART mother
       take little sister out to play in the neighborhood.

       hen kuai jiu hui lai le   a.
       very fast then return come ASP PART
       Mother will come back shortly.

   J1: _Hao_   ma   zaijian.
       HAO mother goodbye
       OK Mom, goodbye.

   X4: _Hao_, zaijian.
       HAO goodbye
       OK goodbye.

In turn X3 the command is issued and in J1 the command is acknow-
ledged and accepted through the use of _hao_. That the social action
is completed from the point of view of the speaker J can be seen
from his following this completion marker with a farewell. Speaker
X then confirms the closure from her perspective following her
completion with her own farewell. This second instance of _hao_
serves only in the Action Structure as a marker of completion of the
social action. The first instance in J1 functions in both the
Exchange Structure as an acknowledgement and assent to a command and
the Action Structure to mark J's completion of his part of the
social action. The other pattern of occurrence of _hao_ found in
commands can be seen below;

3) X4 Dangxin   chezi a,   zhuyi   anquan a.
       be careful cars PART pay attention to safety PART
       Watch out for cars and be careful.

   J2: _Hao_.
       HAO
       OK.

In this pattern _hao_ is used only once by the hearer, the person who
is the recipient of the command. _Hao_ here acts in both the Action
Structure and the Exchange Structure serving at once to complete
the social action and to acknowledge and assent to the command.
    Requests follow the same pattern as the commands described
above. _Hao_ can be used both by the speaker, the initiator of the
action, and by the hearer, the recipient of the request, or it can

be used only by the hearer. Examples 4) and 5) below demonstrate
these respective patterns;

    4)   L2: Ba,   ma,   na women zou ba.
                father mother then we walk PART
                Dad, Mom, then let's go.

          ZT1: <u>Hao</u> ba, Wang xiansheng, zhei zhen buhaoyisi.
                HAO PART Wang   Mr.   this real embarrassing
                Fine, Mr. Wang, this is really embarrassing.

          B2:   <u>Hao</u> le, <u>hao</u> le, bu yong   keqi   le.
                HAO ASP HAO ASP NEG use politeness ASP
                Fine, fine, no need to be polite.

    5)   F1: E,   ayi, kuai yidiar hui   lai a.
                INT Aunt fast a little return come PART
                Hey, Auntie, come back quickly.

          A3:   <u>Hao</u>.
                HAO
                Alright.

The similarities between the command and request social actions can
be clearly seen from the examples above. This similarity should not
be surprising.   My analysis of these social actions and their
inherent felicity conditions reveals that they differ only in the
amount of speaker control over the situation. Hence the difference
in the Participation Framework deriving from the different social
relationships among the participants in these instances does not
appear to impact the Action Structure or the Exchange Structure.
A single <u>hao</u> is used by the hearer as in 5) to assent to the request
and to close the social action. The double <u>hao</u> is used by both the
hearer and the speaker to first assent and close, ZT1, and then to
complete the closure, B2. The following formulaic command made by
B, however, suggests an alternative interpretation. Here the <u>hao</u>
<u>le</u>, <u>hao le</u> can be interpreted as having the propositional content
of 'that's enough, stop' referring to ZT's attempt to be polite.
This alternate interpretation suggests that this other use of <u>hao</u>
may not in fact be too far removed from the usage which is under
discussion here. Such a connection is certainly worthy of further
study.
    The suggestion found in the data examined shows only the
presence of the single use of <u>hao</u> by the listener. The lack of the
reciprocal use of <u>hao</u> may be due to an inherent characteristic of
suggestions or this absence could be due to the small size of the
data examined. Consider the following examples:

    6)   F3: En na women qu caishichang zhao   mama hao bu hao?
                INT then we go   market   find mother good NEG good
                Aw then let's go to the market to find Mom, OK?

J3: Em <u>hao</u> ba.
INT HAO PART
Hmn, OK.

7) L1: Ni kan, nabian you ge kanxiang de, women
you look that side have CL tell fortune NOM we
Look over there, there's a fortuneteller, let's go

guoqu qiaoqiao, hao bu hao?
go over see good NEG good
over and take a look, ok?

C1: Ee, suan la, ai, ni bu jide women xiao shihou
INT forget it INT you NEG remember we little time
Aw, forget it, hey, don't you remember when we were

chang na lai kaiwanxiao de naju hua?
often take come joke NOM that-CL speech
little that joke we used to say?

L2: Shenme hua?
what speech
What joke?

C2: You ming suan dao mei ming.
have fate calculate to NEG fate
Figure your future so often that you have no future.

L3: Aiya, fanzheng shi chulai guang jie, sha shijian
INT anyway be come out wander street kill time
Aw, anyway we came out to wander around and kill

ma!
PART
time!

C3: Ee, <u>hao</u> ba.
INT HAO PART
Oh, ok.

L4: E, ge, ni kan, wo zhei bian zhei ke zhi
INT older brother you look I this side this CL mole
Hey, older brother, look, my mole here, isn't it just

shi bu shi gen ta tushang de zhei yike yiyang?
be NEG be with he chart-on NOM this one-CL same
like the one on his chart?

In both of these examples, _hao_ is used in both the Action Structure
and the Exchange Structure. _Hao_ is used as an answer to the preceding utterance, a question in both cases, thus participating in
the Exchange Structure. Every question requires an answer if the
response is to be felicitous. The _hao_ also serves to complete and
conclude the suggestion social action thus participating in the
Action Structure. Turn L4 shows clearly that the social action has
been completed and that the participants in this conversation
recognize this completion. The next speaker makes an obvious change
of topic and thus initiates a new social action.

Offers also present a difference in patterning from those seen
earlier. In 8) below is an example of the reciprocal use of _hao_
seen above while a new pattern is seen in 9) below. In this new
pattern, the speaker rather than the hearer is the only participant
using _hao_ to mark the completion of the social action.

8) J6: Mmm, na..(?) you le. Women qu shudian   mai tiezhi
INT then   have ASP   we go bookstore buy stickers
Hmn, then...(?) I have it. We can go to the bookstore

lai wan. Nabian,   najia   shudian de tiezhi
come play that-side that-CL bookstore NOM sticker
to buy stickers to play with. That bookstore's

hao piaoliang o.   You meili de hua, you ke-ai
good beautiful PART have pretty NOM flower have cute
stickers are really pretty. They have pretty flowers,

de   xiao dongwu, you katong   renwu   e.
NOM little animal have cartoon personage PART
cute little animals, and cartoon characters.

F7: E, _hao_   a, wo zui xihuan tiezhi le, hmn.. wo yao
INT HAO PART I most like sticker ASP INT   I want
Oh, OK, I like stickers the best, hmn, I want to buy

mai xiao   ji,   xiao niao, hai you xiao yaya.
buy little chicken little bird still have little duck
a little chicken, a little bird, and a little duckie.

J7: _Hao_, na women zou.
HAO then we walk
Fine, then let's go.

9) A1: Women xian bu qu shichang, wo yao qu mai ni yixie
we   first NEG go market   I want go buy you several
We're not going to the market first, I want to go buy

wanju song gei nimen na. Ye yao mai yidian liwu
toy give give you PART also want buy a little gift
some to give to you. I also want to buy a little

song gei ni mama. E   xiaomeimei, ni xihuan
give give you mother INT little sister you like
gift to give to your mother. Hey, little sister,

yangwawa   ne haishi da gouxiong a?
foreign-doll PART or big bear   PART
would you like a doll or a big bear?

F1: Wo xihuan yangwawa.
     I like foreign-doll
     I would like a doll.

A2: Hao, deng yixia   ayi mai yige   zui da zui
     HAO wait a little aunt buy one-CL most big most
     OK, wait a minute and Auntie will buy you the biggest

     piaoliang de yangwawa   gei ni a.
     pretty NOM foreign-doll give you PART
     and prettiest doll.

Again in 8) F7, hao is active in both the Exchange Structure and
the Action Structure. The discourse marker is used to accept the
immediately prior offer and to mark the conclusion of the social
action. While there is a further comment by this speaker, F7, this
comment just serves to reinforce the completion of the social action
by commenting in the Participation Framework on the speaker's
commitment to this agreed upon course of action. In 9) A2 only the
speaker utilizes the marker hao to indicate her closure of the
social action. The hearer, through the propositional content of her
prior statement, F1, in stating her preference has satisfied the
only felicity condition in question, the issue of what would be in
the hearer's "best" interest. The comment following the marker of
completion, hao, as we have seen earlier, addresses the participants' commitment to the agreed-upon action.

4.0 Conclusions

From the above analysis it is clear that hao is a discourse
marker which functions at least in the Action Structure and the
Exchange Structure of discourse. While hao is still not devoid of
propositional content and does participate to a degree in the
propositional content of some exchanges, as a marker its use cannot
simply be explained by its meaning. I have described the function
of hao in the Action Structure as one of marking completion of
social actions. It is important to note that hao marks the satisfactory completion of these social actions. The inherent meaning

of _hao_ derived from its use as a stative verb and a resultative complement would likely be sufficient to keep this marker from functioning to mark the unsuccessful completion of Commissive/-Requestive social actions.

The use of _hao_ also appears to be tied to the commitment on the part of the speaker to a course of action. In all of the examples studied, the speaker who is most clearly committed to action is the one most likely to use _hao_. We have seen in commands, requests and offers where _hao_ is used, while both the speaker and the hearer might use _hao_ to signal completion of the social action, in the cases analyzed at least the person who is committed to act will use _hao_. In the case of offers, this person is the speaker, while in the case of commands and requests, this person is the hearer. In the case of suggestions, this generalization is not so clear. Both of the instances cited involved mutual action on the part of the participants. One could argue that only the commitment of the hearer to action was in question in these instances. This uncertainty would then account for the tendency of the hearer to use _hao_ more than the speaker. Such an explanation would tend to support Geis' (1989b) argument that once the felicity conditions of a social action are satisfied, the social action is completed.

Finally, I should note that _hao_ appears to function in Chinese in a manner similar to that of _OK_ in English (Merritt 1984). Regarding the use of _OK_ in service encounters, typically involving requests, Merritt concludes that _OK_ minimally has two functions:

(1) that of signifying approval, acceptance, confirmation;
(2) that of providing a bridge, a linking device between two stages or phases of the encounter. (144)

Merritt also specifically comments on the use of _OK_ to signal termination of one stage of the service encounter. Within the framework utilized in this paper, these "stage" transition points would typically be identified as the completion point of a social action. The function of _OK_ in English discourse is thus remarkably like that of _hao_ in Chinese conversation. This similarity and the utility of Schiffrin's model of analysis would suggest that Schiffrin's (1987:328) speculation that there may be common characteristics across languages which "allow expressions to be used as markers" has some merit.

Endnotes

1. I would like to thank Michael Geis, Robert Sanders, and James Tai for their comments made on previous versions of this paper.

2. All translations, unless otherwise stated, are my own.

References

BEIJING YUYANXUE YUAN (Beijing Language Institute-BLI). 1982. A
    concise Chinese-English dictionary. Beijing: The Commercial
    Press.
BIQ, YUNG-O. 1984. Indirect speech acts in Chinese polite expres-
    sions. Journal of Chinese Language Teacher's Association
    19(3).1-10.
-----. 1988. From objectivity to subjectivity: The text-building
    function of you in Chinese. Studies in language 12(1).99-102.
BOURGERIE, DANA S. 1987. Particles of uncertainty: A discourse
    approach to the Cantonese final particles. M.A. thesis, Ohio
    State University.
CHAO, YUEN REN. 1968. A grammar of spoken Chinese. Berkeley:
    University of California Press.
LINGUISTIC RESEARCH INSTITUTE, CHINESE SOCIAL SCIENCES INSTITUTE.
    1984. Xiandai hanyu cidian (Modern Chinese dictionary).
    Beijing: Commercial Press.
GEIS, MICHAEL L. 1989a. A linguistically motivated theory of
    conversational sequences. Proceedings of the 25th regional
    meeting of the Chicago Linguistic Society.
-----. 1989b. A new theory of speech acts. To appear in the
    Proceedings of the sixth annual meeting of the Eastern States
    Conference on linguistics.
HANCHER, MICHAEL. 1979. The classification of illocutionary acts.
    Language in Society 8(1).1-14.
HE RONG. 1974. (ed.) Gwoyeu ryhbaw tsyrdean (Mandarin daily news
    dictionary). Taipei: Mandarin Daily News Publishing Division.
INTER-UNIVERSITY PROGRAM FOR CHINESE LANGUAGE STUDIES (IUP). 1984.
    New radio plays.
LI, CHARLES N. AND THOMPSON, SANDRA A. 1981. Mandarin Chinese: A
    functional reference grammar. Berkeley: University of Califor-
    nia Press.
LU SHUXIANG. 1980. Xiandai hanyu babai ci (800 words in modern
    Chinese). Hong Kong: Commercial Press, Hong Kong Division.
MERRITT, MARILYN. 1984. The use of 'okay' in service encounters.
    Language in use, ed. by J. Baugh and J. Scherzer. Englewood
    Cliffs, NJ: Prentice-Hall, 139-47.
OSTMAN, JAN-OLA. 1982. The symbiotic relationship between pragmatic
    particles and impromptu speech. Impromptu speech: A symposium,
    ed. by Nils Enkvist. Abo, Finland: Abo Akademi, 147-77.
SCHIFFRIN, DEBORAH. 1987. Discourse markers. Cambridge: Cambridge
    University Press.
SEARLE, JOHN R. 1969. Speech acts. Cambridge: Cambridge University
    Press.
-----. 1979. Expression and meaning. Cambridge: Cambridge Univer-
    sity Press.
TSAO, FENG-FU. 1979. A functional study of topic in Chinese: a first
    step towards discourse analysis. Taipei: Student Book Company,
    Ltd.

Sentence fragments revisited*

Jerry L. Morgan

University of Illinois

Introduction. Several years ago (Morgan 1973) I examined some empirical problems of 'fragments' like example 1b, interpreted as a response to the question in 1a. I pointed out some syntactic evidence that such fragments are derived by deletion from full sentences, so that 1b would be derived transformationally from the same underlying source as 1c. (I will use 'deletion analysis' as a convenient nickname for this analysis, whose details I will discuss below).

(1) a. What do you see in the window?
  b. A large yellow bird.
  c. I see a large yellow bird in the window.

There were some puzzling aspects to the deletion analysis that were left unresolved. In the meantime, several works have appeared that directly or indirectly challenge the deletion analysis on various grounds, including Yanofsky 1978, Napoli 1982, and the recent book-length treatment by Barton (in press). In this paper I re-examine the deletion analysis, pointing out its most obvious strengths and weaknesses, and taking into account some of the objections that have been raised. My purpose is to survey the generative alternatives for treating fragments, and to discuss the implications of these alternatives for theories of modularity. I will first recapitulate the deletion approach and its obvious competitor, in which fragments are directly generated, and sketch the original evidence in favor of deletion. I will then discuss the residue of unsolved problems for deletion, and the theoretical and empirical objections that have been raised in the literature. I will end with suggestions for a third alternative that treats fragments extra-grammatically, with a discussion of the implications for modularity.

The deletion analysis. The basic facts of fragments are quite simple at first glance; speakers are able to make at least two kinds of judgments for a fragment like that in example 1b: they are able to judge the grammatical well-formedness of the fragment[1], and they are able to judge the appropriateness of the fragment as a direct response to a previous utterance (as in the case of 1b as a response to 1a).

It's obvious that as a response to 1a, 1b is exactly as appropriate as 1c is, because 1b conveys 1c in context 1a; or, more awkwardly but more accurately, 1b can be used to convey directly as a response to 1a what 1c can be used to convey directly as a response to 1a. It's also obvious that interpreting fragments at least sometimes requires reconstructing a larger structure containing the fragment. That people are able to do such reconstruction is shown by the fact that they can make sense of structural puns like those in examples 2 and 3.

(2) a. What are you up to?
  b. Page 32.
(3) a. What did Dracula turn into?
  b. The nearest bar.

But observations of functional equivalence and reconstruction in processing are not by themselves convincing arguments for assigning 1a and 1b identical underlying syntactic structure. Reconstruction in processing is not an unequivocal argument for equivalent underlying representations. To account for the functional equivalence it would suffice to generate fragments directly, and appeal to semantics and/or pragmatics to provide a non-syntactic account for the functional equivalence of 1a and 1b, without assigning them a common syntactic form at any level. In fact I will argue below for the plausibility of a pragmatic, non-syntactic approach for at least some fragments.

There are two obvious alternatives for the syntactic analysis of fragments in generative grammar:

> BASE GENERATION: Fragments are generated directly, by some technical modification of the definition of 'generates', so that grammars no longer generate only S's, but phrases of several categories.

> DELETION: Fragments are generated by deriving them from larger structures, presumably sentences, of which the fragments are constituents

Base generation has been proposed by Brame 1979, Napoli 1982, Yanofsky 1978 and Barton in press, for diverse reasons. The common thread of their proposals is to allow grammars to generate not just sentences, but phrases of several categories; all maximal X-bar categories, for example.

Although I use 'deletion' as a handy name for the second approach, the deletion operation is not the crucial aspect of the analysis; rather, it is the claim that such fragments have the underlying syntactic form of sentences, in which the phonologically realized fragment is a proper sub-constituent. The central idea is that the well-formedness and appropriateness of fragments are derivative of the well-formedness and appropriateness of full sentences containing the fragments. Whether the relation of the fragment to the containing sentence is treated by deletion or by generating sentences consisting mainly of phonologically null elements is neither here nor there for the purposes of this paper. Either variant requires some principles to restrict what elements of the sentence can be phonologically missing.

The main point of Morgan 1973 was to show that syntactic evidence favors deletion over base generation, by showing that appropriateness judgments of fragments involve dependencies between syntactic properties of fragment and linguistic context, in a way that seems to require deriving fragments from full sentences. The syntactic evidence is in two classes: evidence that depends crucially on transformational assumptions, and evidence that holds for mono-stratal theories as well. The transformational evidence consists of fragments that are not constituents in underlying structure, but arise only through the application of transformations; passive and tough-movement are prime examples, as illustrated in these examples from Morgan 1973:

(4) a. If Hubert is hard to follow now, what would he be if he spoke more slowly?
    b. Totally impossible to understand.
(5) a. What is John's goal?
    b. To be killed in combat.

230

It's hard to see how to derive such fragments under the kind of base generation analysis described above, since the fragments do not contain the domain for the transformations in question. But in fact there is a modification to the base generation approach that could reconcile such facts with transformational assumptions: namely, to modify the definition of 'generates' to include non-sentential phrases, in a way that is derivative of the definition of sentence. Suppose the standard formulation of 'generates' for a transformational grammar specifies conditions under which a grammar generates a given string as an S, and assigns it a complex structural description containing a 'surface structure' as a sub-part. Then we add a second clause, to the following following effect:

> G generates a string X, with structural description SD, just in case X is analyzable as SD in the surface structure of some S generated by G.

Thus grammars would generate not only well-formed sentences, but well-formed phrases of every category, as long as the phrase could appear in the surface structure of some sentence[2]. But it's important to note that this modification does *not* make the base generation analysis equivalent to deletion, since even with the modification the well-formedness of the fragment does not depend in any way on syntactic properties of linguistic context. All that's required for a fragment to be well-formed is that the fragment occur in the surface structure of *some* well-formed sentence. There is no additional entailment, as there is in the deletion analysis, that the well-formed sentence be one that is appropriate in context. Thus in the modified base generation analysis, 6b is well-formed due to the well-formedness of sentences like 6d, even though the obvious deletion source 6c is not well-formed.

(6) a. Who did you talk to?
    b. Not to John.
    c. *I talked not to John.
    d. Bill sent your book not to John, but to Harry.

Thus the modified base analysis overcomes the transformational evidence that the simple base analysis faces. The grammar provides to the user an infinite set of phrases of category S, and an infinite set of fragments of various categories whose well-formedness is derivative of the definition of 'surface structure constituent of a well-formed S'; but the well-formedness of such fragments is not relativized in any way to syntactic properties of linguistic context.

Transformational difficulties with passive and tough-movement fragments don't arise for mono-stratal theories like GPSG, of course, since for obvious theoretical reasons the fragments in question *must* be generated as phrases in such theories. But the second class of evidence favoring deletion is independent of this theoretical division. It consists of cases where some property of a fragment appears to depend on properties of a larger, functionally equivalent phrase or sentence containing the fragment. Complementizer choice (like other matters of subcategorization) is a simple case. A fragment is well-formed just in case it satisfies complementizer requirements in the relevant position in the linguistic context; thus 7b is well-formed as a response to 7a, but 7c is not, with the opposite pattern in 8:

(7) a. What does John want?
    b. To come over after dinner.
    c. *Come over after dinner.

(8) a. What did John help you do?
    b. *To wash my car.
    c. Wash my car.

Binding properties are another clear example. Anaphoric elements, including pronouns, reflexives, and 'epithets', are well formed in fragments just in case they would be well-formed in the corresponding larger expressions containing potential binders (I give only a couple of examples here, and refer the reader to Morgan 1973 for more). Thus John is excluded as a possible referent for 'the bastard' in 9b, just as he is in 9c; and 'John' in 10b cannot be construed as coreferential with 'he' in 10a, just as it cannot in 10c. But coreference is possible in 11b, just as it is in 11c.

(9) a. What does John think?
    b. That the bastard is being spied on.
    c. John thinks that the bastard is being spied on.

(10) a. Where is he staying?
    b. In John's apartment.
    c. He is staying in John's apartment.

(11) a. Where is his wife staying?
    b. In John's apartment.
    c. His wife is staying in John's apartment.

As far as I can see, the only way to reconcile such data with the base generation approach is to give up the assumption that the relevant binding conditions are defined on syntactic structure.

Some observations of Pope 1971 also favor deletion: exceptional lexical properties can affect the well-formedness of fragments, as if the fragment were part of a larger structure. Adjectives like 'ill' and 'content' are exceptional in that (for some speakers) they can occur only in predicative position, not attributively:

(12) a. The boy is content/contented.
    b. He is a contented/*content boy.

This distribution is mirrored in fragments in a way that could be explained by a deletion analysis, but not by the base generation analysis:

(13) a. Is the boy unhappy?
    b. No, content/contented.
    c. No, he's content/contented.

(14) a. Is he an unhappy boy?
    b. No, *content/contented.
    c. No, he's a *content/contented boy.

Fragments also show dependencies that appear to be the effect of island constraints, in that the fragment cannot be in a position that is in an island in the corresponding full sentence. As a consequence, in the following examples, the fragment responses are not equivalent to the corresponding sentence responses (for more

232

extensive data, see Morgan 1973):

(15) a. Did John and Bill leave this morning?
b. No, Harry.
c. No, John and Harry left this morning.
(16) a. Was the man who shot Lincoln a Marine?
b. No, Kennedy.
c. No, the man who shot Kennedy was a Marine.
(17) a. Did John's seeing Martha upset the President?
b. No, Thelma
c. No, John's seeing Thelma upset the President.

It's clear that a treatment of such phenomena could be constructed in the deletion approach, where it is possible to talk about the position of the fragment in the larger sentence containing it; but no such solution is available in the base generation approach.

Case marking presents a similar problem, in that in a language like Korean with a healthy case marking system, case marking in fragments is predictable from the position of the fragment in the corresponding sentence, as in the following examples (the asterisk signifies inappropriateness as a direct reply to the question in a):

(18) a. Nu-ka ku chaek-ul sa-ass-ni?
Who this book (acc.) bought?
Who bought this book?
b. Yongsu-ka (nom.)
c. *Yongsu-rul (acc.)
d. Yongsu-ka sa-ass-ta.
Yongsu (nom). bought
Yongsu bought it.

(19) a. Nuku-rul po-ass-ni?
who (acc.) saw?
Who did you see?
b. *Yongsu-ka (nom.)
c. Yongsu-rul (acc.)
d. Yongsu-rul po-ass-ta.
Yongsu (acc.) saw
I saw Yongsu.

Unsolved problems. From facts like these, and others discussed in the earlier paper, the evidence seems to favor a deletion analysis. Unfortunately, the evidence is not unequivocal. It favors the deletion analysis in this respect: the base generation analysis predicts that fragments should have *no* sentence-derivative syntactic properties; this prediction is clearly falsified by the data. The deletion analysis predicts that fragment should have such sentence-derivative properties, which is consistent with the facts to a large extent. Unfortunately, the deletion analysis in its simplest form makes the stronger prediction that fragments should have *all* such properties, save the phonological differences that result from deletion-under-identity. This pre-

diction is too strong, as I pointed out in Morgan 1973. First, the effect of island
constraints in fragments, unlike sentences, is mitigated when the fragment corresponds to a full-sentence position that is at the sentence periphery (see Morgan 1973
for fuller discussion). Second, some fragments are not well-formed even though the
corresponding sentence is fully well-formed. English nominative case pronouns are
a simple illustration of this point. Nominative case pronouns cannot be used as
fragments, as shown in 20 (presumably 'you' is acceptable because it is ambiguous
or unmarked for case):

> (20) a. Who can eat another piece of cake?
> b. *I/*we/*he/*she/you.
> c. Me/?us/him/her.
> d. I/we/he/she/you can eat another piece of cake.
> e. *Me/*us/*he/*she can eat another piece of cake.

Third, some fragments are well-formed in spite of the fact that the corresponding
sentence is ungrammatical. This can be seen in pronouns (example 20c), negated
constituents[3] (example 21), in the combination of prepositions with sentential complements (example 22), in interactions with negative polarity items (example 23),
in 24, which defies labelling; see Morgan 1973 for more examples.

> (21) a. Who shot Cock Robin?
> b. Not Bill/Not I/Not me.
> c. *Not Bill/*Not I/*Not me shot Cock Robin.
> (22) a. Concerning the weather, what can we rely on?
> b. That it will rain.
> c. *You can rely on that it will rain.
> (23) a. Who ever has any money?
> b. My friend Boesky.
> c. *My friend Boesky ever has any money.
> (24) a. What do you like about John?
> b. His nose.
> c. *I like his nose about him.

Some problems of this nature might be solved by exploiting syntactic levels, in a
multi-stratal theory; for example, whatever principle it is that bans $Prep + S'$ might
hold only at S-structure, but not at 'later' levels in which the preposition is missing.
And it's not implausible that English nominative pronouns have structural requirements that are not met in fragments. In short, it's not inconceivable that a more
fully developed deletion analysis could overcome these empirical problems.

Other objections. Nonetheless there are other objections one might raise to the
deletion analysis, beyond the obvious criticism that the conditions of application of
the deletion rule are only alluded to, never explicitly stated. First, there is the theoretical objection that the analysis violates the spirit of autonomy and modularity, in
that the deletion rule is defined on pairs of sentences. The definition of well-formed
fragment is not given in terms of formal properties of the fragment itself, but in a
way that depends on formal properties of another sentence: a fragment is syntac-

tically well-formed just in case it can be derived by deletion-under-identity from a well-formed sentence.

The system might better be viewed, then, as generating not well-formed phrases, but well-formed discourse pairs, certainly a profound deviation from the theoretical foundations of generative grammar. Personally I don't find such theoretical objections compelling; if the facts require such an analysis, so be it. But for those with more fastidious theoretical tastes than mine, I think there is a way to re-construe the deletion analysis that partially overcomes the objection. As originally described, the deletion analysis simultaneously accounts for both the well-formedness and the appropriateness of fragments, by reducing both to the well-formedness and appropriateness of corresponding sentences containing the fragments. But suppose we separate these functions: the well-formedness could be treated syntactically, independent of linguistic context, by some version of the base-generation approach. Appropriateness of sentences in context should follow from a general theory of pragmatics. Then the appropriateness of fragments could be attributed to a component of pragmatic competence that assigns discourse appropriateness to context-fragment pairs, by relating the fragment to some full sentence.

But there is still a troublesome aspect to this approach: the pragmatic system must reconstruct, for each context-fragment pair, one (or more, in the case of ambiguity) full sentence whose appropriateness the fragment inherits. The problem is, the evidence suggests that the reconstruction process deals in syntactic properties defined in sentence grammar. One would expect discourse appropriateness to depend on syntactic properties only insofar as syntactic properties determine semantic properties, which in turn partially determine use properties like speech act potential and appropriateness-in-context. But for fragments of the kind discussed so far, appropriateness judgements depend on syntactic properties of sentences containing the fragments, in a way that seems to violate this expectation.

Another objection to deletion, due originally to Yanofsky (Yanofsky 1978, and in her unpublished dissertation) is that there are fragments whose appropriateness cannot be treated as derivative of full sentences. Yanofsky gives a number of interesting types of such fragments whose interpretation requires no prior linguistic context, like the following:

(25) a. One hot dog, please.
　　 b. John, your face!
　　 c. The door.
　　 d. Thief!
　　 e. Fire!
　　 f. Sharks!
　　 g. Idiot!
　　 h. Cold Beer!
　　 i. That damn dog.

Yanofsky argues persuasively that the well-formedness and appropriateness of fragments like these are not derivative of properties of containing sentences. Then presumably such cases must be generated directly, rather than by deletion from sentences. From this premise Yanofsky criticizes the deletion analysis on the grounds that it would not provide a unified analysis of fragments, since some would be directly generated, others derived by deletion[4]. Her criticism is motivated by the observation that a sound theory of pragmatics ought to provide an account of fragments anyway. I believe she is correct on this point, though I disagree with the conclusion she draws from it. Her reasoning, if I understand correctly, goes roughly like this:

1. There are fragments like those in 25 whose well-formedness and appropriateness properties are not plausibly derived from properties of sentences.

2. Therefore there must be syntactic rules to generate NP's and other non-sentential phrases directly.

3. Various sub-systems of linguistic and/or pragmatic competence must assign use properties (speech act potential, appropriateness, ...) to such fragments directly, not derivatively from properties of sentences.

4. Any system (or conglomerate of systems) that can do this much will automatically provide an analysis for the cases that do involve linguistic context.

5. Therefore every such fragment receives dual treatment. The deletion analysis is redundant, since its domain is a subset of the domain of the more general pragmatic system.

6. Therefore, on grounds of theoretical parsimony, the deletion analysis is wrong and should be abandoned.

Points 1 through 3 are probably correct, and I will not discuss them further. The remaining points are problematic, and I will spend some time on them, arguing that point 5 is correct. I will show some data from Korean that suggest that there are two strategies available for interpreting fragments, one entirely pragmatic and the other involving syntactic reconstruction.

Toward a redundant account of fragments. By *pragmatics* I mean the general approach to interpretation inspired by the work of H. P. Grice, especially Grice 1975. In this view, the heart of pragmatics is not another specialized module of the language faculty, but common-sense interpretation of intentional actions: the every-day human ability to make sense of events by interpreting them as goal-directed actions carried out by beings with intentions. One application of this general ability is its application to linguistic events: the ability to interpret utterances of linguistic expressions as intentional actions. Working from non-linguistic observations of the facts of context (including the observable facts of the event of utterance) and from the semantic properties assigned by grammar to the expression uttered, the hearer reconstructs the goals and intentions behind the speaker's acts of utterance. Knowledge-of-language in the Chomskyan sense has only a small role in this process, albeit an indispensable one.

Given the obvious generality of such an intepretive ability, it is inevitable that it would give an account of the kind of fragments Yanofsky discusses, without deriving their properties from properties of sentences. To begin with, it is plausible to think that expressions smaller than sentences have associated speech-act potential. Assuming some assignment of speech-act potential to noun phrases, every utterance of a noun phrase can be interpreted as an intentional act, even when the utterance is not embedded as a sub-part of the utterance of a sentence. Then it should be possible to interpret some noun phrase utterances without reconstructing containing sentences. A thought experiment may make this point clearer. Suppose we are in a room together, and English is our only common language. Suppose further that I am on the phone with a third party, speaking Albanian to her, and narrating to you the events of our phone conversation. I say something in Albanian to her, then turn to you and say "I just asked her who's with her." She says something to me in Albanian, and I turn to you and say "She just uttered the name of her son." Without knowing Albanian, it should be pretty clear to you what the import of her second utterance is, without having to reconstruct a full Albanian sentence containing her reply. Knowing the semantic and use properties of names, assuming that the intent of her utterance was to reply cooperatively to my question, the goal and communicative import of her act of utterance is plain.

So I'm willing to concede to Yanofsky point 4: that the right pragmatic theory, if we had one, would automatically provide an account of (at least some) fragment utterances, without reconstructing containing sentences. It follows immediately, then, that to maintain the deletion approach is to maintain that some fragments, perhaps all, receive two accounts: one from pragmatics alone, one via deletion from a containing sentence. But I'm not willing to concede that this is grounds for abandoning the deletion analysis. Occam's razor has to be wielded with great care in psychology, since, as Sadock points out (Sadock 1983), redundancy is common in living systems. It's unwise, then, to rule out *a priori* the possibility of two independent systems of fragment interpretation.

In fact there is some evidence from Korean that suggests that there are two parallel systems. The phenomenon involved is case-marking. In some languages, like German, every noun phrase[5] bears some linguistic manifestation of case. The morphology and syntax interact in such a way that no caseless noun phrases are generated. But in Korean, case-marking is optional under a diverse set of conditions. First, in some colloquial styles, nominative and accusative case markers may be omitted in certain syntactic positions. Second, case markers may be omitted in non-final conjuncts of coordinate structures, as in 26, and must be omitted in combination with the verb 'ita', as in 27[6].

(26) a.
Yongsu-ka	kuriko	Suni-ka	chip-e kassta
Yongsu (nom.)	and	Suni (nom.)	home-to went

b.
Yongsu	kuriko	Suni-ka	chip-e kassta
Yongsu (no case)	and	Suni (nom.)	home-to went

Yongsu and Suni went home

(27) a.   I kos-i   chaek   ita
           This (nom.)   book (no case)   is

      b.   *I kos-i   chaek-i   ita
           This (nom.)   book (nom.)   is
           This is a book

The upshot is that the morpho-syntax of Korean must generate both case-marked noun phrases and noun-phrases that are not marked for case. And this grammatical distinction corresponds to the distinction between two kinds of fragments. There are Korean fragments that are like Yanofsky's English fragments (example 25) in requiring no linguistic context. Such fragments appear without case in Korean, as in 28. The kind of fragment discussed in Morgan 1973, which show dependencies on syntactic properties of linguistic context, may occur in Korean with or without case, as in 29 through 31 (in these examples the asterisk signifies that the form is inappropriate for the use indicated).

(28) a.   phyo   han-cang   (no case)
           ticket   one
           *phyo   han-cang-i   (nom.)
           *phyo   han-cang-ul   (acc.)
           One ticket! (to order a ticket)

      b.   nae   cha!   (no case)
           *nae   cha-ka   (nom.)
           *nae   cha-rul   (acc.)
           My car! (On finding my stolen car)

      c.   pul! pul!   (no case)
           *pul-i! pul-i!   (nom.)
           Fire! Fire!

(29) a. Nu-ka ku chaek-ul sa-ass-ni? *Who bought the book?*

          Yongsu-ka (nom.)   Yongsu-ka (ku chaek-ul) sassta
      b. Yongsu (no case)   *Yongsu (ku chaek-ul) sassta
          *Yongsu-rul (acc.)   *Yongsu-rul (ku chaek-ul) sassta
          Yongsu   *Yongsu bought the book*

(30) a. Nuku-eke ku chaek-ul ponaess-ni? *Who did you send the book to?*
          Yongsu-eke (dat.)   (na-nun) (ku chaek-ul) Yongsu-eke ponaessta
      b. Yongsu (no case)   *(na-nun) (ku chaek-ul) Yongsu ponaessta
          *Yongsu-ka (nom.)   *(na-nun) (ku chaek-ul) Yongsu-ka ponaessta
          Yongsu   *(I) sent (the book) to Yongsu*

(31) a. Muos-uro phyonci-rul ssoss-ni? *With what did you write the letter?*
          Yonphil-lo (instr.)   Yonphil-lo ssoss-ta
      b. Yonphil (no case)   *Yonphil ssoss-ta.
          Pencil   *(I) wrote (it) with a pencil*

The distribution of case in these examples is very interesting. The first kind of fragment, whose interpretation is independent of linguistic context, appears without case. In the second kind, interpreted relative to linguistic context, the fragment may appear with the case one would expect from the deletion analysis. Or it may appear without case, *even when case is obligatory in the corresponding sentence.* The facts suggest parallel systems: one for caseless noun phrases, which interprets fragments without reconstructing containing sentences, and one for case-marked noun phrases, which interprets fragments by reconstruction. Accounting for the unacceptability of the starred case-marked fragments in examples 29b and 30b requires one additional assumption: the presence of case marking *forces* the reconstruction strategy. The acceptability, then, is a consequence of the failure of reconstruction. The reconstruction process attempts to use syntactic information from context and fragment to reconstruct a full sentence that is an appropriate response to the context. Reconstruction fails, and the case-marked fragment is judged unacceptable.

The absence of case, on the other hand, doesn't force reconstruction, but allows the pragmatic system to proceed without reconstruction. Whether absence of case in fact *blocks* reconstruction is impossible to tell from these data.

Discussion: speculations on a synthesis. So far I have argued for a redundant solution, based on the Korean evidence, involving both a pragmatic, non-reconstruction strategy, and a syntactic strategy that involves reconstruction from linguistic context. I have identified the latter with syntactic deletion, so that the reconstruction is treated as a matter of grammar proper.

But the reconstruction approach could also be reformulated extra-grammatically, with fragments generated directly in the syntax, and interpreted by processing strategies that involve reconstruction in context. This seems to be consistent with the proposals of Barton, though many details of her theory remain to be worked out, and it is hard to see at this point how she would account for all the sentence-like properties of fragments. Still, I believe that this approach is very promising, since it may be more consistent with the most troublesome kind of data for the syntactic deletion approach: partiality. As I have pointed out (see examples 21 through 24 and accompanying discussion), fragments have some, but not all, of the properties one would expect them to have if they were sub-constituents of sentences. Taken as a complete account of fragments, neither base generation nor deletion is consistent with this partiality. The base generation analysis falsely predicts that fragments don't behave in any way as if they were sub-constituents of sentences. The syntactic deletion approach avoids this false prediction, but errs in the other direction, in that in its simplest form it predicts that such fragments behave in every way as if they were sub-constituents of sentences. The data make it clear that this prediction is also false, though the door is left open to explain the discrepancies in grammatical terms, say in terms of constraints that do and do not hold at the post-deletion level of analysis.

The processing-strategy approach could be made consistent with this partiality if the linguistic processing module and the system of pragmatic interpretation interacted in such a way that reconstruction is partial. What's required is a system that can 'turn off' reconstruction at a point before a full sentence is reconstructed, with the result that only some sentential properties will be manifested in acceptability judgements.

If we view the pragmatic system (PS) as a consumer of information produced by the linguistic processor (LP), then the question is of the flow of information between the two. In the simplest view, LP takes in a linguistic form and works to a complete linguistic analysis of it, which is then fed to PS[7]. PS is entirely passive, with no control over the workings of LP. But suppose that the interaction is more complex, and that LP feeds partial information to PS as processing unfolds. Suppose further that PS is able to determine when the information it receives from LP is sufficient for needs at hand, and is able at that point to 'turn off' LP before the linguistic input is fully processed. The problematic partiality of sentential properties of fragments could then be explained in terms of the interaction of PS and LP. This picture of things requires a very complex model of inter-modular interaction, but it preserves the heart of modularity, in that the pragmatic system does not deal in grammatical properties.

But deciding between the grammatical approach of syntactic deletion and an extra-grammatical approach involving complex modular interaction will require much more research, both by linguistic and psycholinguistic methods. Future research should be directed toward discovering the unifying features that distinguish the sentence-like properties fragments do have from those they don't have, and examining how the difference relates to the flow of information in processing.

Footnotes

* I am indebted to Georgia Green for extended comments, to Jae Ohk Cho for help with the Korean data, and to Ellen Barton for her comments and the impetus of her work to make me take another look at this problem.

1. Judgments may of course be influenced by the manner of presentation. In my experience, non-linguists tend to reject examples like (i)a presented out of context, but will accept them as well-formed and functionally equivalent to (i)b when a context like (i)c is supplied.

    (i) a. I used to think lobster.
       b. I used to think lobster is the most delicious seafood.
       c. What is the most delicious seafood dish?

2. It might be necessary to add further restrictions; for example, that the phrase must be X-bar maximal, in light of examples like (ii), contrasted with (iii):

    (ii) a. Did John borrow your book, or my book?
       b. *My.
       c. John borrowed my book.
    (iii) a. Did John borrow yours, or mine?
        b. Mine.
        c. John borrowed mine.

If such a restriction is necessary, then a counterpart restriction would be necessary in the deletion approach.

3. Note that despite first appearances, the negated constituent fragments here

are not inconsistent with the modified base generation proposal presented above, in which fragments are generated derivatively of sentences, though not, strictly speaking, *derived from* sentences. Though the sentences here are not grammatical, nonetheless there are grammatical sentences in which such negated constituents *can* occur, which is all that's required for the fragments to count as grammatical:

(iv) In the corner stood not Bill, but a frightened deer.
(v) It was Harry, not I, who stole the tarts.

4. James D. McCawley suggests that Yanofsky's premises can be turned against her: her observation that some cases are not dependent on linguistic context can be taken as evidence that such cases deserve a different treatment from fragments which do involve linguistic context. I am still ruminating on this point.

5. Well, almost every noun phrase. It's not obvious whether to consider proper names, for example, as inherently caseless, or ambiguous for case. The point is, Korean noun phrases have caseless forms, which is not generally true in German.

6. Although only nominative is shown here, the example with 'ita' is ungrammatical with *any* case marker on the preceding noun phrase. The caselessness of the noun phrase is an idiosyncratic requirement of the verb 'ita', and   a consequence of compounding or incorporation. The negative of 'ita', 'anita', requires that the noun phrase be marked with nominative case.

7. A common complaint against this simple view is that the flow of information is uni-directional, which conflicts with the theory that linguistic processing can make use of non-linguistic information; for example, that syntactic processing makes use of semantic and pragmatic information. The complaint may well be justified, but it is independent of the point I'm trying to make here: that the flow of information is incremental and partial, and can be 'turned off' before it reaches completion.

References

Barton, E. in press. *A theory of the grammatical structure and pragmatic interpretation of nonsentential constituents.* John Benjamins, Amsterdam.

Brame, M. 1979. A note on COMP S grammar vs. sentence grammar. *Linguistic analysis*, 5:383–386.

Grice, H. P. 1975. Logic and conversation. In P Cole and J Morgan (Eds.), *Syntax and semantics, volume 3: speech acts*, pages 41–58, Academic Press, New York.

Morgan, J. 1973. Sentence fragments and the notion 'sentence'. In B Kachru et al. (Eds.), *Issues in linguistics: papers in honor of Henry and Renée Kahane*, pages 719–751, University of Illinois Press, Urbana.

Napoli, D. J. 1982. Initial material deletion in English. *Glossa*, **16**:85–111.

Pope, E. 1971. Answers to yes-no questions. *Linguistic Inquiry*, **2**(2):69—82.

Sadock, J. 1983. The necessary overlapping of grammatical components. In J Richardson et al. (Eds.), *Papers from the parasession on the interplay of phonology, morphology and syntax*, pages 198–221, Chicago Linguistic Society, Chicago.

Yanofsky, N. 1978. NP utterances. In D Farkas et al. (Eds.), *Papers from the four-teenth regional meeting, Chicago Linguistic Society*, pages 491–502, Chicago Linguistic Society, Chicago.

Grammatical Person and Social Agency
in the New Guinea Highlands

Alan Rumsey

University of Sydney

This paper concerns some of the social uses of grammatical categories of person and number in Ku Waru, a Papuan
language spoken in the Nebilyer Valley, in the Western
Highlands of Papua New Guinea, where Francesca Merlan and I
have done linguistic and anthropological fieldwork.[1] One of
our main concerns has been with the oratorical uses of
language at large scale ceremonial exchange events, which
play a central part in the social life of Ku Waru people, as
elsewhere in New Guinea and Melanesia more generally (see
Merlan and Rumsey forthcoming, Rumsey 1986, Merlan, this
volume). What I will be focussing on here are particular
forms of personal reference and address within that oratory
which seem problematical for the cross-linguistic characterization of concepts of speaker and addressee. To see how
they might be problematical, let me first briefly review
some of the limitations of those notions, and some recent
attempts to overcome them.
    Classical structuralist analyses of the grammatical
category of *person* (e.g. Benveniste 1971, Jakobson 1971)
have taken these concepts of speaker and addressee as
primitive terms. While this may suffice for distinguishing
paradigmatically among person categories in particular
languages, it has begun to look inadequate for understanding
the various *uses* of those categories in situated discourse.
Goffman (1981) argued that, in order to account for what
goes in everyday English, one must recognize at least two
kinds of hearer/addressee: addressed and non-addressed
recipient; and at least three kinds of speaker: 'author',
'animator', and 'principal'. He also made a cross-cutting
distinction between 'ratified' and 'non-ratified' participants in the speech event. Systematizing and elaborating
upon Goffman's framework, Levinson (1987) has proposed a
feature analysis allowing us to capture what he claims are
empirically motivated distinctions among at least 17 different participant roles. Our ordinary notion of speaker, for
example, is specified by plus values along four distinct
dimensions of potential contrast, viz.; +PARTICIPANT (in the
speech event), +TRANSMISSION (i.e. actual utterer or transmitter of the message), +MOTIVE (i.e. having the motive or
desire to communicate some particular message), and +FORM
(i.e. being the one who has devised the form or format of
the message). Minus values along some of these dimensions
allow us to distinguish this 'ordinary' sort of speaker

242

from, for example, a 'ghostee', i.e. someone reading or
reciting a speech written for them (-FORM), or a 'spokesman', who is responsible for the form of the utterance but
is not its motivator (-MOTIVE). In a recent critique of
Levinson's approach, Irvine (ms.), while recognizing the
usefulness of Levinson's distinctions, and suggesting that
even they may not suffice, argues against his strategy of
decomposing speaker and hearer into a set of other, analytically primary components, and proposes instead to derive the
more subtle subtypes via a notion of intersecting frames.
For example, she proposes that the special status of the
Wolof Griot as 'spokesman' (see Irvine 1974) at weddings can
be accounted for by the fact that her message is contextualized with respect to two distinct speech events: the present
one, in which she is speaker, and a prior one, in which she
was an addressee, and was instructed in what to say.

Let us now turn to the oratory used at Ku Waru exchange events and consider what its implications might be
for this debate. In order to understand the relevant forms
of person reference used within that oratory, we must first
consider some other aspects of the social formation in which
it plays a part.

Despite Ku Waru people's present political encapsula-
tion within the nation-state of Papua New Guinea, and their
increasing involvement in the cash economy (their first
contact with the outside world having occurred in the
1930s), gift exchange among them still functions as what
Marcel Mauss (1966) called a 'total social phenomenon', in
our terms at once political, economic, and religious in its
ramifications. The organizing bases of exchange even in this
one society are various, and include both what we can gloss
as an *interpersonal* dimension and an *inter-group* one. On the
interpersonal side, exchange takes place between individual
trading partners, who are usually related to each other
through ties of matrilateral kinship or affinity -- eg.
between a man and his mother's brother's son, or his wife's
brother. On the intergroup side, exchange takes place between *talapi*, a kind of segmentary social unit which can for
present purposes be roughly glossed as 'tribe' or 'clan'.
Talapi are, however, unlike some segmentary units found,
e.g. in Africa and Polynesia in that there are within them
no inherited or otherwise ascribed positions of leadership
(see Merlan and Rumsey forthcoming, Chapter 3, for other
differences and further details concerning the nature of
talapi). Instead of chiefs or chiefly lineages, within each
talapi, there is more-or-less open competition for 'big man'
status -- a status which is understood to be achieved largely through demonstrating skill in the practice of oratory
and ceremonial exchange. These two activities -- oratory and
gift exchange -- are closely interrelated in that exchange
transactions between *talapi* are always accompanied by exten-

sive speechmaking.

Exchange in its inter-*talapi* aspect cannot be thought of as mutually exclusive with interpersonal exchange. Rather, most exchange transactions between *talapi* consist of, or have an alternate identity as, a congeries of transactions between individual partners identified with each of the two *talapi*. Thus, for example, a major payment in 1981 by a *talapi* called Kubuka to one called Poika (both to figure in the examples below) consisted of 33 distinct interpersonal payments made by particular members of Kubuka (or small consortia of them) to particular partners in Poika. Now what would-be bigmen compete at is not so much the maximization of their own 'interpersonal' exchanges, nor their personal contributions to inter-*talapi* ones; rather, they struggle to coordinate their fellow clansmen's inter-personal transactions into an inter-*talapi* one. Or, more generally, as I shall try to demonstrate below, they struggle for control of the meaning of events for inter-group politics (cf. Lederman 1980).

It is in this context that the person and number categories of the Ku Waru language take on certain values which seem problematical for some standard notions of speaker and addressee. The language distinguishes three grammatical numbers -- singular, dual and plural -- and the usual three person categories, with conflation of second and third person in the non-singular numbers, as shown in Table One.

Table 1. Ku Waru Personal Pronouns

	Singular	Dual	Plural
First Person	na 'I'	olto 'we two'	olyo 'we'
Second Person	nu 'you'(sg.)	elti 'you two' or	eni 'you' (pl.)
Third Person	yu 'he'/'she'	'they two'	

Exactly the same distinctions are shown in the verb, which agrees with its subject in person and number. Now in Ku Waru as in English, socio-political entities, e.g. the sides in a war, can be referred to in the singular or the plural number (e.g. 'Germany was at war with Poland'/'The Germans fought the Poles'). But unlike in English, in Ku Waru, the singular usages are not limited to the third person, but are also common in the first and second. That is, words which we would otherwise translate as 'I' or 'you' (sg.) (and verbs which are marked for 1sg. or 2sg. subject) can be used

to refer not to individual, physically present 'speaker' and
his 'addressee', but to whole segmentary units. 'I' (*na*) in
this context can be glossed as: 'the segmentary unit with
which the orator uttering this instance of *na* is identified'; and 'you' (*nu*) as 'the segmentary actor to which this
utterance is addressed'. This does not necessarily imply
that the physically present, speaking individual is included
among the referents of his 'I', nor that the referents of
his 'you' include individuals present at the speech event,
for what is sometimes being referred to are activities which
took place well before any of these people were born. For
example, 'I' fought with 'you' can mean: 'my ancestors *qua*
segmentary unit fought with yours'.[2] These uses are instances of what Francesca Merlan and I (forthcoming, chapter
5) call 'segmentary person'.
     An example is the following:

> midipu kujilyi nu-n yi kare aki-yl-nga suku tekin
>   turun-kiyl
> Midipu Kujilyi, you (sg.) have killed some of the men
>   within [this tribe]

This example shows a segmentary use of the second
person singular pronoun, *nu* (followed by ergative marker
-n), whereby the leading bigman of his tribe, Midipu Kujilyi, is picked out in direct address (he was present at
this event) as what we might see as a kind of synecdochic
figure for his whole tribe -- in fact for a whole congeries
of five fairly small tribes, among all of which he is the
leading bigman. Kujilyi himself could not have actually
killed anyone at the war which is here being referred to, as
he would have been just a young boy at the time. Another,
textually related example is as follows:

> pilyikimil el turum-uyl topa-kin epola-alya-sil
>   lyirim-a
> you (pl.) know that when there was fighting, Epola-
>   Alya took (sg.) it
>
> pi tepa oba na-nga kangi-na nosinsirum
> then 'he' came and put it on my skin
>
> jika-kungunuka sirid
> I gave it to Jika-Kungunuka

Here the speaking orator is Kujilyi himself (the same
man nominated as addressee in the previous example). There
are instances of segmentary person references in every line.
In the first line, the expression *epola-alya-sil* 'the pair
of Epola and Alya' occurs as the singular subject of the
verb *lyi-* 'take', describing the recruitment of those tribes

into the same war referred to in the first example. In the
second line, this tribe-pair becomes the grammatical subject, again referred to with singular number. 'Put it upon
my skin' here is an idiom for 'make me liable for', meaning
that Kujilyi's tribe pair, Kusika-Midipu, were recruited as
allies. Note the grammatically singular form na-nga, my
(skin). In the third line, Kujilyi then refers to his own
tribe's (or tribe pair's) recruitment of the Jika-Kungunuka
using a first person singular form (of the verb si- 'to
give') which translates as though he himself had done the
recruiting. But Kujilyi, recall, was a young boy at the
time, and cannot himself have played any part in these acts
of recruitment (which would have been negotiated by the big
men of that time).

　　While in this example it is fairly clear that the
individual orator cannot be identified as the sole 'referent' of his 'I', more commonly, in the 'segmentary' uses of
these forms, it is ambiguous, or a moot point, whether the
speaker is talking about 'himself' or a whole segmentary
unit. This can be illustrated with a more extended example,
taken from a transcript of the same exchange event from
which the others are taken.

　　In order for the reader to make sense of the transcript, I need to provide some background information concerning the nature of Ku Waru warfare, and this episode of
it in particular. Warfare -- then as now fought mainly with
bow and arrow, ax, and spear -- was endemic in the New
Guinea Highlands before enforced pacification by the coloni-
al government in the 1950s, and has undergone a resurgence
since independence in 1975. In the Ku Waru area at least, it
is the inter-talapi transaction par excellence, in that
talapi, or blocs of them, are always involved as the protagonists. One of the talapi on each side is always identified
as the 'fight source' (el pul), the others being recruited
in chain-like series such as those shown in the first line
of the following figure:

Chain of Recruitment

A ────> B ────> C

Chain of Compensation Payments

C <──── B <──── A

The acts of recruitment, or the resulting injuries and
deaths among allies recruited, must later be compensated
for, in a series of transactions which reverses the order of

recruitment, as shown in the second row of this figure. In other words, if fight source A recruits B and B then recruits C, B must later present compensation to C, and then A to B. In these terms, the *talapi* involved in the events to be discussed below are as follows:

A	B	C
Epola	Kopia	Laulku
Alya	Kubuka	(Mujika)
Lalka		
Kusika		
Midipu		

The war took place in 1982. The five tribes named under A were the 'fight source' on their side, in that it originally broke out as a fight between them and another tribe-pair, the Tea-Dena (who were thus the 'fight source' among all the tribes on the opposing side). Bloc A then recruited the Kopia-Kubuka, and the Kopia-Kubuka in turn recruited the Laulku (or, arguably, the pair of Mujika and Laulku -- for details, see Merlan, this volume, and Merlan and Rumsey forthcoming, 6.2.6). The exchange event from which all the oratorical examples in this paper are taken is the one at which the Kopia-Kubuka (B) were presenting compensation to (Mujika-) Laulku.

As has been widely noted in highlands ethnography, when a segmentary unit (such as the Ku Waru *talapi*) is nominally involved in warfare, it is seldom if ever the case that every adult male of that unit joins in the fighting. In general, the further out a tribe is from the 'fight source' along the chain of allies (e.g. C as opposed to B in Figure 1), the lower the proportion of men who participate. Furthermore, some men invariably join in from *talapi* which are not, qua *talapi*, recruited as allies. In general, these men, if recruited at all, are recruited along lines of close matrilateral kinship or affinity (just the kind of relationships which figure in 'interpersonal exchange', as discussed above). But there is always room for disagreement about the basis of their participation.

This can be illustrated from the transcript with reference to the role of the Poika and Palimi tribes in these proceedings. In the past, these two tribes have been the main allies of the Kopia-Kubuka (B). In the fighting for which compensation is here being paid, by Kopia-Kubuka, several men from these tribes (Poika and Palimi) did participate, and at least two of the Poika were wounded. On the day of compensation, many people from those tribes turned up. A big man from Kubuka called Tamalu gave a speech in which he tried to justify the Poika-Palimi not being paid compensation at this time. The speech began as follows:

633   poika kang nyikim, eee! laulku kang nyikim
       he says 'a Poika fellow' or 'a Laulku fellow'

634   ilyi nyikin pel pora nyikim, poika kang-te el munsurum
           aki-yl
       what you (sg.) are talking about, cousin, that's
           finished, a Poika was wounded

635   olto-nga ung-iyl kornga pilyipa lyilym
       as for these words of us two he [the Poika] already
           understands about that

636   el ya naa telybolu i kupulanum ilyi, ime-nga pansip
           tep ime-nga pansip tep
       we two do not fight on this 'road' [i.e., within the
           Kopia-Kubuka-Poika-Palimi alliance]; we do it
           together thither and yon

637   na nanu poika-palimi-sil-kin molup telyo
       I myself stay with Poika and Palimi

638   ya yu-nga ul-uyl malysip malysip modup te midi kim mi
           tuyl-te pirim
       we've got all of his matters cleaned up except for one
           old 'rotten vegetable' that still remains

639   ilyi naa pelka-ja i wiyl-ola ilyi-nga pubu na mokabu
           naa lyibu nyilka
       if it hadn't been for that, I wouldn't be demanding
           compensation [from bloc A] so soon

In this excerpt (and elsewhere in the speech as well),
Tamalu makes subtle use of segmentary person forms, so as to
group the Palimi and Poika together with the Kopia-Kubuka as
relative 'insiders' vis à vis the Laulku -- so that the
Kopia-Kubuka accept responsibility for compensating the
Laulku as a *talapi*, but not for compensating the Poika as
one. Shortly before this speech of Tamalu's, someone in the
audience has made an offstage remark about the injury received in the fighting by one of the Poika participants.
Tamalu's first move (line 633) is to address the general
assemblage, telling them about this remark. Starting in line
634, he addresses the man who has made the remark, using the
first person dual pronoun *olto* (line 635) to refer not to
two individuals, but to whole segmentary units. 'We two' in
this context means 'we Kopia-Kubuka and Laulku'. *Olto-nga
ung* 'The word of us two' means 'the things you Laulku and we
Kopia-Kubuka are talking about between us today'. The implication of line 635 is that these are matters which have
already been thoroughly canvassed between Poika and Kopia-
Kubuka before the payment was given in this form. In line

636, the reference of the first person dual category then
shifts to another segmentary pair: the pair of Kopia-Kubuka
and Poika-Palimi -- just those tribes among whom the matter
has purportedly already been discussed. These are people who
fight on the same side as a matter of course. The first
person singular pronoun (*na*) in 637 can be construed as
referring to Tamalu himself, to the Kubuka tribe, or to the
pair of Kopia and Kubuka.

In any case, the effect is to point to bonds of
coresidence which identify Kopia-Kubuka and Poika-Palimi
together in a way that Laulku is not identified with any of
them. But, having made this identification, he then goes on
to explain (in line 638) that there is one outstanding debt
(metaphorically referred to as a 'rotten vegetable') that
remains to be paid within this alliance. That is a compensation payment which is owed for the death of a Poika man in a
previous war. It was explained to us privately that this
outstanding debt was the reason why the Poika were not
recruited *as a talapi* to assist the Kopia-Kubuka in the 1982
war, the idea being that it would be wrong to incur a another compensation debt to them before the earlier one had been
discharged. That was presumably one reason for Tamalu's
mentioning it in this context -- as an explanation ostensi-
bly addressed to the Laulku for why the Poika were not now
being compensated. But discussion of this transcript with
participants in this event, and our own experience of these
matters, suggests that the 'private agreement' with Poika on
this score was probably not as secure as Tamalu suggests,
and his remark was also covertly aimed ('targeted' in Levinson's terms) at the Poika, to preempt any claim they might
be thinking about pressing at this time. He is presumably
also trying to reassure them by suggesting that his tribe,
the Kubuka, will later use the compensation they get from
those who recruited them into the fight, to pay their
'rotten vegetable' debt to Poika, and that he will press for
this compensation to be paid soon.

Later on in these proceedings, some of the money was
in fact presented to some men from Poika. But this speech of
Tamalu's helped to assure that that money could not be
construed as having been given to 'Poika' as such. What
happened instead was that a relatively small payment was
given to particular men from Poika for the role they played
in the fighting.

One can see from this example that the question of
whether the Poika participated as a *talapi* in the fighting
-- and therefore in the compensation event -- is not one
which can be addressed independently of how the matter was
discursively constructed by these concerned. Particular men
identified with a particular *talapi* are agreed to have taken
part, and to have incurred injury for which compensation
would ordinarily be paid. But from this the conclusions to

be drawn for segmentary politics are not self-evident. The men's actions are subjected to various competing constructions using both explicit appeals to a relationship of close identification or 'sameness' among the relevant *talapi*, and the more subtle device of segmentary person to *presuppose* such a relationship. This is a prime example of what I mean by 'struggle for control of the meaning of events for inter-group politics', a struggle which has very real material consequences in that it may create or decisively alter the exchange obligations of relevant *talapi* -- wealth exchange being canonically transacted among segmentary units which are 'different', and requiring joint participation among those which are 'same'. The segmentary first person singular is the ultimate linguistic device for constructing relations of the latter sort, as its use not only presupposes singularity of reference, but directly instantiates singularity of social agency in the act of speaking, and by implication, in the act of exchange in which that speaking plays a part. In other words, in its situated use, the segmentary *I* 'personifies' the social unit or units to which it refers.[3]

But equally, in so doing, it 'amplifies' the persona of the would-be 'big man' who uses it. Thus, note how in the present example, Tamalu's first person references work in such a way as to identify himself totally with his *talapi*, the Kubuka, or with the pair of Kopia and Kubuka, so that it becomes a moot point whether he is *really* talking about himself or his *talapi* (as attested by the frequent exasperation of Ku Waru informants to whom we dutifully persisted in putting such questions, even as we already suspected what their answers confirmed -- that our questions had simply missed the point). Thus, even while would-be big men compete to speak as entire *talapi*, in effect they also collaborate to reproduce a social order in which *talapi* figure crucially -- often lethally -- as relevant agents (cf. Rumsey 1986).

To return now to the questions raised above about the cross-linguistic status of concepts of 'speaker' and 'addressee', I would argue that neither Goffman's framework nor Levinson's is capable of accounting for the differences between the segmentary and non-segmentary uses of Ku Waru first person singular and dual forms.[4] The difference between segmentary and non-segmentary uses of the first person singular cannot be captured by Goffman's distinctions among author/animator/principal, because in both of the former, the 'speaker' is identified as all three of the latter. The same goes for Levinson's distinctions as outlined above, since the segmentary 'I' who speaks is, no less than the everyday one, understood to be a present, fully participating, self-motivated transmitter of the message precisely as formulated. As we can see from the examples I have discussed, a basic feature of this kind of oratory is not that the orator is acting as a kind of ratified 'spokeman' or 'mouthpiece' for his *talapi*, but that, through it, he works to merge his own persona with that of the *talapi* with which he is identified -- amplifying the former while personifying the latter.[5]

If Goffman's and Levinson's dimensions of contrast are indeed insufficient to capture the relevant difference here, could we think of others that might do the job instead? Certainly so, but how *ad hoc* should we be willing to let them be? A feature +/- SEGMENTARY would suffice for this instance, but how useful would it be for any other? My own inclination would be *not* to try to use these data to motivate any further putatively universal dimensions of contrast (cf. Irvine ms.), but to account for the relevant differences in this case as aspects of the culturally specific construction of inter-*talapi* oratory as what Levinson (1987:167 et passim) calls a 'speech event' type (as opposed to 'utterance event'). Or rather, as aspects of inter-*talapi* exchange as a form of social action, since I don't want to accept any *a priori* distinction between speech and other forms or moments of social action.[6] Here I think I am in agreement with at least part of Levinson's argument, which is that we must insist on a distinction between speech *roles*, which are what we are trying to relate in some universally applicable way to grammatical categories of person/number, and the *incumbents* of those roles, which we can expect to be culturally far more specific and variable than the roles themselves.

To return to one of the 'classical' formulations of person mentioned above, Benveniste would seem to have already allowed for enormous variability of the latter sort when he said that: ' "pronominal" forms do not refer to "reality" or to "objective" positions in space or time but to the utterance, unique each time, that contains them' (Benveniste 1971:219).

Here Benveniste may have even overstated the case, insofar as the speaking subject or agent, while a culturally variable construction, belongs to, or is constructed in relation to, a more or less limited range of definite types within each culture or social formation, and so can never belong only to a single instance of discourse. But he provides a valuable reminder of the fact that the nature and historical continuity of the speaking subject, whether as type or as token, can never be taken for granted as a brute fact about the world, whether that of linguistics conferences or of segmentary transactors in the New Guinea Highlands.

Notes

1. This fieldwork, conducted over sixteen months between 1981 and 1986, was funded by the Australian Research Grants Council, and by the (U.S.) National Science Foundation (Research Grant #BNS-8024174), to which patrons our gratitude is hereby expressed. We also want to thank the many people in the Western Highlands who helped us during our time there.

2. These usages are also attested among the neighboring Melpa people, and the Huli people in the Southern Highlands. For textual examples see Strathern 1975:199 and Goldman 1983:134, line 294 respectively.

3. This is consistent with the fact that properly efficacious *talapi* are said to have 'one mind' or 'one will' (*numan tilupu*). The same thing is also said of a successful bigman, as opposed to men of lower status, and women, both of whom are said to be of 'many minds' or 'many wills' (*numan ausiyl*). For more details see Rumsey 1986 and Strathern 1981.

4. The same holds for the second person forms, but space does not permit me here to take up Goffman's and Levinson's proposals concerning the notions of 'addressee'. Suffice it to say that both of their analyses rely on a distinction between immediate 'addressee' and ultimate 'recipient', which is here irrelevant for much the same reason as the distinction between transmitter-animator and motivator -principal which I take up below.

5. This not to deny the possiblity that two (or even more) levels of relevant agency may be distinguished here, either by us as analysts, or by Ku Waru people in other contexts. The point is rather that what is publicly 'ratified' in *this* context is the identification of the speaking big man with, or as, his *talapi*.

6. I don't claim to have presented anything but the bare bones of such an account in the limited space available here. For fuller details see Merlan and Rumsey forthcoming.

References

Benveniste, E. 1971[1956]. 'The nature of pronouns'. In his *Problems in General Linguistics*. Coral Gables: University of Miami Press.

Goffman, E. 1981[1976]. 'Footing'. In his *Forms of Talk*. Oxford: Basil Blackwell.

Goldman, L. 1983. *Talk Never Dies: The Language of Huli Disputes*. London: Tavistock.

Irvine, J. 1974. 'Strategies of status manipulation in the Wolof greeting'. In Bauman, R. and Sherzer, J. (eds.) *Explorations in the Ethnography of Speaking*. Cambridge: Cambridge University Press.

Irvine, J. ms. 'The implicated dialogue: structures of participation in discourse'. Unpublished paper presented at the 1988 meetings of the American Anthropological Association.

Jakobson, R. 1971[1957]. 'Shifters, linguistic categories, and the Russian verb'. In his *Collected Papers*, vol. 2. The Hague: Mouton.

Lederman, R. 1980. 'Who speaks here? Formality and the politics of gender in Mendi, Highland Papua New Guinea'. *Journal of the Polynesian Society* 89:479-98.

Lederman, R. 1986. *What Gifts Engender: Social Relations and Politics in Mendi, Highland Papua New Guinea*. Cambridge: Cambridge University Press.

Levinson, S., 1987. 'Putting linguistics on a proper footing'. In Drew, P. and Wootton, A. (eds.) *Erving Goffman: Exploring he Interaction Order*. Boston: Northeastern University Press.

Mauss, M. 1966[1925]. *The Gift: Forms and Functions of Exchange in Archaic Societies*. New York: Norton.

Merlan, F. and Rumsey, A. forthcoming. *Ku Waru: Language and Segmentary Politics in the Nebilyer Valley of Papua New Guinea*. Cambridge: Cambridge University Press.

Rumsey, A. 1986. 'Oratory and the politics of metaphor in the New Guinea Highlands'. In Threadgold, T., Grosz, E., Kress, G., and Halliday, M.A.K. (eds.) *Semiotics, Ideology, Language*. Sydney: Sydney Society for Studies in Society and Culture.

Strathern, A. 1975. 'Veiled speech in Mt. Hagen'. In Bloch, M. ed., *Political Language and Oratory in Traditional Society*. London: Academic Press.

Strathern, A. 1981. 'Noman: representations of identity in Mount Hagen'. In Holy, L. and Stuchlik, M. (eds.) *The Structure of Folk Models*. London: Academic Press.

GEN: AN AFFECT/EVIDENTIAL PARTICLE
IN AUSTRALIAN CREOLE ENGLISH

Margaret S. Steffensen

Illinois State University

In Australian languages, a variety of affect/evidential particles perform a number of discourse functions (Dixon, 1980). In Walpiri, for example, Laughren (1982) has found four major categories of particles. (Laughren, 1982). Particularly interesting are the propositional particles, which allow speakers to encode their judgments about the truth of a proposition and information about its source. The particles may be used to disclaim responsibility for a proposition, to indicate a logical conclusion, or to overtly mark the relationship between the speaker and the semantic content of the utterance.

Wilkins (1986), in his study of the Mparntwe Arrernte particles of criticism and complaint, proposes that such speech acts are generated through the interaction of the lexical meaning of the particle, the propositional content of the utterance and the cultural logic that dictates the lexical choices. Through these particles, the speakers encode their affective response to propositional content. Complaints are communicated when the particles are attached to a first-person argument. When attached to a non-first-person argument, criticism or compassion may be conveyed. To understand such utterances, the listener must have knowledge of what is considered good and bad in the Arrernte cultural context. This is especially true in the case of three particles which have different primary evidential force but can convey criticism or complaint. These are the "hearsay" particle, kwele, which attributes a proposition to someone else; the clitic -kathene, which marks mistaken belief; and -me, an interrogative. By using these forms in appropriate contexts, their semantic range is extended.

In this study, I will discuss a particle, gen, that has wide distribution in a creole English spoken in the Northern Territory of Australia. This form fulfills a number of discourse functions and, in one of its uses, clearly shows age grading. I will conclude by commenting briefly on its history.

The Australian Creole English dialect I am analyzing is spoken in a small Aboriginal settlement, Barunga (formerly Bamyili), which is near Katherine, in

the Northern Territory. At the time of the research,
several different Aboriginal languages were represented
in the community, none of which had clear dominance.
The principal substratum languages were Ngalkbun,
Djauwan, and Maiali/Gunwinggu. Other languages, such
as Arrernte, Gunei, Jinba, Mangarai, Rembarrnga, and
Wogaid, had only small numbers of speakers. It would
be useful to be able to show that particles exist in
these languages that perform the functions found for
the particle in the creole. Unfortunately, descriptions of the principal substratum languages are not
available. According to Dixon, "Australian languages
typically have a set of a score or so `particles' that
provide logical modal-type qualification of a complete
clause" (1980:284). Since evidential particles are
present in related substratum languages, it is reasonable to assume they occur in the languages spoken at
Barunga. This being the case, they would be present to
affect the development of the evidential/affect particle in the creole.

     Let us now consider the particle itself and its
functions. There are two major meaning clusters in
which gen has epistemological modality or attitudinal
value and there is a lexical form. Unlike research
with Aboriginal languages, in the creole we do not have
the benefit of phonological shape to help identify the
pragmatic force of the items. However, the two core
meanings are quite clear. From these central meanings,
there are diffuse groupings of meaning and usage which
demonstrate the process of lexical formation in creole
languages as well as particular characteristics associated with the development of such particles. Even
cases that involve different words, there is a continuum of meanings and, not surprisingly, this is also
the case in the Barunga Creole (BC). A somewhat arbitrary line must be drawn between the evidential,
affect, and lexical forms, but such a distinction will
be made since it aids in the analysis.

     One set of meanings is clearly an evidential
function. Evidentials provide speakers with a means of
encoding how certain they are about the truth of the
propositional content of an utterance. They are a
means of distancing oneself from the statement and
attributing the responsibility or authorship to either
an implied or stated source. In Aboriginal languages,
greater distance from the proposition content is marked
with different particles. In BC, however, gen covers
the continuum ranging from those assertions the speaker
may believe to be true but not know on the basis of
personal knowledge or experience to those s/he believes

to be false.

Reported speech is marked with gen because the speaker does not have first-hand knowledge. This fact is redundantly encoded both by the matrix sentence, 'They said...' and the presence of gen at the beginning of the embedded sentence. In these cases, there is no reason beyond the lack of firsthand experience for doubting the truth of the proposition:

> 1. De bin tok gen de bin gilim ganggaru.
>   they PST say EVI they PST kill + TRANS
>   kangaroo

Verbs of cognition may be similarly marked when they refer to another person. Rather than simply commenting upon authorship of the proposition, the speaker is making an inference and marking it with gen. The lack of certainty about truth value springs not from lack of firsthand knowledge but from the communicative risks inherent in making inferences about other people's mentation. As in reported speech, gen occurs before the proposition being qualified:

> 2. Gen im dinggid im gona ren na.
>   EVI he think + TRANS it gonna rain now

These two types of modality are marked in Walpiri with different morphemes (Laughren, 1982), a fact which supports the analysis of two different functions for gen.

Gen is also used in telling Aboriginal myths of creation, the Dreamtime:

> 3. Gen imin olwez sey, "Ai garrem big
>   wan wing, not laik yubala, yubala
>   garrem lil wan lil wan wing not
>   laik mi...(D. Gentian, 1975)
>
>   EVI he + PST always say I have big ADJ wing
>   not like you + PL you + PL have little ADJ
>   little ADJ wing not like me..."

Willett (1988), in his cross-linguistic survey of evidentiality, considers folklore and mythology a type of reported content, noting that in such cases the event is also remote in time. Example (3) would fall into this category both because it is embedded under the higher verb sey and because it is mythic.

In another analysis of epistemological modality,
Chung and Timberlake (1985) propose four categories:
1) Experiential refers to knowledge that springs from
events witnessed or experienced by the speaker.   2)
Inferential is the result of direct observation of
evidence by the speaker.   3) Quotative is propositional
content reported by someone else.   And 4) Construct is
reality that is mentally constructed by the speaker, as
a dream or thought.   It can be argued that examples
from the Dreamtime cycle should be included under construct because they represent thought and are created,
rather than reported, reality.   On the other hand, if
the speaker literally believes these myths, and I think
many do, then they should be considered reported information.   A third option is that such usage falls in
both categories, showing what Haviland (1987) has
called the "multifunctionality" of these particles.
     There are indisputable examples of the construct
parameter in BC.   Counterfactual worlds embedded under
higher world-creating verbs are marked by <u>gen</u>, changing
the modality of the embedded sentence:

    4. Ai bin drim gen ai bin go langa
        United States. I PST dream EVI I
        PST go to the United States

    5. Maidbi gen imin drim gen imin
        ganggaru. it might be EVI he
        PST dream EVI he PST kangaroo

The double use of <u>gen</u> in 5 encodes both the speaker's
assessment of the claim that someone had a particular
dream and the constructed world itself.
     Unlike these cases in which the speaker simply
cannot vouch for the truth on the basis of personal
experience, there are cases reflecting speaker doubt or
negativity about propositional content.   In BC, questions are formed with the particles <u>ai</u> or <u>indid</u>.   In
(6), doubt can be attributed to the speaker because of
the use of <u>gen</u>:

    6. Gen dad olmen imin dai, ai?
        EVI that old man he + PST die QUES
        That old man didn't die, did he?

     Further along the continuum toward "false" are
those propositions that the speaker considers incorrect.   In an experimental situation, one informant was
pressed unduly for answers about a story she had just
heard.   Because the task was an unfamiliar one and

because she felt she had to respond, she generated
answers that had no basis in the text. They were
marked sentence finally with gen. To a question about
what made the child in the story sick, she incorrectly
responded, "It was starved, gen." Other causes she
suggested were "Rubbish lying there, gen" and "Heat,
gen." She proposed that the mother "Gave him a bath,
gen" as part of the treatment. The fact that the
speaker knew these answers were incorrect was indicated
by such paralinguistic behaviors as long pauses and
sighs before answering, as well as the presence of the
evidential. An appropriate gloss for this use of the
particle is:

> 7. I know I am expected to reply in this
>   situation.
>   I do not know the correct answers to
>   your questions.
>   I am providing plausible answers based
>   on my world knowledge.
>   Since I am sure they are not correct,
>   I am marking them with gen.

This particular speech event demonstrates an
interesting example of the multifunctionality of gen.
The demands of the speech situation were forcing the
speaker to provide incorrect answers and were creating
stress and embarrassment. Her feelings, as well as her
judgment about propositional content, were communicated
through the use of the particle. While the evidential
use of gen was probably the primary one, the affective
function of gen was also present. Such pragmatic ambiguity occurs when the act of encoding information about
truth value has high emotional loading.
    This is similar to the use of the Arrernte parti-
cles encoding criticism and complaint (Wilkins, 1986).
One infers the speaker's emotional state in the light
of cultural norms and the denotative meaning of the
particle itself. The affective impact of the particle
can be inferred from the meaning of the particle itself, the content of the utterance, and the cultural
context.
    In all of the above cases, gen expresses speak-
ers' assessments of the truth of their own utterances.
This evidential function can be explained in terms of
Grice's cooperative principle (1975). The maxim of
quality, "1. Do not say what you believe to be false.
2. Do not say that for which you lack adequate evidence" (Grice 1975:46) has been violated. By using the
evidential gen, the speaker is able to reconcile the

demands of the social situation and the cooperative
principle.

Sarcasm can be encoded using <u>gen</u>. In sarcasm,
the speaker produces a sentence that is the opposite of
the intended message, deliberately violating Gricean
principles. The use of <u>gen</u>, tone of voice and extralinguistic information, all indicate to the listener
that an implicature is involved:

> 8. Gen dad lil boi im jimadwan.
>   EVI that little boy he smart + ADJ
>   That kid is <u>really</u> stupid.

There are several extensions of the strict reading of the evidential. It is used to self-repair false
starts. The utterance is interrupted with the particle, which refers anaphorically to the preceding proposition. Unlike cases 1-4, in which the clause following <u>gen</u> is modified, in these cases the speaker is
certain that what follows <u>gen</u> is true and what precedes
is not:

> 9. Wen imin bol daun - gen- wen
>   imin ban... wen it + PST fall
>   down - EVI - when it + PST
>   burn

A complex instance of language play occurred when
a group of women were trying to translate (literally)
the religious truism, "He loves us very much." One
proposed:

> 10. Im luv us tumac, gen.

This rendering was greeted with shouts of laughter by
her creole listeners, who understood the inevitable
misinterpretation by low proficiency creole speakers.
This speech event can be glossed as:

> 11. The correct BC translation is
>   <u>Im</u> <u>luv</u> <u>us</u> <u>tumac</u>.

> A speaker who does not know BC well will
> translate this as 'He loves us too much (for
> our own good).'
> This is an incorrect back translation.
> Therefore, even though it is correct, I am
> marking the translation with <u>gen</u> to show
> that repair is needed because of the cross-
> cultural speech context.

This usage to initiate linguistic repairs has further generalized to the extralinguistic context. It marks blunders in a manner equivalent to the English oops, as when a speaker was playing pool and marked a missed shot with gen.

> 12. Are you sending a letter--gen--to
> your sister?

In another case, the speaker dropped a toy as she was trying to place it on a shelf:

> 13. I'm gonna put it there--gen.

These examples show the integration of the evidential with the context of the speech event. Not only does it mark truth value and affective state, but it can also be used to comment upon intended actions.

The second major group of uses encodes affect. Gen may be used to convey the speaker's attitude that a behavior is inappropriate or ridiculous. One Dreamtime myth explains that the emu cannot fly because he danced too close to a fire and burned his wings. Gen conveys the information that the emu's dancing was awkward and foolish:

> 14. En den afta gen imiyu bin dens na.
> (Gentian, 1975) and then after
> AFF emu PST dance now

Informants said that gen introduces a humorous element in this sentence. Both evidential and affective function are present, but here the affective function was judged as the primary one.

Gen may mark an inappropriate behavior in the extralinguistic context and mildly censure it. Such a case occurred when a teenager accidentally made a toddler she was playing with fall down. When the young girl laughed, the baby's mother commented:

> 15. Gen imin lab, daran dea.
> AFF she + PST laugh that+one there

The girl was clearly upset by this comment and hid behind her mother for several minutes.

Gen as a comment on inappropriate behavior, is probably the source of another purely affective usage. It occurs in the speech of preadolescent and adolescent girls with stupefying frequency in any situation consi-

dered embarrassing. For example, if a young girl no-
tices an adult looking at her, she glances down and
shyly murmurs gen. When questioned, teenagers explained that gen means you're ashamed and volunteered
that one might use it, for example, if one's boyfriend
approached. When adults express embarrassment with
gen, it is integrated with the evidential function.
Adults also use gen to comment on inappropriate or
embarrassing behavior which is not affectively loaded
for the speaker (a speaker-exclusive function). For
younger speakers, gen is a pragmatically simple interjection that conveys information about the speaker's
emotional state (speaker-inclusive function). This
usage by teenagers has been identified by adult informants as a recent extension. This may reflect a general ontogenetic process from pure affect to multifunctionality.

There is one final usage of the affective gen to
be noted: It expresses praise or approbation. This is
similar to the inversion found in Black English Vernacular, where bad (with vowel lengthening) can mean
'extraordinarily good'. Stress and the intonation
contour also mark inversion.

> 16. Gen, Gladys gada nu dres.
>   AFF Gladys gotta new dress

We have now considered gen in its evidential and
affect functions. The third form is a lexical item
with the meaning 'pretend'. It is most commonly used
to describe children's play and encodes redundantly
information that is obvious from the extralinguistic
context:

> 17. Mindubala grugman gen.
>   we two (exclusive) crook pretend
>   We two are make-believe robbers.

In this usage only, there are examples of gen
being reduplicated:

> 18. Gengen we ple kauboi.
>   pretend + REDUP we play cowboy
>   We're playing make-believe cowboys.

Reduplication of intransitive verbs is used in BC to
encode continuous aspect while reduplication of modifiers encodes plurality of the modified noun
(Steffensen, 1979). In 18, however, continuous aspect
is carried through reduplication of gen.

I will now briefly consider the historic development of this form. Gen can be traced to the English slang gammon, which means 'to deceive, feign or pretend'. Gamon occurs in limited usages in BC as an alternate form of gen. Like gen, it can be reduplicated to convey continuous aspect in the 'pretend' meaning. This process is problematic since it also occurs in sentences which undergo the more common process of verbal reduplication to form the continuous:

> 19. Yu megim gamongamon haus.
>   you make + TRANS pretend + REDUP
>   house
>   You're building a make-believe house.

> 20. Im lablab gamon.
>   he laugh + REDUP pretend
>   He's pretending to laugh.

Gamon can also be used, like gen, to show approval or approbation. Finally, it is used to mean 'liar' or 'a lie', for which there is no alternate form.

Gamon is widespread throughout the South Pacific. According to Hall (1943), it was used in Neo-Melanesian, with the meanings 'false, deceitful, to be fooling, to lie'. Churchill (1911) in the glossary of his small treatise on Beach-La-Mar gives several references for it and reports that it was heard in New Zealand as early as 1815. His list of meanings extends beyond Hall's and includes 'to joke, to exaggerate, to cheat'. It was documented in 1834 in the pidgin spoken in Sydney by the Reverend Lancelot Threlkeld (reported in Dixon, 1980).

In his analysis of the diachronic sources of the evidentials, Willett (1988) argues that they are derived from sensory verbs, verbs of speaking and observation, and perfectives through a process of generalization. Because metaphoric extension is a pervasive aspect of language that widens the meaning of a lexical item, Willett proposes that this is the actual process of derivation. Syntactic and phonological fusion and reduction also occur during their formation.

These processes can account for the development of the particle gen. It can be derived from gamon by syncope. Such a rule appears to have operated in BC for two other pairs, the locative preposition langa ~ la, < probably from along and the possessive morpheme blanga ~ bla, 'belong'.

The first usage in the creole was probably the meaning 'false', which evolved to the milder 'pretend'.

The same meaning was adopted as a particle marking
reported speech, questionable and incorrect propositions, all of which violate the maxim of quality to
varying degrees and could therefore be considered
false. Through extension of its pragmatic range, the
particle gen became a marker of false starts and extralinguistic blunders. Over time, because of the speech
events it was marking, we can hypothesize that gen
acquired the connotative values associated with lack of
composure and awkwardness. As its affective value
increased, it became a marker of both ridiculous behavior and personal embarrassment. In its most recent
extension, it functions solely as an interjection of
affect.

To summarize, we can represent schematically the
two uses of the particle derived from the original use
of 'pretend.' As an evidential, gen follows the
patterns found in other Aboriginal languages, forming a
continuum from true to false:

                    TRUE
            Reported speech
                Inferences
              Constructions
         Doubtful propositions
                  Sarcasm
                  Repairs
                   FALSE

Multifunctionality, or pragmatic ambiguity, is apparent
when the particle has both epistemological modality and
affective force. This can occur when someone is forced
to verbalize about something s/he does not understand.
Sarcasm also clearly involves both affect and evidential functions. The repair function for false starts
and propositional errors has been extended to extralinguistic false steps.

In a second cluster of meanings, affect is the
principle component. Gen is used to mark what the
speaker considers inappropriate behaviors, either in
narratives or in the extralinguistic situation. It can
be used as an expression of embarrassment on the speaker's part. In a form of inversion, it conveys approbation. These uses can be captured in a tree diagram
representing self-reflective or other-directed attitudes:

AFFECT

OTHER-DIRECTED   SELF-DIRECTED

Inappropriate   Censure   Approbation   Embarrassment
Behavior

    The functions and distribution of <u>gen</u> provide an
insight into creole languages. In the formation of
creoles, the substratum languages generally have a
greater impact on the phonological and syntactic systems, while many of the words may be traced to the
superstratum. Like many other creole words, <u>gen</u> is
polysemous. A superstratum word has been adopted and
extended to meet the semantic needs of BC speakers.
<u>Gen</u> performs various linguistic functions which are
absent in English but which can be traced to Aboriginal
sources. This suggests that the substratum also contributes significant aspects of its pragmatic system to
a creole, making the creole both formally and pragmatically a creation of the indigenous population.

REFERENCES

Fieldwork was supported by the Australian Institute of
Aboriginal Studies. I am heavily indebted to Niko
Besnier, whose insights and suggestions greatly im-
proved this paper. Bruce Hawkins' comments were also
most appreciated.

Churchill, William. 1911. Beach-La-Mar: The jargon
     or trade speech of the Western Pacific.
     Washington: The Carnegie Institution.
Dixon, Robert M. W. 1980. The languages of Australia.
     New York: Cambridge University Press.
Chung, Sandra and Alan Timberlake. 1985. Tense,
     aspect, and mood. Grammatical categories and the
     lexicon (Language typology and syntactic
     description 3), ed. by Timothy Shopen, 202-257.
     New York: Cambridge University Press.
Gentian, David. 1975. Bamyili school newsletter.
     Mimeo.
Grice, Paul. 1975. Logic and conversation. Syntax
     and semantics III: Speech acts, ed. by Peter Cole
     & Jerry Morgan, 41-58. New York: Academic Press.
Hall, Robert A., Jr. 1943. Melanesian Pidgin English.
     Baltimore, Md.: Linguistic Society of America.
Haviland, John B. 1987. Fighting words: Evidential

particles, affect and argument. Proceedings of
the Thirteenth Annual Meeting, 343-54. Berkeley:
Berkeley Linguistics Society.
Laughren, Mary. 1982. A preliminary description of
propositional particles in Warlpiri. (Working
papers of SIL, Series A, 16:129-163.) Darwin:
Summer Institute of Linguistics, Australian
Aborigines Branch.
Steffensen, Margaret S. 1979. Reduplication in
Bamyili Creole. Pacific Linguistics: Papers in
Pidgin and Creole Linguistics 2: 119-134.
Wilkins, David. 1986. Particle/clitics for criticism
and complaint in Mparntwe Arrernte (Aranda).
Journal of Pragmatics 10: 575-96.
Willett, Thomas. 1988. A cross-linguistic survey of
the grammaticization of evidentiality. Studies in
Language 12: 51-97.

Interpreting Interruption in Conversation

Deborah Tannen
Georgetown University

A joke has it that a woman sues her husband for divorce. When the judge asks her why she wants a divorce, she explains that her husband has not spoken to her in two years. The judge then asks the husband, "Why haven't you spoken to your wife in two years?" He replies, "I didn't want to interrupt her."

This joke reflects the commonly held stereotype that women talk too much and interrupt men. On the other hand, one of the most widely cited findings to emerge from research on gender and language is that men interrupt women far more than women interrupt men. This finding is deeply satisfying insofar as it refutes the misogynistic stereotype and seems to account for the difficulty getting their voices heard that many women report having in interactions with men. At the same time, it reflects and bolsters common assumptions about the world: the belief that an interruption is a hostile act, with the interrupter an aggressor and the interrupted an innocent victim. Furthermore, it is founded on the premise that interruption is a means of social control, an exercise of power and dominance.

This research has been questioned on methodological grounds, can be questioned on sociolinguistic grounds, and must be questioned on ethical grounds, as it supports the stereotyping of a group of people on the basis of their conversational style. I here examine each of these objections in turn, juxtaposing the research that claims to find men interrupt women with my own and others' research on ethnicity and conversational style.

Males interrupt females: The research. Most widely cited for the finding that men interrupt women is the work of Candace West and Don Zimmerman (for example, Zimmerman and West 1975, West and Zimmerman 1983, 1985). This is not, however, the only research coming to the conclusion that males interrupt females. Others include Bohn and Stutman (1983), Eakins and Eakins (1976), Esposito (1979), Gleason and Greif (1983), and McMillan, Clifton, McGrath and Gale (1977).[1]

Zimmerman and West (1975) recorded naturally-occurring casual conversations on campus locations. They report that 96% of the interruptions they found (46 out of 48) were perpetrated by men on women. (The

range is from no interruptions in one conversation to
13 in another). Following up with an experimentally
designed study in which previously unacquainted first
and second year undergraduates talked in cross-sex
dyads, West and Zimmerman (1983) report a similar,
though not as overwhelming, pattern: 75% of
interruptions (21 of 28) were instances of men
interrupting women.
     Eakins and Eakins (1976) examined turntaking
patterns at seven faculty meetings and found that "men
generally averaged a greater number of active
interruptions per meeting than women, with eight being
the highest average and two the lowest. For women the
range was from two to zero" (p. 58).
     Some of the research finding that males interrupt
females was carried out with children rather than
adults. Esposito (1979:215) randomly assigned forty
preschool children to play groups and found that boys
interrupted girls two to one. Examining the speech of
16 mothers and 16 fathers, Gleason and Greif
(1983:147) found that fathers interrupt their children
more than mothers, and that both interrupt female
children more than male children.

Interruption as dominance. West and Zimmerman
(1983:103) are typical in calling interruption "a
device for exercising power and control in
conversation" and "violations of speakers' turns at
talk." But they also claim that silence is a device
for exercising dominance. They cite (p. 108)
Komarovsky (1967:353) to the effect that the
"dominant" party in a marriage is often the more
silent one, as revealed by the wife who says of her
husband, "He doesn't say much but he means what he
says and the children mind him." That men control and
dominate women by refusing to speak is the main point
of Sattel (1983), who illustrates with a scalding
excerpt from Erica Jong's novel Fear of Flying in
which a wife becomes increasingly more desperate in
her pleas for her husband to tell her what she has
done to anger him. If both talking and not talking are
dominating strategies, one wonders whether power and
domination reside in the linguistic strategy at all or
on some other level of interaction.

Methodological objection. All researchers who report
that males interrupt females more than females
interrupt males use mechanical definitions to identify
interruptions. This is a function of their research
goal: Counting requires coding, and coding requires
"operational" definitions. For example, Zimmerman and

West, following Schegloff,[2] define an interruption as
a violation of the turn exchange system, an overlap as
a misfire in it. If a second speaker begins speaking
at what could be a transition-relevance place, it is
counted as an overlap. The assumption is that the
speaker mistook the potential transition-relevance
place for an actual one. If a second speaker begins
speaking at what could not be a transition-relevance
place, it is counted as an interruption: The second
speaker had evidence that the other speaker did not
intend to relinquish a turn, but took the floor
anyway, consequently trampling on the first speaker's
right to continue speaking.

Most others who have studied this phenomenon have
based their definitions on Zimmerman's and West's.
For example, Esposito (1979) considered that
"Interruptions occur when speaker A cuts off more than
one word of speaker B's unit-type." Leffler,
Gillespie and Conaty (1982:156) did not distinguish
between overlap and interruption. They included as
interruptions "all vocalizations where, while one
subject was speaking, the other subject uttered at
least two consecutive identifiable words or at least
three syllables of a single word." They eliminated,
however, instances of repetition.

Operationally defined criteria, requisite and
comforting to experimentally-oriented researchers, are
anathema to ethnographically-oriented ones.
Interruptions provide a paradigm case for such
objections. Bennett (1981) points out that overlap
and interruption are, in Russell's sense, logically
different types. (Barbara Johnstone [p.c.] suggests
the linguistic terms "etic" and "emic" may serve here
as well.) To identify overlap, one need only
ascertain that two voices are going at once.
(Overlap, then, is an "etic" category.) But to claim
that a speaker interrupts another is an interpretive,
not a descriptive act (an "emic" category). Whereas
the term "overlap" is, in principle, neutral (though
it also has some negative connotations), the label
"interruption" is clearly negative. Affixing this
label accuses a speaker of violating another speaker's
right to the floor, of being a conversational bully.
Claiming that one has "observed" an interruption is
actually making a judgment, indeed what is generally
perceived to be a moral judgment.

One of West's and Zimmerman's (1983:105) examples
of interruption is a case of an overlap that seems
justified in terms of interactional rights:

```
(1)   Female: So uh you really can't bitch when you've
              got all those on the same day (4.2) but I
              uh asked my physics professor if I
              couldn't chan[ge that ]
      Male:             [Don't   ] touch that
        (1.2)
      Female: What?
        (#)
      Male: I've got everything jus'how I want it in
            that notebook (#) you'll screw it up
            leafin' through it like that.
```

This interruption is procedural rather than substantive. Many would argue that if the male feels that the female's handling of his notebook is destroying his organization of it, he has a right to ask her to desist immediately, without allowing further damage to be done while he awaits a transition-relevance place.[3]

Stephen Murray has mounted a number of attacks on Zimmerman and West on methodological grounds (Murray 1985, 1987, Murray and Covelli 1988). He argues, for example, that there can be no "absolute syntactical or acoustical criteria for recognizing an occurrence of 'interruption'," because a speaker's "completion rights" depend on a number of factors, including length or frequency of speech, number of points made, and special authority to speak on particular topics (Murray 1985). He observes, too, that whether or not a speaker feels interrupted is not absolute but varying by degree. His example, however, of what he considers a "prototypical case of interruption" -- one in which a speaker has not been "allowed to make one point at all" -- is equally questionable:

```
(2)   H: I think [that
      W:         [Do you want some more salad?
```

Harvey Sacks observed that offering food often takes priority at a dinner table, and is heard not as an interruption but an aside. I would add that in this as in all matters of conversational rights and obligations, there are individual and cultural differences. Some people would feel interrupted if overlapped by an offer of salad; others would not. Many similar examples can be found of what might appear to be interruptions but are actually procedural metacomments that many consider rightful to override ongoing substantive talk.

Sociolinguistic objection. Interpreting interruption as evidence of power or dominance assumes that interruption is a single-handed speech act, something one speaker does to another. But sociolinguistic research (for example Duranti and Brenneis 1986, Erickson 1986, Goodwin 1981, McDermott and Tylbor 1983, Schegloff 1982, 1988) establishes that conversation is a joint production: Everything that happens is the doing of all participants. For an interruption to occur, two speakers must act: One must begin speaking, and another must stop. If the first speaker does not stop, there is no interruption. Thus even if an overlap is experienced as an interruption by a participant, it is wrongheaded for a researcher to conclude that the interruption is the doing of one party.

Furthermore, the contention that interruption is a sign of dominance reflects two assumptions that are neither universal nor obvious. One is that conversation is a fight for the floor. The validity of this contention varies with subcultural, cultural and individual predisposition as well as with the context of interaction. Yamada (1989), for example, argues that Japanese speakers prefer not to speak in potentially confrontational situations, since talk is seen as a liability. A similar view is attributed to Finns by Lehtonen and Sajavaara (1985).

Moreover, in light of the methodological objection that one cannot interpret the "meaning" of an overlap on the basis of its occurrence, many instances of overlap are supportive rather than obstructive. When students in one of my classes counted overlaps in half-hour casual conversations they had taped, the vast majority of overlaps, roughly 75%, were judged by the students who had taped the conversations to be cooperative rather than obstructive. Greenwood (1989) found that a high rate of interruption was a sign of social comfort in conversations among preadolescent boys and girls having dinner with their friends: The more comfortable the children reported feeling with their age-mate dinner guests, the more interruptions Greenwood observed in the transcript of their conversation.

Not only is it the case that a transcript might evidence overlap where participants did not feel that their speaking rights had been infringed upon, but participants might feel that their rights have been infringed upon where the transcript indicates they have not. For example, Greenwood discusses a segment in which Dara (age 12) and her sister Stephanie (11)

have performed a humorous routine which climaxes with
the utterance of a tongue twister for the benefit of
their brother's dinner guest, Max (14). Although this
routine sparked delighted laughter on other occasions
among other friends, Max did not laugh and claimed not
to get the joke. Dara and Stephanie try to explain it
to him. Max recalls a tongue twister that he knows.
When Dara and Stephanie continue their explanation,
Max complains about being interrupted:

```
(3)   1 Dara:   Listen, listen, listen, listen.
      2 Max:    Say it in slow motion, okay?
      3 Steph:  Betty bought a bit of bitter butter and
      4         she said this butter's bitter.  If I
      5         put it in my batter, it will make my
      6         batter bitter.  So Betty bought a bit
      7         of better butter to⌐
-->   8 Dara:                      ⌊You never heard
      9         that before?
     10 Max:    No.  Never.
     11 Dara:   Max, seriously?
     12 Max:    Seriously.
     13 Dara:   It's like the famous to⌐
--> 14 Steph:                          ⌊tongue twister.
     15 Max:    No.  The famous tongue twister is
     16         Peterpiperpicked⌐
--> 17 Dara:                    ⌊Same thing.  It's like
     18         that.  It's like that one.
     19 Max:    You keep interrupting me.
```

Though Dara and Stephanie repeatedly cut each other
off, there is no evidence that either resents the
other's intrusions. Rather, they are supporting each
other, jointly performing one conversational role --
the common phenomenon that Falk (1980) calls a
conversational duet. Though Max complains of being
interrupted, the turn he has taken in 15-16 ("No. The
famous tongue twister is Peterpiperpicked-") can
easily be seen as an interruption of the girls'
explanation, even though there is no overlap. In this
interchange, the girls are trying to include Max in
their friendly banter, but by insisting on his right
to hold the floor without intrusions, he is refusing
to be part of their friendly group, rejecting their
bid for solidarity. It is therefore not surprising
that Dara later told her mother that she didn't like
Max. Although Dara does "interrupt" Max at 17 to tell
him he's got the idea ("Same thing. It's like
that."), there is no evidence that she is trying to
dominate him. Furthermore, though Dara and Stephanie
intrude into each other's turns, there is no evidence

that either one of them is trying to dominate the
other either.

An assumption underlying the interruption-as-
dominance paradigm is that conversation is an
arrangement in which one speaker speaks at a time.
Posited as an operational tenet by the earliest work
on turntaking (Sacks, Schegloff and Jefferson 1974),
this reflects ideology more than practice. Most
Americans believe one speaker ought to speak at a
time, regardless of what they actually do. I have
played back to participants tape recordings of
conversations that they had thoroughly enjoyed when
they participated in them, in which many voices were
heard at once, only to find that they are embarrassed
upon hearing the recording, frequently acting as if
they had been caught with their conversational pants
down.

My own research demonstrates that simultaneous
speech can be "cooperative overlapping" -- that is,
supportive rather than obstructive, evidence not of
domination but of participation, not power, but the
paradoxically related dimension, solidarity. Applying
the framework that Gumperz (1982) developed for the
analysis of cross-cultural communication, I have shown
apparent interruption to be the result of style
contact -- not the fault or intention of one party,
but the effect of style differences in interaction.

In a two-and-a-half hour dinner table
conversation that I analyzed at length (Tannen 1984),
interruptions resulted from conversants' differing
styles with regard to pacing, pausing, and overlap.
The conversation included many segments in which
listeners talked along with speakers, and the first
speakers did not stop. There was no interruption,
only supportive, satisfying speaking together. For
these speakers in this context, talking together was
cooperative, showing understanding and participation.
In the framework of politeness phenomena (Brown and
Levinson 1987), overlaps were not perceived as
violating speakers' negative face (their need not to
be imposed on) but rather as honoring their positive
face (their need to know that others are involved with
them). It is an exercise not of power but of
solidarity. The impression of dominance and
interruption was not their intention, nor their doing.
Neither, however, was it the creation of the
imaginations of those who felt interrupted. It was
the result of style contact, the interaction of two
differing turntaking systems.

I characterized the styles of the speakers who
left little or no inter-turn pause, and frequently

began speaking while another speaker was already
speaking, as "high-involvement," because the
strategies of these speakers place relative priority
on the need for positive face, to show involvement.
When high-involvement speakers used these (and other
strategies I found to be characteristic of this style)
with each other, conversation was not disrupted.
Rather, the fast pacing and overlapping served to
grease the conversational wheels. But when they used
the same strategies with conversants who did not share
this style, the interlocutors hesitated, faltered, or
stopped, feeling interrupted and, more to the point,
dominated. I characterized the style of these longer-
pause-favoring, overlap-aversant speakers as "high-
considerateness," because their strategies place
relatively more emphasis on serving the need for
negative face, not to impose.

    I present here two examples to illustrate these
two contrasting situations and the correspondingly
contrasting effects of overlap on interaction. (4)
shows overlapping that occurs in a segment of
conversation among three high involvement speakers
that has a positive effect on the interaction. (5)
shows overlapping that occurs between high involvement
and high considerateness speakers that results in mild
disruption. (4) occurred in the context of a
discussion about the impact of television on children.
Steve's general statement that television has damaged
children sparks a question by Deborah (the author)
about whether or not Steve and his brother Peter (who
is also present) grew up with television:[4]

```
(4)    1 Steve:   I think it's basically done damage to
       2          children.  .... That what good it's
       3          done is ... outweighed by ... the
       5          damage.⌐
-->    6 Deborah:        ⌊Did you two grow up with
       7          television?
       8 Peter:   Very little.  We had a tv in the
       9          ⌐quonset
--> 10 Deborah: ⌊How old were you when your parents got
      11          it?⌉
--> 12 Steve:        ⌊We had a tv but we didn't watch it
      13          all the time.  .... We were very young.
      14          I was four when my parents got a
      15          tv.⌉
--> 16 Deborah:      ⌊You were four?
      17 Peter:   I even remember that.  ......
      18          ⌐I don't remember /??/
--> 19 Steve:     ⌊I remember they got a tv before we
```

```
20          moved out of the quonset huts. In
21          1954.⌐
-->  22 Peter:      └I remember we got it in the
23          quonset huts.
24 Deborah: [chuckle] You lived in quonset huts?
25          .... When you were how old?
            .....
26 Steve:   Yknow my father's dentist said to him
27          "What's a quonset hut." ... And he said
28          "God, you must be younger than my
29          children. .... He was. ....
30          Younger than both of us.
```

This interchange among three high-involvement speakers evinces numerous overlaps and latchings (turn exchanges with no perceptible intervening pause). Yet the speakers show no evidence of discomfort. As the arrows indicate, all three speakers initiate turns that are latched onto or intruded into others' turns. Peter and Steve, who are brothers, operate as a duet, much as Dara and Stephanie did in (3).

Note, for example, lines 8-15: Peter's statement in 8 that begins **"We had a tv** in the quonset," is cut off by my question 10 "How old were you when your parents got it?" Prior to answering my question, Steve repeats his brother's sentence beginning and completes it: 12 **"We had a tv** but we didn't watch it all the time." This statement blends smoothly into an answer to my question: 13-15 "We were very young. I was four when my parents got a tv." The change in focus from completing Peter's previous statement to answering my question can be seen in the change from first person plural in **"We** had a tv" to first person singular in "I was four when **my** parents got a tv," as well as in the change in focus from **the children** having a tv (repeated from Peter's unfinished statement) to **the parents** getting it (repeated from my question). That Steve finished another thought (the one picked up from his brother) before anwering my question, and the smoothness of the transition from one to the other, is evidence that he did not find the overlapped question intrusive.

A similar, even more striking example of the cooperative   effect of overlapping in this example is seen in 26-30 where Steve ignores my question 24-25 "You lived in quonset huts? When you were how old?" in favor of volunteering a vignette about his father that the reference to quonset huts has reminded him of. Part of the reason he does not find my questions intrusive is that he does not feel compelled to attend to them. Finally, the positive effect of overlapping

in this interchange was supported by the participants'
recollections during playback.

   In (5) overlapping and latching were asymmetrical
and unintentionally obstructive. David, an American
Sign Language interpreter, is telling about ASL. As
listeners, Peter and I used overlap and latching to
ask supportive questions, just as I did in (4). (Note
that the questions, in both examples, show interest in
the speaker's discourse rather than shifting focus.)[5]

```
(5)   1 David:    So: and this is the one that's
      2            Berkeley.  This is the Berkeley ...
      3            sign for .. ⌐Christmas
-->   4 Deborah:              └Do you figure out those ..
      5            those um correspondences? or do-
-->   6                           David: └ /?/ ┘
      7            when you learn the signs, /does/
      8            somebody tells you.
      9 David:    Oh you mean ⌐watching it? like
--> 10 Deborah:              └Cause I can imagine
     11            knowing that sign, ... and not ..
     12            figuring out that it had anything to do
     13            with the decorations.
     14            ....
     15 David:    No. Y- you know that it has to do with
     16            the decorations.⌝
--> 17 Deborah:                   └'Cause somebody tells
     18            you?  Or you figure⌐it out?
--> 19 David:                        └No.    Oh. ...
     20            You you talking about me, or a deaf
     21            person.⌝                     ⌐
--> 22 Deborah:                                 └ Yeah
     23                   └You. You.
     24 David:    Me? Uh: Someone tells me, usually. ...
     25            But a lot of 'em I can tell.  I mean
     26            they're obvious. ....  The better I get
     27            the more I can tell.  The longer I do
     28            it the more I can tell what they're
     29            talking about. .....
     30                   Deborah:   Huh.
     31            Without ⌐knowing what the sign is.⌝
--> 32 Deborah:          └ That's interesting.┘
--> 33 Peter:                                     ⌐But
     34            how do you learn a new sign?
                   ....
     35 David:    How do I learn a new sign?⌝
     36 Peter:                              └Yeah.  I
     37            mean supposing ... Victor's talking and
     38            all of a sudden he uses a sign for
     39            Thanksgiving, and you've never seen it
     40            before.
```

In this interchange, all Peter's and my turns are
latched or overlapped on David's. In contrast, only
two of David's seven turns overlap a prior turn;
furthermore, these two utterances: an inaudible one at
6 and David's "No" at 19 are probably both attempts to
answer the first parts of my double-barreled preceding
turns (4-5 "Do you figure out those .. those um
correspondences?" and 17 "'Cause somebody tells
you?"). David shows evidence of discomfort in his
pauses, hesitations, repetitions, and circumlocutions.

During playback, David averred that the fast pace
of the questions, here and elsewhere, caught him off
guard and made him feel borne in upon. It is
difficult for me to regard this interchange in the
merciless print of a transcript, because it makes me
look overbearing. Yet I recall my good will toward
David (who remains one of my closest friends) and my
puzzlement at the vagueness of his answers. The
comparative evidence of the other example, like
numerous others in the dinner conversation, makes it
clear that the fast paced, latching, and overlapping
questions (which I have dubbed "machine-gun
questions") have exactly the effect I intended when
used with co-stylists: They are taken as a show of
interest and rapport; they encourage and reinforce the
speaker. It is only in interaction with those who do
not share a high-involvement style that such questions
and other instances of overlapping speech create
disruptions and interruptions.

Cultural variation. As Scollon (1985) argues,
whenever interactants have different habits with
regard to pacing, length of inter-turn pause, and
attitudes toward simultaneous speech, unintended
interruptions are inevitable, because the speaker
expecting a shorter pause perceives and fills an
uncomfortable silence while the speaker expecting a
longer pause is still awaiting a turn-signalling
pause. This irritating phenomenon has serious
consequences because the use of these linguistic
strategies is culturally variable. It is no
coincidence that the speakers in my study who had
high-involvement styles were of East European Jewish
background and had grown up in New York City, whereas
the speakers whose styles I have characterized as
high-considerateness were Christian and from
California.

It is crucial to note that pacing, pausing, and
attitude toward simultaneous speech have relative
rather than absolute values. Characteristics such as
"fast pacing" are not inherent values but result from

the styles of speakers in interaction <u>relative to each other.</u> Whereas Californians in my study appeared to use relatively longer inter-turn pauses relative to the New Yorkers, Scollon and Scollon (1981) show that in conversations between midwestern Americans and Athabaskan Indians in Alaska, the Midwesterners become aggressive interrupters and Athabaskans their innocent victims, because the length of inter-turn pause expected by the midwesterners, while longer than that expected by Jewish New Yorkers, is significantly shorter than that expected by Athabaskans. In conversation with Scandinavians, most Americans become interrupters, but Swedes and Norwegians are perceived as interrupting by the longer pause-favoring and more silence-favoring Finns who, according to Lehtonen and Sajavaara (1985), are themselves divided by internal regional differences with regard to length of pausing and pacing.

Labov and Fanshel (1977) claim that Rhoda, the 19-year-old psychotherapy patient in the therapeutic discourse they analyze, never ends her turn by falling silent. Rather, when she has said all she has to say, she begins to repeat herself, inviting the therapist to take a turn by overlapping her. This is an effective device for achieving smooth turn exchange without perceptible inter-turn silence, a high priority for speakers of a conversational style that sees silence in conversation, rather than simultaneous speech, as evidence of conversational trouble. It is not coincidental that the therapeutic interaction analyzed by Labov and Fanshel took place in New York City between Jewish speakers.

Reisman (1974) was one of the first to document a culturally recognizable style in which overlapping speech serves a cooperative rather than obstructive purpose. He coined the term "contrapuntal conversations" to describe this phenomenon in Antigua. Watson (1975) borrows this term to describe Hawaiian children's jointly produced verbal routines of joking and "talk story." As part of these routines, "turn-taking does not imply individual performance" but rather "partnership in performance" (p. 55). Moerman (1988) makes similar observations about Thai conversation. Hayashi (1988) finds far more simultaneous speech among Japanese speakers than among Americans. Shultz, Florio, and Erickson (1982) find that an Italian-American boy who is reprimanded at school for unruly behavior is observing family conventions for turn-taking that include simultaneous speech.

Lein and Brenneis (1978) compared children's arguments in three speech communities: "white American children in a small town in New England, black American children of migrant harvesters, and rural, Hindi-speaking Fiji Indian children" (299). Although they found no overlaps in the arguments of the black American children and only occasional overlaps in the arguments of the white American children, the Fiji Indian children evidenced a great deal of overlap, continuing for as long as thirty seconds. Lein and Brenneis do not interpret these as misfires or errors but as "deliberate attempts to overwhelm the other speaker" (307). Although not cooperative in the sense of supportive, this use of sustained overlap is cooperative in the sense of playing by rather than breaking rules.[6]

Paradoxically (in light of the men-interrupt-women research), another group that has been described as favoring overlapping talk in in-group conversation is women. One of the first to make this observation was Kalcik (1975). Edelsky (1981), setting out to determine whether women or men talked more in a series of faculty committee meetings, found that she could not tackle this question without first confronting the question of the nature of a conversational floor. She found two types of floor: a singly developed floor in which one person spoke and the others listened silently, and a collaboratively developed floor in which more than one voice could be heard, to the extent that the conversation seemed, at times, like a "free-for-all." Edelsky found that men tended to talk more than women during singly developed floors, and women tended to talk as much as men in collaboratively developed floors.[7] In other words, this study implies that women are more comfortable talking when there is more than one voice going at once.

The following excerpt (6) shows women in casual conversation overlapping in a highly cooperative and collaborative interchange. It is taken from a naturally-occurring conversation that took place at a kitchen table, recorded by Janice Hornyak.[8] Peg is visiting relatives in Washington DC, where her daughter Jan now lives and is confronting snow for the first time. Peg and Marge, who are sisters-in-law, reminisce about the trials of having small children who like to play in the snow, for Jan's benefit:

```
(6)   1 Peg:    The part I didn't like was putting
      2         everybody's snow pants and boots
      3        ⌈and
-->   4 Marge:  ⌊Oh yeah that was the worst part,
```

```
     5 Peg:    ┌and scarves
-->  6 Marge:  └and get them all bundled up in boots
     7          and everything and they're out for half
     8          an hour and then they come in and
     9          they're all covered with this snow and
    10          they get that shluck all over┐
--> 11 Peg:                                  └All that
    12          wet stuff and
--> 13 Jan:     That's why adults don't like snow huh?
    14 Marge:   That's right.
    15 Peg:     Throw all the stuff in the dryer
    16          and then they'd come in and sit for
    17          half┌an hour
--> 18 Marge:        └And in a little while they'd want
    19          to go back out again.
    20 Peg:     Then they want to go back out again.
```

As in the example of Steve, Peter, and me, all three
speakers in this brief segment initiate turns that
either latch onto or intrude into other speakers'
turns. Like Dara and Stephanie in (3) and Steve and
Peter in (4), Peg and Marge jointly hold one
conversational role, overlapping without exhibiting
(or reporting) resentment at being interrupted.
Furthermore, Hornyak points out that these speakers
often place the conjunction "and" at the end of their
turns in order to create the appearance of overlap
when there is none, as seen for example in 11-12 (Peg:
"All that wet stuff and").[9]
    It is clear, then, that many, if not most,
instances of overlap -- at least in casual
conversation among friends -- have cooperative rather
than obstructive effects. And even when the effect of
overlap is perceived to be obstructive, the intent may
still have been cooperative.

Ethical Objection: Stereotyping and conversational
style. When people who are identified as culturally
different have different conversational styles, their
ways of speaking become the basis for negative
stereotyping. Anti-Semitism classically attributes
the characteristics of loudness, aggressiveness, and
"pushiness" to Jewish speakers. The existence of this
stereotype hardly needs support, but I provide a brief
example that I recently encountered. In describing a
Jewish fellow writer named Lowenfels, Lawrence Durrell
wrote to Henry Miller, "He is undependable, erratic,
has bad judgment, loud-mouthed, pushing, vulgar,
thoroughly Jewish..." (Gornick 1988:47).
    It is clear that the evaluation of Jews as loud
and pushy simply blames the minority group for the

effect of the interaction of differing styles.[10]
Kochman (1981) demonstrates that a parallel style
difference, which he calls the "rights of
expressiveness" in contact with the "rights of
sensibilities," underlies the stereotyping of
community Blacks as inconsiderate, overbearing, and
loud. Finally, the model of conversation as an
enterprise in which only one voice should be heard at
a time is at the heart of misogynistic stereotypes as
well. It is likely because of their use of
cooperative overlapping in in-group talk that women
are frequently stereotyped as noisily clucking hens.

Gender, Ethnicity, and Conversational Style. The
juxtaposition of these two lines of inquiry: gender
and interruption on the one hand, and ethnicity as
conversational style on the other, poses a crucial and
troubling dilemma. If it is theoretically
wrongheaded, empirically indefensible, and morally
insidious to claim that speakers of particular ethnic
groups are pushy and dominating because they appear to
interrupt in conversations with speakers of different,
more "mainstream" ethnic backgrounds, can it be valid
to embrace research which "proves" that men dominate
women because they appear to interrupt them in
conversation? If the researchers who have observed
that men interrupt women in conversation were to
"analyze" my audiotapes of conversations among New
York Jewish and Christian Californian speakers, they
would no doubt conclude that the New Yorkers
"interrupted" and "dominated" -- the impression of the
Californians present, but not, I have demonstrated,
the intention of the New Yorkers, nor the effect of
their conversational styles in in-group interaction.
My brief analysis here and extended analysis elsewhere
(Tannen 1984) makes clear that the use of overlapping
speech by high-involvement speakers does not create
interruption in interaction with other like-style
speakers. In short, the "research" would do little
more than apply the ethnocentric standards of the
majority group to the culturally different behavior of
the minority group.
    The research on gender and interruption presents
a sociolinguistic parallel, but a political contrast.
Although not a minority, women are at a social and
cultural disadvantage. This transforms the political
consequences of blaming one group for dominating the
other. Most people would agree that men dominate
women in our culture, as in most if not all cultures
of the world. Therefore many would claim (as do
Henley and Kramarae 1988) that sociolinguists like

Maltz and Borker (1982) and me (Tannen 1986) who view gender differences in conversation in the framework of Gumperz' (1982) paradigm for cross-cultural communication, are simply copping out -- covering up real domination with a cloth of cultural difference. Though I am sympathetic to this view, my conscience tells me we cannot have it both ways. If we accept the research in one paradigm -- the men-interrupt-women one -- then we are forced into a position that claims that high-involvement speakers, such as Blacks and Jews and, in many circumstances, women, are pushy, aggressive, or inconsiderately or foolishly noisy.

Finally, given the interaction among gender, ethnicity, and conversational style, what are the consequences for American women of ethnic backgrounds which favor high-involvement conversational styles -- styles perceived by other Americans as pushy, aggressive, and dominating? The view of conversational style as power from the men-interrupt-women paradigm yields the repugnant conclusion that many women (including many of us of African, Caribbean, Mediterranean, South American, Levantine, Arab, and East European backgrounds) are dominating, aggressive, and pushy -- qualities, moreover, that are perceived as far more negative in women than in men. It was just such a standard that resulted in Geraldine Ferraro being labeled a bitch when she spoke in ways accepted, indeed expected, in male politicians.

Conclusion. As a woman who has personally experienced the difficulty many women report in getting heard in some interactions with men, I am tempted to embrace the studies that find that men interrupt women: It would allow me to explain my experience in a way that blames others. As a high-involvement style speaker, however, I am offended by the labeling of a feature of my conversational style as loathsome, based on the standard of those who do not share or understand it. As a Jewish woman raised in New York who is not only offended but frightened by the negative stereotyping of New Yorkers and women and Jews, I recoil when scholarly research serves to support the stereotyping of a group of speakers as possessing negative intentions and character. As a linguist and researcher, I know that the workings of conversation are more complex than that. As a human being, I want to understand what is really going on. Such understanding, I conclude, remains to be delivered by discourse analysts concerned with investigating patterns of turntaking in conversation.

Notes

1. Deborah James is currently conducting a review of the literature on gender and interruption.
2. Schegloff (1987) takes issue with Zimmerman's and West's imposition of gender as a category on transcripts in which there is no evidence that the participants' gender is a live issue. He does not, however, take issue with their definition and identification of interruptions.
3. There are other aspects of this excerpt that lead one to conclude this male speaker may be a conversational bully, other than the fact of interrupting to protect his property.
4. Overlapping is shown by brackets; brackets with reverse flaps show latching. Two dots (..) indicate perceptible pause of less than a half second. Three dots indicate a half second pause; each extra dot indicates an additional half second of pause. /?/ indicates indecipherable utterance. All the questions in (4) are spoken with fast pace and high pitch. Quonset huts were temporary housing structures provided by the American government for returning veterans following World War II.
5. The question was posed whether David's discomfort was caused by his role as spokesperson for ASL. Although this may have exacerbated it, the pattern of hesitation exhibited in this excerpt is typical of many involving David and another participant, Chad, as shown in the longer study (Tannen 1984) from which these brief examples are taken.
6. It cannot be assumed that apparent conflict is necessarily truly agonistic. Corsaro (in press), for example, demonstrates that children in an Italian nursery school deliberately provoke highly ritualized, noisy disputes when they are supposed to be quietly drawing because, as he puts it, they would rather fight than draw. Schiffrin (1984) demonstrates that apparent argument serves a sociable purpose among working class Jewish speakers in Philadelphia.
7. Edelsky notes that her initial impression had been that women "dominated" in the collaboratively-developed floors, but closer observation revealed they had not. This supports the frequently heard claim (for example Spender 1980) that when women talk as much as men they are perceived as talking more.
8. Hornyak recorded and analyzed this excerpt as part of her coursework in my Discourse Analysis class Spring 1989. I thank her for her data, her insights, and her permission to use them here.

9. Hornyak claims this is a family strategy which is
satisfying and effective when used among family
members but is often the object of complaint by non-
family members when used with them. Though she thinks
of this as a family strategy, I wonder whether it
might not be a cultural one. The family is of
Hungarian descent, and evidence abounds that
cooperative overlapping is characteristic of many East
European speakers.
10. No group is homogeneous; any attempt to
characterize all members of a group breaks down on
closer inspection. The high-involvement style I refer
to here is not so much Jewish as East European.
German Jews do not typically exhibit such style, and
of course many American Jews have either abandoned,
modified, or never acquired high-involvement styles.

References

Bennett, Adrian. 1981. Interruptions and the
    interpretation of conversation. Discourse
    Processes 4:2.171-88.
Brown, Penelope and Stephen C. Levinson. 1987.
    Politeness: Some universals in language usage.
    Cambridge: Cambridge University Press.
Bohn, Emil and Randall Stutman. 1983. Sex-role
    differences in the relational control dimension
    of dyadic interaction. Women's Studies in
    Communication 6.96-104.
Corsaro, William and Thomas Rizzo. In press.
    Disputes in the peer culture of American and
    Italian nursery school children. Conflict talk,
    ed. by Allen Grimshaw. Cambridge: Cambridge
    University Press.
Duranti, Alessandro and Donald Brenneis (eds.) 1986.
    The audience as co-author. Special issue of Text
    6:3.239-47.
Eakins, Barbara and Gene Eakins. 1976. Verbal turn-
    taking and exchanges in faculty dialogue. The
    sociology of the languages of American women, ed.
    by Betty Lou Dubois and Isabel Crouch, 53-62.
    Papers in Southwest English IV. San Antonio, TX:
    Trinity University.
Edelsky, Carol. 1981. Who's got the floor? Language
    in Society 10.383-421.
Erickson, Frederick. 1986. Listening and speaking.
    Languages and linguistics: The interdependence of
    theory, data, and application. Georgetown
    University Round Table on Languages and
    Linguistics 1985, ed. by Deborah Tannen, 294-

284

319. Washington, DC: Georgetown University
     Press.
Esposito, Anita. 1979. Sex differences in children's
     conversations. Language and Speech 22, Pt 3, 213-
     20.
Falk, Jane. 1980. The conversational duet.
     Proceedings of the Sixth Annual Meeting of the
     Berkeley Linguistics Society, 507-14. Berkeley,
     CA: University of California.
Gleason, Jean Berko and Esther Blank Greif. 1983.
     Men's speech to young children. Language, gender
     and society, ed. by Barrie Thorne, Cheris
     Kramarae, and Nancy Henley, 140-50. Rowley, MA:
     Newbury House.
Gornick, Vivian. 1988. "Masters of Self-Deception."
     Review of The Durrell-Miller Letters 1935-80, ed.
     by Ian S. MacNiven. The New York Times Book
     Review November 20, 1988, 3, 47.
Greenwood, Alice. 1989. Discourse variation and
     social comfort: A study of topic initiation and
     interruption patterns in the dinner conversation
     of preadolescent children. PhD dissertation,
     City University of New York.
Goodwin, Charles. 1981. Conversational organization:
     Interaction between speakers and hearers. New
     York: Academic Press.
Gumperz, John J. 1982. Discourse strategies.
     Cambridge: Cambridge University Press.
Hayashi, Reiko. 1988. Simultaneous talk -- from the
     perspective of floor management of English and
     Japanese speakers. World Englishes 7:3.269-88.
Henley, Nancy and Cheris Kramarae. 1988.
     Miscommunication - Issues of gender and power.
     Paper presented at the annual meeting of the
     National Women's Studies Association,
     Minneapolis.
Kalcik, Susan. 1975. "...like Ann's gynecologist or
     the time I was almost raped": Personal narratives
     in women's rap groups. Journal of American
     Folklore 88:3-11. Rpt Women and folklore, ed. by
     Claire R. Farrer. Austin: University of Texas
     Press, 1975.
Kochman, Thomas. 1981. Black and White styles in
     conflict. Chicago: University of Chicago Press.
Komarovsky, Mirra. 1962. Blue-Collar Marriage. New
     York: Vintage.
Labov, William, and David Fanshel. 1977. Therapeutic
     discourse. New York: Academic Press.
Lehtonen, Jaakko and Kari Sajavaara. 1985. The
     silent Finn. Perspectives on silence, ed. by

Deborah Tannen & Muriel Saville-Troike, 193-201. Norwood, NJ: Ablex.

Leffler, Ann, D.L. Gillespie and J.C. Conaty. 1982. The effects of status differentiation on nonverbal behavior. Social Psychology Quarterly 45:3.153-61.

Lein, Laura and Donald Brenneis. 1978. Children's disputes in three speech communities. Language in Society 7.299-323.

Maltz, Daniel N., & Ruth A. Borker. 1982. A cultural approach to male-female miscommunication. Language and social identity, ed. by John J. Gumperz, 196-216. Cambridge: Cambridge University Press.

McDermott, R.P. and Henry Tylbor. 1983. On the necessity of collusion in conversation. Text 3:3.277-297.

McMillan, Julie R., A. Kay Clifton, Diane McGrath and Wanda S. Gale, 1977. Women's language: uncertainty or interpersonal sensitivity and emotionality. Sex Roles 3:6.545-59.

Moerman, Michael. 1988. Talking culture: Ethnography and conversation analysis. Philadelphia: University of Pennsylvania Press.

Murray, Stephen O. 1985. Toward a model of members' methods for recognizing interruptions. Language in Society 13:31-41.

Murray, Stephen O. 1987. Power and solidarity in "interruption": A critique of the Santa Barbara School conception and its application by Orcutt and Harvey (1985). Symbolic Interaction 10:1.101- 110.

Murray, Stephen O. and Lucille H. Covelli. 1988. Women and men speaking at the same time. Journal of Pragmatics 12:1.103-11.

Reisman, Karl. 1974. Contrapuntal conversations in an Antiguan village. Explorations in the ethnography of speaking, ed. by Richard Bauman & Joel Sherzer, 110-124. Cambridge: Cambridge University Press.

Sacks, Harvey, Emanuel Schegloff and Gail Jefferson. 1974. A simplest systematics for the organization of turn-taking for conversation. Language 50:696-735.

Sattel, Jack W. 1983. Men, inexpressiveness, and power. Language, gender and society, ed. by Barrie Thorne, Cheris Kramarae, and Nancy Henley, 119-24. Rowley, MA: Newbury House.

Schegloff, Emanuel. 1982. Discourse as an interactional achievement: Some uses of 'uhuh' and other things that come between sentences.

Analyzing discourse: Text and talk. Georgetown University Round Table on Languages and Linguistics 1981, ed. by Deborah Tannen, 71-93. Washington, DC: Georgetown University Press.

Schegloff, Emanuel. 1987. Between micro and macro: Contexts and other connections. The micro-macro link, ed. by Jeffrey C. Alexander, Bernhard Giesen, Richard Munch and Neil J. Smelser, 207-234. Berkeley: University of California Press.

Schegloff, Emanuel. 1988. Discourse as an interactional achievement II: An exercise in conversation analysis. Linguistics in context: Connecting observation and understanding, ed. by Deborah Tannen, 135-158. Norwood, NJ: Ablex.

Schiffrin, Deborah. 1984. Jewish argument as sociability. Language in Society 13:3.311-335.

Scollon, Ron. 1985. The machine stops: Silence in the metaphor of malfunction. Perspectives on silence, ed. by Deborah Tannen and Muriel Saville-Troike, 21-30. Norwood, NJ: Ablex.

Scollon, Ron and Suzanne B.K. Scollon. 1981. Narrative, literacy and face in interethnic communication. Norwood, NJ: Ablex.

Shultz, Jeffrey, Susan Florio, and Frederick Erickson. 1982. Where's the floor? Aspects of the cultural organization of social relationships in communication at home and at school. Ethnography and education: Children in and out of school, ed. by Perry Gilmore and Alan Glatthorn, 88-123. Washington, DC: Center for Applied Linguistics. (Distributed by Ablex Publishing, Norwood, NJ.)

Spender, Dale. 1980. Man made language. London: Routledge and Kegan Paul.

Tannen, Deborah. 1981. New York Jewish conversational style. International Journal of the Sociology of Language 30.133-39.

Tannen, Deborah. 1984. Conversational style: Analyzing talk among friends. Norwood, NJ: Ablex.

Tannen, Deborah. 1986. That's not what I meant!: How conversational style makes or breaks your relations with others. New York: William Morrow.

Watson, Karen A. 1975. Transferable communicative routines. Language in Society 4:53-72.

West, Candace and Don H. Zimmerman. 1983. Small insults: A study of interruptions in cross-sex conversations between unacquainted persons. Language, gender and society, ed. by Barrie Thorne, Cheris Kramarae, and Nancy Henley, 103-117. Rowley, MA: Newbury House.

West, Candace and Don H. Zimmerman. 1985. Gender, language, and discourse. Handbook of discourse analysis, Vol. 4, Discourse analysis in society, ed. by Teun A. van Dijk, 103-124. London: Academic Press.

Yamada, Haru. 1989. American and Japanese topic management strategies in business conversations. PhD dissertation, Georgetown University.

Zimmerman, Don H. & Candace West. 1975. Sex roles, interruptions and silences in conversation. In: Barrie Thorne & Nancy Henley (eds.), Language and sex: Difference and dominance. Rowley, Mass.: Newbury House, pp. 105-129.

Visual Input, Auditory Input and Word Order

Yael Ziv
The Hebrew University

1. Introduction

Despite increasing recognition of the linguistic relevance of context, the pertinent contextual features are far from being fully specified. Most studies involving context-dependent properties of language contain an ad-hoc description of certain, apparently relevant, contextual characteristics. Thus, questions concerning well-formedness, interpretation and appropriateness of given sentences were all shown to involve a variety of contextual considerations, but so far no principled, non-controversial specification of the features required for a full characterization of the pertinent contextual factors exists. The present paper will not achieve the ultimate goal, of course, but will constitute one step towards exposing certain necessary contextual distinctions, without which no account will be satisfactory.

In this paper I will be concerned with a contextual distinction that seems to be functional in descriptions of word order options in Colloquial Israeli Hebrew (CIH). Specifically, the need will be shown to distinguish visual from non-visual situational contexts. The former will be shown to act somewhat like <u>situationally given</u> information, while the latter will manifest the properties otherwise associated with <u>new</u> (<u>non-background</u>) information. Suggestions concerning explanations along the lines of iconicity and the predominance of certain sentential positions as correlating with the structure of our memory will be investigated as well.

2. Background

Chomsky's concern with 'the ideal speaker-hearer's linguistic competence' (Chomsky 1965) left 'context' outside of the realm of scientific linguistic investigation for a significant period of time. In theory, then, contextual considerations were not regarded as relevant and hence were neglected. In practice, however, judgements of well-formedness have often been based on the extent to which a given utterance could be contextualized, and accounts had to be provided for the alleged ill-formedness of sentences for which no contextualization seemed plausible.

To take a specific example, consider the following sequence (discussed and analyzed in Mittwoch (1985)):

(1) I think you should perjure myself.

The sentence in (1) would be judged as ill-formed, violating conditions on anaphora, under the assumption that it was uttered by a single speaker. If, however, the context of utterance is altered and the same sequence is regarded as being uttered by two distinct speakers as in (2)

(2a) I think you should
(2b) perjure myself. (I know.)

it would display different acceptability properties and would not be rejected as ill-formed. The contextual information is, thus, involved in the determination of the type of account that is required: syntactic, semantic or pragmatic.

In semantics, too, strict context-independence was advocated and practiced initially, 'context' being conceived of as extra-linguistic (e.g. Katz and Fodor 1964). Context-dependent semantics with variables such as the time and place of the utterance and details about the speaker(s) and the audience currently provide serious alternatives to the context-independent approach (e.g. Barwise and Perry 1983). In the general domain of interpretation it has long been recognized that meaning underdetermines interpretation and that extensive reference to contextual information is required for full interpretation. The relevant contextual contributions, however, have been treated on an ad-hoc basis lacking predictive power and allowing for after-the-fact accounts only.

The problem of specifying the linguistically relevant contextual factors is shared by linguists who admit pragmatic considerations into their linguistic description. Thus, this issue is elegantly avoided in Sperber and Wilson's (1986) account of relevance. Sperber and Wilson stand the whole picture on its head by adopting the presumption of relevance and the consequent search for the most appropriate context yielding the largest number of contextual implicatures at a minimum cost in terms of effort of processing. Still, they state that encyclopaedic knowledge, background assumptions based on the discourse at hand as well as information about the immediately observable environment constitute the kind of context against which the relevance of a given linguistic expression is evaluated. Sperber and Wilson's notion of context, then, is not very explicit.

3. Linguistically Relevant Contextual Factors
In their 'Definite reference and mutual knowledge'

Clark and Marshall (1981) distinguish a variety of
contextual features under the guise of different types
of 'mutual knowledge'. The distinctions they draw are
between (a) community membership with the accompanying
assumption of universality of knowledge, (b) physical co-
presence, which is further sub-divided into immediate,
potential and prior, (c) linguistic co-presence where
potential and prior constitute sub-divisions and (d)
indirect co-presence with its physical and linguistic
subsets. Clark and Marshall's divisions are offered from
a cognitive perspective, in that they are based on the
source and strength of evidence utilized by the
interlocutors. Their attempt to provide the various
linguistic correlates of their particular contextual
features indicates that some of their classifications are
of no linguistic consequence. Thus, their fourth
category, indirect co-presence, is, in fact, a conceptual
category based on inferences, or the construction of
'bridges', to use Clark and Haviland's (1977) term, and
it is parasitic on the other three sources of 'mutual
knowledge'. The fact that it is based on the so-called
community membership and that it may be either physical
or linguistic (its two subtypes) is evidence of its non-
independent status. It is not surprising, therefore,
that it has no particular linguistic realization, unlike
the other contextual features distinguished (e.g. proper
nouns indicating community membership, deictics
indicating physical co-presence and anaphoric pronouns
indicating linguistic co-presence).

An alternative characterization of the
linguistically relevant contextual factors is provided
by Ariel (1985 and forthcoming). Ariel draws on both
Clark and Marshall (1981) and Prince (1981) and succeeds
in establishing a correlation between the types of so-
called 'givenness' (defined in terms of context types)
and their potential linguistic manifestations on the one
hand, and between the various types of givenness and
their cognitive counterparts on the other.[2]

Thus, she discusses three types of Givenness:
Knowledge Givenness (KG) (akin to Clark and Marshall's
community membership), Physical Givenness (PG) and
Linguistic Givenness (LG), and suggests that the present
discourse is criterial in the determination of linear
word order, while general knowledge is relevant in
accounting for the speaker's decision to introduce a
piece of information as Given rather than as New.[3]

In this paper I will largely adopt Ariel's
characterization of the various linguistically relevant
contextual features, but I would like to introduce a
further distinction concerning situational or physical
contexts, one having to do with the visual/non-visual

axis.   Such a distinction seems to be required in
accounting for certain word order options in Colloquial
Israeli Hebrew (CIH).

4.   Visual vs. Auditory Situational Context and Word Order

The phenomenon under investigation may be subsumed
under the general category of presentationals.
Presentationals are known to involve constructions where
subjects do not occur initially in SVO languages.
Various alternatives exist depending on the type of
presentational and the particular language concerned (cf.
Berman 1980, Firbas 1971, Givón 1976 and 1977, Hetzron
1975, Ziv 1982a, 1982b, 1988 inter alia for general
discussions as well as specific references to Hebrew).

In the case at hand I wish to discuss a variety of
constructions in CIH serving introductory, identifying
or reminding functions in the discourse.   The common
denominator in the present context is the fact that these
constructions are used to introduce or identify the
entity in question in a particular type of situational
context, where no visual clues are available.   I will
show that in the corresponding situations where visual
input is admitted different properties are evident.   In
the cases where visual input is available the nature of
identification or introduction is significantly
different.   I would like to propose that in such cases
we are dealing with establishing a correspondence between
visual information, supplied by the situational context,
and the details of the particular identity of the entity
in question.[4]

In the following I will describe a variety of what
I believe to constitute situational contexts where no
relevant visual input is available.   It will be shown
that in each of these cases auditory input is the sole
pertinent factor in the discourse context and the
introductory statement involves a characteristic word
order not evident in related situations showing visual
inputs. The first such instance concerns the difference
between radio and television reports of on-going sports
events with respect to certain word order options when
introducing a player performing a particular maneuver.
Thus in the television-aired game we witness the
canonical SVO word order in CIH in the report whether the
player is introduced on the scene or whether his moves
are described subsequent to his introduction.   Hence the
following

    (3)   miki berkovich tofes   et hakadur
          Miki Berkowich catches   the ball

can occur in the report either when the player, Miki, appears on the scene (in the sense that he was not present in the focus of attention immediately preceding the reported event) or as a description of a non-initial move in a sequence portraying the player's maneuvers.[5] In the radio-transmitted report of the on-going game, where there are obviously no visual clues, the introduction of the player on the scene does not show the canonical word order, but rather structures like the following, where the constituent denoting the name of the player is non-initial in the sentence, are operative.

(4) tofes et hakadur axshav miki berkovich,
     catches the ball now Miki Berkowich[6]

Such structures cannot be used in non-introductory contexts, where the player in question has been mentioned immediately prior to the current occurrence and his subsequent moves are reported. Rather, the canonical word order structure is appropriate under those circumstances. Before I engage in an attempt to shed some light on the distinction between the two sub-types of situational context, the one involving visual input and the other involving auditory input only, I would like to present a few more instances of auditory and non-visual contexts where introductions are evident.

A context similar to the one just discussed again concerns television vs. radio. In introducing or identifying the announcer or correspondent who is about to read a news item, the radio style in CIH always shows the name of the introduced person non-initially as in:

(5) harey haxadashot   mipi   yicxak   ro'e
     here the news from the mouth (of) Y.   Ro'e
(6) baulpan   Alex Anski
     in the studio

The introduction may be performed by self or others. The version where the name of the announcer or correspondent occurs initially, e.g. in subject position, as in

(7) yicxak   ro'e kore   / makri et haxadashot
     Yitschak Ro'e is reading / is reading the news
                                   (causative)

is infelicitous in this case. (7) could be used felicitously in reporting the state-of-affairs in the studio, but not in introducing the announcer. In the television version of this situation we witness an interesting corroboration of our observation. Thus, when the anchorperson first appears on the screen no name is

provided. In introducing a correspondent who is about
to present his news item there are two basic states on
television: one where the correspondent is not yet
visible and the other where (s)he is. In the instance
where the correspondent is invisible at the time of the
introduction by the anchorperson the same pattern holds
as is evident in the auditory context on the radio;
however, in the case where the reporter is visible the
canonical order with the name of the correspondent in
initial position (when it is the subject) holds. (8a)
and (8b) below may be used in these two contexts
respectively:

> (8a) medaveax   katavenu   yarin kimor
>   (is) reporting our correspondent Yarin Kimor
> (8b) katavenu   yarin kimor medaveax
>   our correspondent Yarin Kimor (is) reporting

(8b) may also be used in indirectly reporting the content
of the relevant news item.
    Yet another instance exhibiting the properties in
question is evident when upon inviting a performer who
is backstage to perform on the stage the M.C. announces

> (9) veaxshav   yofia   lefanenu   Mati Kaspi
>   and now will perform in front of us Mati Kaspi

thereby introducing the performer. The canonical SVO
construction is clearly inappropriate as an introduction
in such a case; it may, however, be used as a description
of the coming attractions. If the performer is already
on the stage, and if he is sufficiently distinct as the
entity to be focused on, an introduction like the one in
(9) would seem infelicitous. If, however, there is a
group of performers on the stage such that the performer
in question cannot be reasonably expected to be salient,
then an introduction like that evident in (9) would be
appropriate.
    Closely related to this state of affairs is the
following setting from the Jewish tradition. When a
person is called to the reading of the Torah in the
synagogue during services, the formula used shows a clear
VS structure of the type evident in the other cases
discussed so far. Thus:

> (10a) ya'ale   moshe ben   shaul
>   will come up Moshe son of Saul
> (10b) ya'amod   NP (= name of a person)
>   will stand up NP

The person called upon is a part of the crowd of prayers

before he is introduced. So he cannot reasonably be
expected to be in the visual focus or otherwise be
significantly distinct. Hence the formula in such
contexts falls under the same generalization as our other
cases. The last two examples seem to force us into a
refinement of our criterion of visual input. It appears
to be the case that the relevant aspect of the visual
input is visual saliency.

We will come back to this property of the visual
input shortly. Before we do that I would like to mention
one other situational context sharing the lack of visual
input and showing identification using the types of
structures characterized in this study. I am referring
specifically to telephone conversations.

In telephone conversations, where lack of visual
input is evident, the caller introduces himself using
such structures as in

    (11a) shalom.   medaber   rotem.
           hi/hello. (is) speaking Rotem (= proper name)
    (11b) shalom.   kan   rotem.
           hi/hello here   Rotem

where the NP subject designating the name of the caller
does not introduce the relevant sentence. In fact, the
canonical counterparts of these sentences such as the
ones in (12)

    (12a) shalom.   rotem medaber.
           hi/hello Rotem (is) speaking
    (12b) shalom.   rotem kan.
           hi/hello Rotem (is) here

are infelicitous in such instances. Rather, (12a) and
(12b) can be used to describe the facts portrayed in
them. They serve as descriptions by others, as is
evident from the lack of first person pronoun as the
subject.[8] Likewise, the sentences in (11) cannot be used
in contexts other than self-introductions by callers.
In particular, they cannot be used by the caller to
confirm his identity in response to the callee's query.
Thus the exchange in (13) is impossible.

    (13a) Callee: Is Rotem speaking?
    (13b) Caller: ken.   medaber   rotem.
                    yes   (is) speaking Rotem

In such cases the alternative in (12) is an appropriate
answer on the part of the caller.

An objection may be raised at this point with regard
to the relevance of such examples as the ones involving

set phrases or formulae to the argument under discussion.
I would like to propose in this context that the formulae
in question are not as arbitrary as is evident elsewhere,
and in fact their pattern is predictable on the basis of
our general observation.

The fact that precisely the word order option that
they allow is the available one and not the other way
around is predictable, or, minimally, follows rather
naturally from our generalization.

5. Conclusions

We have observed that in CIH a variety of
constructions that serve an identifying or introductory
discourse purpose display a non-canonical word order
whereby the NP designating the name of the introduced
entity does not occur in initial position even when it
is the subject of the sentence. Such sentences were
shown to function in a particular type of situational
context, namely, where visual clues are not available.
In addition to the need that these observations suggest
to distinguish two varieties of situational contexts in
any coherent description of this phenomenon in CIH, and
hence presumably in the pragmatics of natural language
in general, there seems to be an interesting conclusion
that follows from the state of affairs described. The
conclusion has to do with the status of entities that we
come to possess knowledge of via visual clues. Such
entities appear to act as though they were Physically
Given in the sense of Ariel (1985 and forthcoming), and
as such behave with respect to word order determination
as do other given entities, namely, they favor initial
position. The entities mentioned in the situational
contexts characterized by auditory input but lacking
visual clues apparently function as new, in the sense of
non-given physically, and as such indeed seem to favor
non-initial, and sometimes even final position, in line
with new entities elsewhere.

The correlation between the explicit visual clues
and physical givenness is intuitively clear, and it is
substantiated by the fact that visual clues are perceived
at a faster speed than auditory clues. The information
perceived visually thus acts as though it were already
given, the information expressed verbally does not.
Hence, with respect to situational contexts lacking
visual input, introductions of entities count as
introductions of new material, and follow the linguistic
conventions involved in such cases. However, full-
fledged situational contexts involving visual input do
not seem to call for introductions of new material; the
relevant material in them is conceived of as given, and
hence the entity in question could function topically,

in the 'aboutness' sense of Reinhart (1981). In such cases a match is established between a Physically Given entity and a name; this is not an introduction and as such does not display the properties associated with introductions.

Notes

1. I am indebted to Mira Ariel and Rachel Giora for certain comments they made on an earlier version of this paper.

2. Prince (1981) draws interesting conceptual distinctions in the context of discussing her scale of assumed familiarity. Not all the detailed properties, however, turn out to be of linguistic consequence.

3. Ariel claims that natural languages do not codify the source of givenness directly, but rather what is being codified by givenness markers is the degree of accessibility of the referent in question to the addressee. KG markers (e.g. proper names and definite descriptions) are associated with the general store of knowledge which is clearly not located in activated memory, but is presumably stored in long-term memory and is therefore not immediately accessible. PG markers (e.g. deictics and demonstratives) depend on the speech situation for their referents and are thus more readily accessible than the KG referents. LG markers (e.g. third person pronouns and gaps) are restricted to highly accessible referents, occurring in the immediately preceding text, and are, in all probability, associated with short-term memory.

4. Note that I am discussing non-visual context as an instance of physical or situational context. An objection may be raised to this designation on the grounds that in fact the lack of visual input in the cases at hand renders them non-physical or non-situational. However, it is clear that despite the lack of crucial visual input, the context in question preserves the necessary contemporaneousness and in addition shows attendance to the same circumstances by all interlocutors, a feature which is not self-evident in situational contexts elsewhere. In some situational contexts the attention of the addressee might have to be specifically directed towards attending to the same circumstances (e.g. looking at the same object in the environment).

No classification of the context under examination is possible as an instance of the general knowledge context, neither is it sensible to consider it an instance of linguistic discourse context. Establishing a separate contextual category unrelated to the existing

three seems highly inadvisable in light of the similarity
it bears to some of the crucial characteristics of
physical/situational context. Supporting evidence might
come from considerations of communication between blind
people. It is intuitively clear that when blind people
engage in verbal interchanges when they are in the same
location, it is accurate to attribute to such interchanges the properties associated with physical/situa-
tional contexts.

5. I would like to point out the problematicity of
determining the relevant notion of 'newly introduced
entity' in the context of on-going sports games. Thus
a player could have been mentioned prior to the report
of the current move but still be considered newly
introduced or, more accurately, reintroduced, simply
because a variety of other players were actively engaged
in the game and were mentioned in the report between the
two mentions of the player in question. The question
here is essentially the same as the one evident in
instances of long distance anaphora. An answer in terms
of Chafe's (1976) notion of 'being in the addressee's
consciousness' as well as Prince's (1981) notion of
'saliency' seems to be required.

6. I will not discuss the syntactic properties of
the construction in question in any detail here. Suffice
it to say in the present context that it seems to display
properties evident in inversions elsewhere (cf. Green
1980 and 1985 and Ziv 1988).

7. The type of utterances under examination should
be clearly distinguished from the closing formulae of
news items whether they be delivered by television or by
radio:

(i) kan yoram ronen Paris
     here Yoram Ronen Paris

These represent fixed formulae designating the
termination of the piece in question.

8. Note that the sentences in (11), which are used
in self-identification or introduction, do not contain
first person pronouns in referring to the speaker. From
the pragmatic point of view of the discourse function of
the utterance it is evident that for identification to
be successful it has to provide the maximal relevant
information such that the entity introduced will,
consequently, be easy to identify. Clearly, personal
pronouns are not sufficiently identifying.

From the syntactic point of view, it has been
claimed that the VS order is not an available option when
S is pronominal. (See Givón 1976 but cf. Ziv 1988 for
systematic exceptions.)

9. Attempts may be made to assign an iconic function
to the word order in such instances, such as suggesting
that the predominance of end position correlates with the
structure of our memory and thus entities we need to keep
in prominent position notionally would be more
effectively presented in a structurally and intonation-
ally predominant position. Such attempts are immature
at the current state of our knowledge. More
specifically, in the absence of a relatively worked out,
principled and predictive theory of iconicity in
language, references to iconicity are at best a
speculation.

References

Ariel, M. 1985. Givenness Marking. Unpublished Ph.D.
dissertation. Tel-Aviv University.
_____. Forthcoming. Accessing NP Antecedents.
Routledge: Croom Helm Linguistics Series.
Barwise, J. and J. Perry. 1983. Situations and
Attitudes. Cambridge, Mass: The M.I.T. Press.
Berman, R. 1980. 'The case of an (S)VO language',
Language 56: 4, 759-776.
Chafe, W. 1976. 'Givenness, Contrastiveness,
Definiteness, Subjects, Topics and Point of View',
in C.N. Li (ed.), Subject and Topic. New York:
Academic Press, pp. 25-55.
Chomsky, N. 1965. Aspects of the Theory of Syntax.
Cambridge, Mass: The M.I.T. Press.
Clark, H. and S.E. Haviland. 1977. 'Comprehension and
the Given-New contract', in R. Freedle (ed.),
Discourse Production and Comprehension. Hillsdale,
N.J.: Lawrence Erlbaum Associates, pp. 1-40.
Clark, H. and C.R. Marshall. 1981. 'Definite reference
and mutual knowledge', in A.K. Joshi (ed.), Elements
of Discourse Understanding. Cambridge: Cambridge
University Press, pp. 10-63.
Firbas, J. 1971. 'On the concept of Communicative
Dynamism in the theory of Functional Sentence
Perspective', Sbornik Prac'i Filosofick'e Fakulty
Brnensk'e University. A. 19: 135-144.
Givón, T. 1976. 'On the VS order in Israeli Hebrew:
Pragmatics and typological change', in P. Cole
(ed.), Studies in Modern Hebrew Syntax and
Semantics. Amsterdam: North-Holland, pp. 153-181.
_____. 1977. 'The drift from VSO to SVO in Biblical
Hebrew: The pragmatics of tense-aspect', in C.N. Li
(ed.), Mechanisms of Syntactic Change. Austin:
University of Texas Press, pp. 181-254.
Green, G. 1980. 'Some wherefores of English
inversions', Language 56: 582-601.

_____. 1985. 'The description of inversions in Generalized Phrase Structure Grammar', in M. Niepokuj et al. (eds.), Proceedings of the 11th Annual Meeting of the Berkeley Linguistics Society, pp. 117-146.

Hetzron, R. 1975. 'The presentative movement or Why the ideal word order is V.S.O.P.', in C.N. Li (ed.), Word Order and Word Order Change. Austin: University of Texas Press, pp. 345-388.

Katz, J.J. and J.A. Fodor. 1964. 'The structure of a semantic theory', in J.A. Fodor and J.J. Katz (eds.), The Structure of Language: Readings in the Philosophy of Language. Englewood Cliffs, N.J.: Prentice-Hall, pp. 479-518.

Mittwoch, A. 1985. 'Sentences, utterance boundaries, personal deixis and the E-hypothesis', Theoretical Linguistics 12:2, 137-152.

Prince, E. 1981. 'Toward a taxonomy of Given-New information', in P. Cole (ed.), Radical Pragmatics. New York: Academic Press, pp. 223-255.

Reinhart, T. 1981. 'Pragmatics and linguistics: An analysis of sentence topics', in Philosophica 27, 1: 53-94.

Sperber, D. and D. Wilson. 1986. Relevance: Communication and Cognition. Oxford: Basil Blackwell Ltd.

Ziv, Y. 1982a. 'Another look at definites in existentials', Journal of Linguistics 18: 73-88.

_____. 1982b. 'Getting more mileage out of existentials in English', Linguistics 20: 747-762.

_____. 1988. 'Word order in children's literature: FSP and markedness', in Y. Tobin (ed.), The Prague School and its Legacy. Amsterdam: John Benjamins, pp. 123-144.

Language Index